When you see something like this, you gotta climb it...

- Takeshi Konomi, 2004

About Takeshi Konomi

Takeshi Konomi exploded onto the manga scene with the incredible **THE PRINCE OF TENNIS.** His refined art style and sleek character designs proved popular with **Weekly Shonen Jump** readers, and **THE PRINCE OF TENNIS** became the number one sports manga in Japan almost overnight. Its cast of fascinating male tennis players attracted legions of female readers even though it was originally intended to be a boys' comic. The manga continues to be a success in Japan and has inspired a hit anime series, as well as several video games and mountains of merchandise.

THE PRINCE OF TENNIS
VOL. 26
The SHONEN JUMP Manga Edition

STORY AND ART BY
TAKESHI KONOMI

Translation/Joe Yamazaki
Consultant/Michelle Pangilinan
Touch-up Art & Lettering/Vanessa Satone
Design/Sam Elzway
Editor/Leyla Aker

Editor in Chief, Books/Alvin Lu
Editor in Chief, Magazines/Marc Weidenbaum
VP of Publishing Licensing/Rika Inouye
VP of Sales/Gonzalo Ferreyra
Sr. VP of Marketing/Liza Coppola
Publisher/Hyoe Narita

Printed in the U.S.A.

Published by VIZ Media, LLC
P.O. Box 77010
San Francisco, CA 94107

SHONEN JUMP Manga Edition
10 9 8 7 6 5 4 3 2 1
First printing, July 2008

SHONEN JUMP Manga

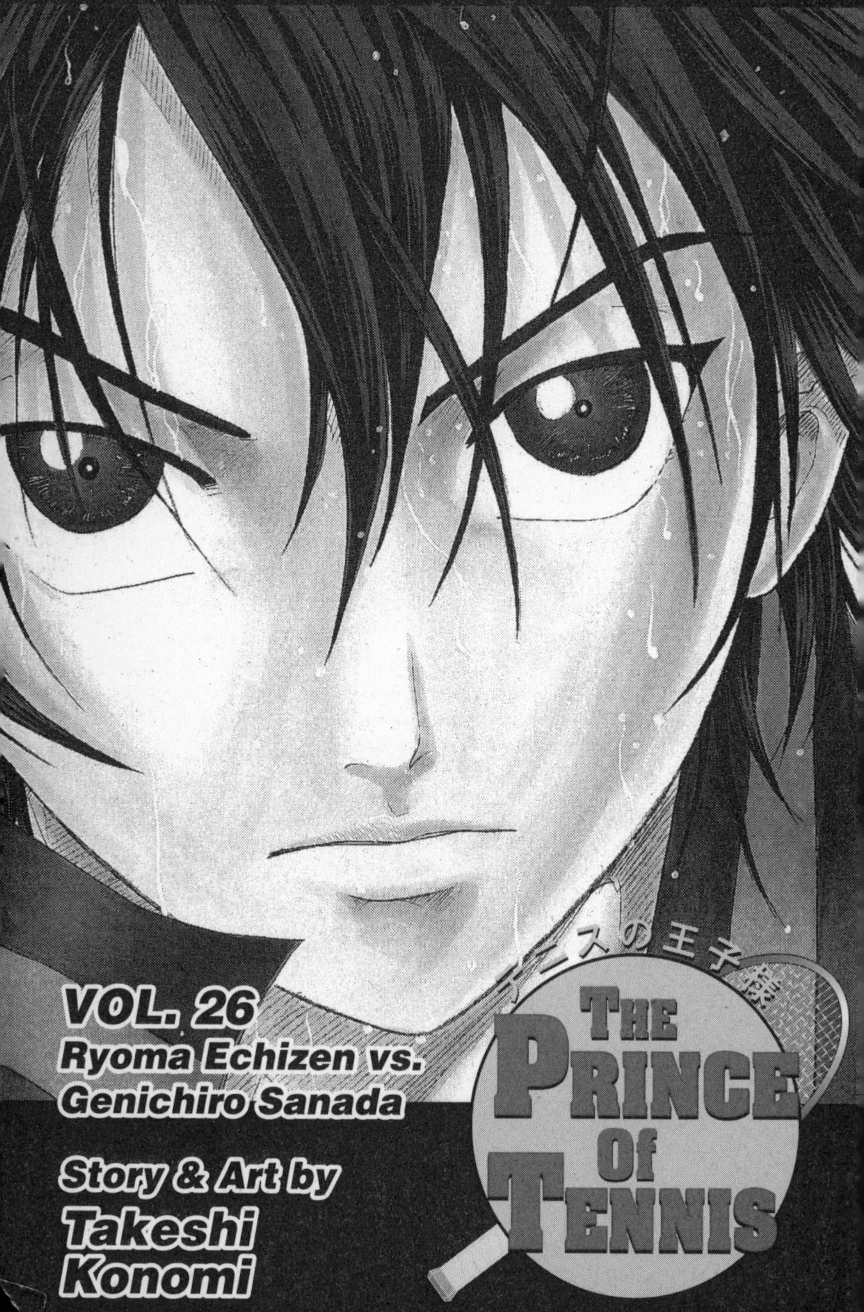

THE PRINCE OF TENNIS

VOL. 26
Ryoma Echizen vs. Genichiro Sanada

Story & Art by
Takeshi Konomi

ENNIS CLUB

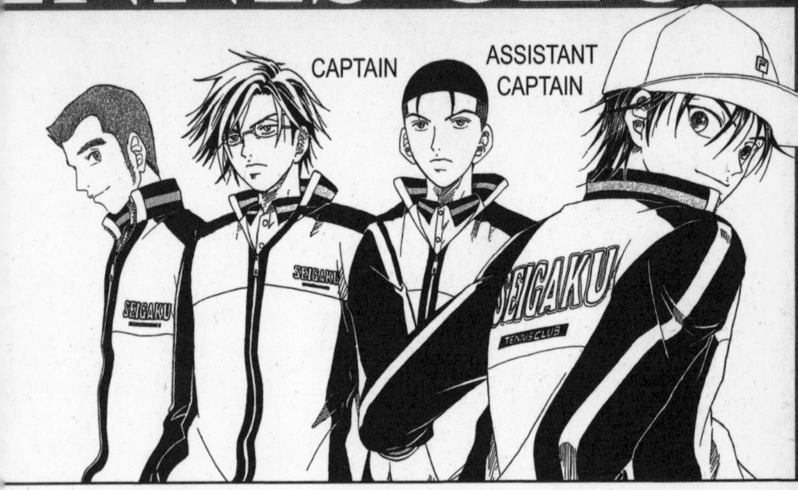
CAPTAIN
ASSISTANT CAPTAIN

• TAKASHI KAWAMURA • KUNIMITSU TEZUKA • SHUICHIRO OISHI • RYOMA ECHIZEN •

STORY & HARACTERS

Seishun Academy student Ryoma Echizen is a tennis prodigy, with wins in four consecutive U.S. Junior Tennis Tournaments under his belt. He became a starter as a 7th grader and led his team to the District Preliminaries! Despite a few mishaps, Seishun won the District Prelims and the City Tournament, and even earned a ticket to the Kanto Tournament. The team comes away victorious from its first-round matches against Hyotei, but Kunimitsu injures his shoulder and goes to Kyushu for treatment. Despite losing captain Kunimitsu and assistant captain Shuichiro to injury, Seishun defeats Midoriyama and Rokkaku, not only reaching the finals of the tournament but also earning a slot at the Nationals!

Their Kanto Tournament finals opponent is the number-one ranked champion, Rikkai. Seishun loses both doubles matches but gains their first win when Sadaharu defeats Renji in No. 3 Singles. In the No. 2 Singles match between Shusuke and Akaya, Shusuke manages to hold off Rikkai's ace to win the first game. But Akaya retaliates with a malicious shot and deliberately strikes Shusuke in the head! Now a temporary loss of sight from the blow has put Shusuke in a precarious situation...

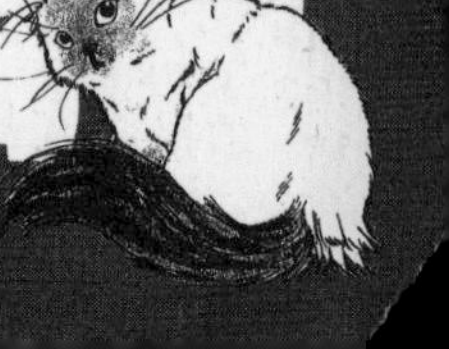

SEIGAKU T

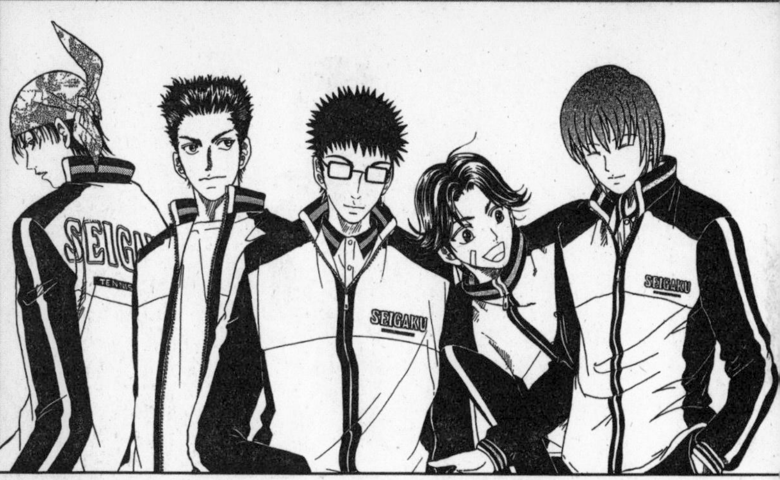

●KAORU KAIDO ● TAKESHI MOMOSHIRO ● SADAHARU INUI ● EIJI KIKUMARU ● SHUSUKE FUJI ●

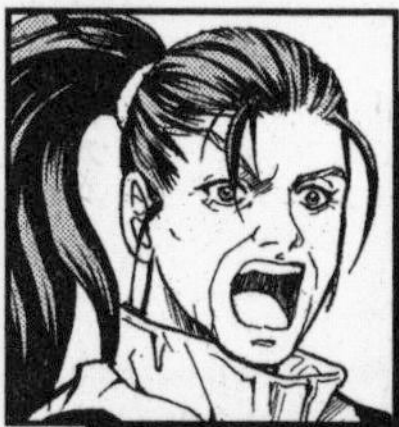

SEISHUN ACADEMY TENNIS COACH

SUMIRE RYUZAKI

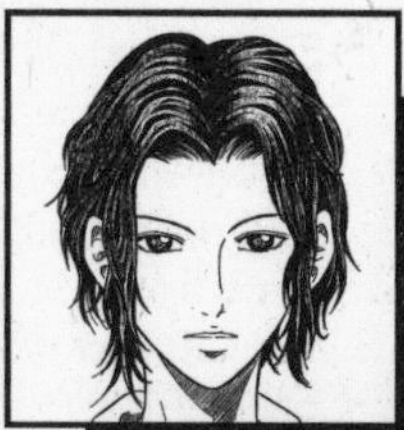

RIKKAI

SEIICHI YUKIMURA

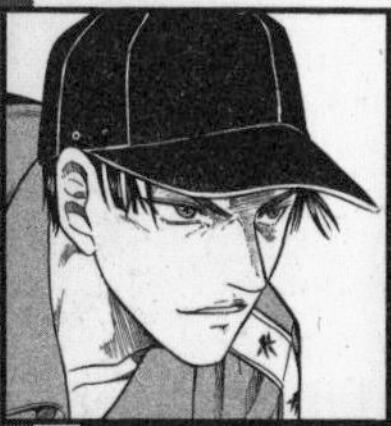

RIKKAI

GENICHIRO SANADA

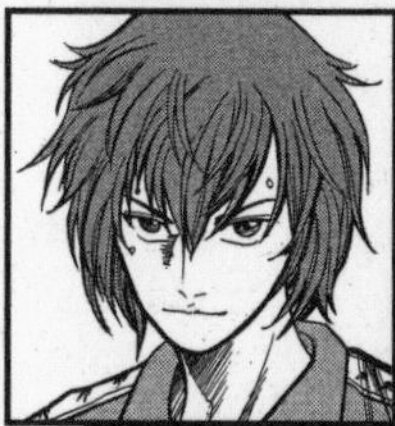

RIKKAI

BUNTA MARUI

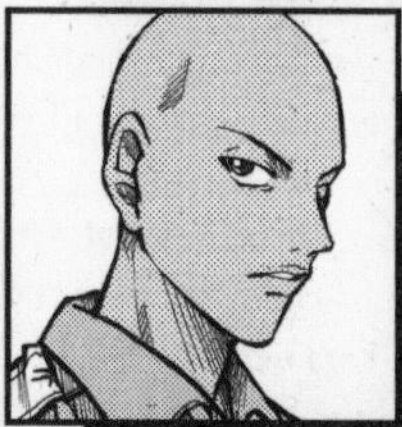

RIKKAI

JACKAL KUWAHARA

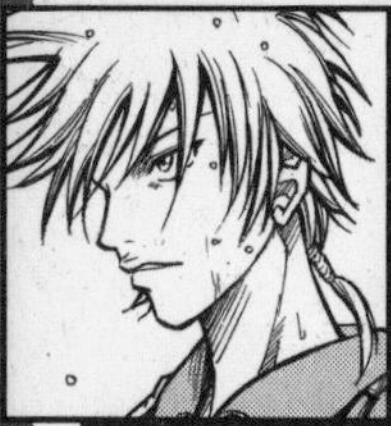

RIKKAI

MASAHARU NIO

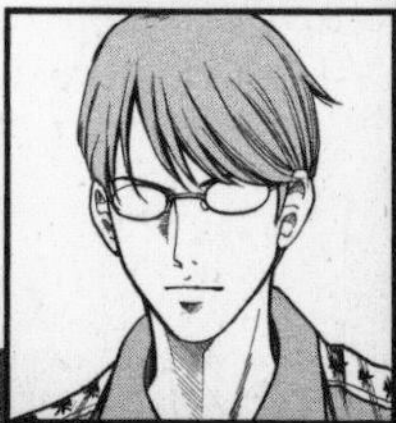

RIKKAI

HIROSHI YAGYU

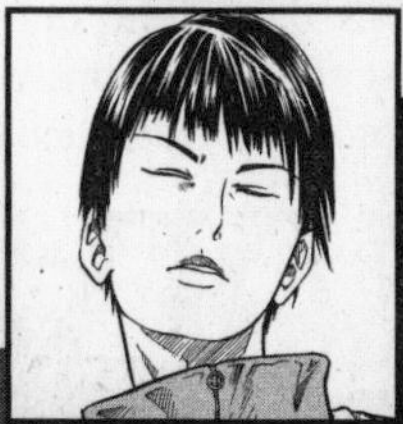

RIKKAI

RENJI YANAGI

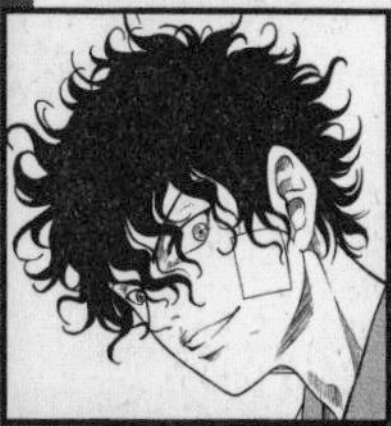

RIKKAI

AKAYA KIRIHARA

CONTENTS

Vol. 26
Ryoma Echizen vs.
Genichiro Sanada

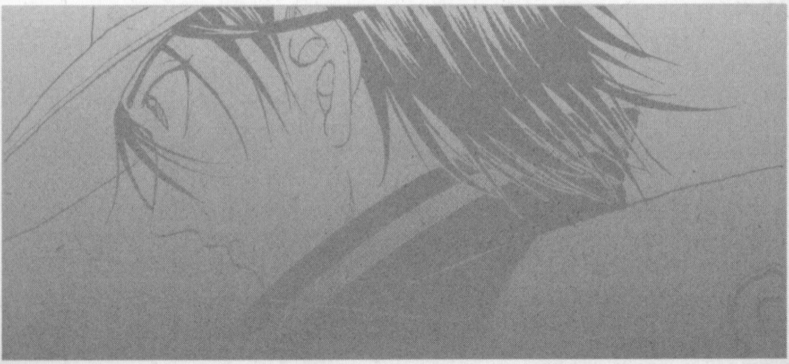

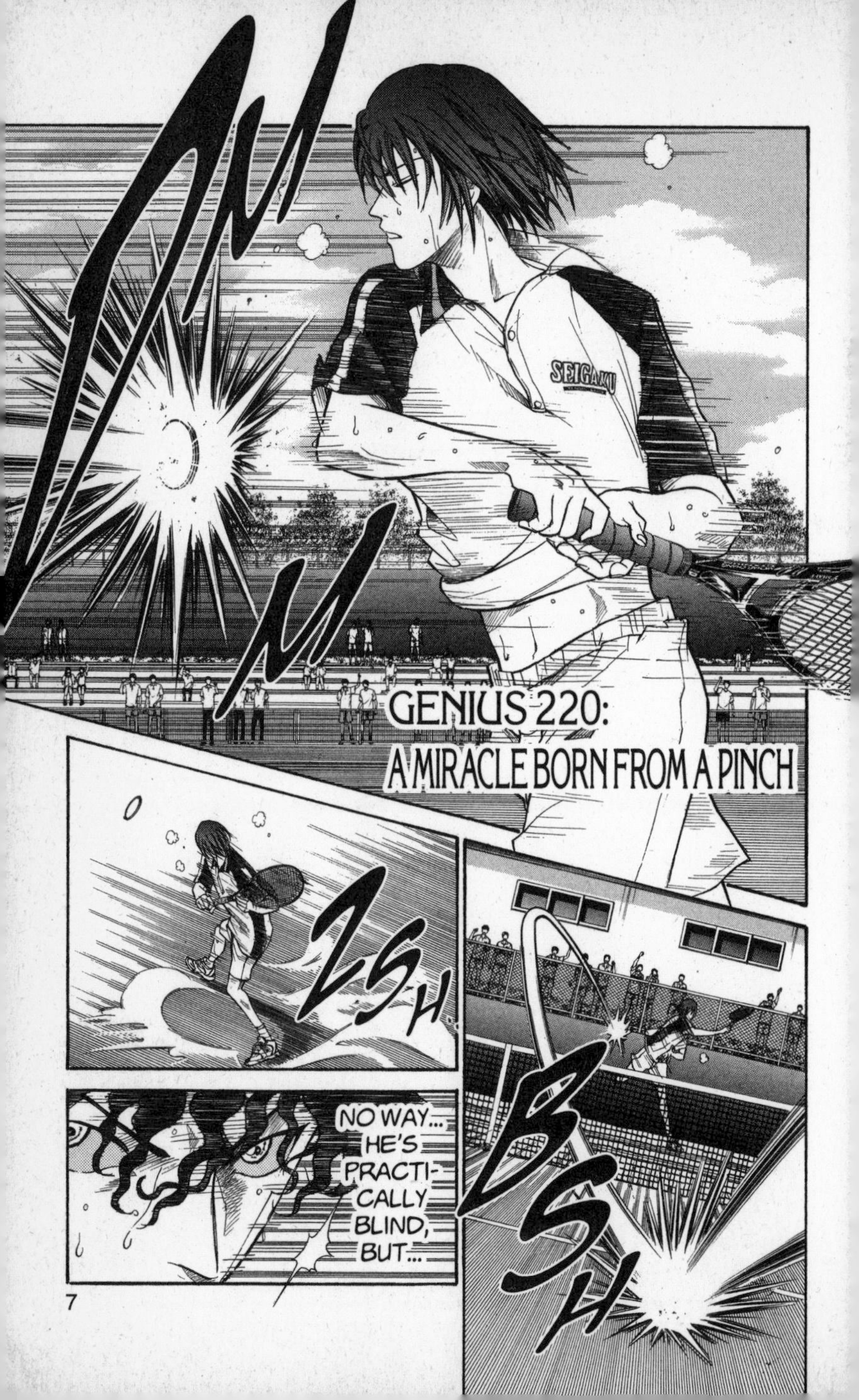
GENIUS 220:
A MIRACLE BORN FROM A PINCH
SEIGAKU
NO WAY... HE'S PRACTI-CALLY BLIND, BUT...

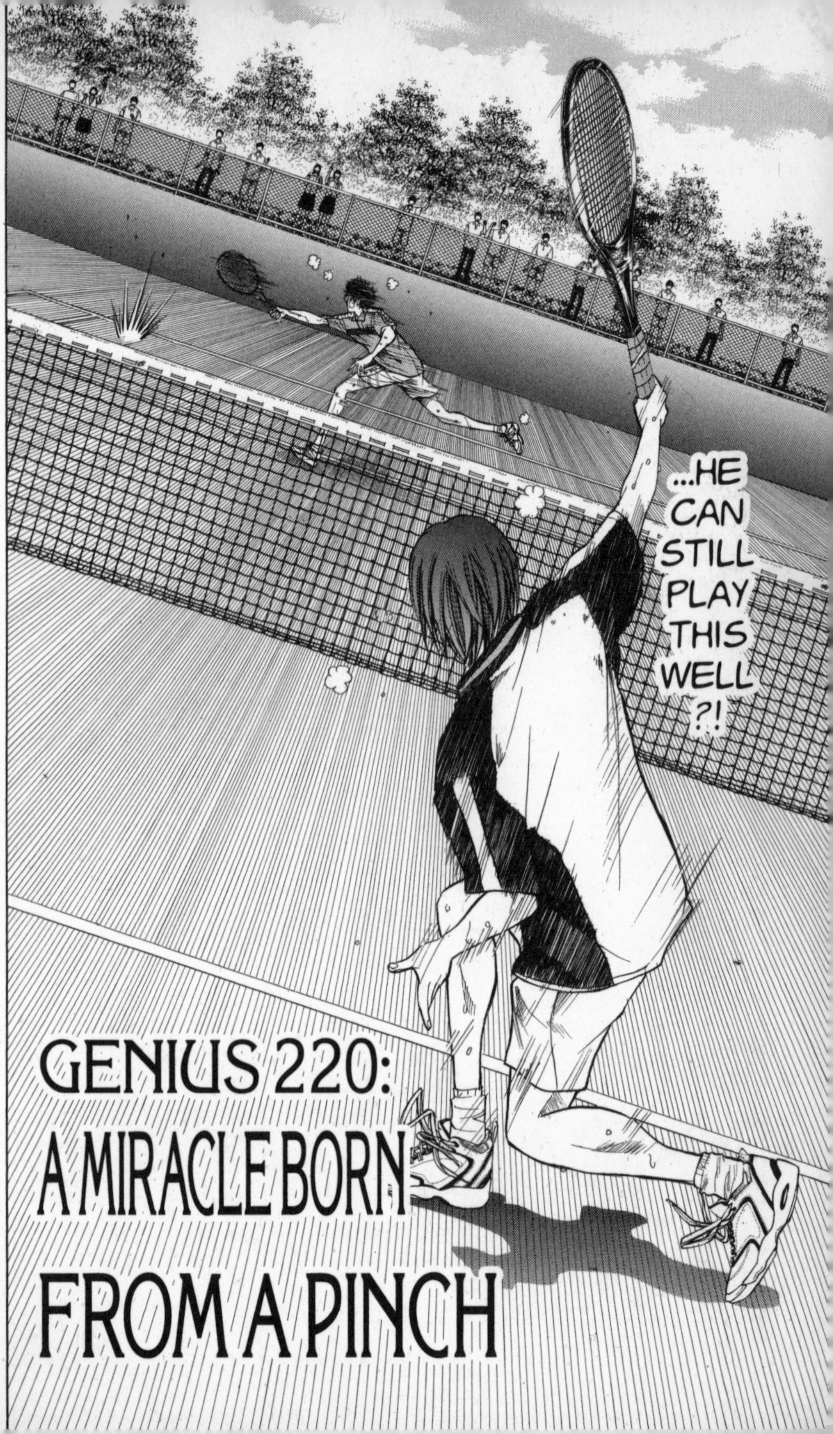
...HE CAN STILL PLAY THIS WELL?!
GENIUS 220:
A MIRACLE BORN FROM A PINCH

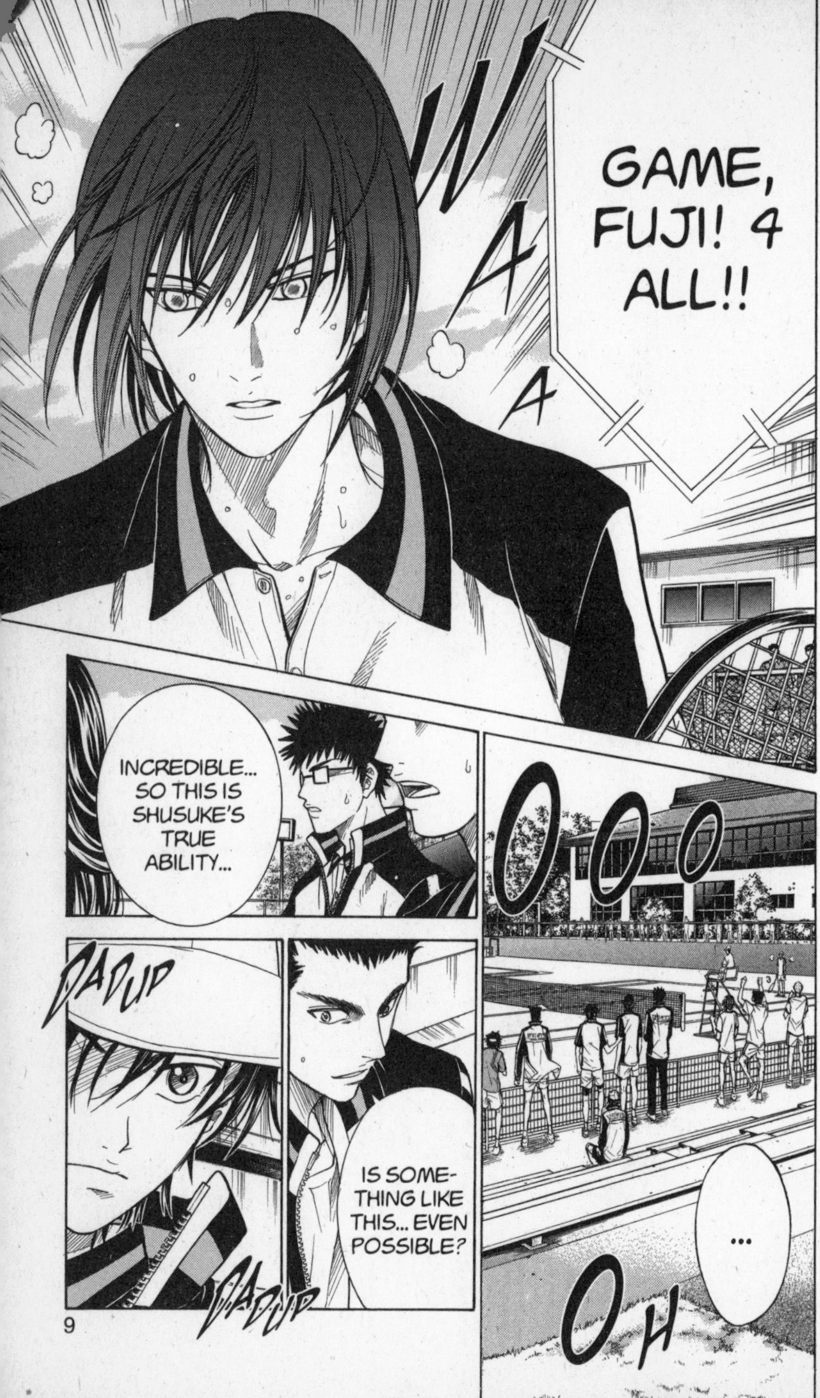
GAME, FUJI! 4 ALL!!
WAAA
OOO
...
OH
INCREDIBLE... SO THIS IS SHUSUKE'S TRUE ABILITY...
IS SOME-THING LIKE THIS... EVEN POSSIBLE?
DADUP
DADUP

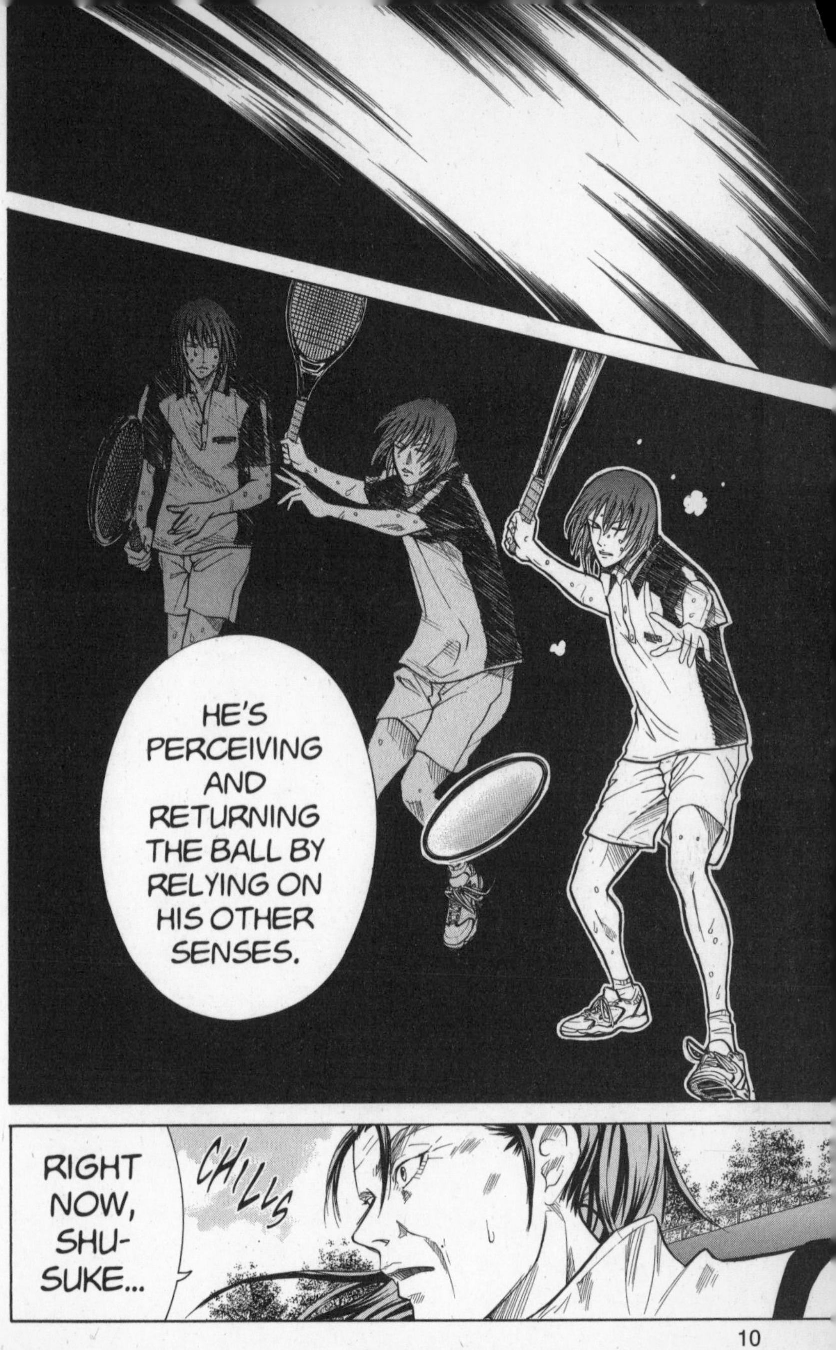
HE'S PERCEIVING AND RETURNING THE BALL BY RELYING ON HIS OTHER SENSES.
CHILLS
RIGHT NOW, SHU-SUKE...

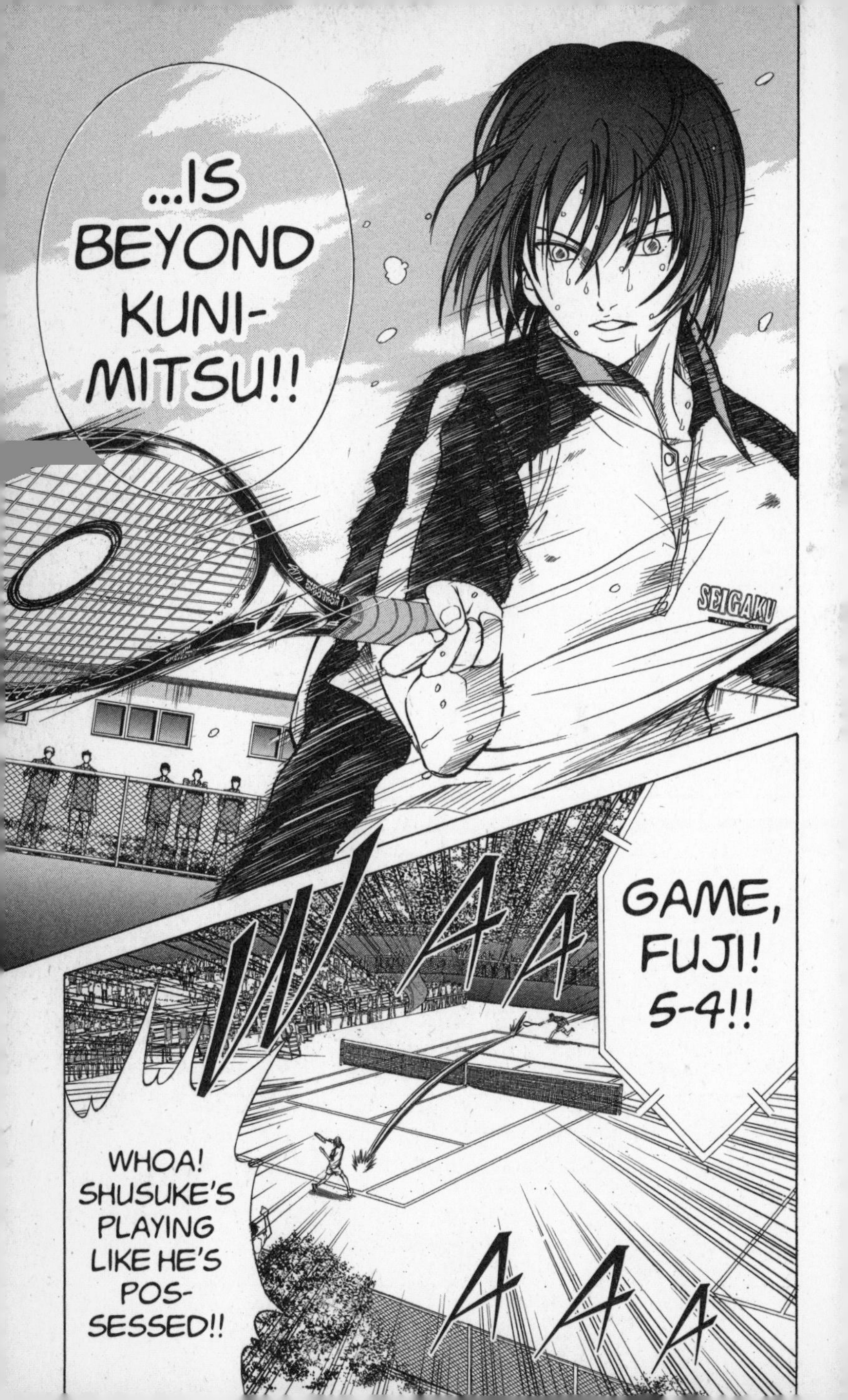
...IS BEYOND KUNI-MITSU!!
GAME, FUJI! 5-4!!
WAA
AAA
WHOA! SHUSUKE'S PLAYING LIKE HE'S POS-SESSED!!

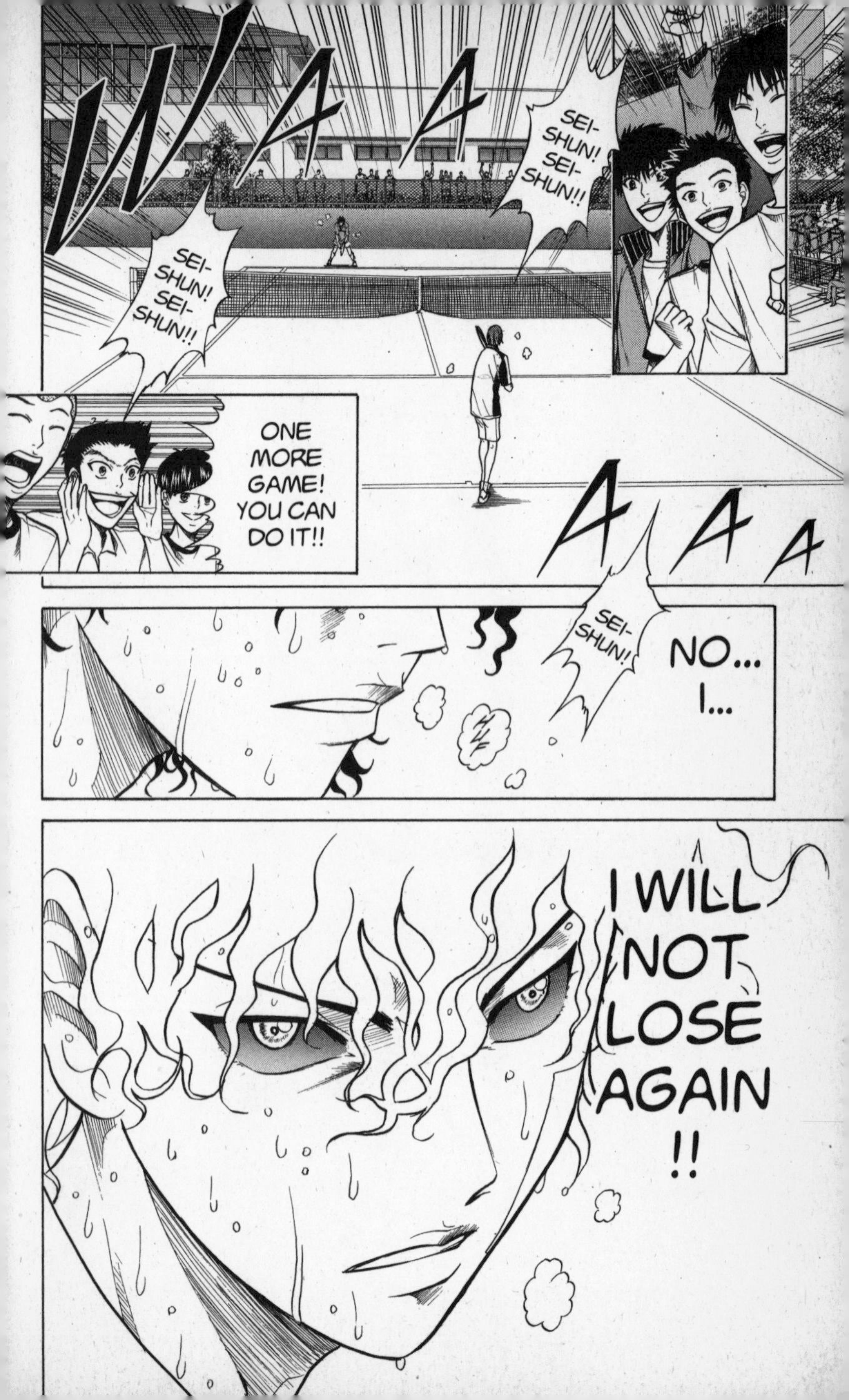
SEI-SHUN! SEI-SHUN!!
WAA
SEI-SHUN! SEI-SHUN!!
AAA
ONE MORE GAME! YOU CAN DO IT!!
SEI-SHUN!
NO... I...
I WILL NOT LOSE AGAIN!!

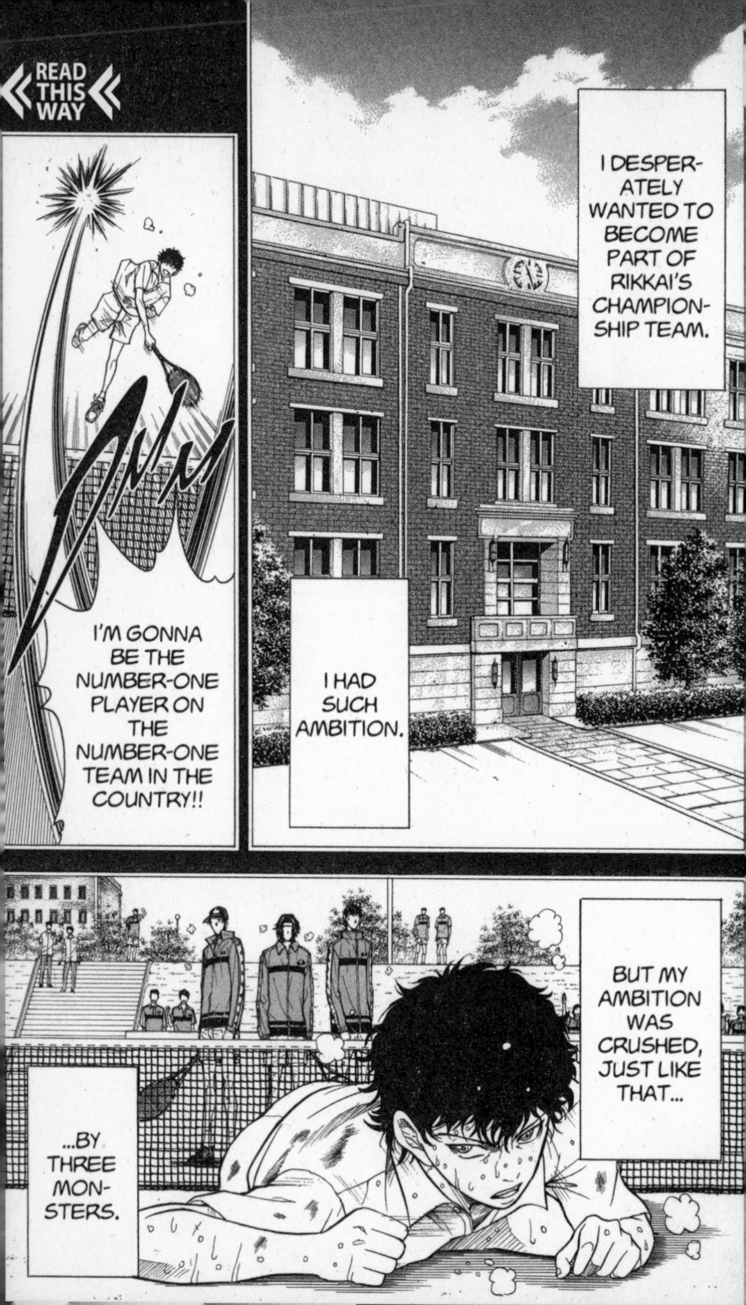
READ THIS WAY
I DESPERATELY WANTED TO BECOME PART OF RIKKAI'S CHAMPIONSHIP TEAM.
I HAD SUCH AMBITION.
I'M GONNA BE THE NUMBER-ONE PLAYER ON THE NUMBER-ONE TEAM IN THE COUNTRY!!
BUT MY AMBITION WAS CRUSHED, JUST LIKE THAT...
...BY THREE MONSTERS.

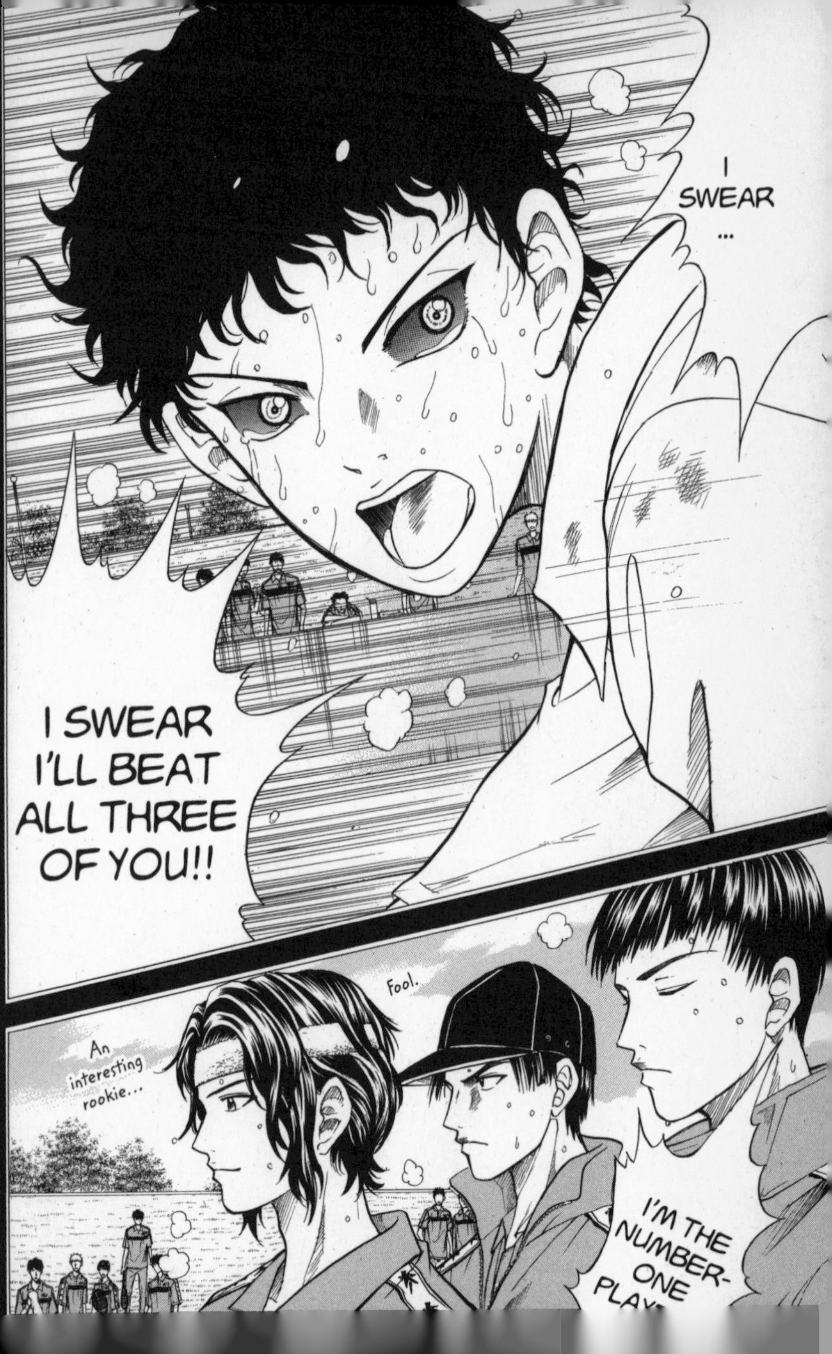
I SWEAR...
I SWEAR I'LL BEAT ALL THREE OF YOU!!
I'M THE NUMBER-ONE PLAY
Fool.
An interesting rookie...

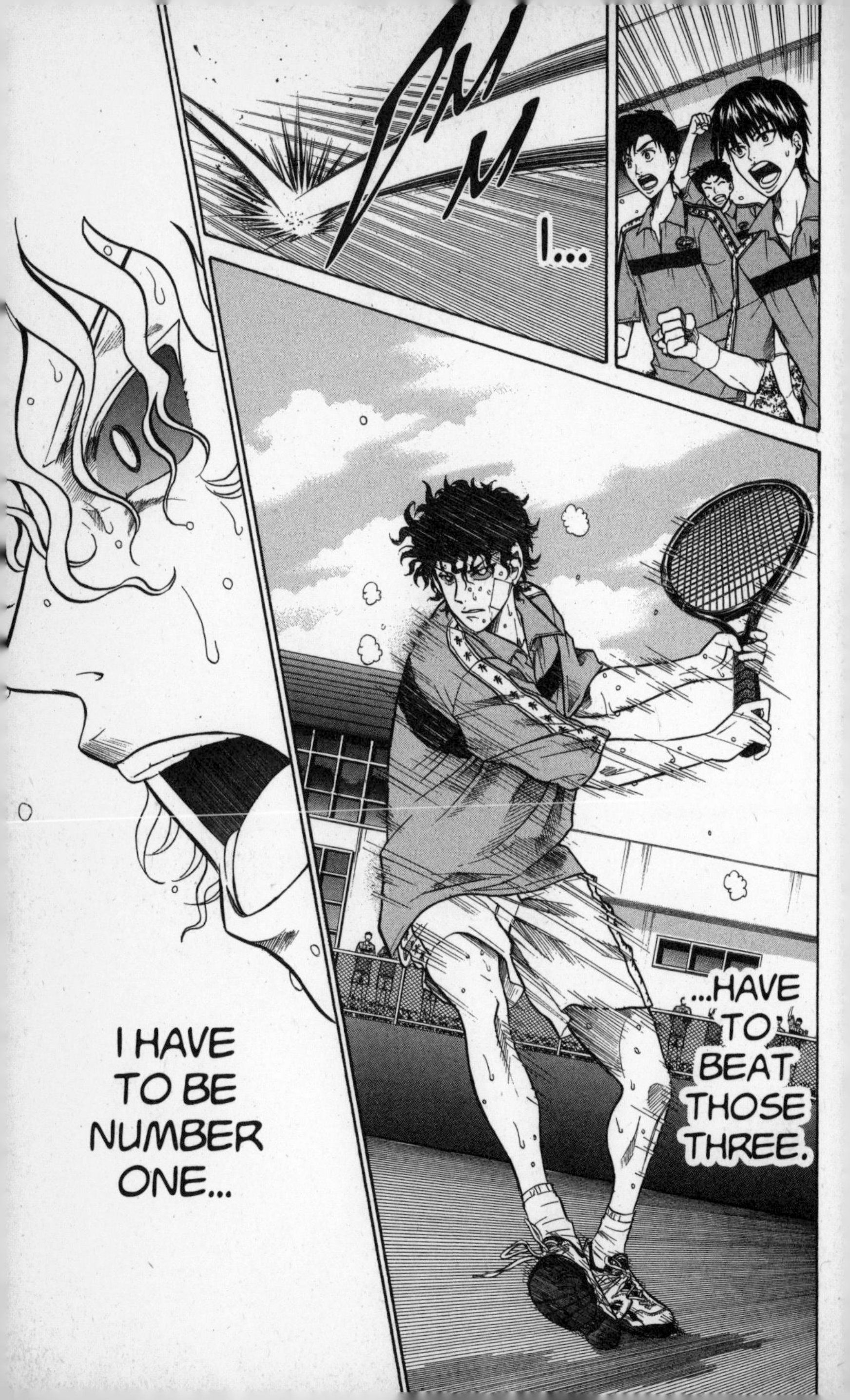
I...
...HAVE TO BEAT THOSE THREE.
I HAVE TO BE NUMBER ONE...

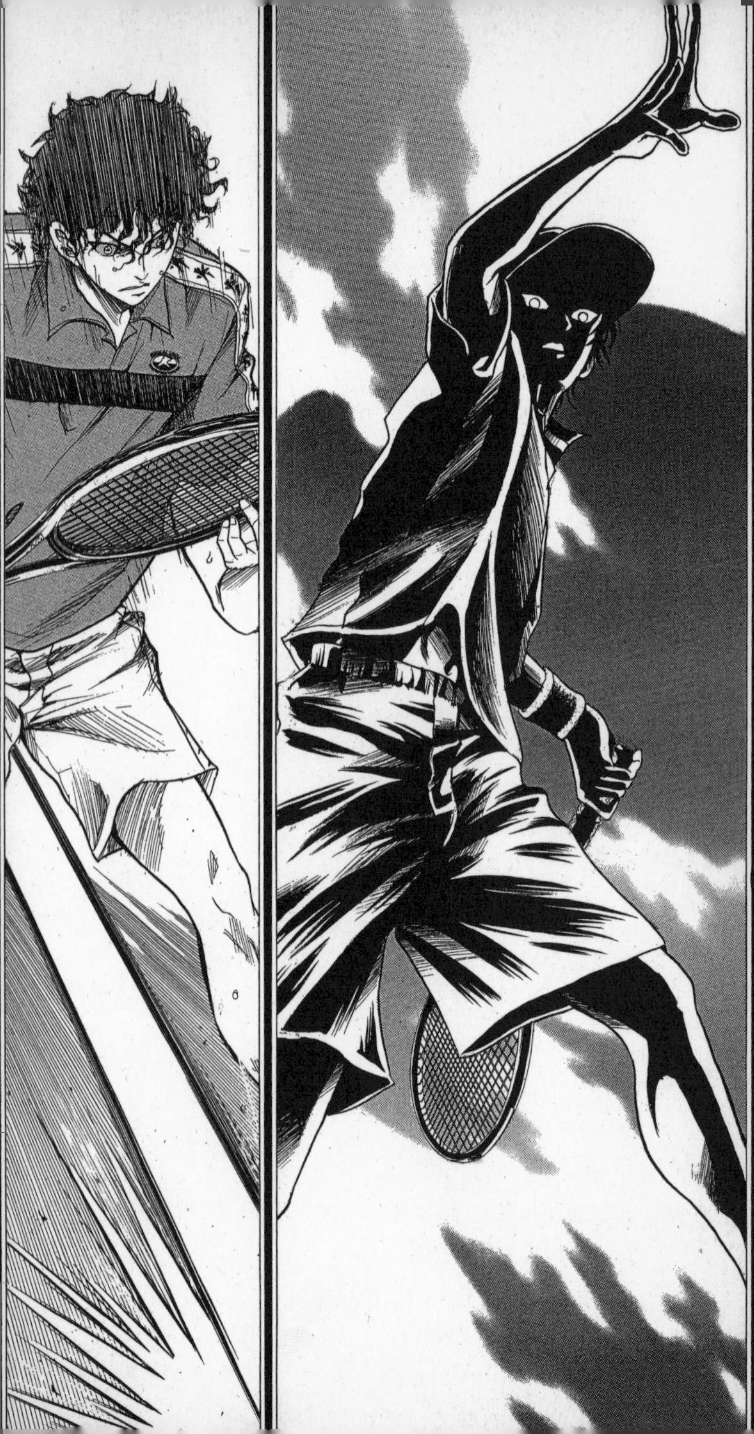

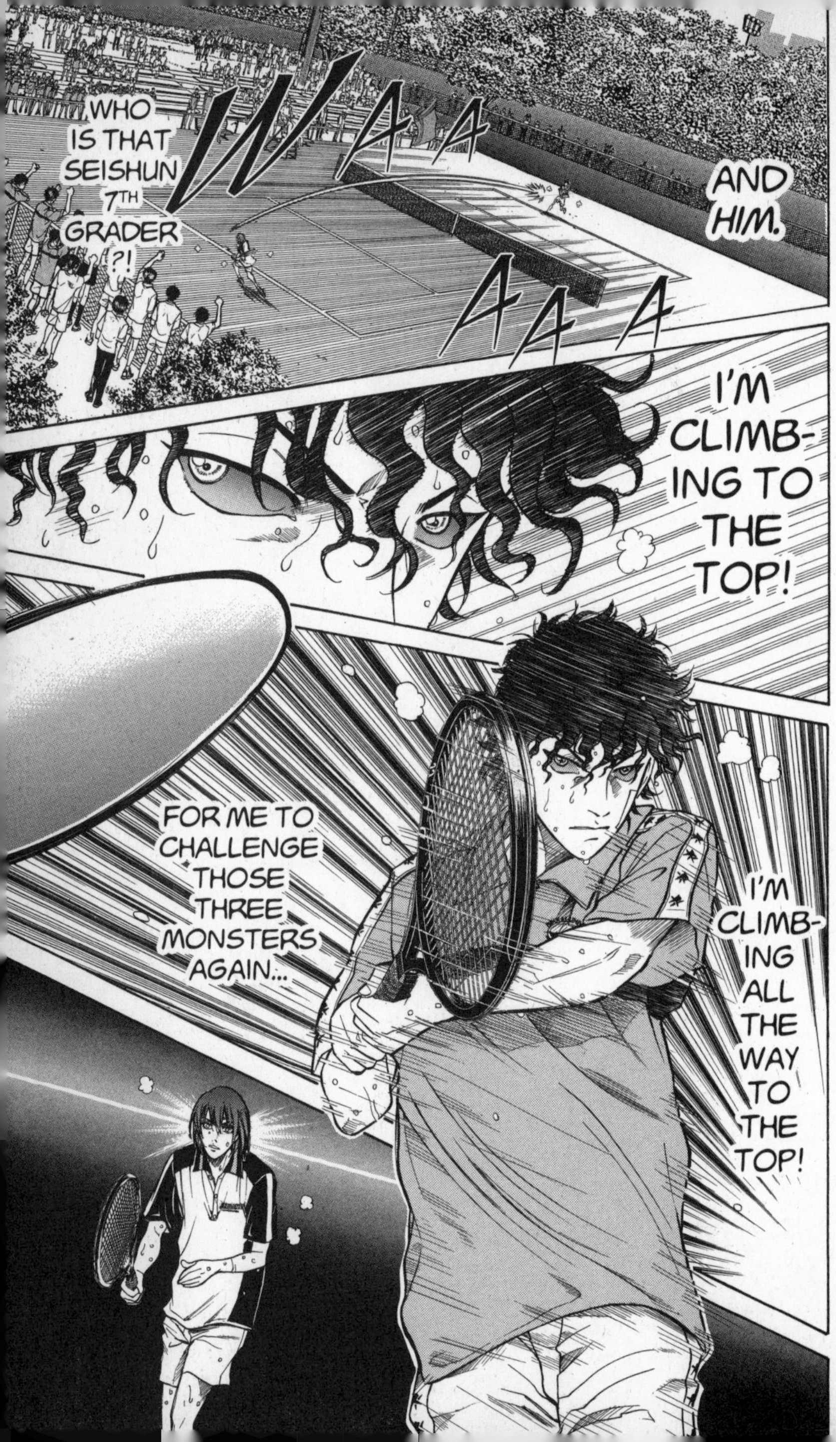
WAAAAAA
AND HIM.
WHO IS THAT SEISHUN 7TH GRADER?!
I'M CLIMBING TO THE TOP!
I'M CLIMBING ALL THE WAY TO THE TOP!
FOR ME TO CHALLENGE THOSE THREE MONSTERS AGAIN...

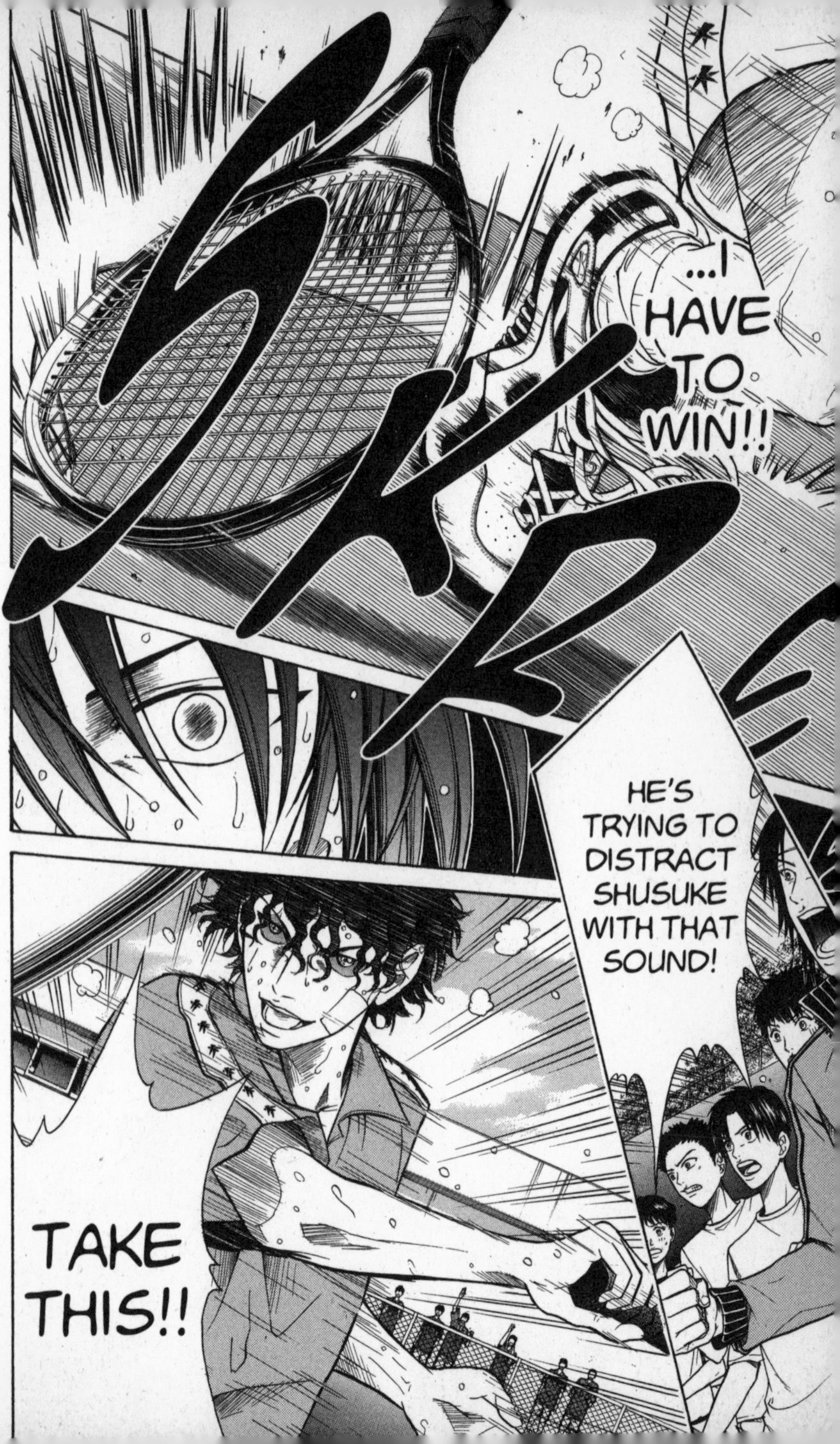
...I HAVE TO WIN!!
HE'S TRYING TO DISTRACT SHUSUKE WITH THAT SOUND!
TAKE THIS!!

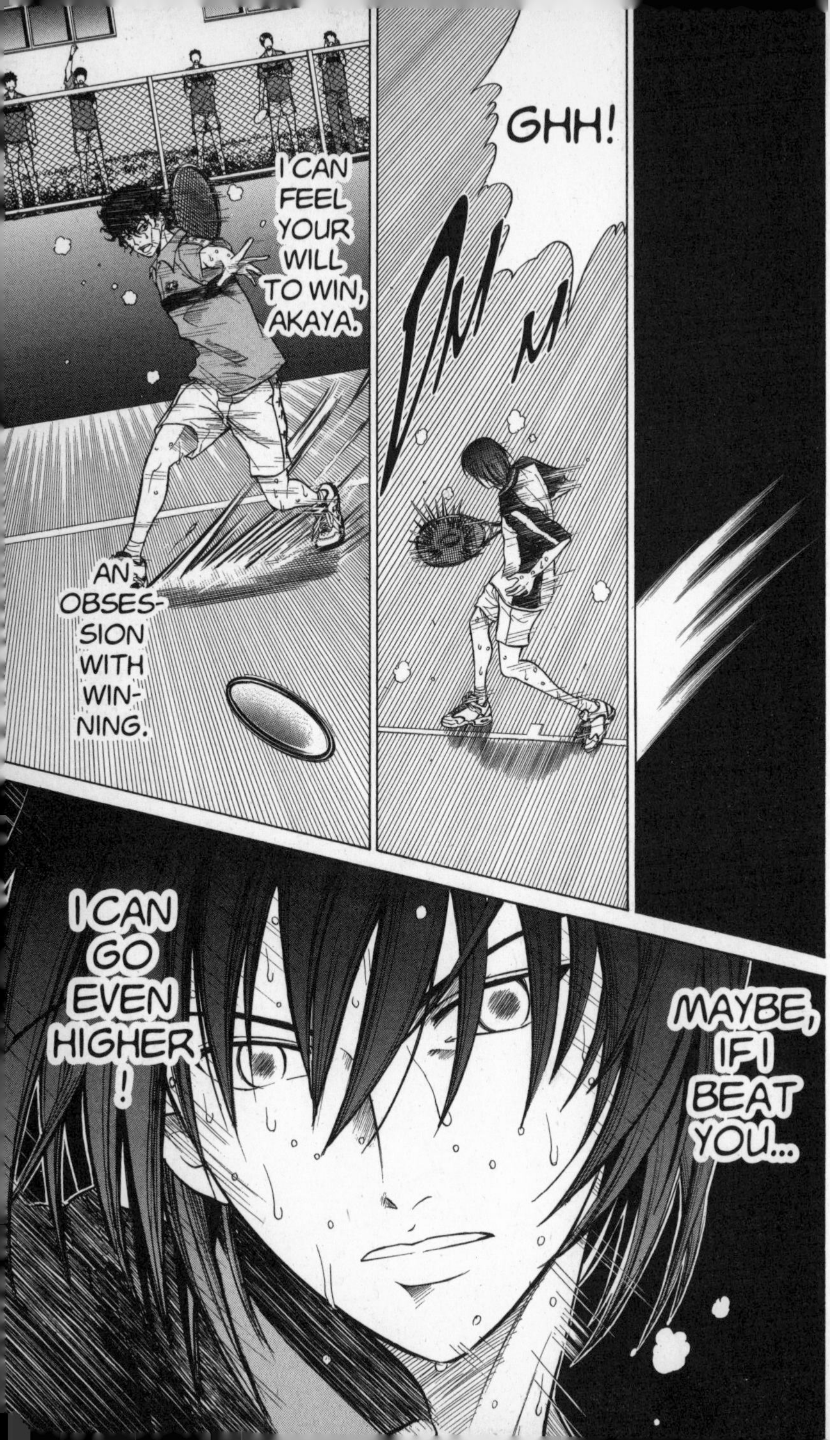
GHH!
I CAN FEEL YOUR WILL TO WIN, AKAYA.
AN OBSES-SION WITH WIN-NING.
MAYBE, IF I BEAT YOU...
I CAN GO EVEN HIGHER!

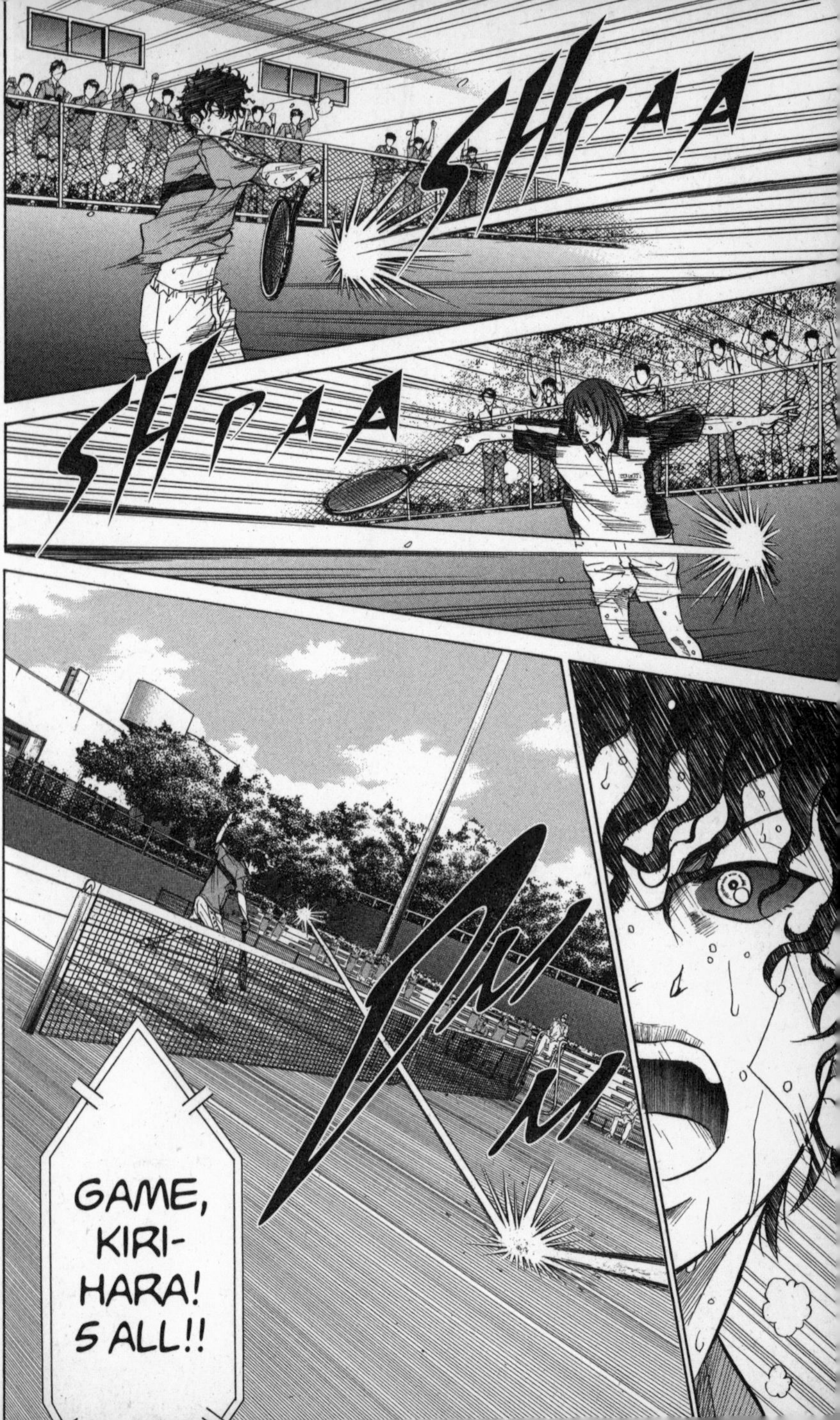
SHPAA
SHPAA
GAME, KIRI-HARA! 5 ALL!!

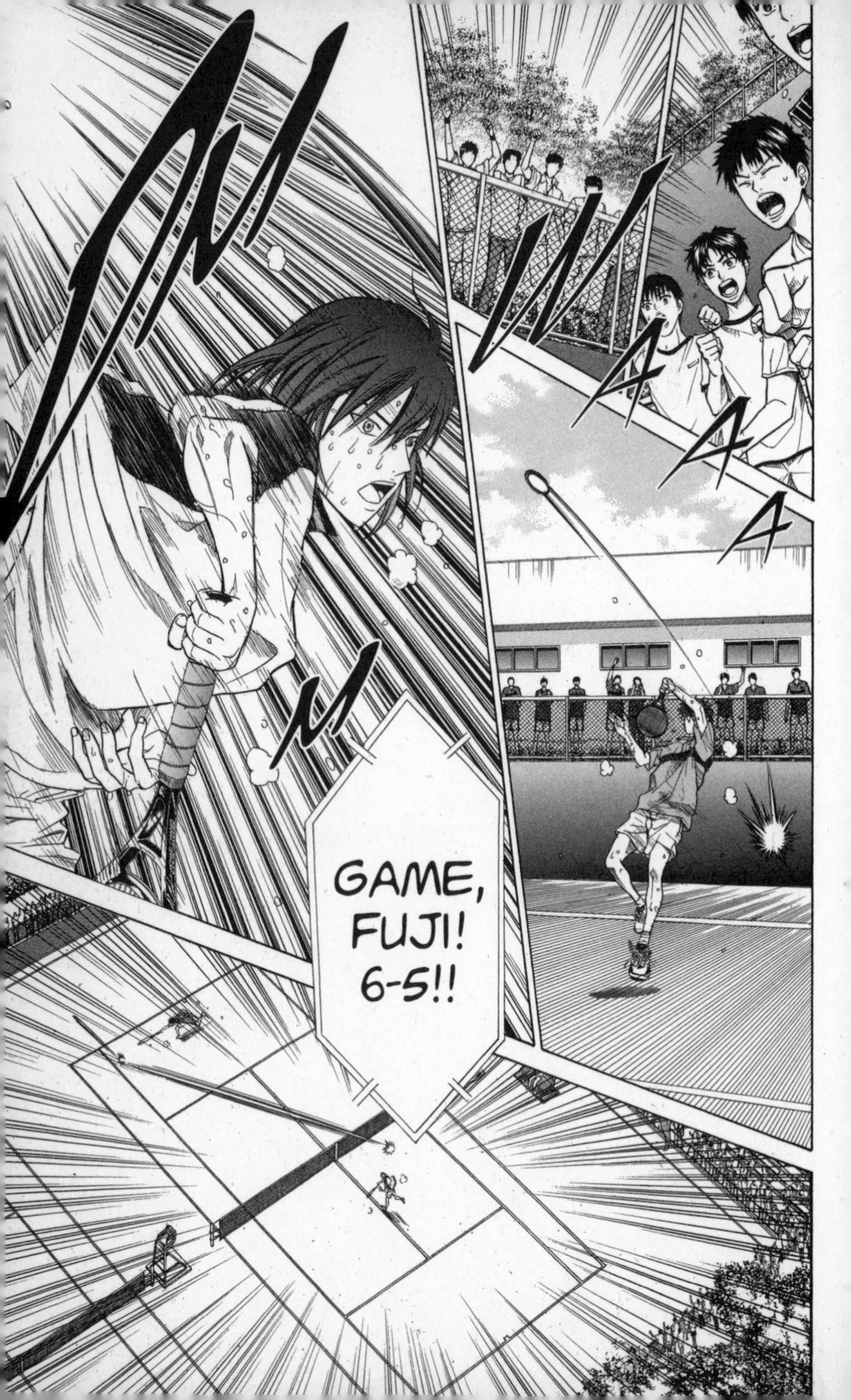
WAAA
GAME, FUJI! 6-5!!

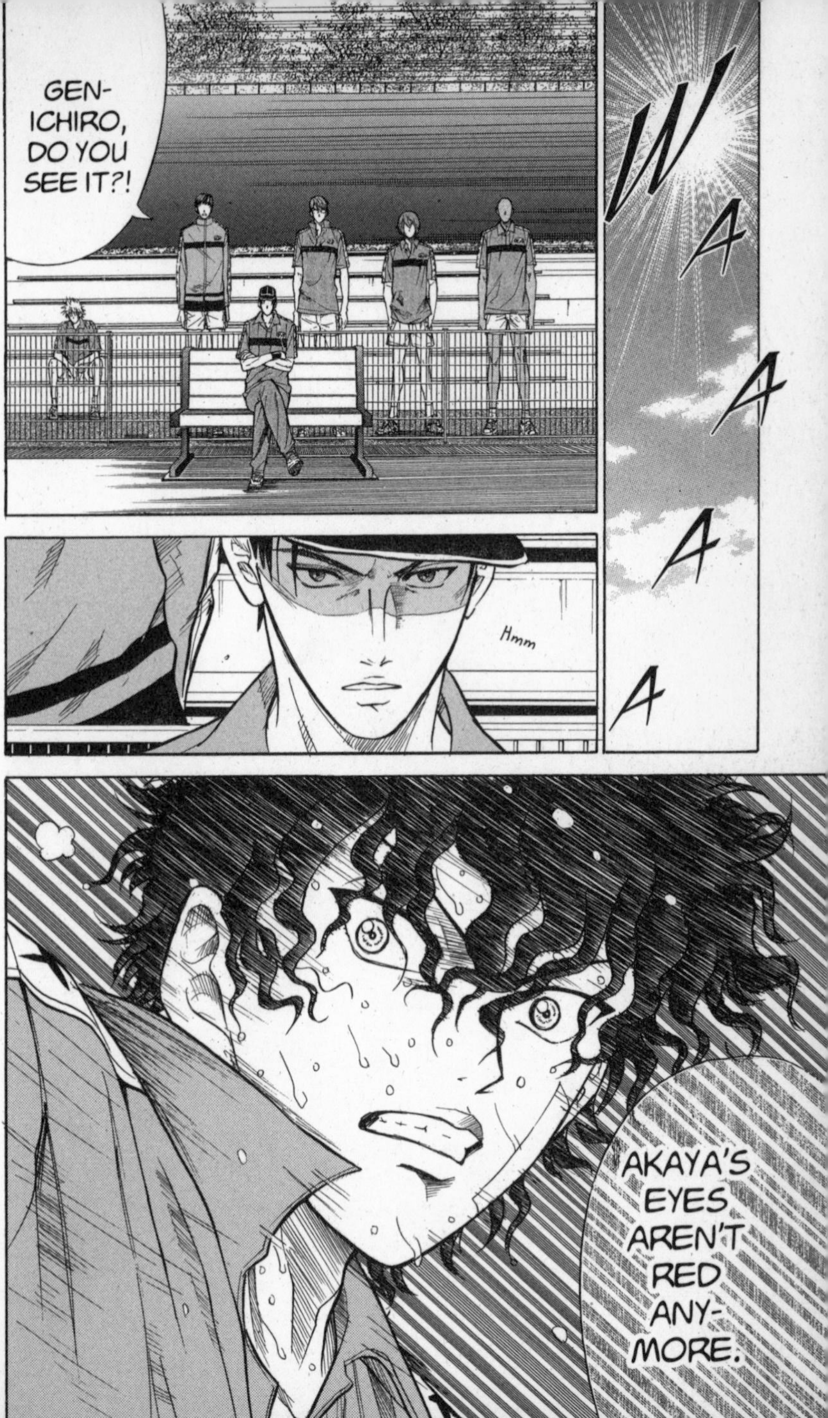
WAAAAA
GEN-ICHIRO, DO YOU SEE IT?!
Hmm
AKAYA'S EYES AREN'T RED ANYMORE.

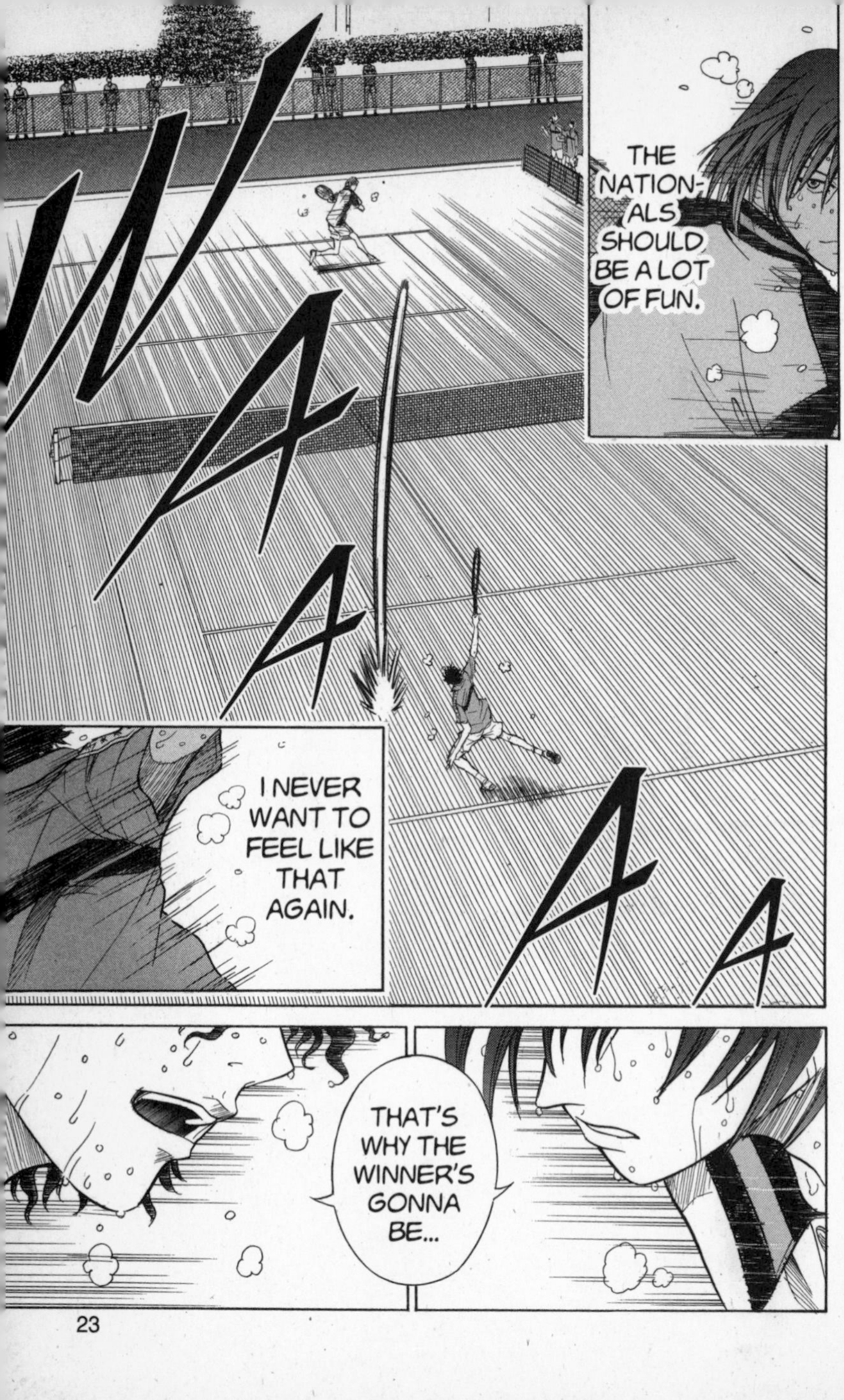
THE NATION-ALS SHOULD BE A LOT OF FUN.
WAAAA
I NEVER WANT TO FEEL LIKE THAT AGAIN.
THAT'S WHY THE WINNER'S GONNA BE...

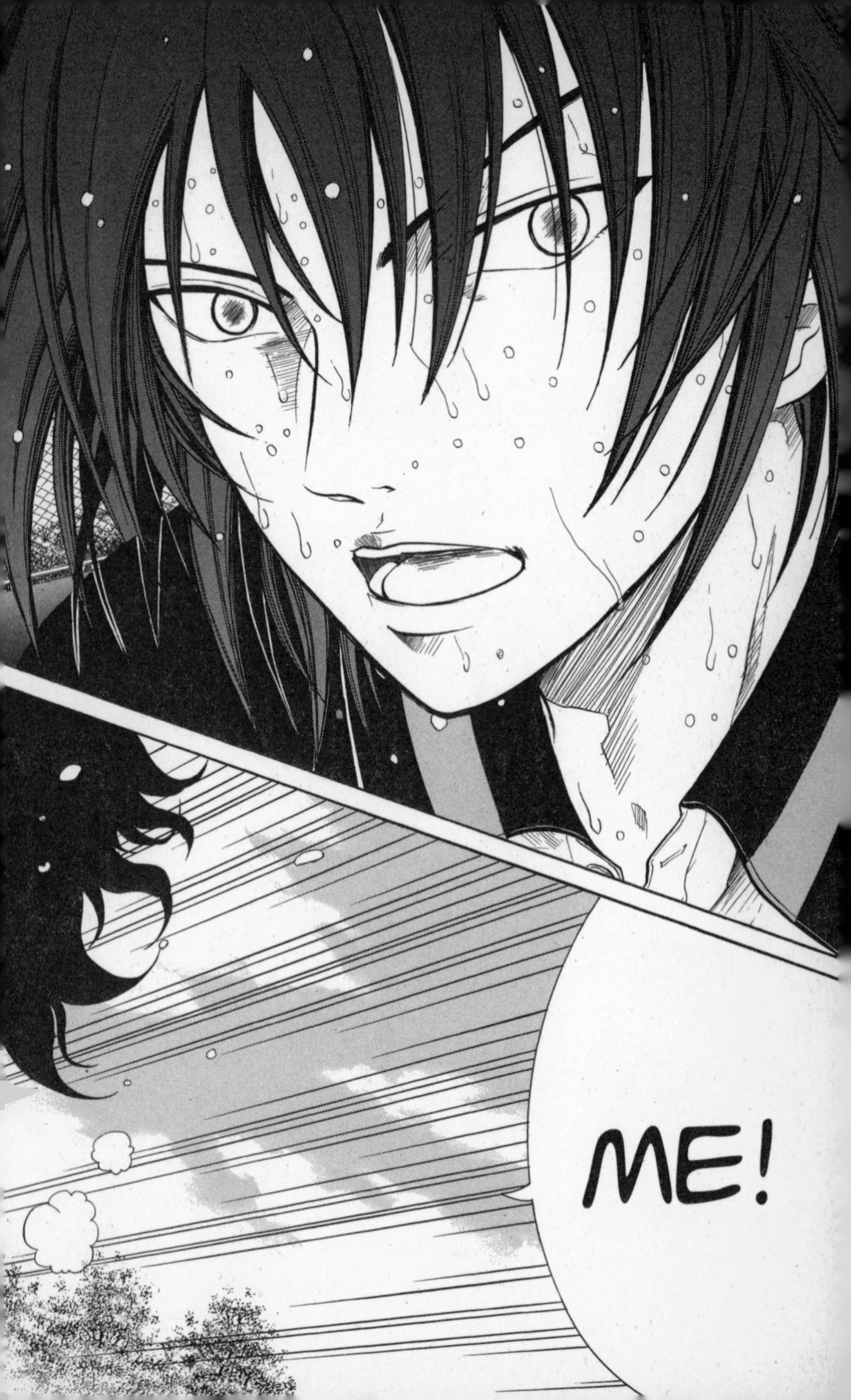
ME!

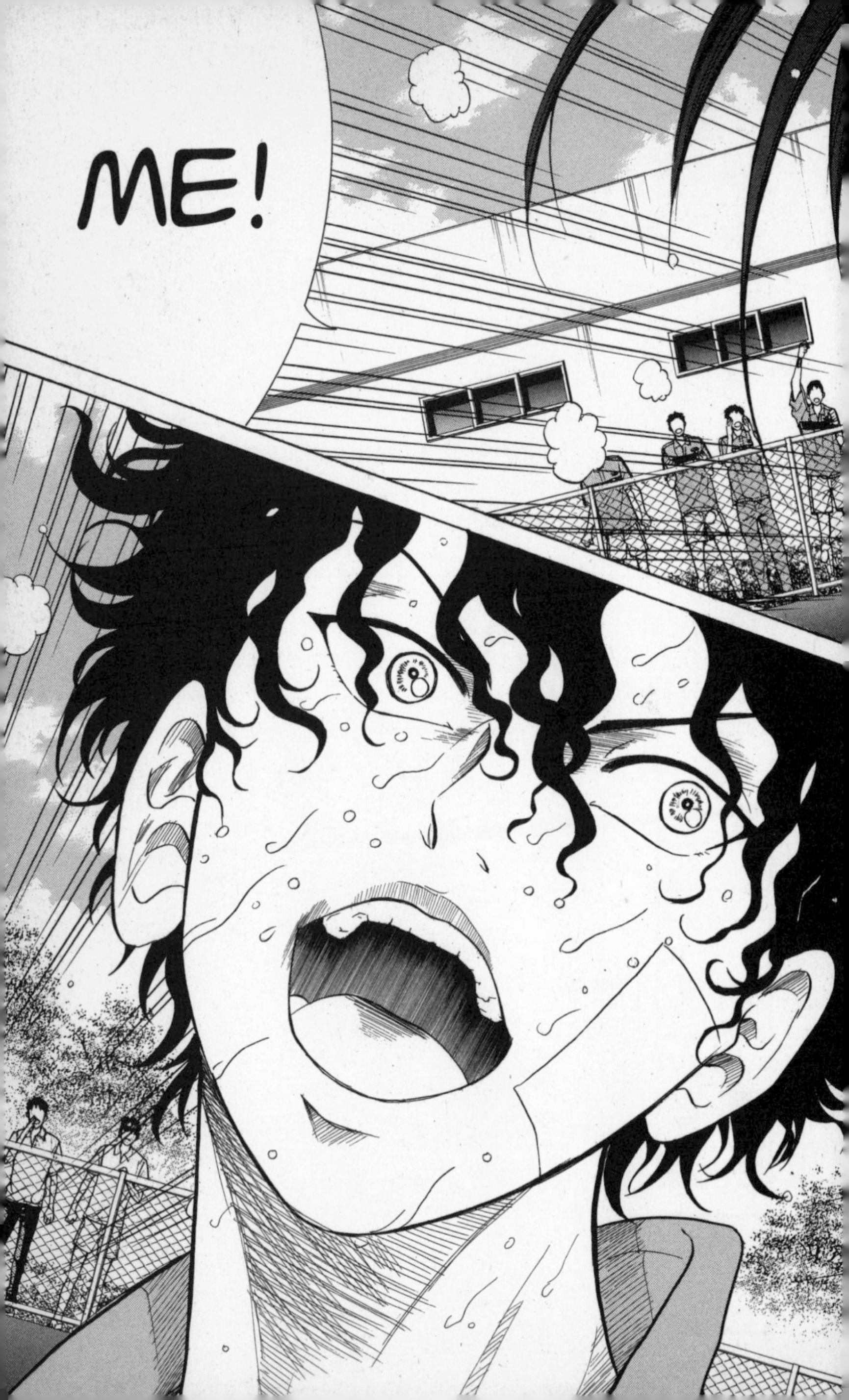
ME!

RIKKAI QUESTION CORNER

It's Back!!

Part 1

RIKKAI UNIV. JUNIOR HIGH SCHOOL TENNIS CLUB

Thanks for all your kind letters!! It's been a while since we last had this segment, but the members of Rikkai's team are here with us today and will be responding to your questions themselves!

Q: I was completely fooled by "The Con Artist," Masaharu Nio! At what point did he and Hiroshi make the switch? I gotta know!! (Y.I., Saitama)

 I don't know what you're talking about… *cough*.

 Hey, hey. Hiroshi's playin' dumb!

 A "gentleman" conning people? Sure that's okay?

 …..Fwee ♪

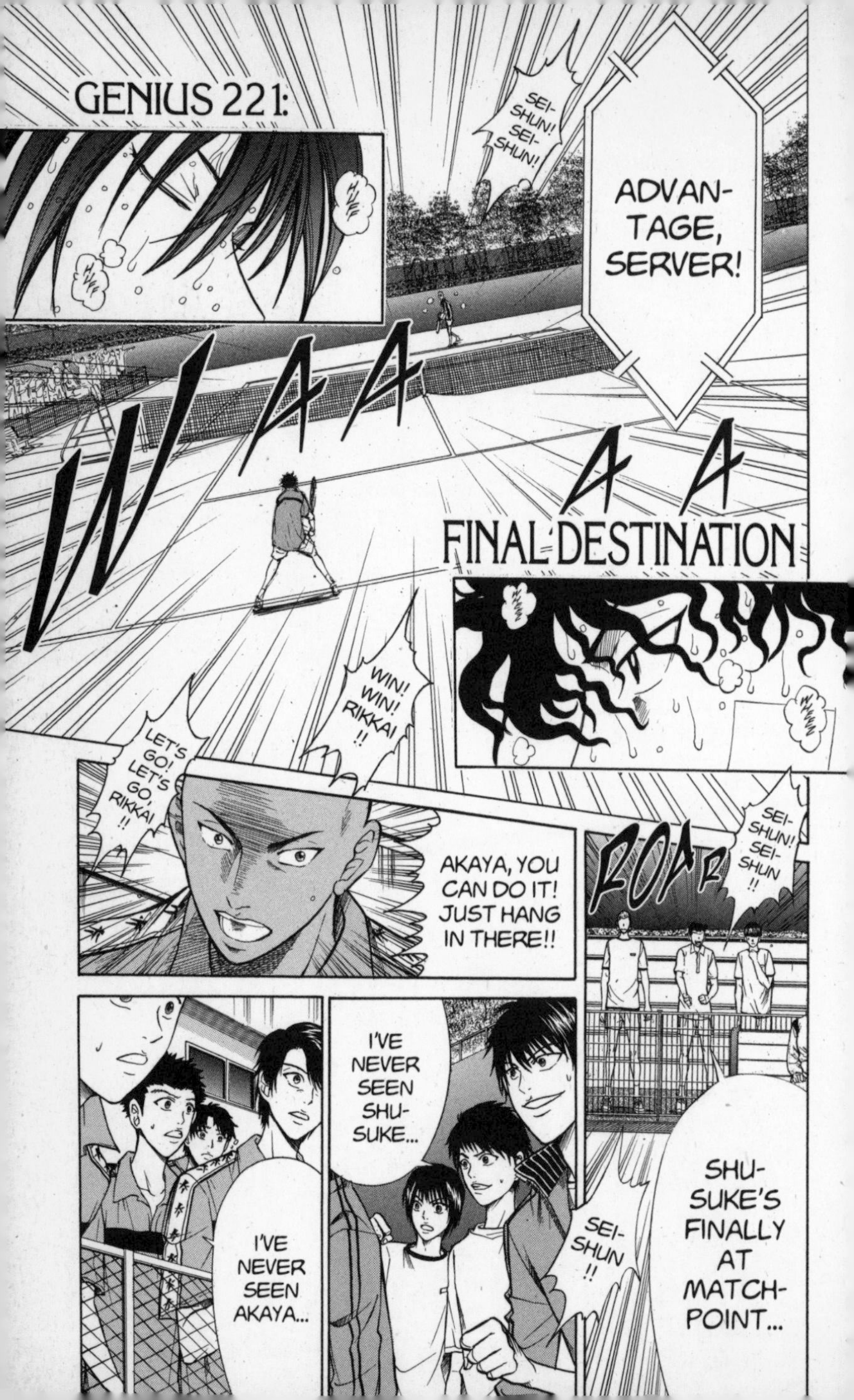
SEI-SHUN! SEI-SHUN!
ADVAN-TAGE, SERVER!
GENIUS 221:
HUFF
HUFF
WAAAA
FINAL DESTINATION
SEI-SHUN! SEI-SHUN!!
ROAR
AKAYA, YOU CAN DO IT! JUST HANG IN THERE!!
WIN! WIN! RIKKAI!!
LET'S GO! LET'S GO, RIKKAI!!
SHU-SUKE'S FINALLY AT MATCH-POINT...
SEI-SHUN!!
I'VE NEVER SEEN SHU-SUKE...
I'VE NEVER SEEN AKAYA...

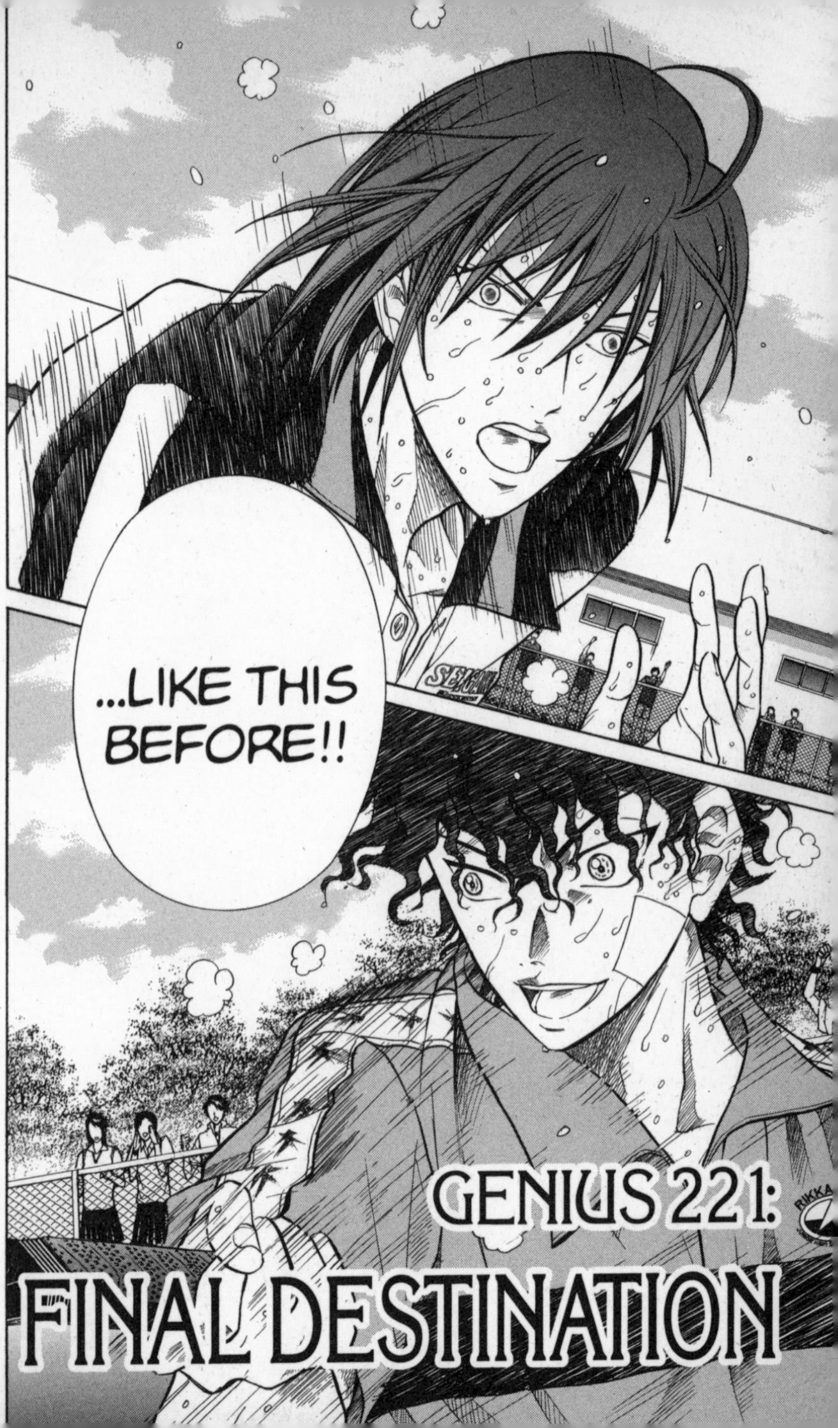
...LIKE THIS BEFORE!!
GENIUS 221:
FINAL DESTINATION

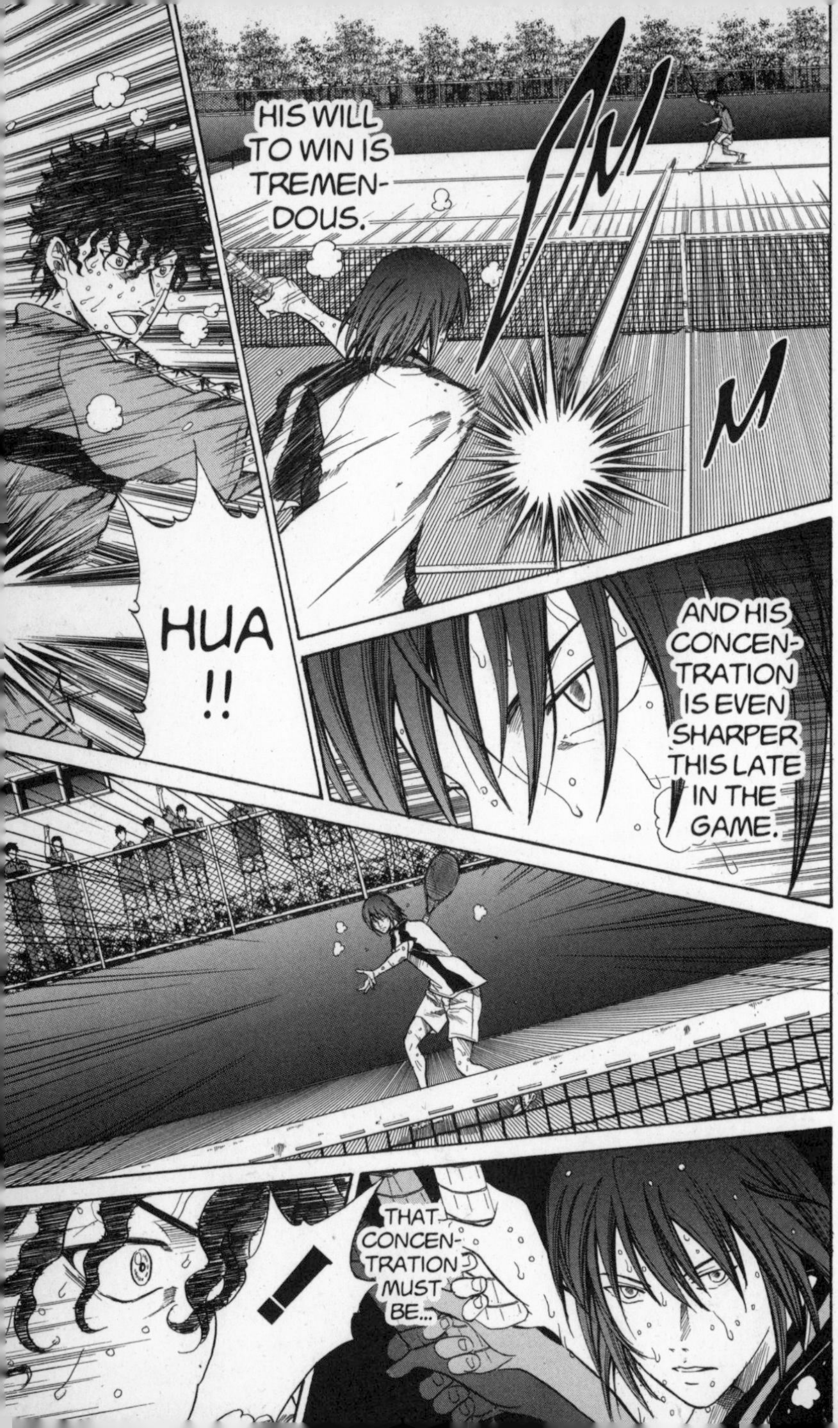
HIS WILL TO WIN IS TREMEN-DOUS.
M
HUA !!
AND HIS CONCEN-TRATION IS EVEN SHARPER THIS LATE IN THE GAME.
THAT CONCEN-TRATION MUST BE...
!

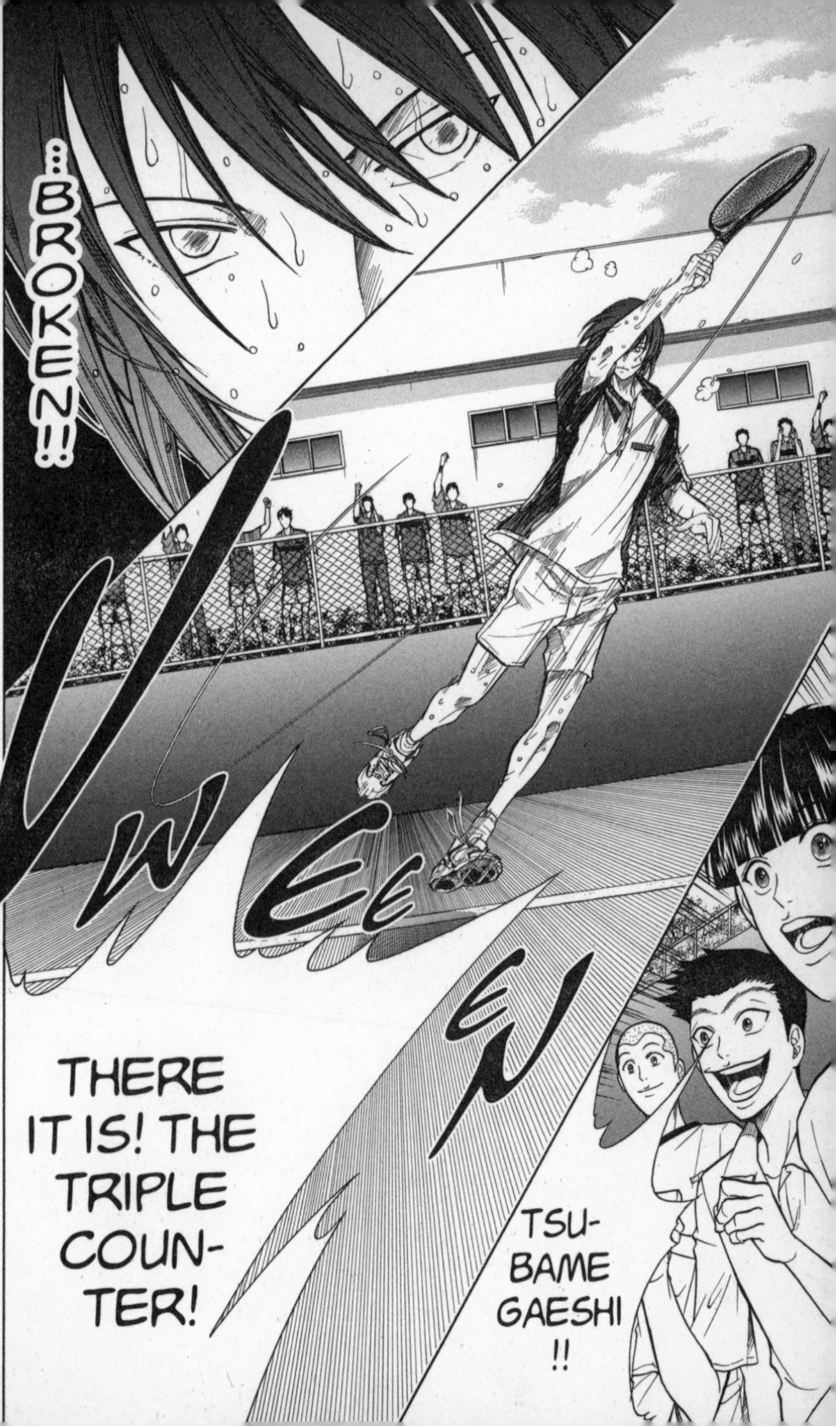
...BROKEN!!
TSU-BAME GAESHI!!
THERE IT IS! THE TRIPLE COUN-TER!

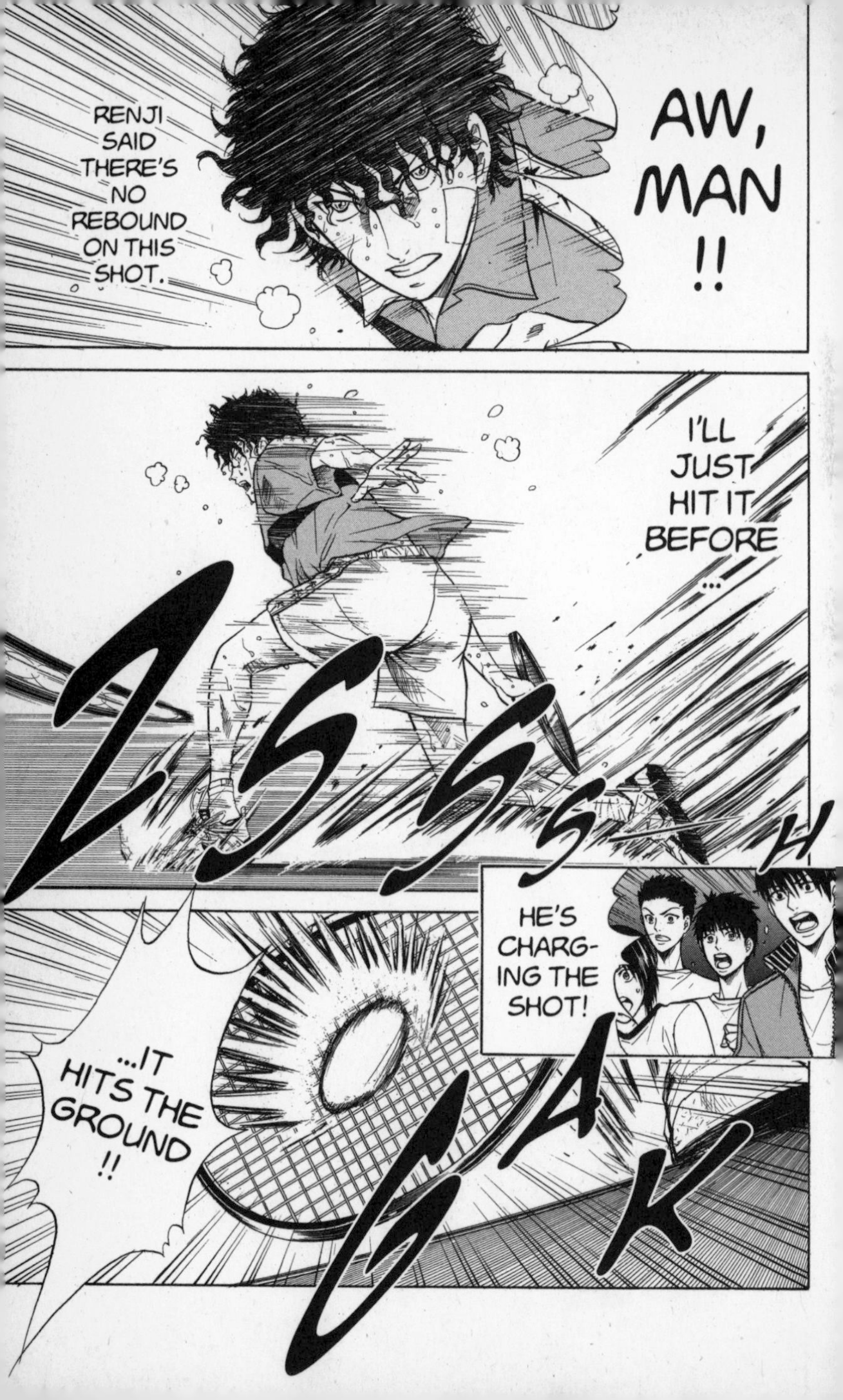
AW, MAN!!
RENJI SAID THERE'S NO REBOUND ON THIS SHOT.
I'LL JUST HIT IT BEFORE...
ZSSSSH
HE'S CHARG-ING THE SHOT!
...IT HITS THE GROUND!!

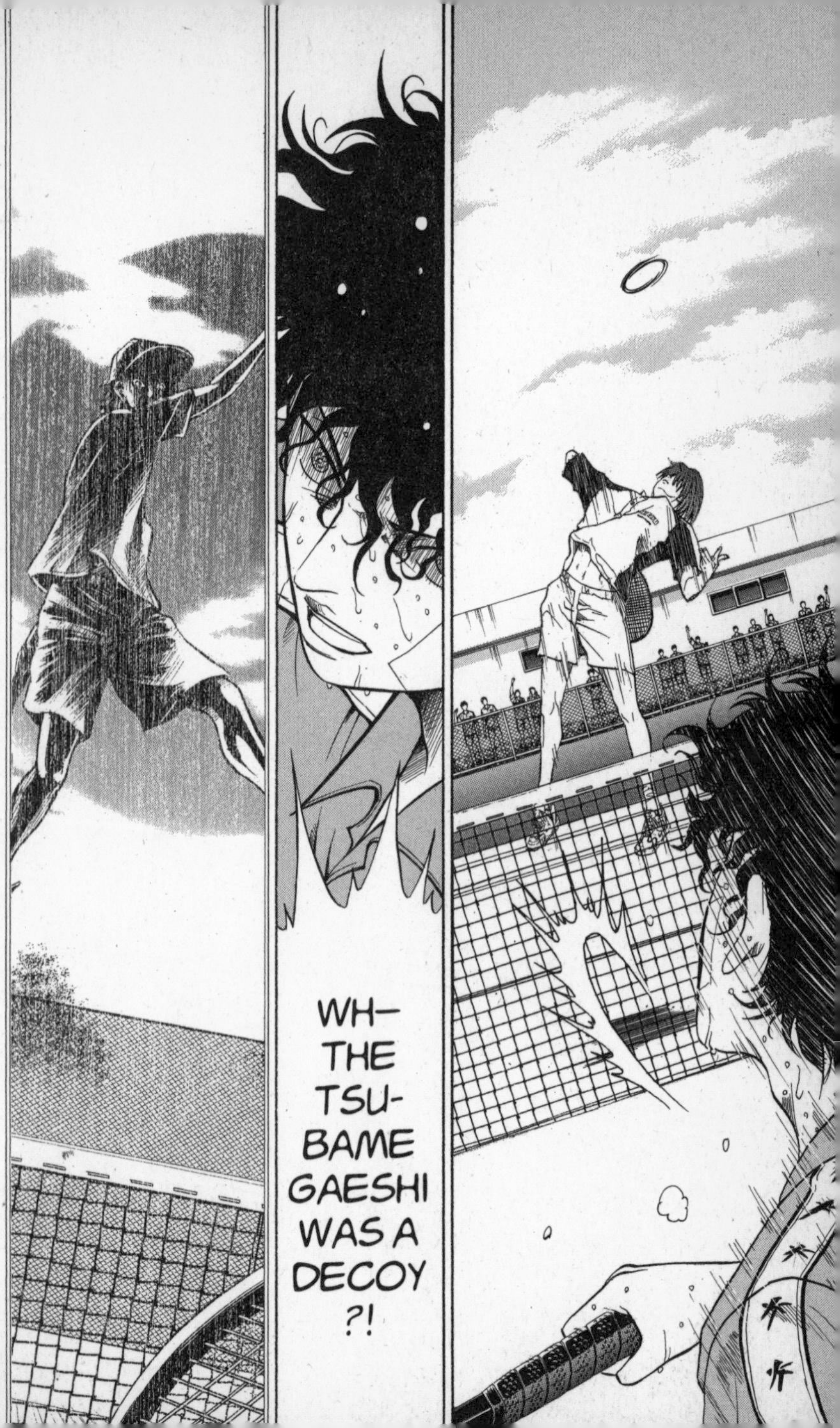
WH-
THE
TSU-
BAME
GAESHI
WAS A
DECOY
?!

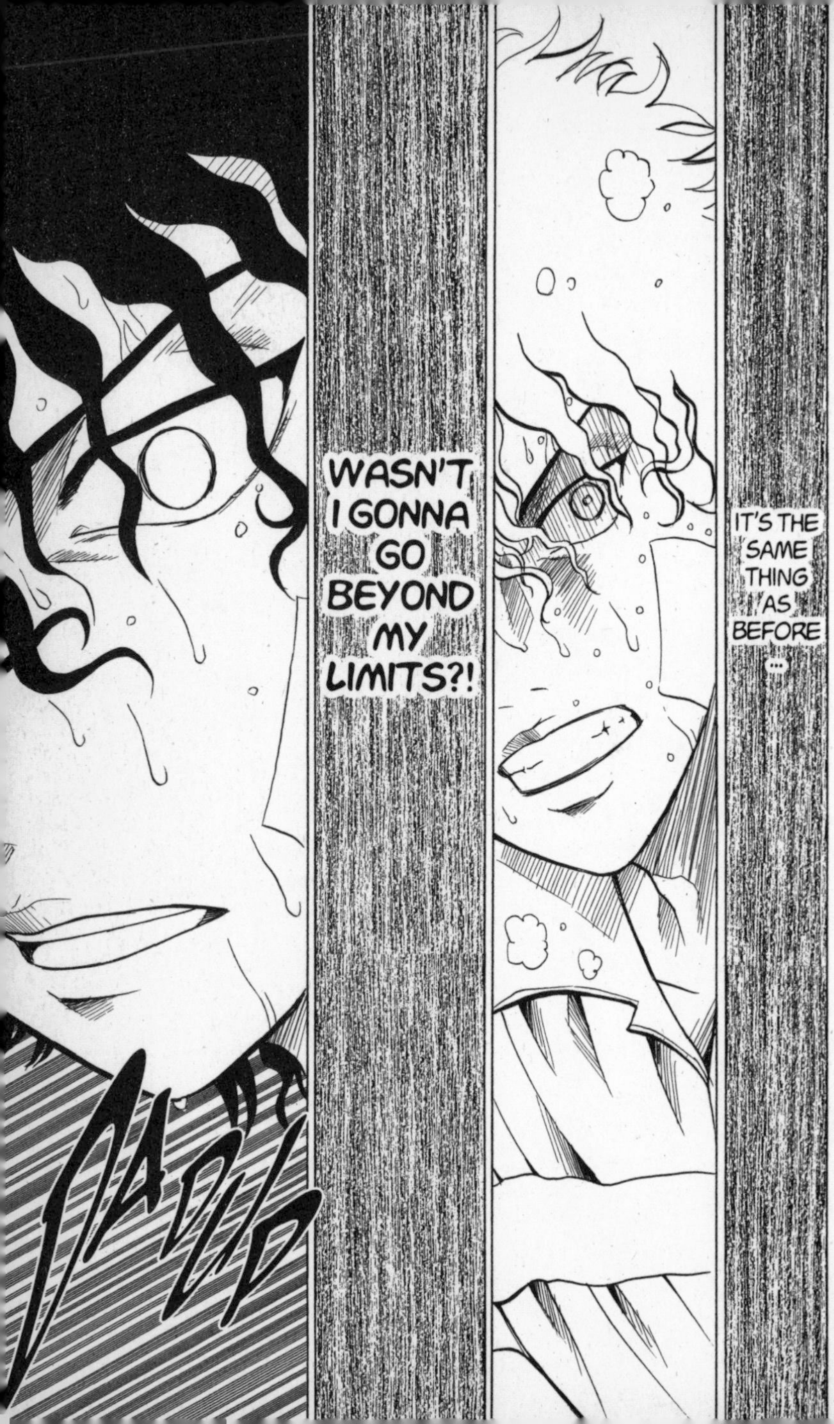
IT'S THE SAME THING AS BEFORE...
WASN'T I GONNA GO BEYOND MY LIMITS?!

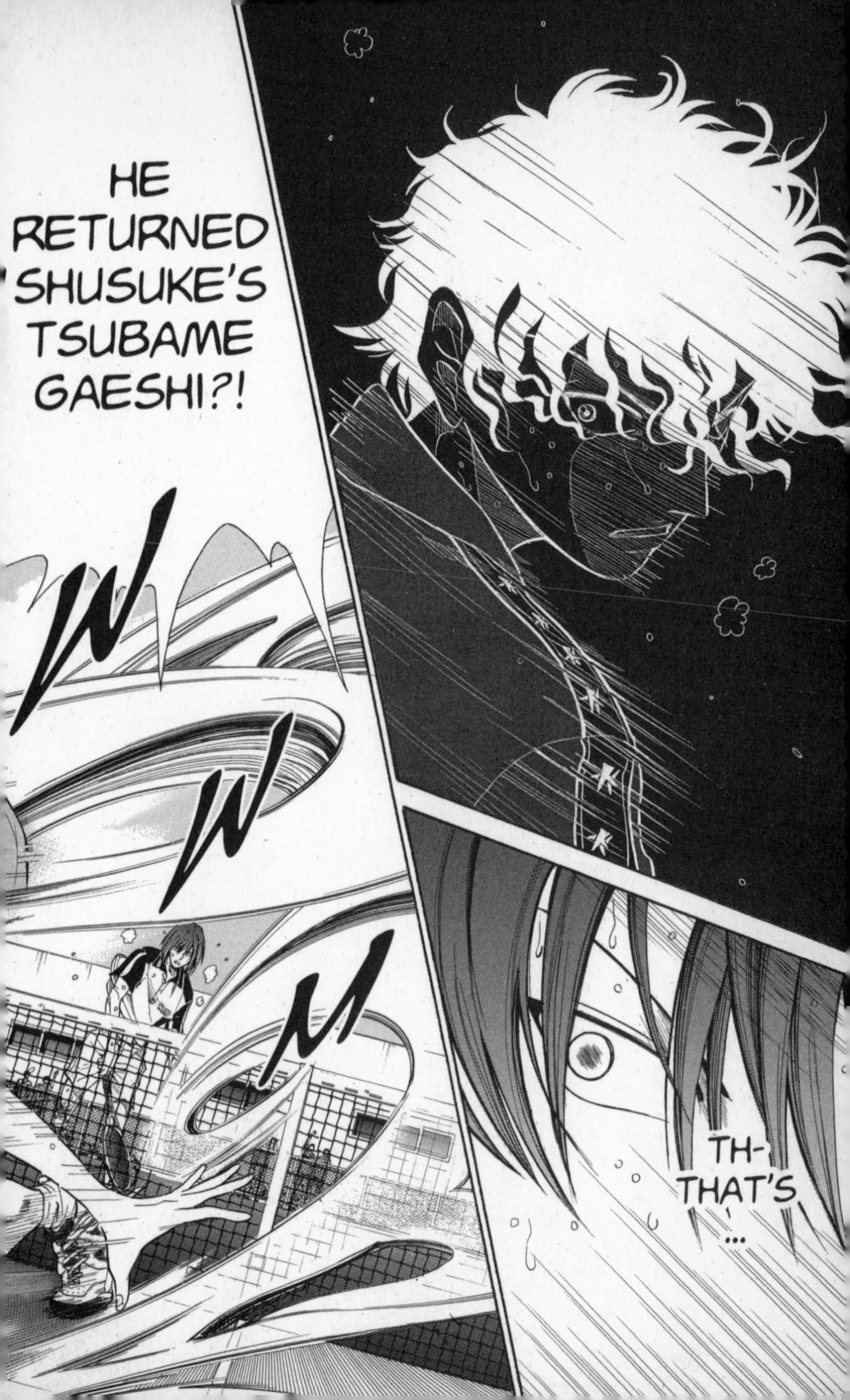
TH-THAT'S...
HE RETURNED SHUSUKE'S TSUBAME GAESHI?!
W
W
M

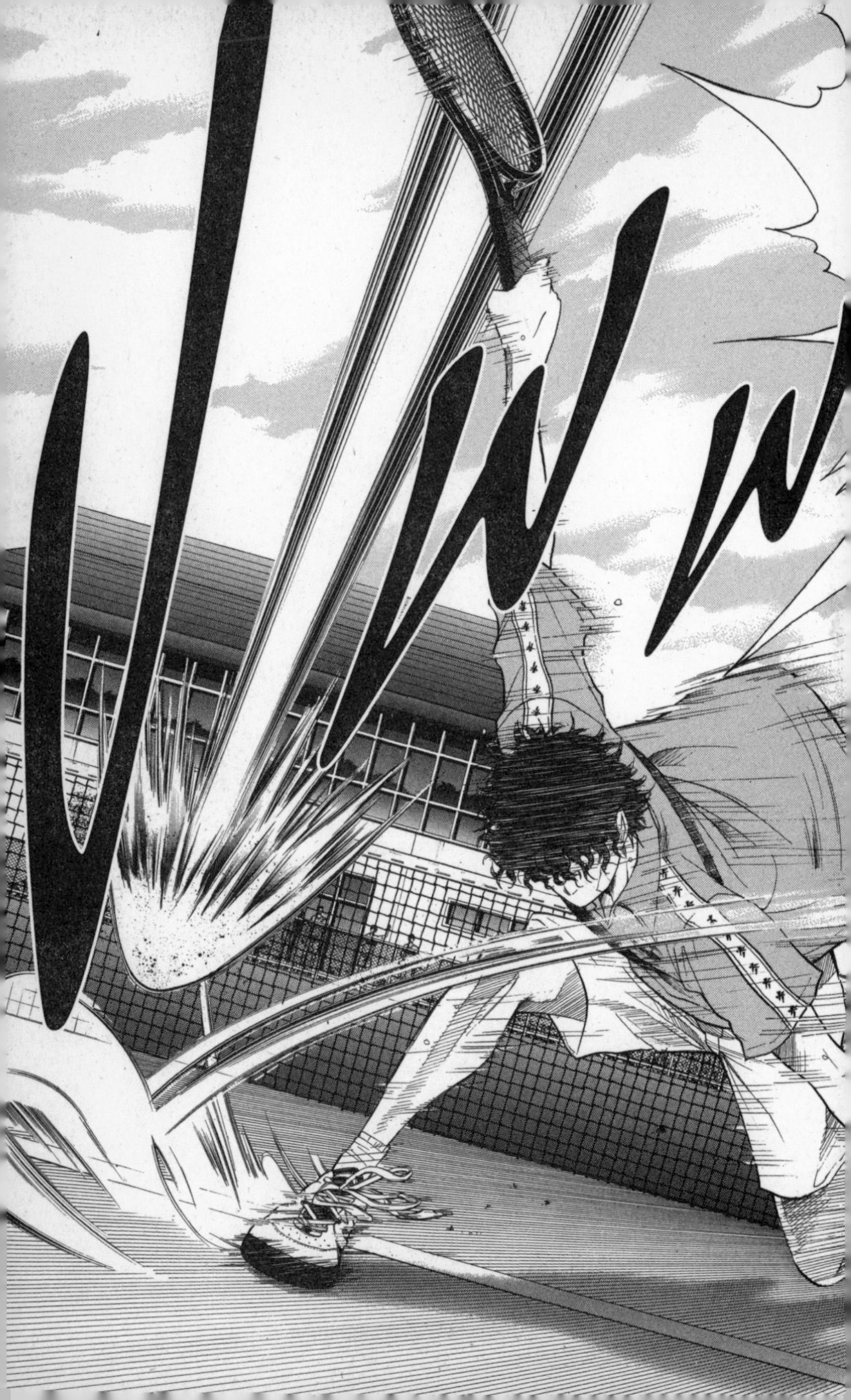

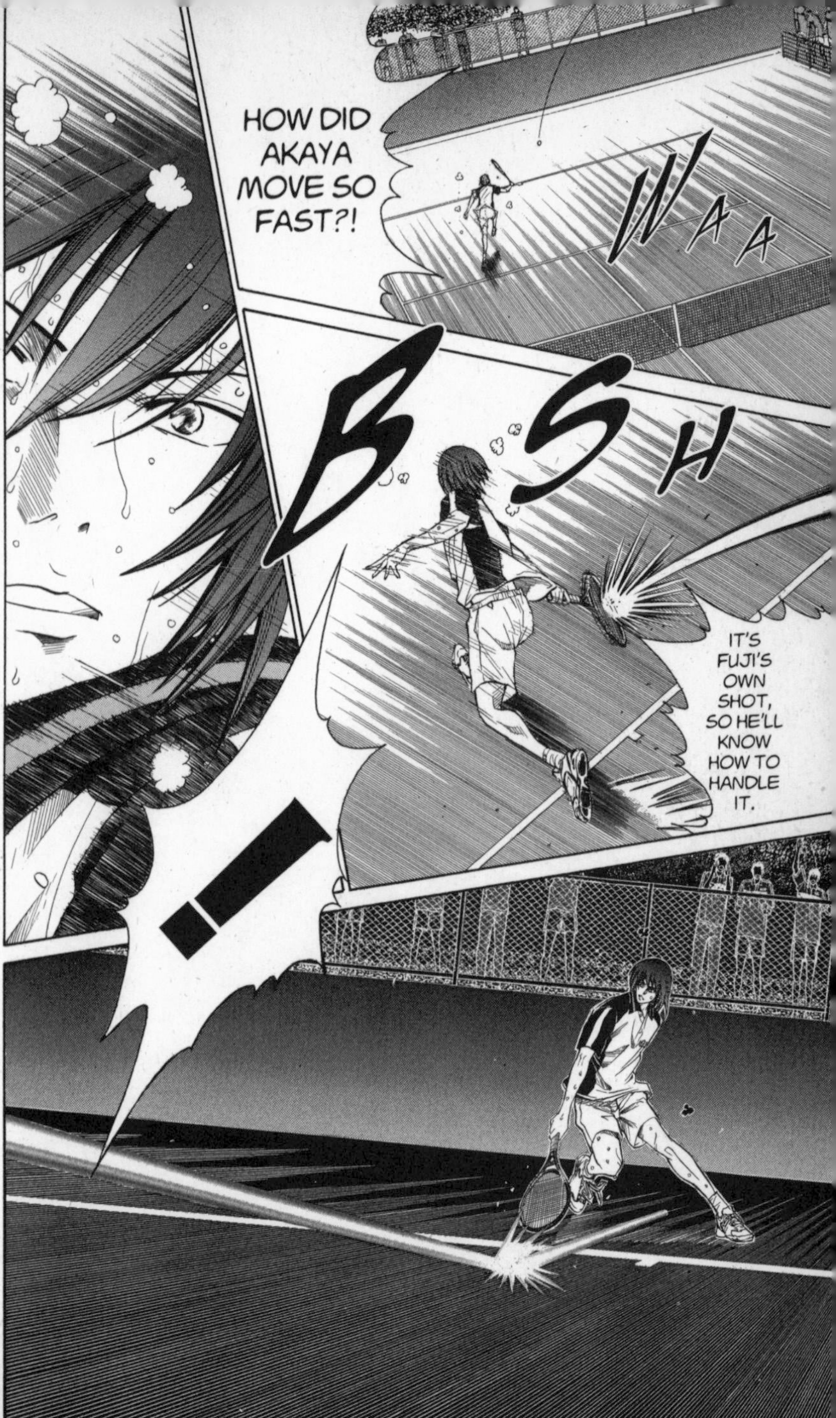
WAA
HOW DID AKAYA MOVE SO FAST?!
BSH
IT'S FUJI'S OWN SHOT, SO HE'LL KNOW HOW TO HANDLE IT.
!

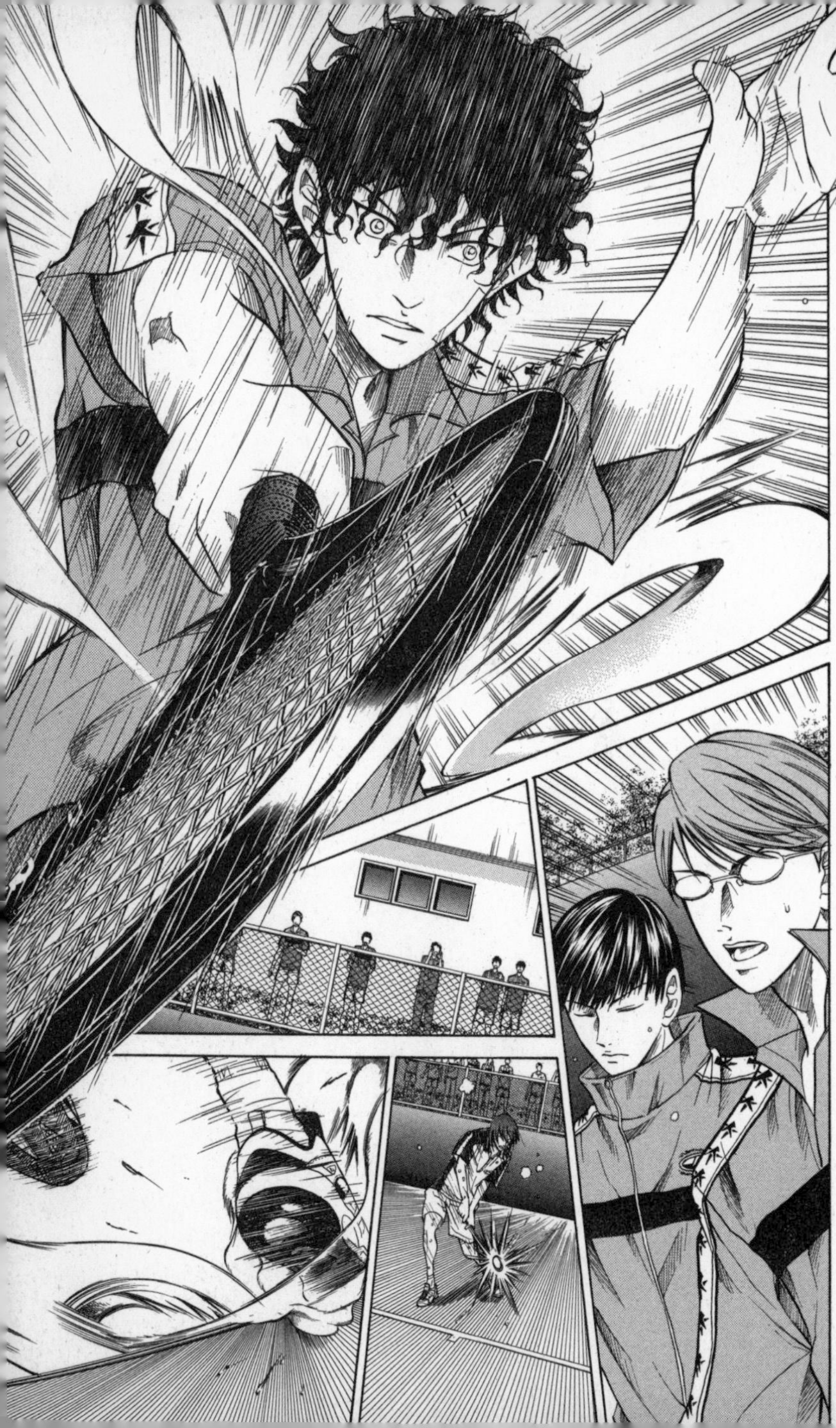

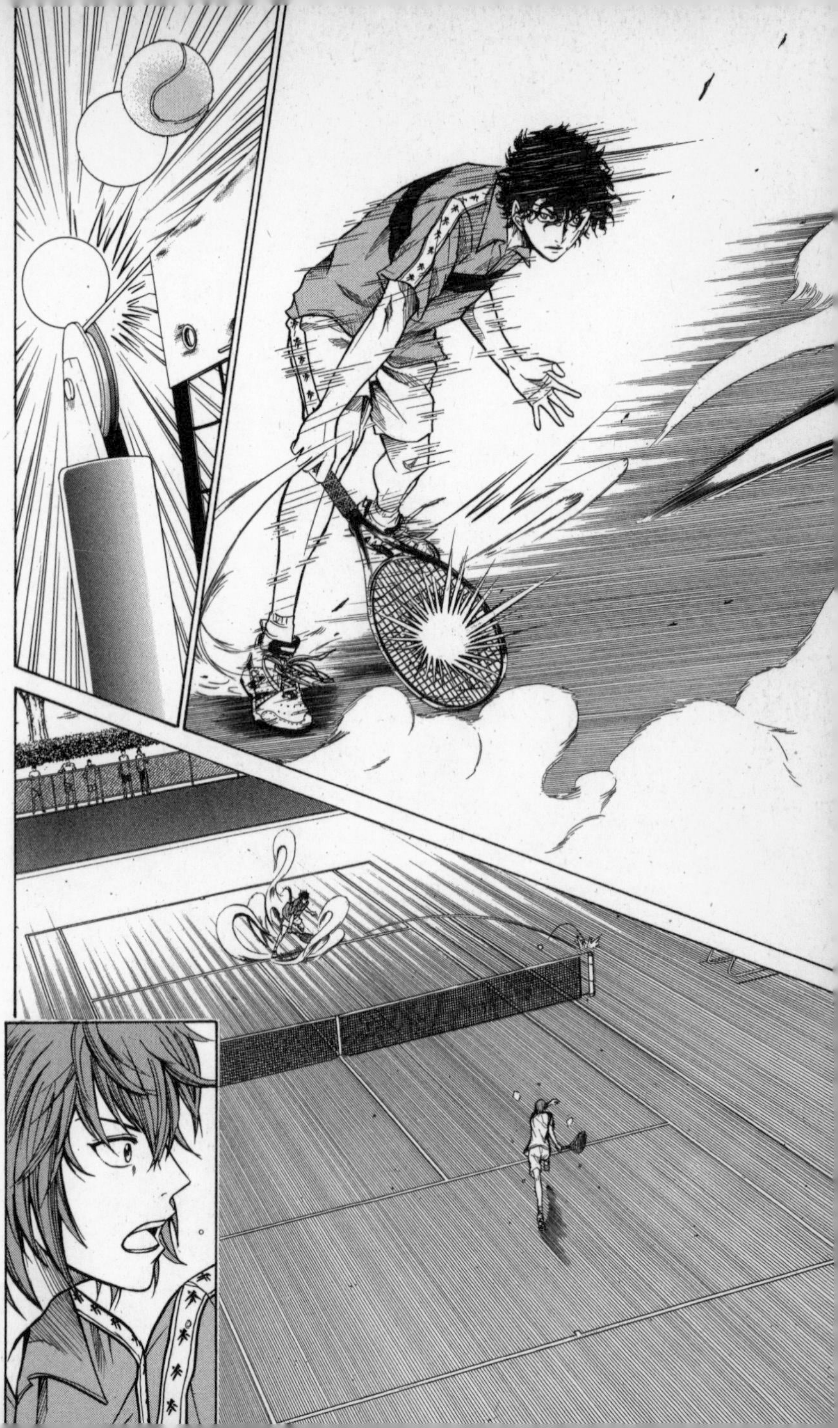

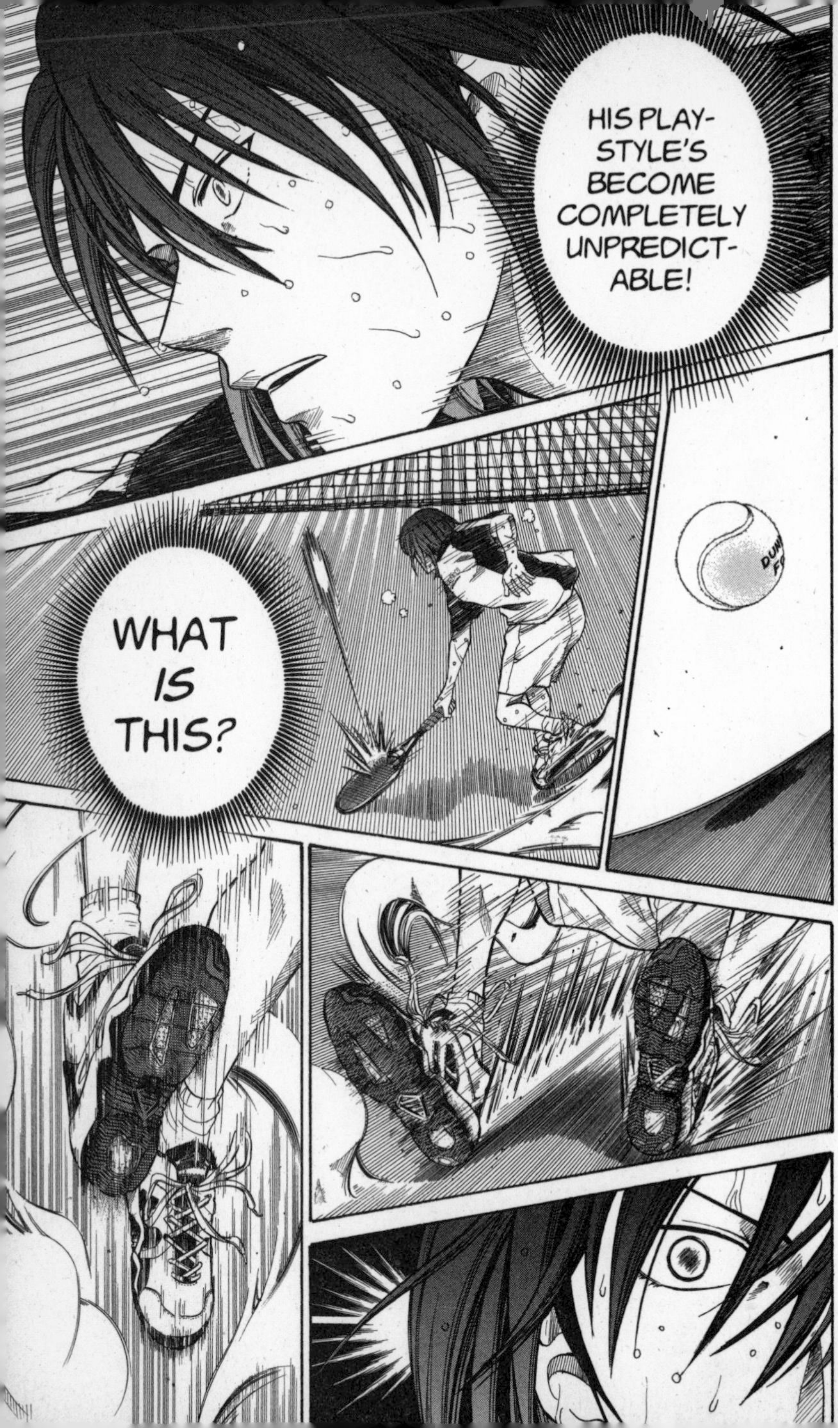
HIS PLAY-STYLE'S BECOME COMPLETELY UNPREDICT-ABLE!
WHAT IS THIS?

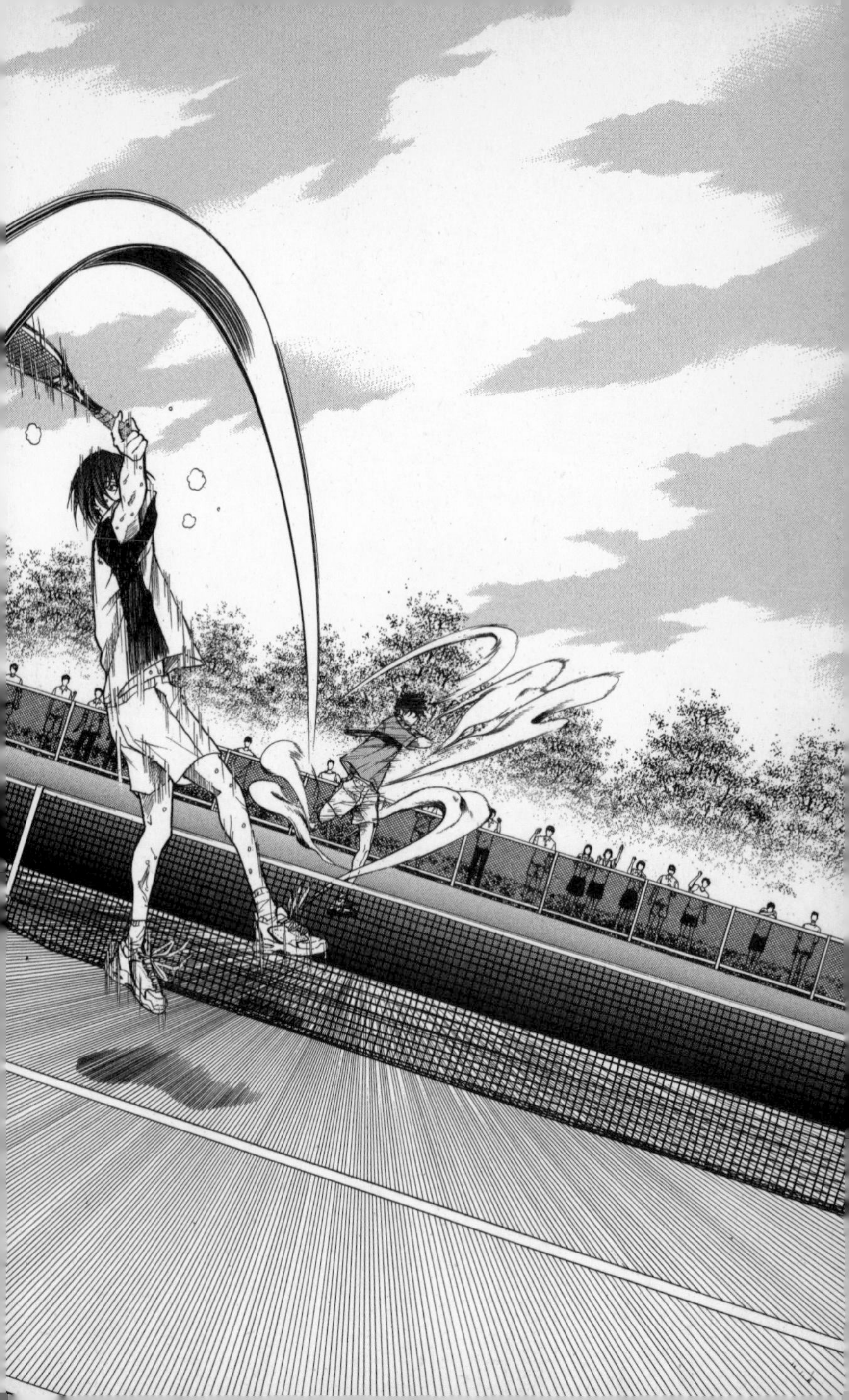

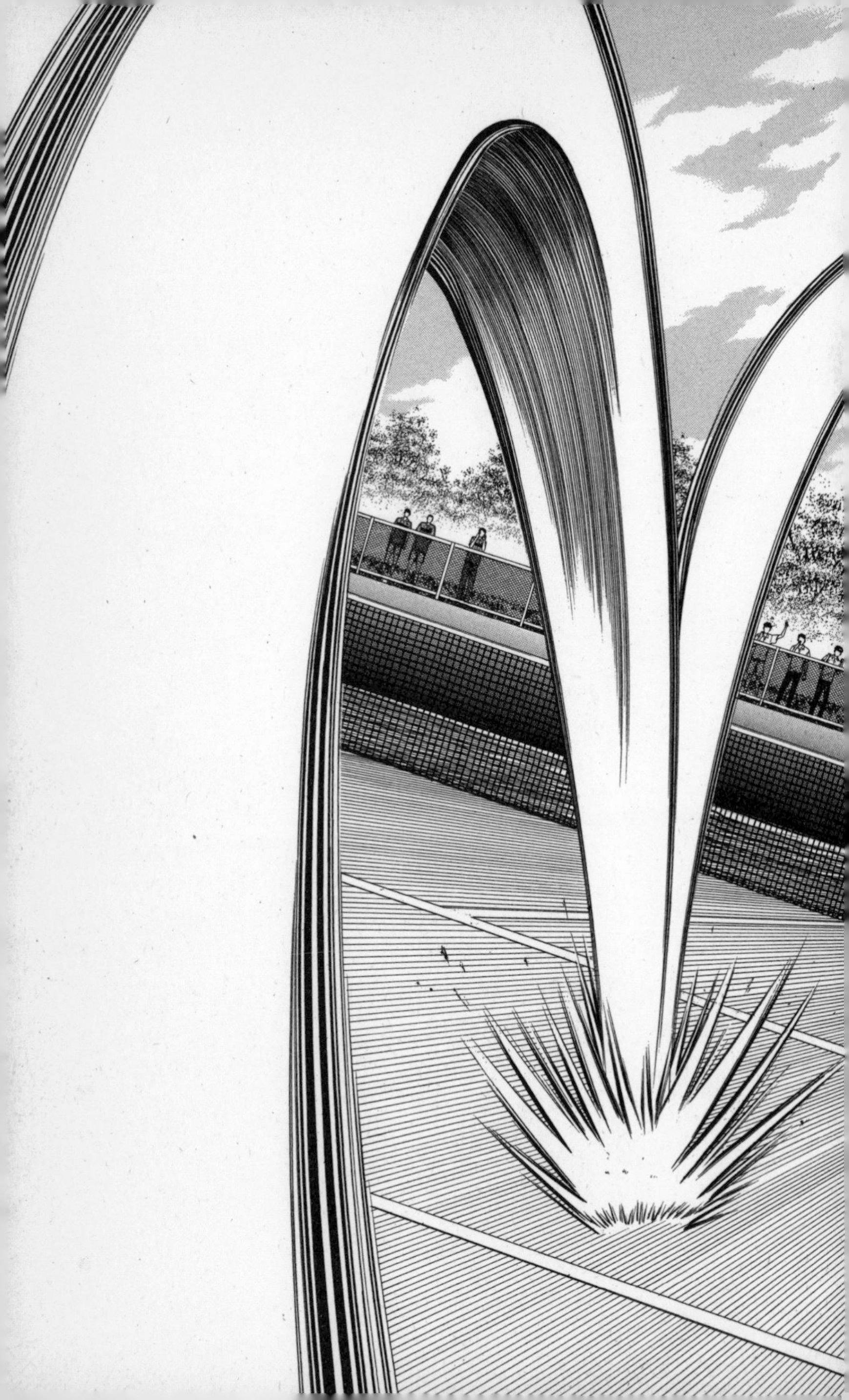

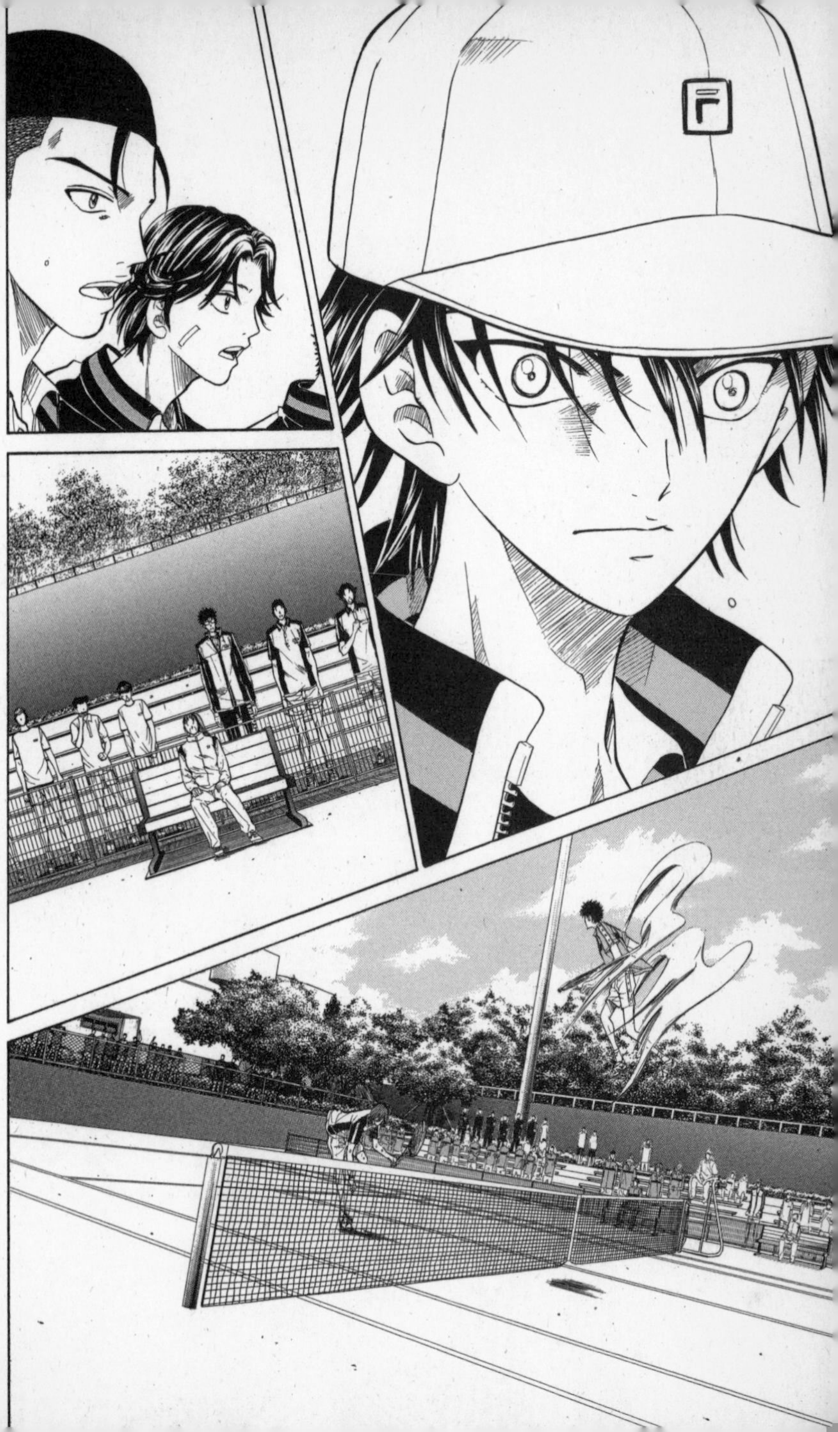

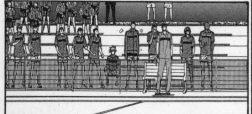

IM...
IMPOS-
SIBLE.
AKAYA...

...FINALLY
ACHIEVED
THE...

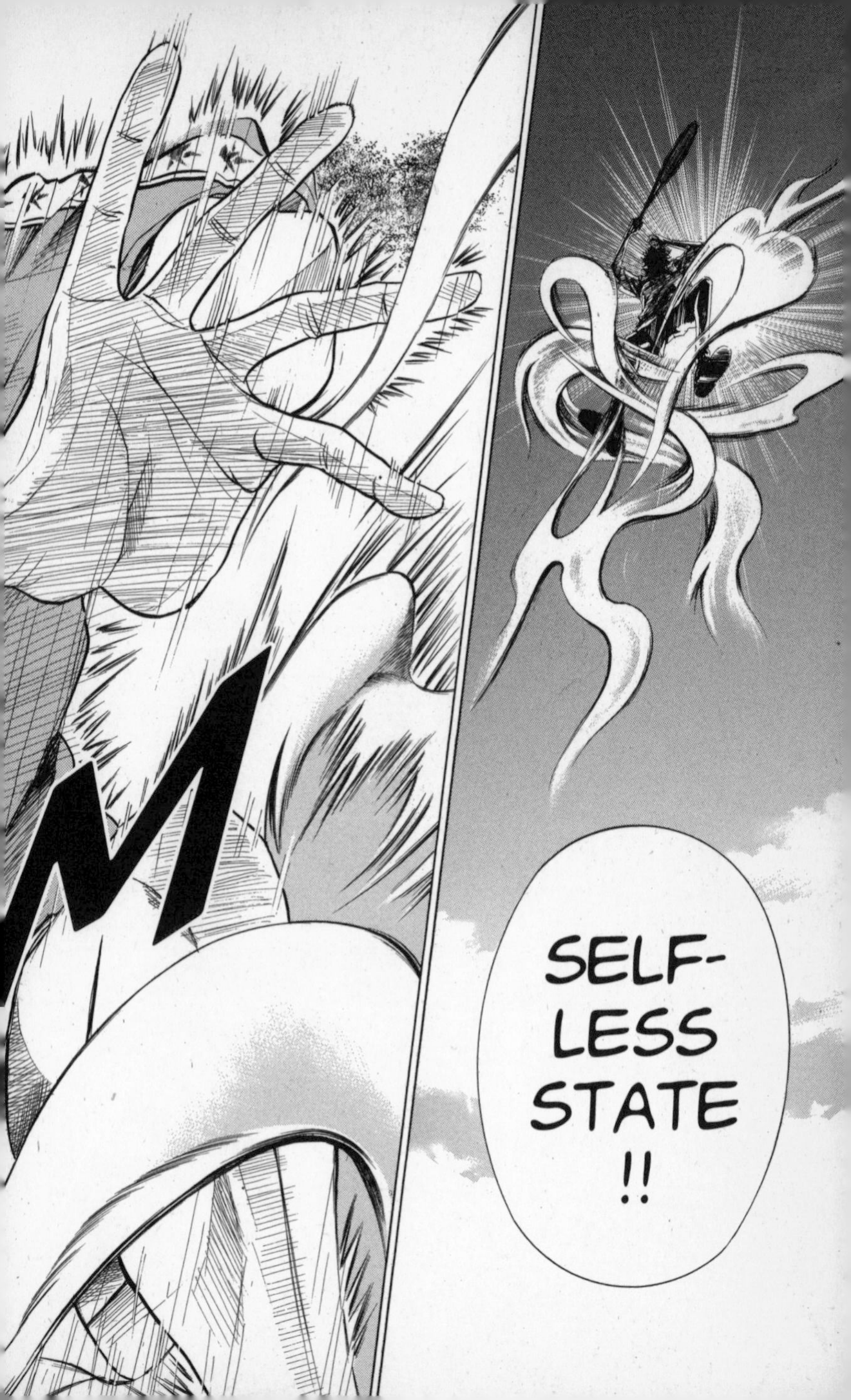
SELF-LESS STATE !!
M

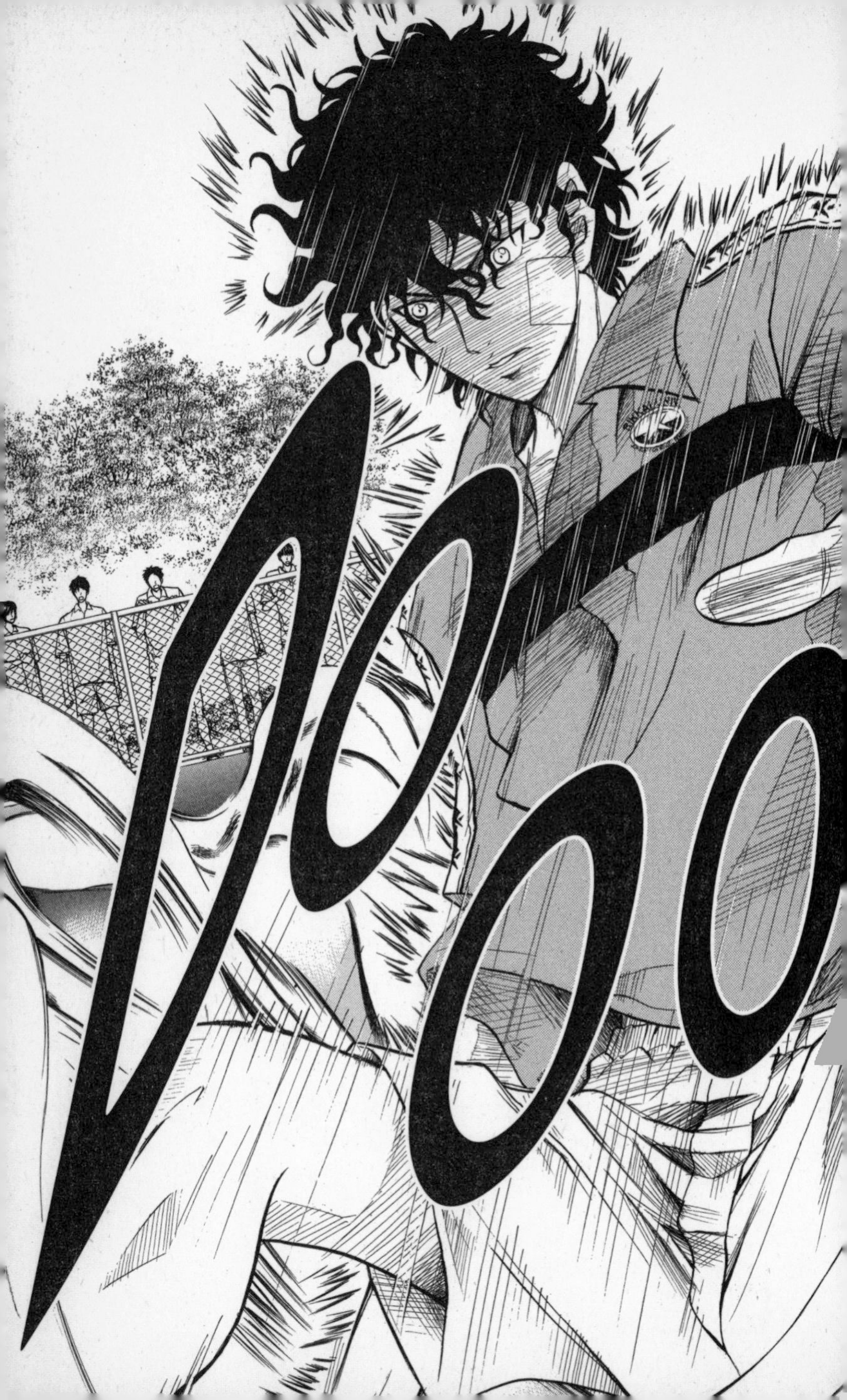
ZOOO

RIKKAI QUESTION CORNER

Part 2

It's Back!!

RIKKAI UNIV. JUNIOR HIGH SCHOOL TENNIS CLUB

We're back with another segment of the Rikkai Question Corner, the special section where members of the team answer your questions themselves!!

Q: I'm a fan of Renji's! I was surprised when he actually opened his eyes in the game against Sadaharu [laughs]. I like him with his eyes closed, but now I like him with his chilling open eyes, too!
(A.O., Tokyo)

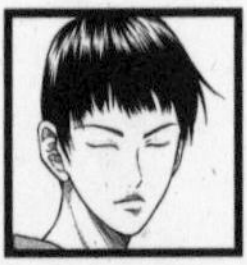

Thanks...

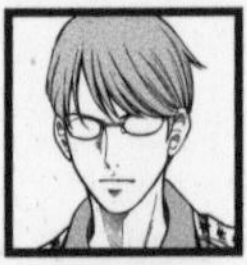

Hmm... Renji, are you blushing?

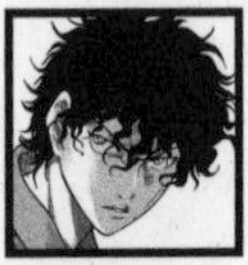

I heard that anyone who looks into Renji's open eyes turns into stone... [pales].

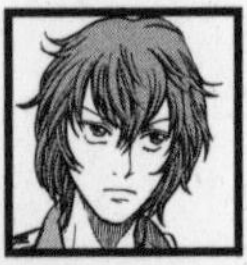

Y'know, this wasn't actually a question.

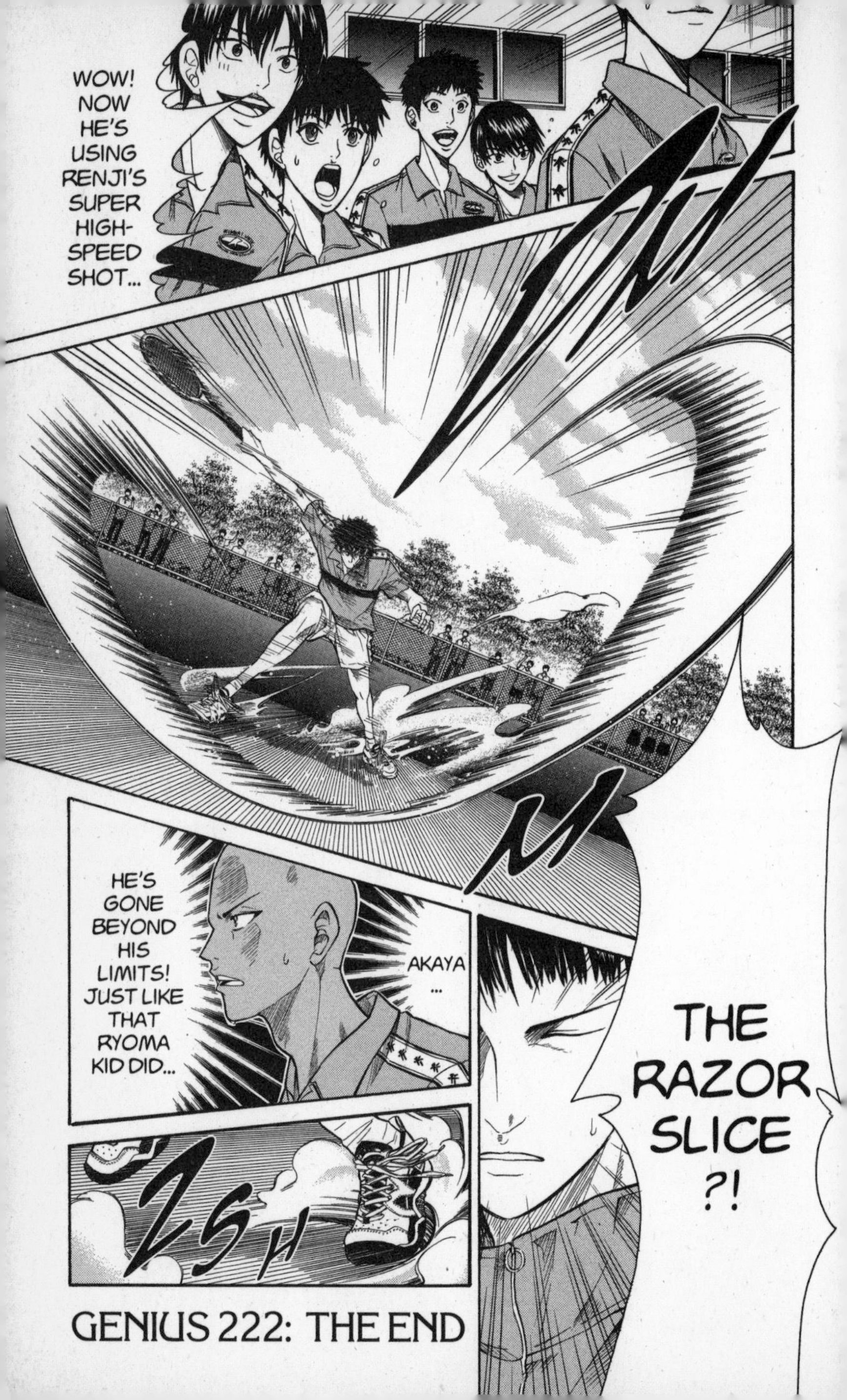
WOW! NOW HE'S USING RENJI'S SUPER HIGH-SPEED SHOT...
THE RAZOR SLICE ?!
AKAYA ...
HE'S GONE BEYOND HIS LIMITS! JUST LIKE THAT RYOMA KID DID...
ZSH

GENIUS 222: THE END

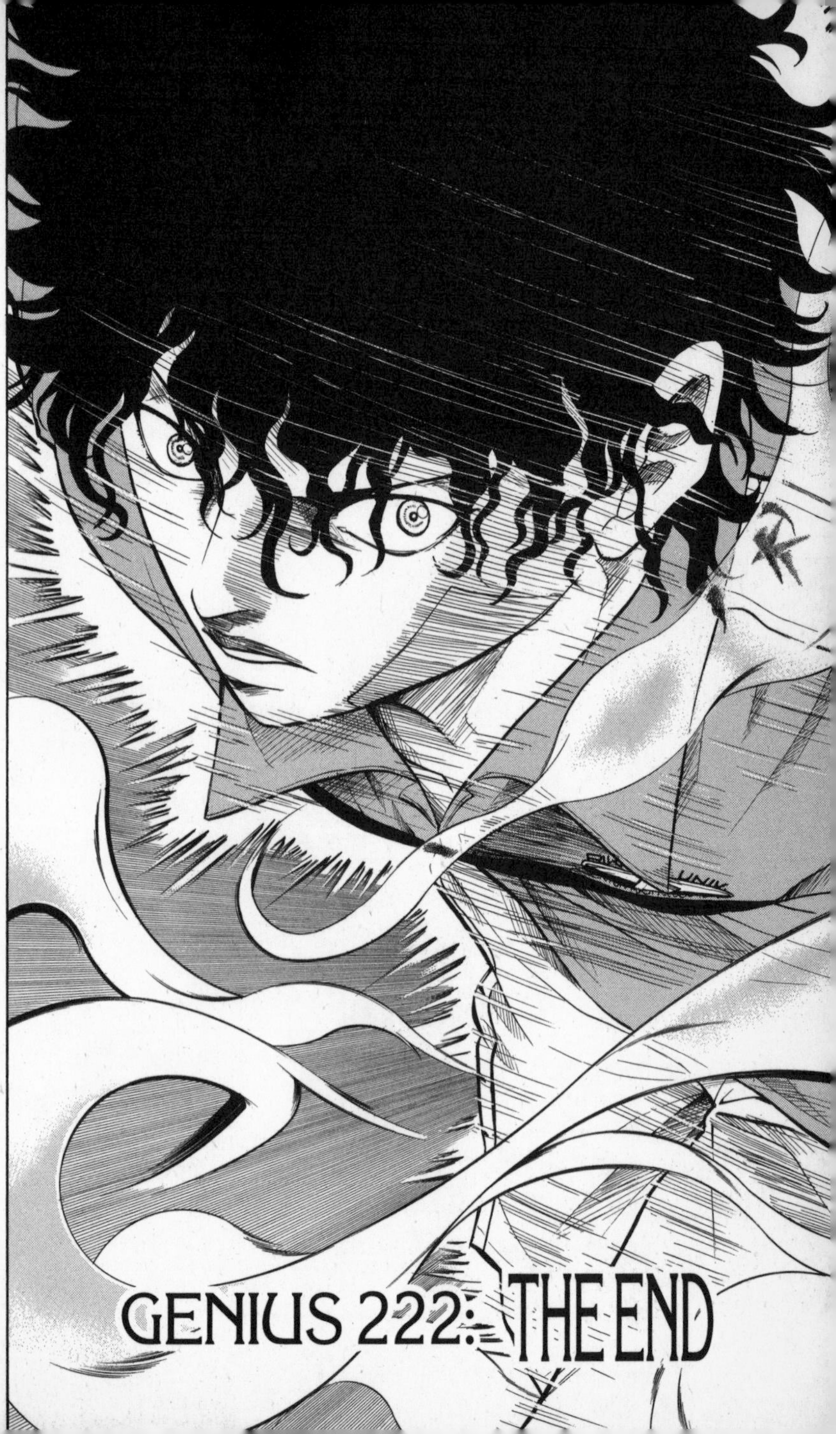
GENIUS 222: THE END

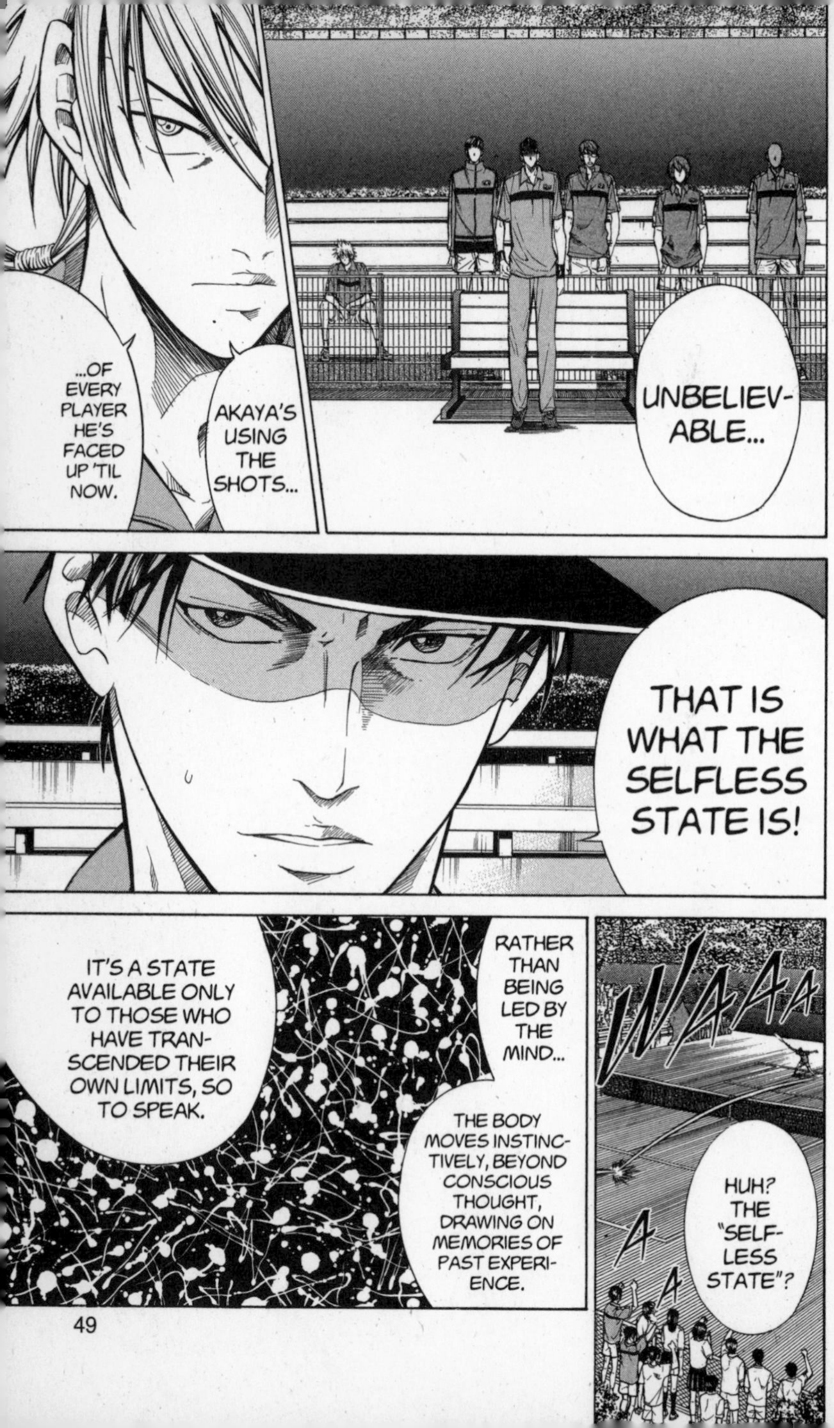
UNBELIEVABLE...
AKAYA'S USING THE SHOTS...
...OF EVERY PLAYER HE'S FACED UP 'TIL NOW.
THAT IS WHAT THE SELFLESS STATE IS!
WAAAA
A
A
HUH? THE "SELFLESS STATE"?
RATHER THAN BEING LED BY THE MIND...
THE BODY MOVES INSTINCTIVELY, BEYOND CONSCIOUS THOUGHT, DRAWING ON MEMORIES OF PAST EXPERIENCE.
IT'S A STATE AVAILABLE ONLY TO THOSE WHO HAVE TRANSCENDED THEIR OWN LIMITS, SO TO SPEAK.

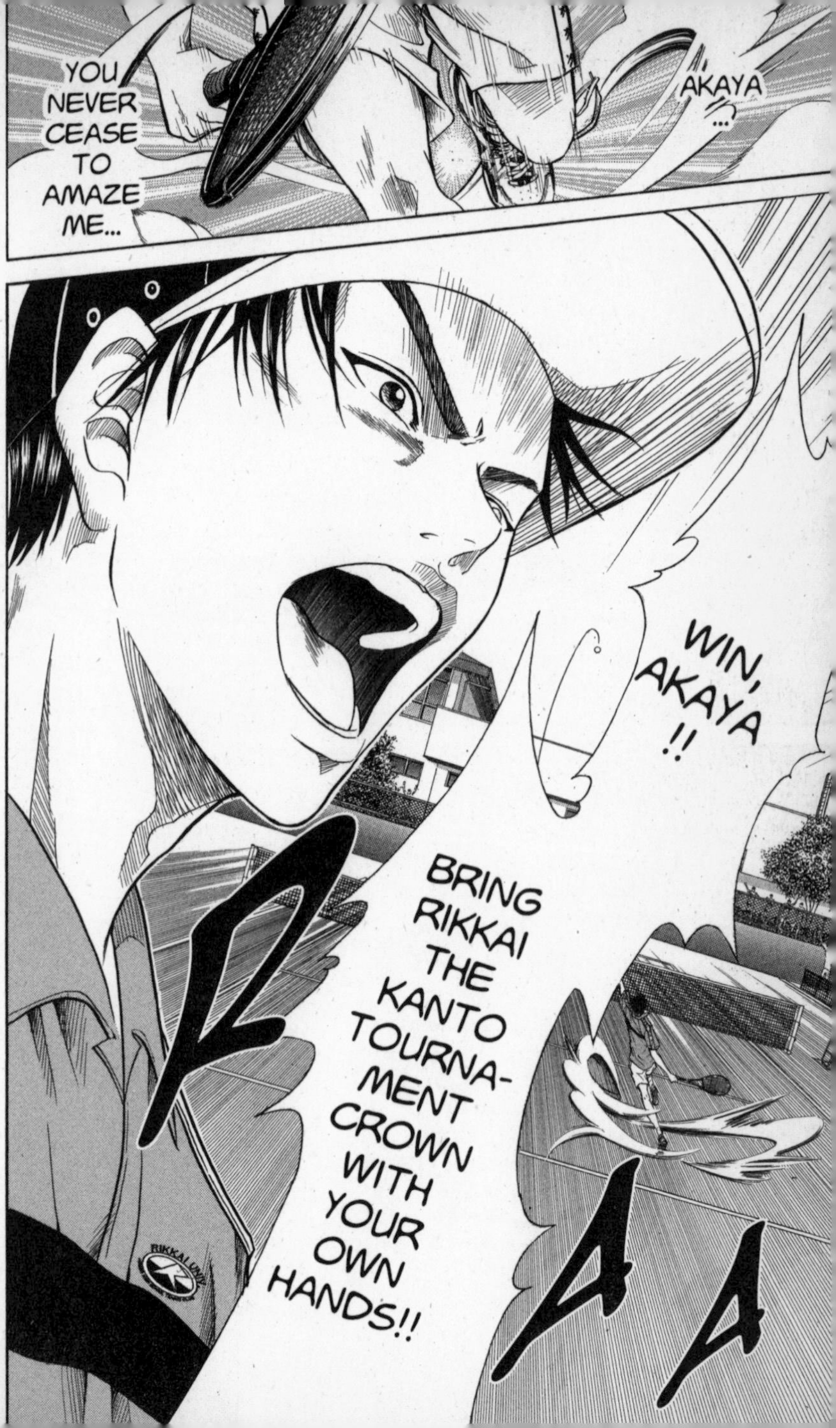
AKAYA...
YOU NEVER CEASE TO AMAZE ME...
WIN, AKAYA!!
BRING RIKKAI THE KANTO TOURNAMENT CROWN WITH YOUR OWN HANDS!!
RIKKAI UNIV.

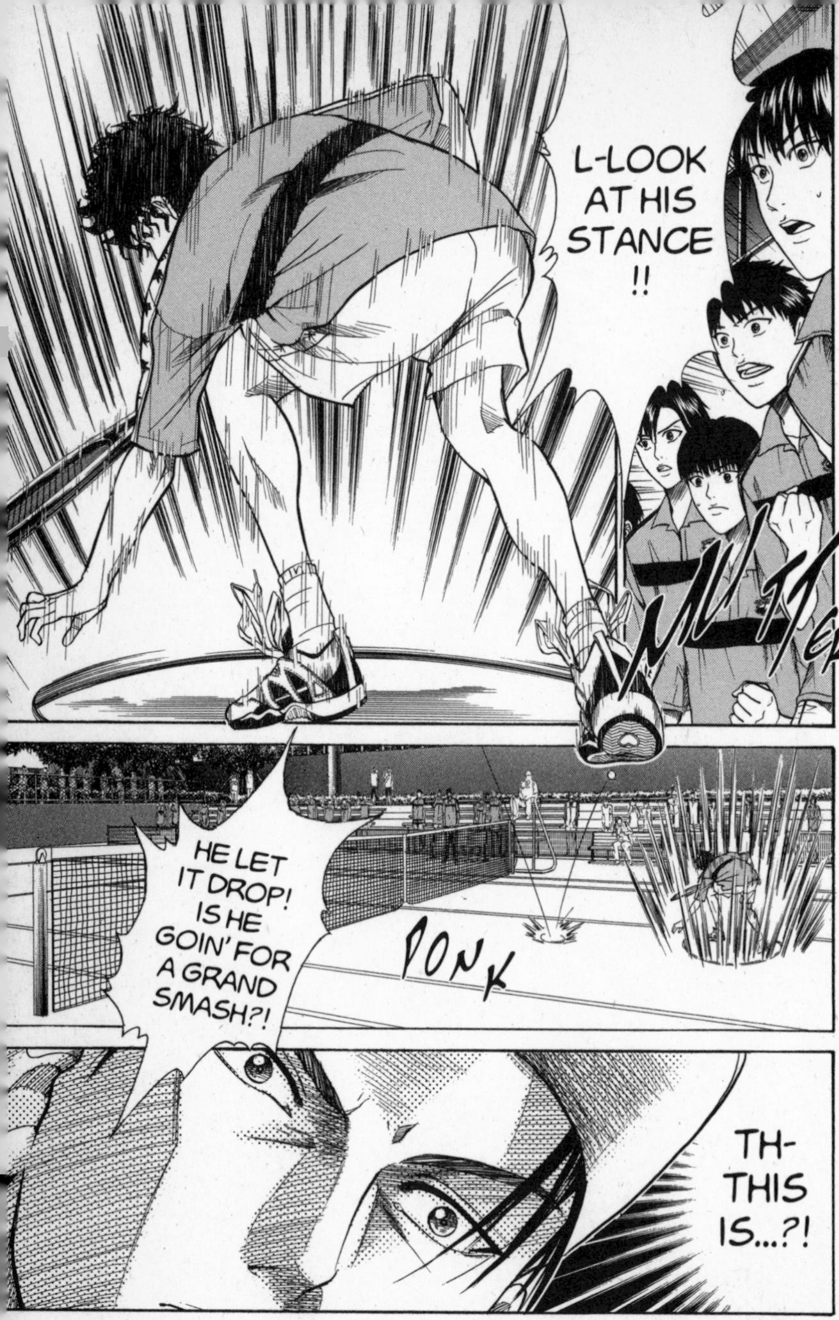
L-LOOK AT HIS STANCE !!
MUTTER
HE LET IT DROP! IS HE GOIN' FOR A GRAND SMASH?!
PONK
TH-THIS IS...?!

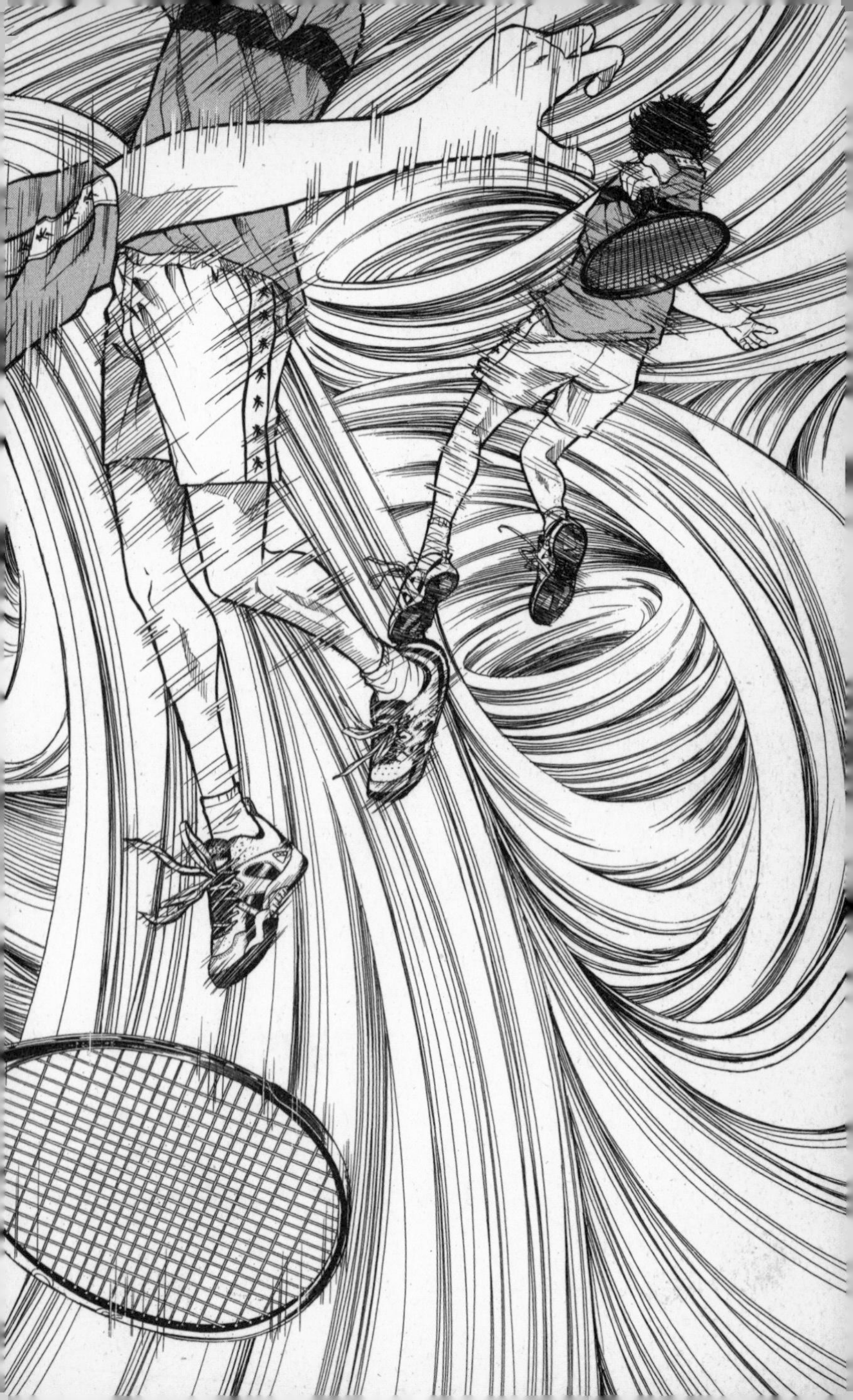

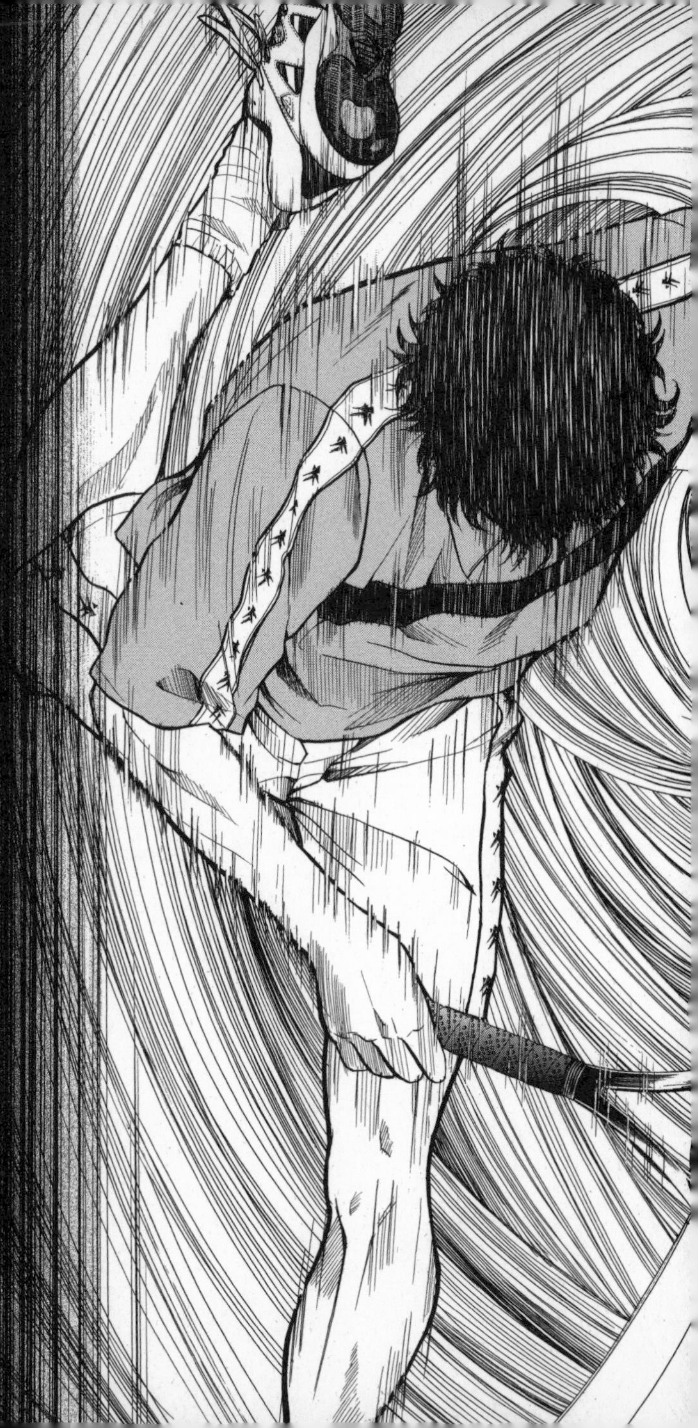

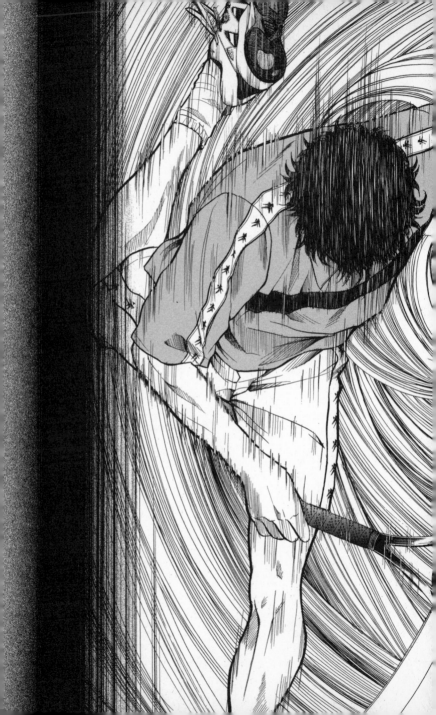

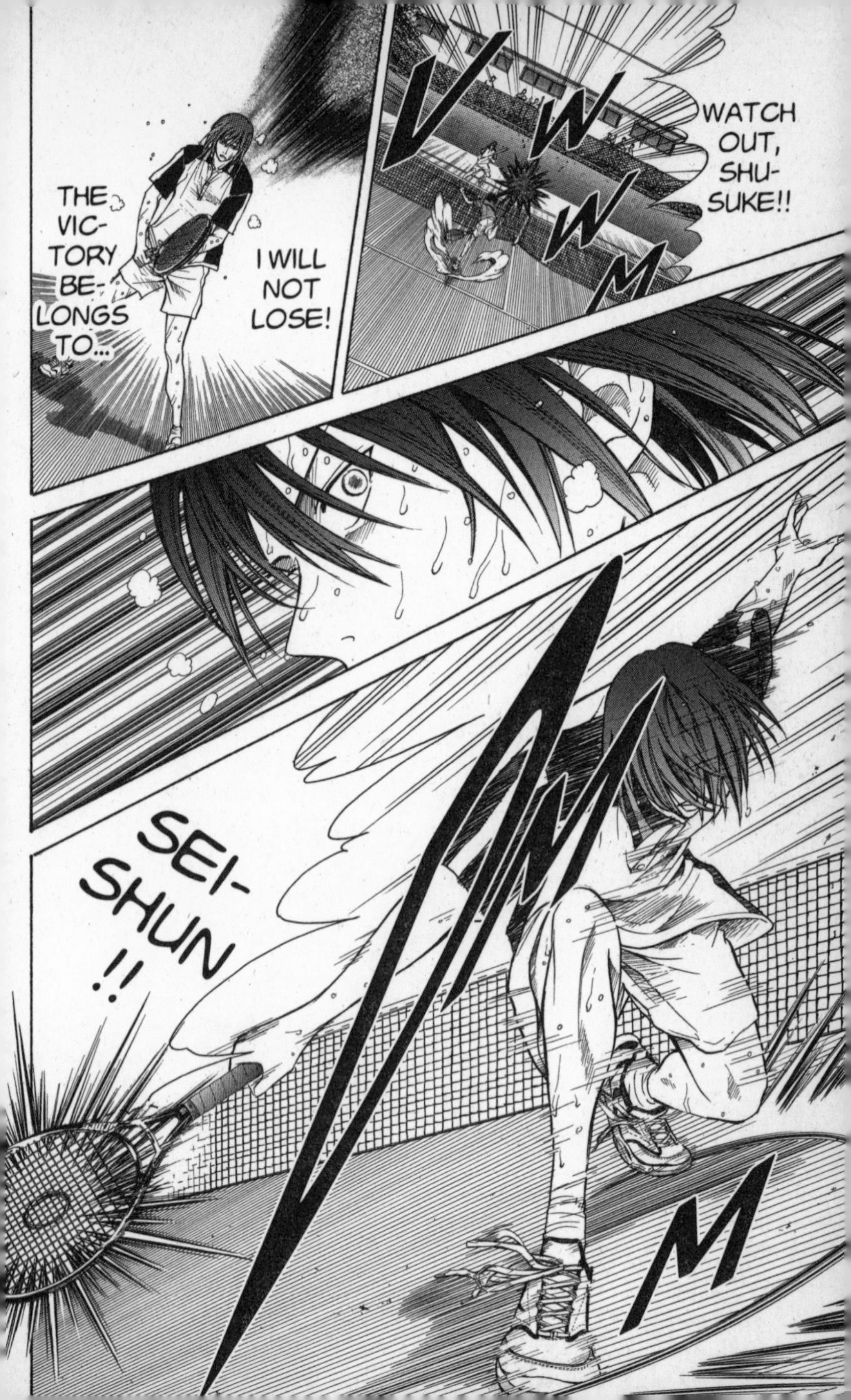
VWWM
WATCH OUT, SHUSUKE!!
I WILL NOT LOSE!
THE VICTORY BELONGS TO...
SEI-SHUN!!
M

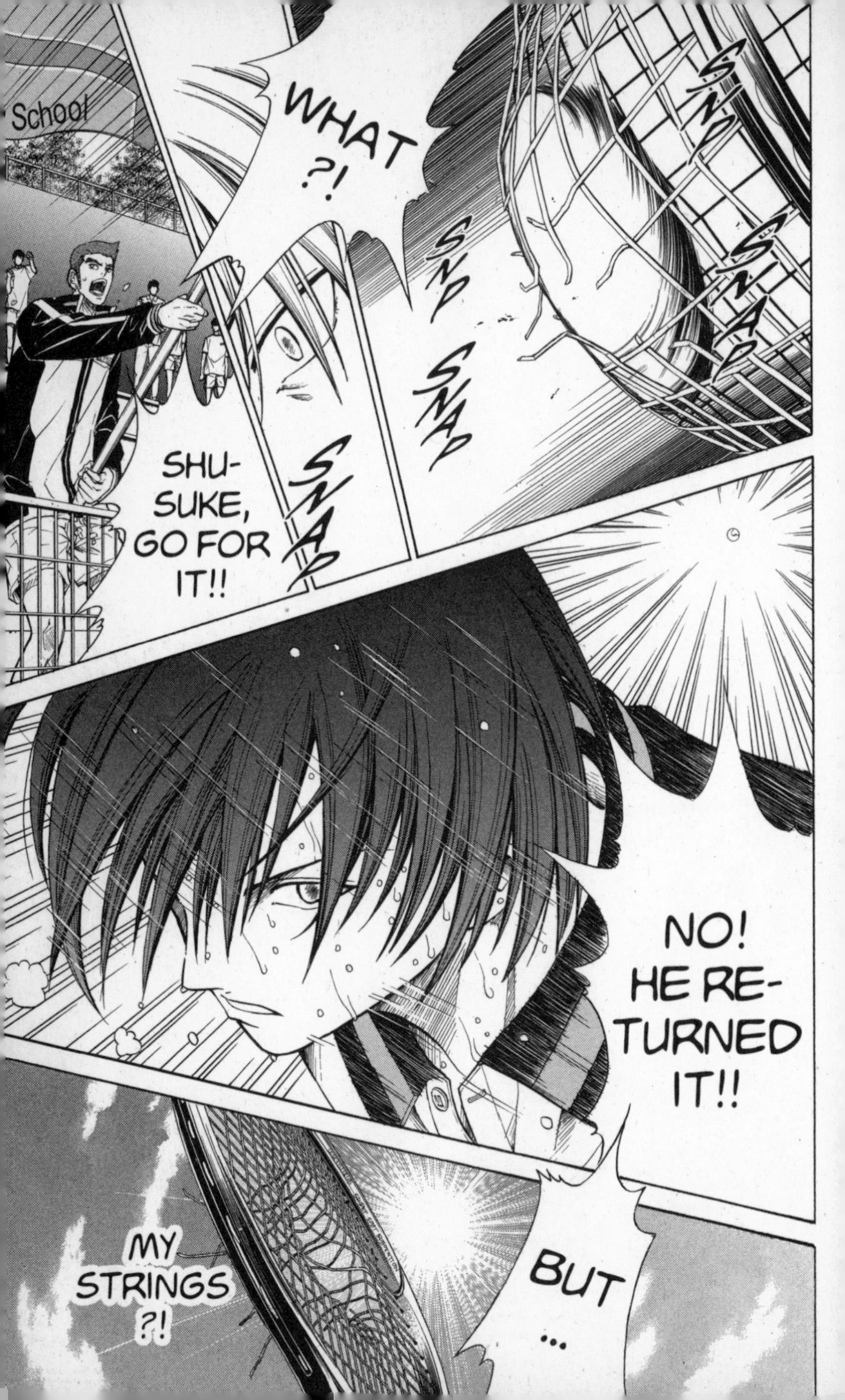

SNAP
SNAP
WHAT?!
SNAP
SNAP
SNAP
SHU-SUKE, GO FOR IT!!
School
NO! HE RE-TURNED IT!!
BUT...
MY STRINGS?!

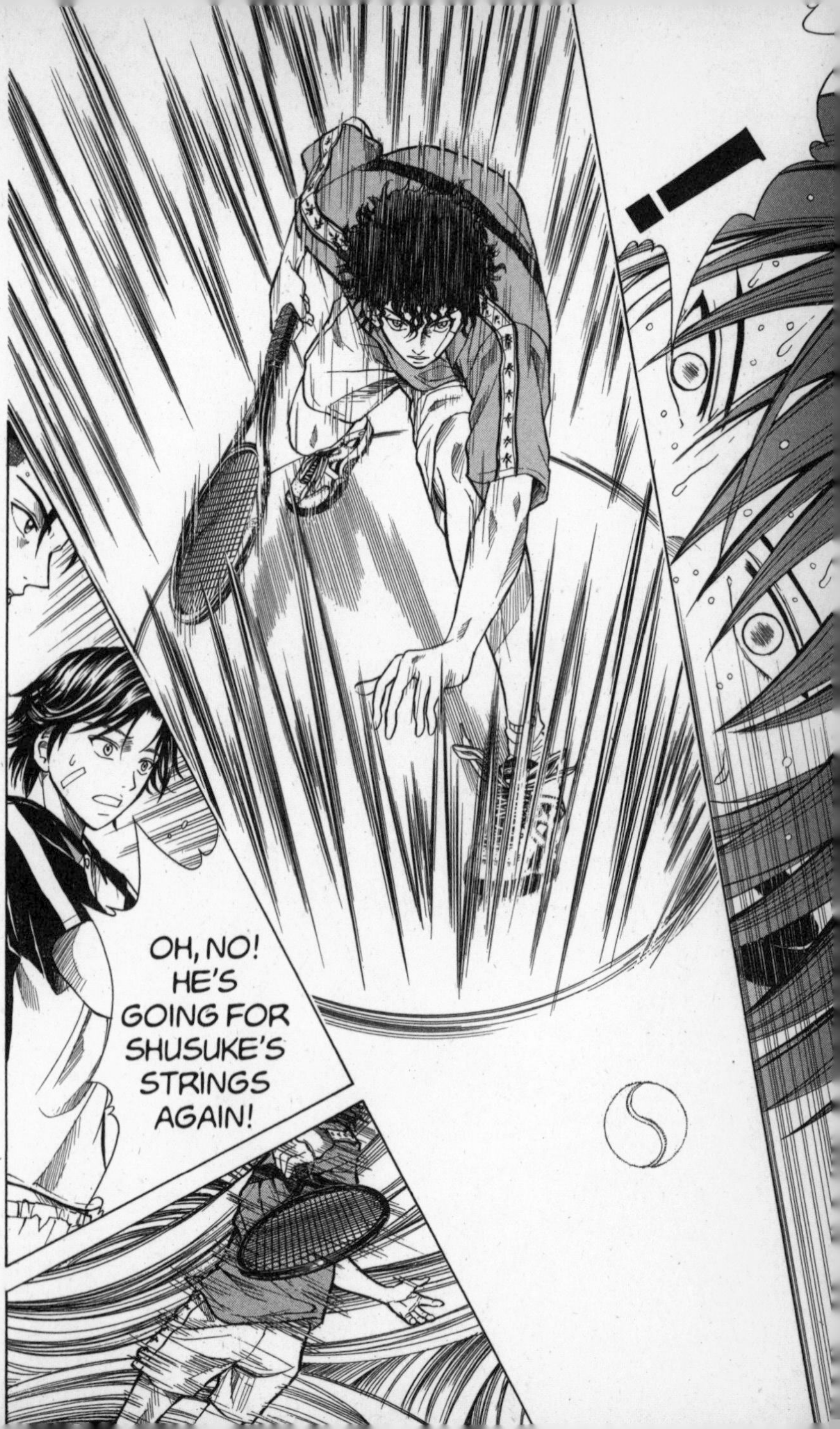
OH, NO! HE'S GOING FOR SHUSUKE'S STRINGS AGAIN!

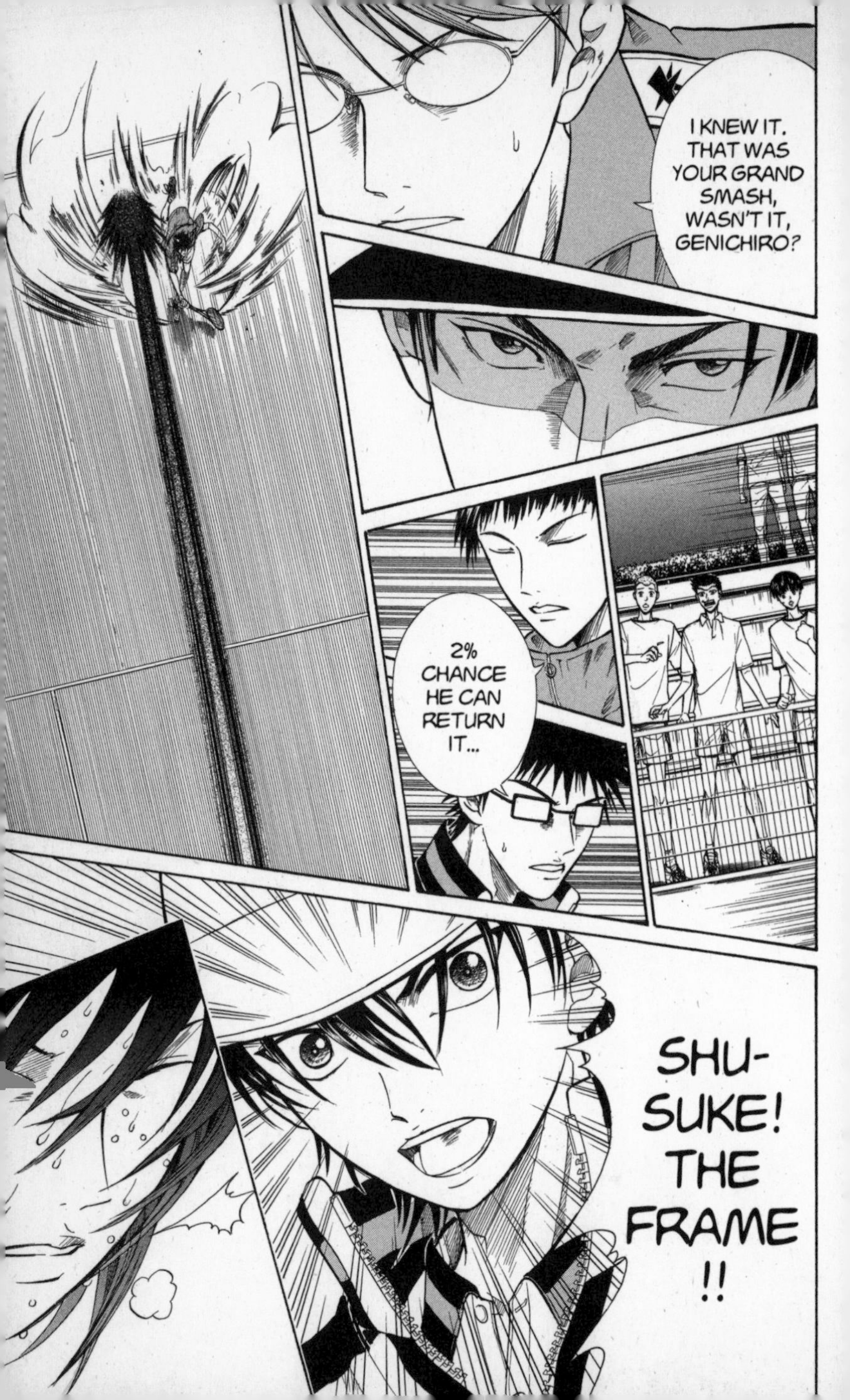
I KNEW IT. THAT WAS YOUR GRAND SMASH, WASN'T IT, GENICHIRO?
2% CHANCE HE CAN RETURN IT...
SHU-SUKE! THE FRAME !!

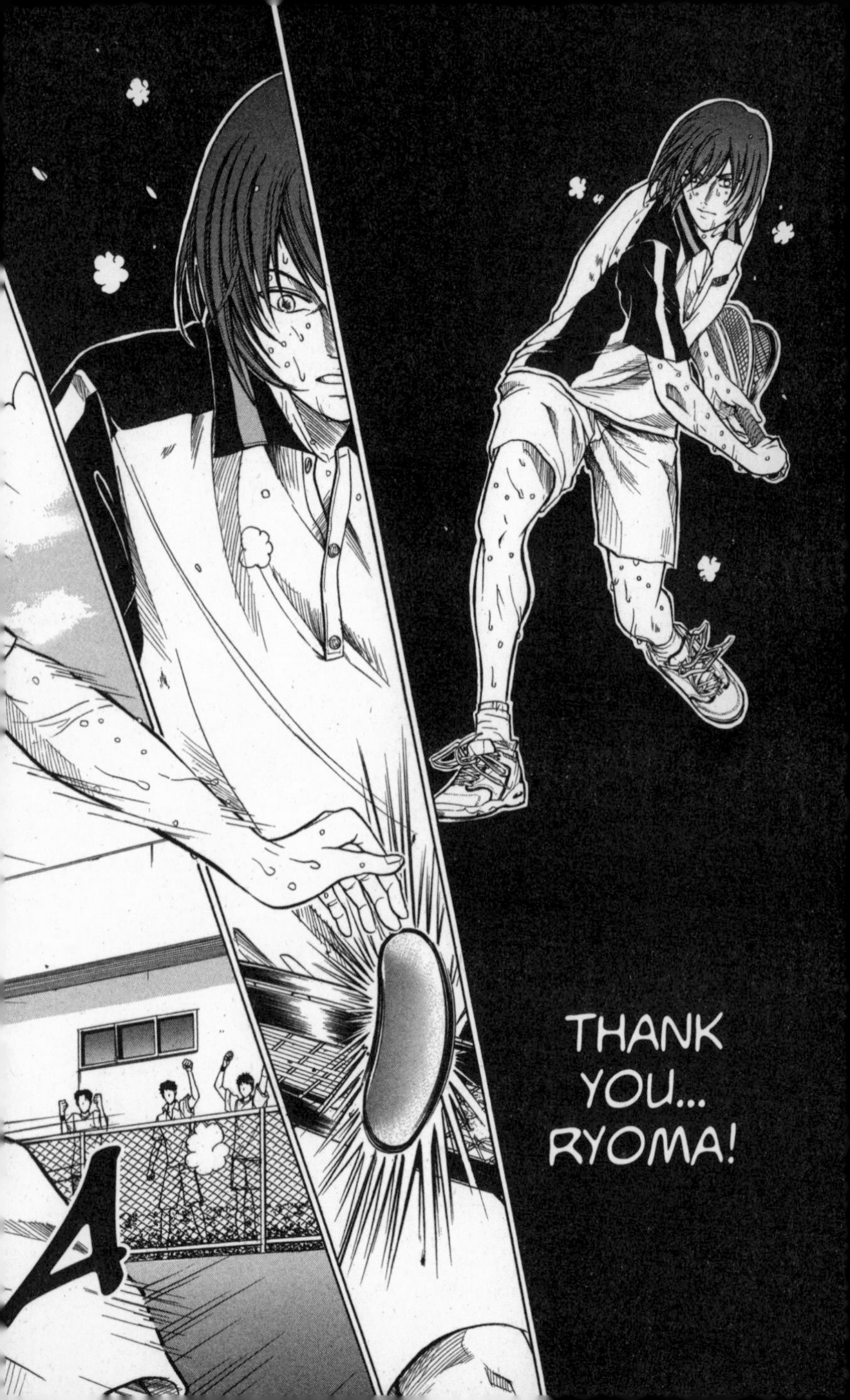
THANK YOU... RYOMA!

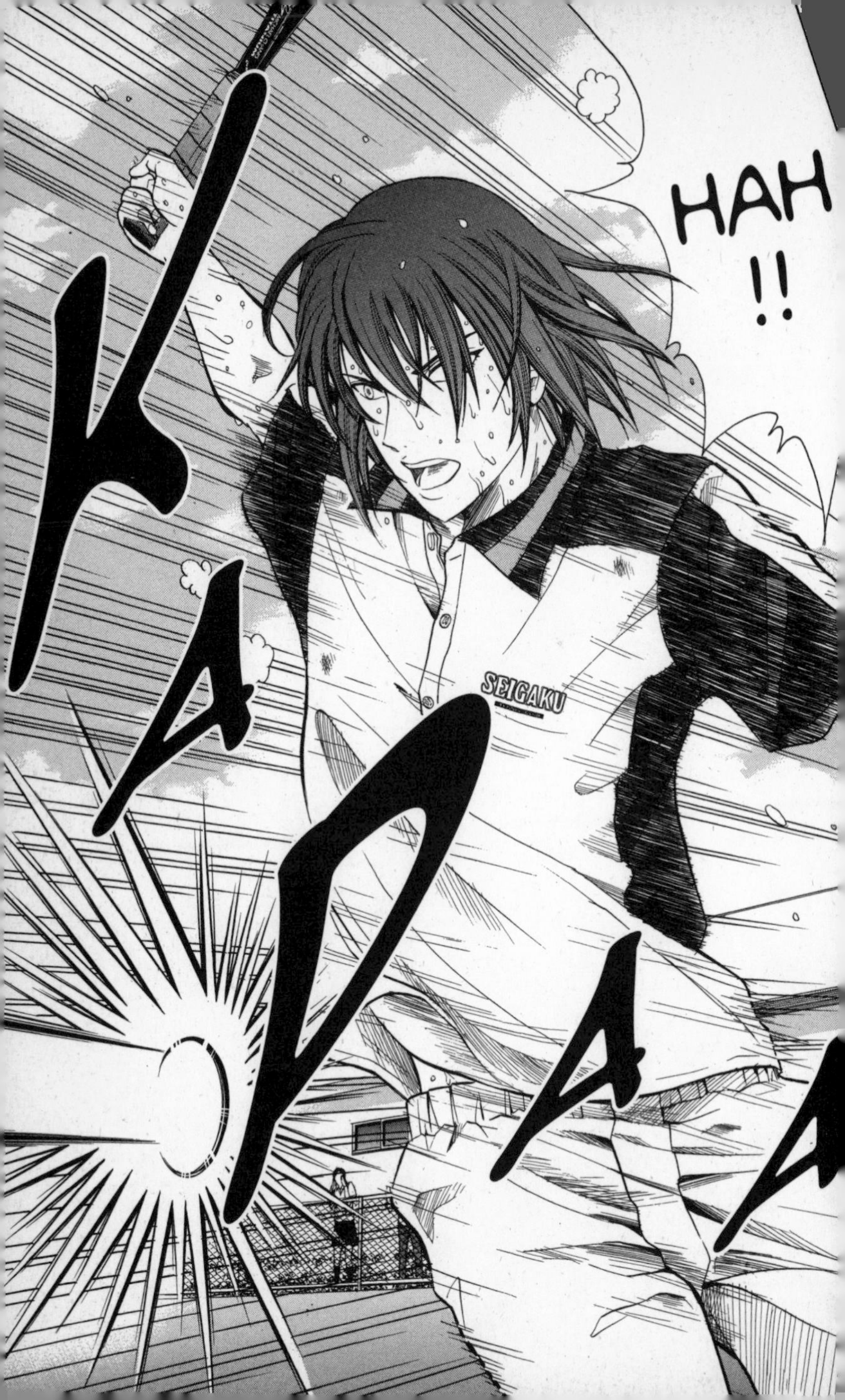
HAH !!
SEIGAKU

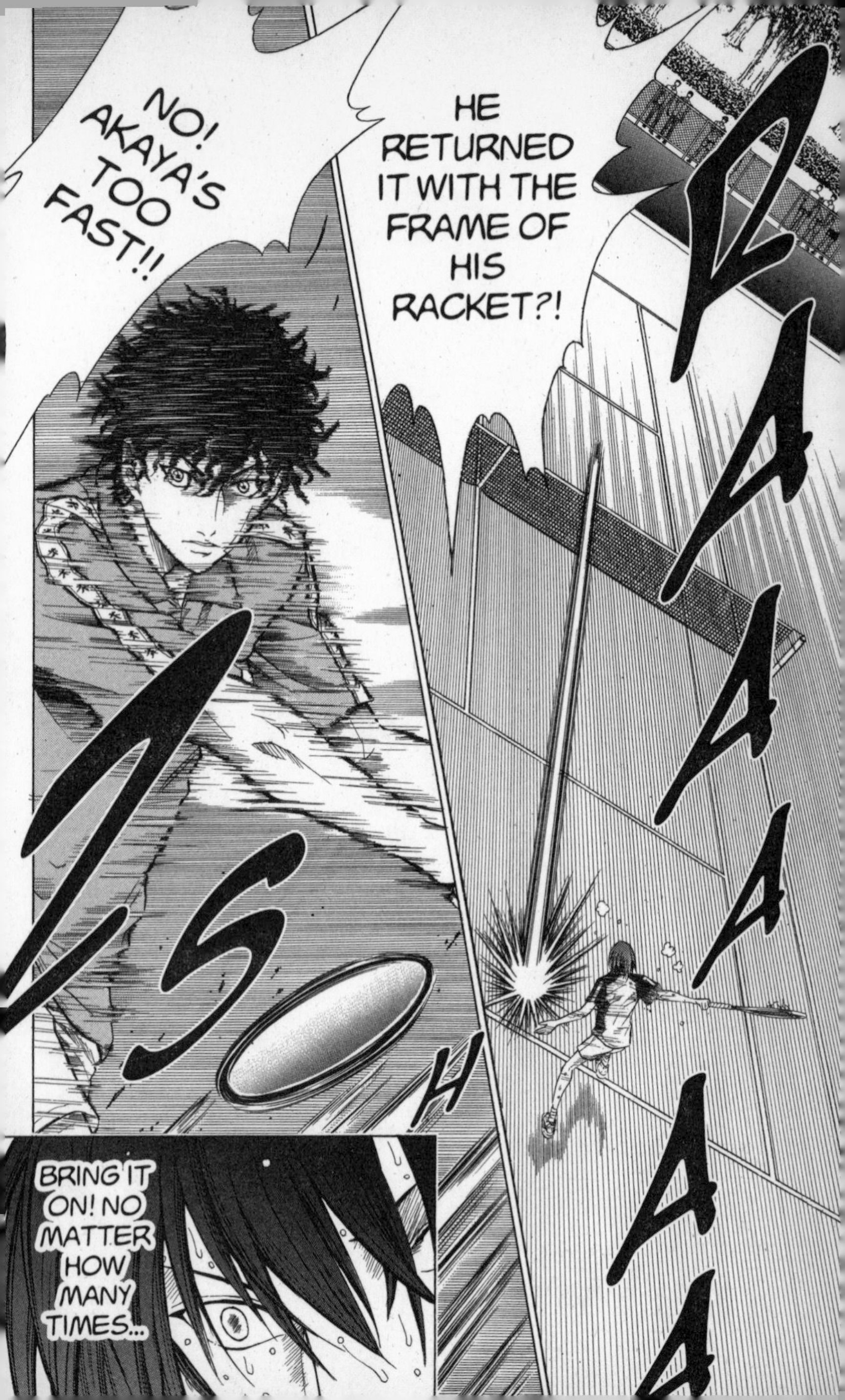
HE RETURNED IT WITH THE FRAME OF HIS RACKET?!
NO! AKAYA'S TOO FAST!!
BRING IT ON! NO MATTER HOW MANY TIMES...

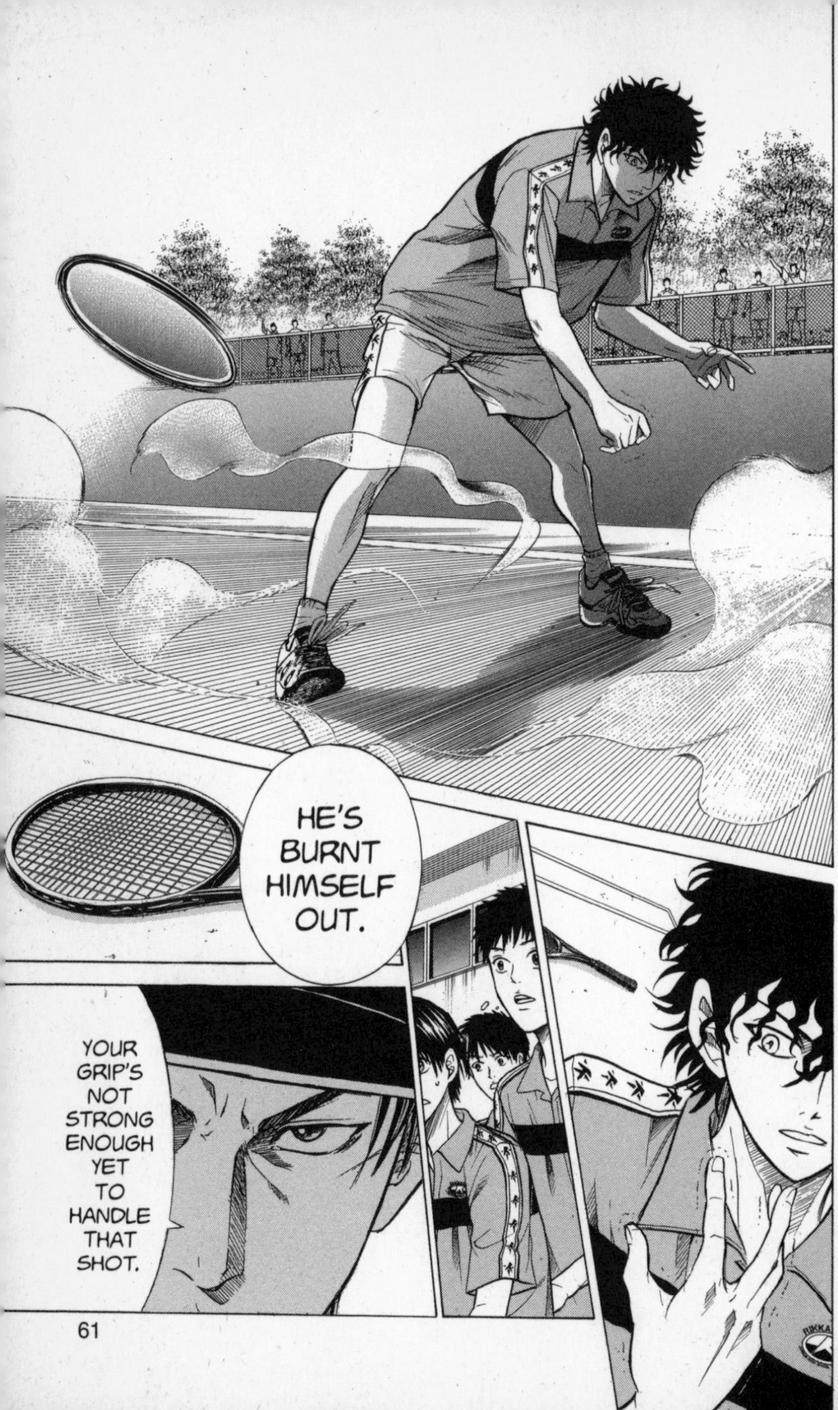
HE'S BURNT HIMSELF OUT.
YOUR GRIP'S NOT STRONG ENOUGH YET TO HANDLE THAT SHOT.

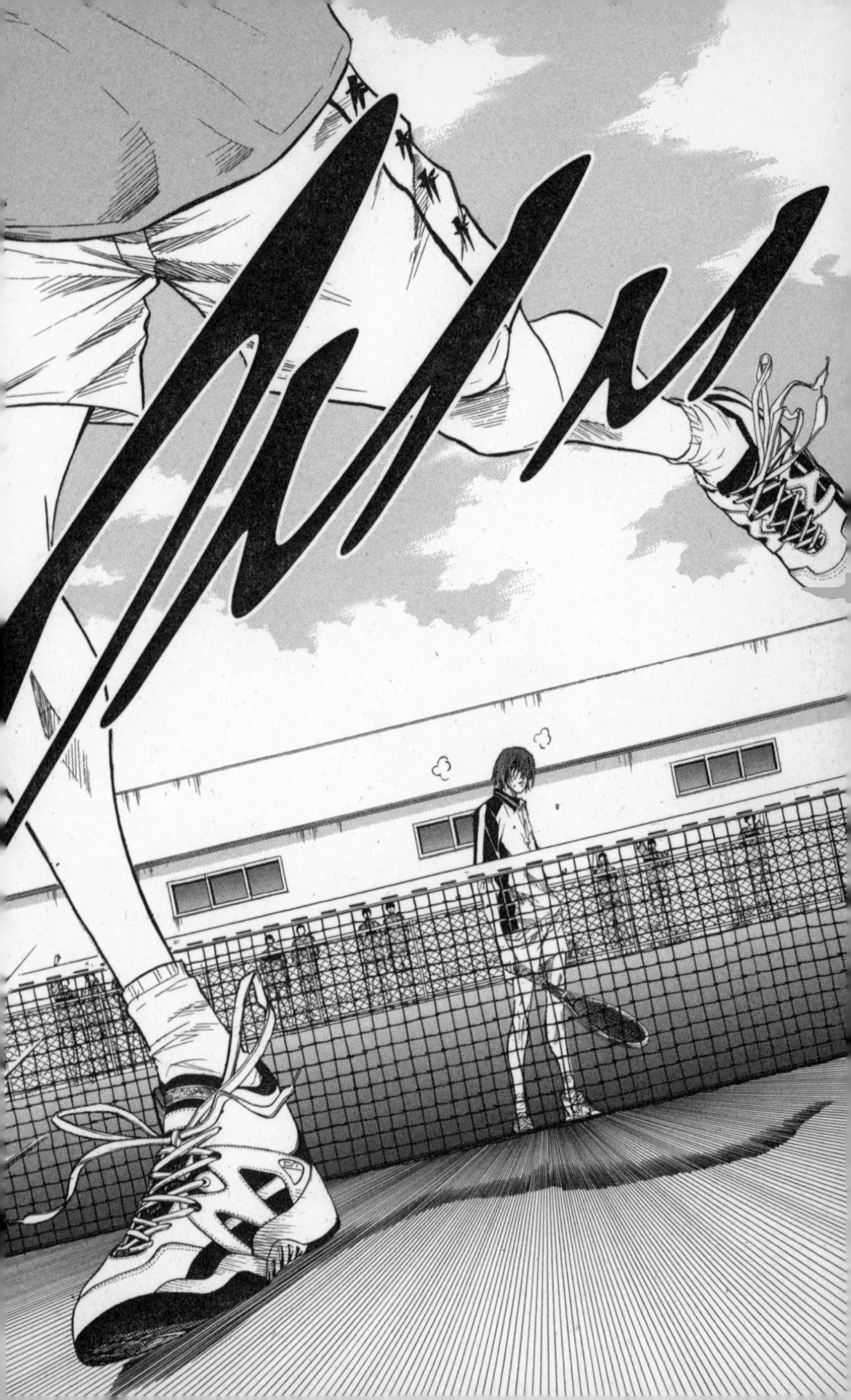

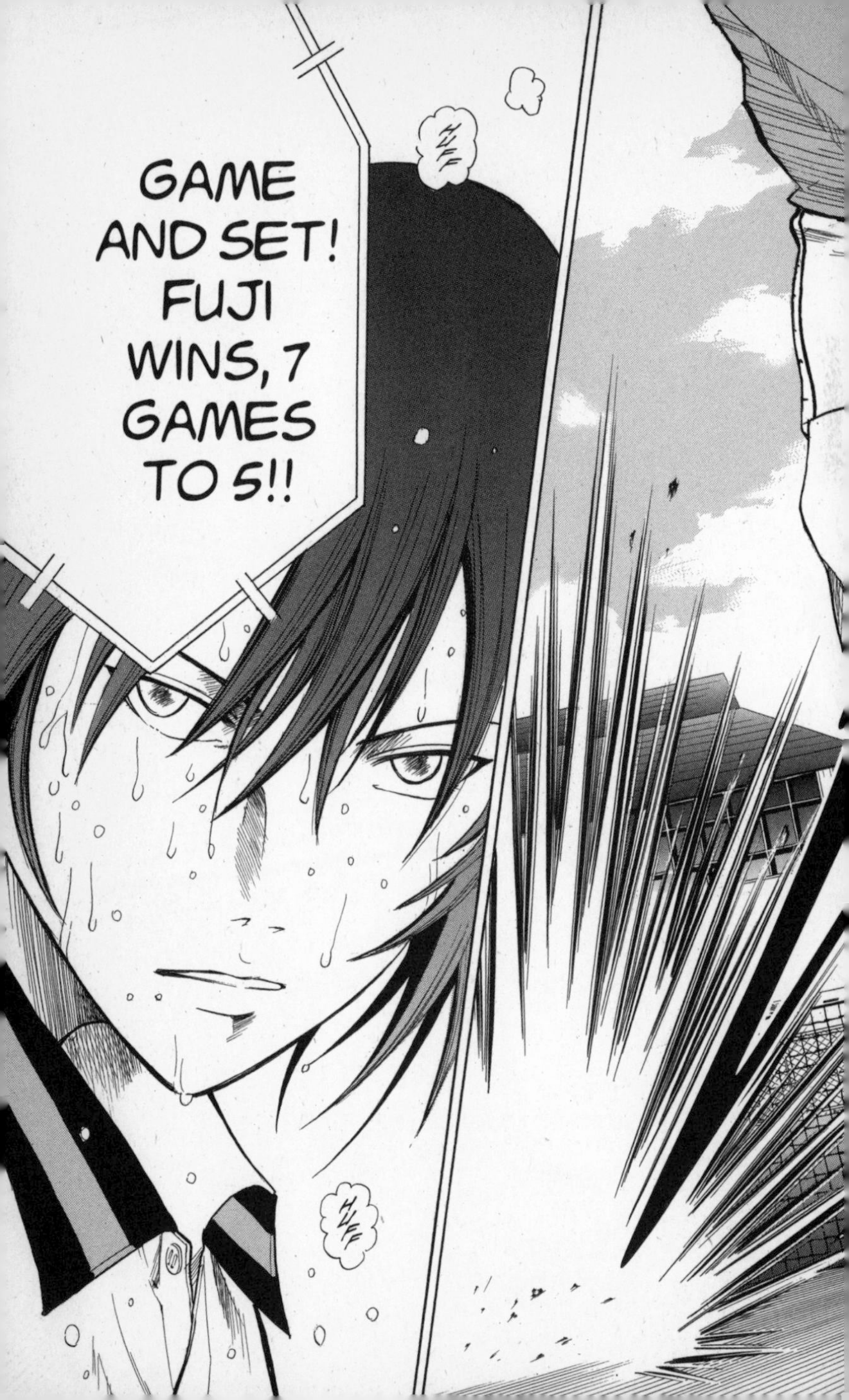
HUFF
GAME AND SET! FUJI WINS, 7 GAMES TO 5!!
HUFF

RIKKAI QUESTION CORNER

It's Back!!

Part 3

RIKKAI UNIV. JUNIOR HIGH SCHOOL TENNIS CLUB

We're back with another segment of the Rikkai Question Corner, the special section where members of the team answer your questions themselves!!

Q: Where is Masaharu from? I think he's from the West, but it's hard to tell...

(S.K., Yamaguchi)

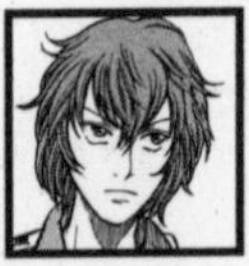

You know...don't you, Jackal?

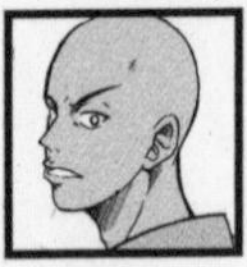

Me?! [More flustered than he should be.]

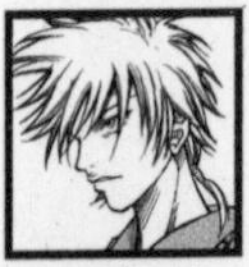

Nobody can know where I'm from! Phwee♪

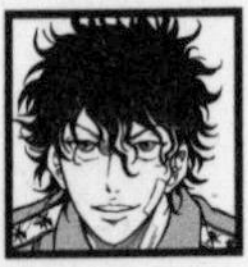

What was that all about?

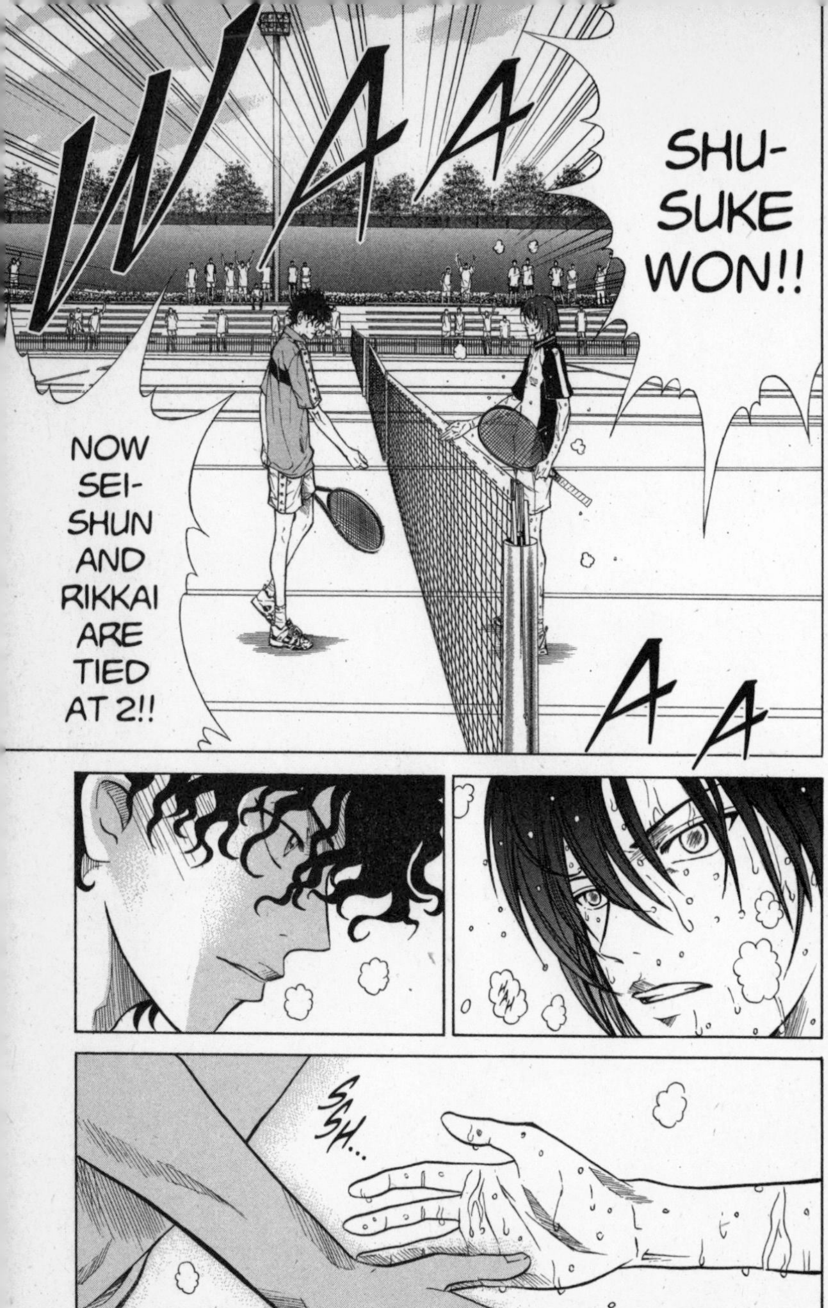
WAA
SHU-SUKE WON!!
NOW SEI-SHUN AND RIKKAI ARE TIED AT 2!!
AA
HAH
SSH...

GENIUS 223: PRESENCE

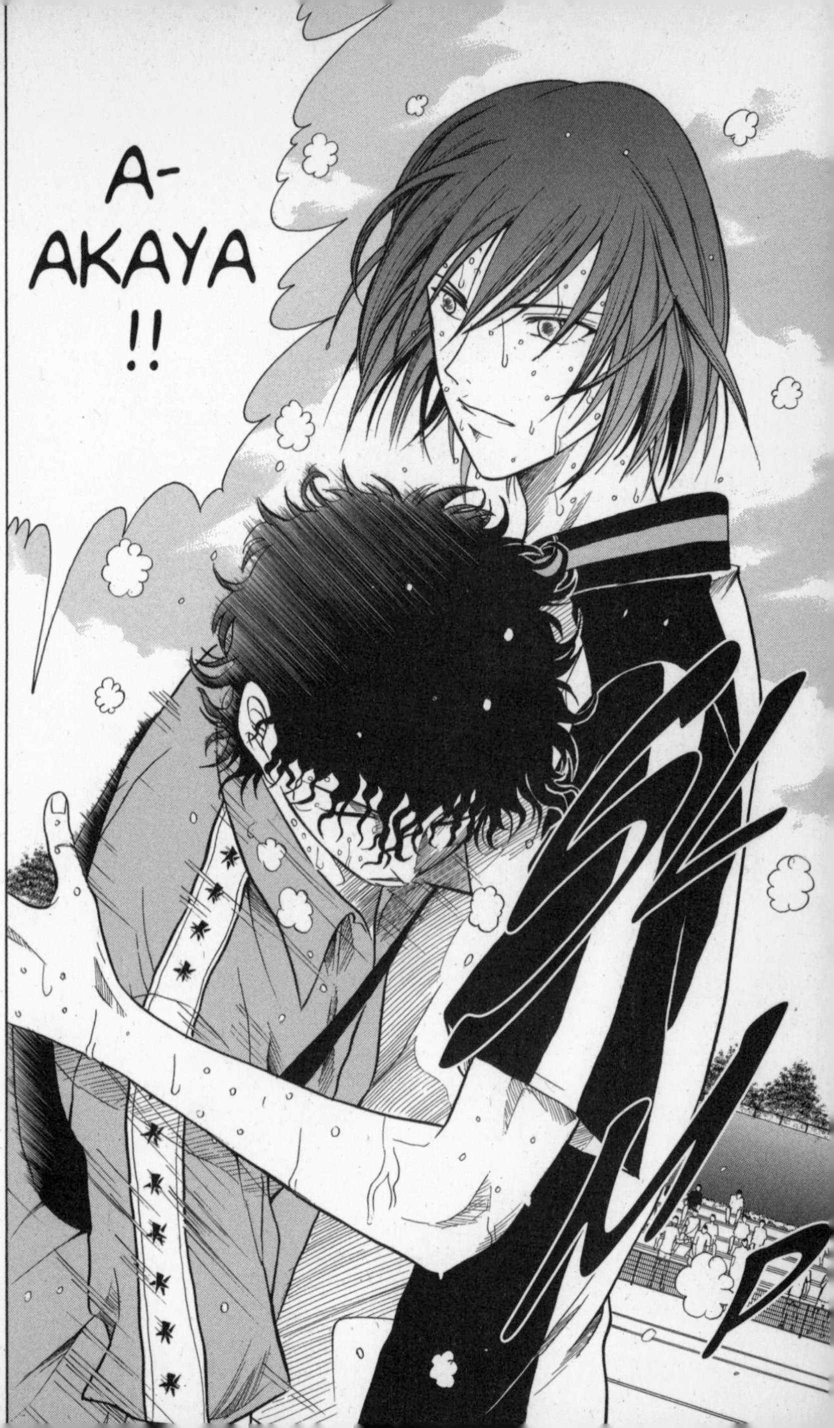
A- AKAYA !!

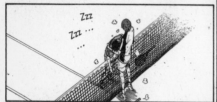

Zzz...
Zzz...
...

DON'T WORRY... HE'S JUST SLEEPING.

GENIUS 223:
PRESENCE

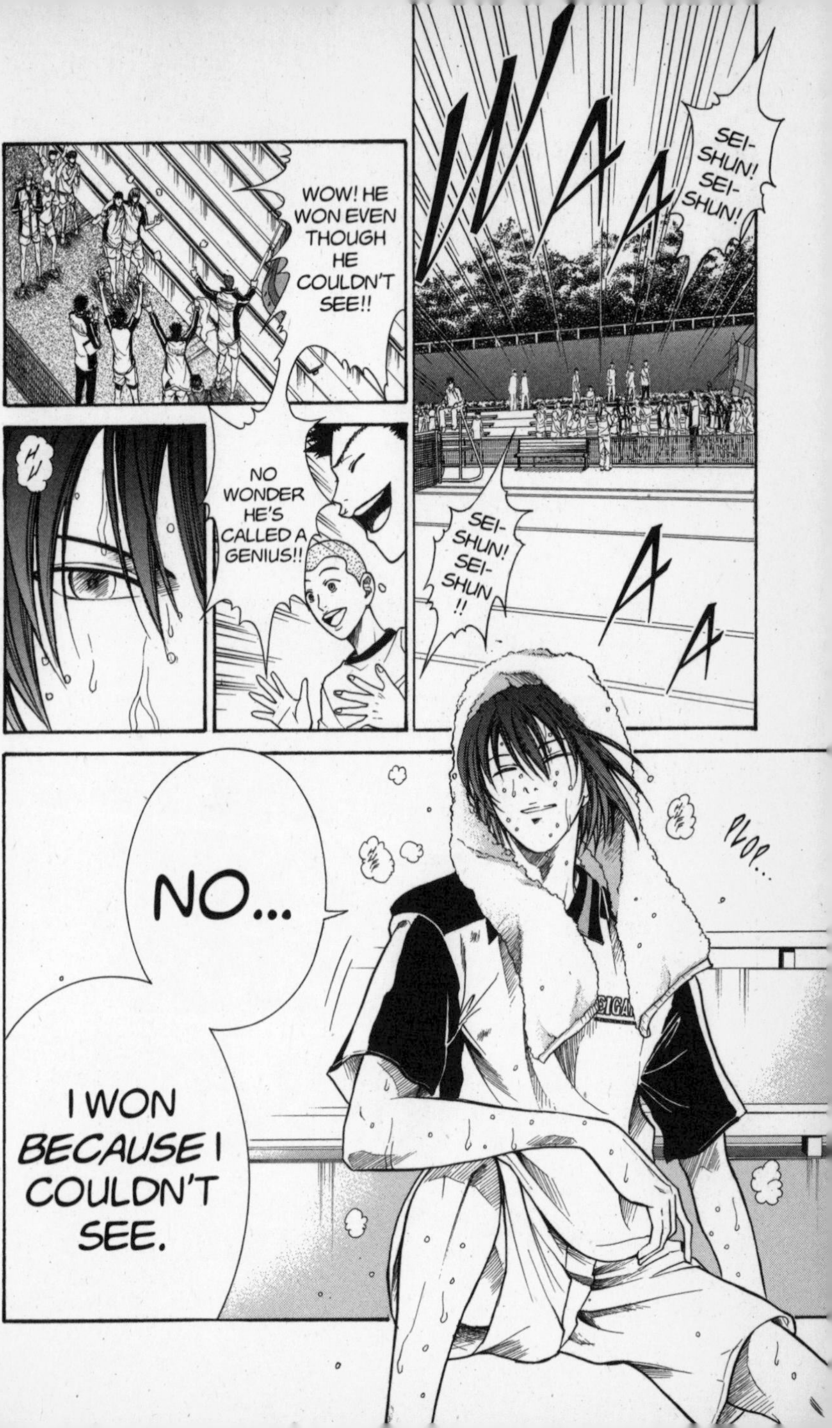
WAA
SEI-SHUN! SEI-SHUN!
SEI-SHUN! SEI-SHUN!!
AA
WOW! HE WON EVEN THOUGH HE COULDN'T SEE!!
NO WONDER HE'S CALLED A GENIUS!!
PLOP...
NO...
I WON *BECAUSE* I COULDN'T SEE.

READ THIS WAY

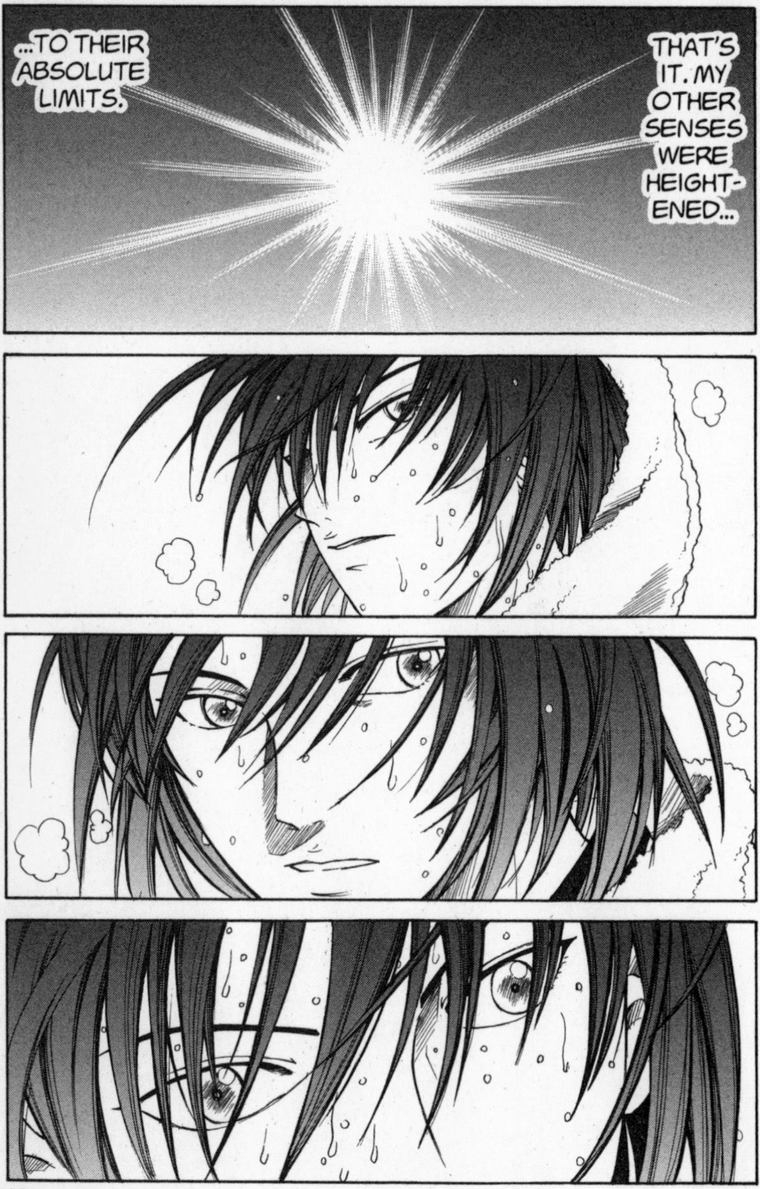

THAT'S IT. MY OTHER SENSES WERE HEIGHT-ENED...
...TO THEIR ABSOLUTE LIMITS.

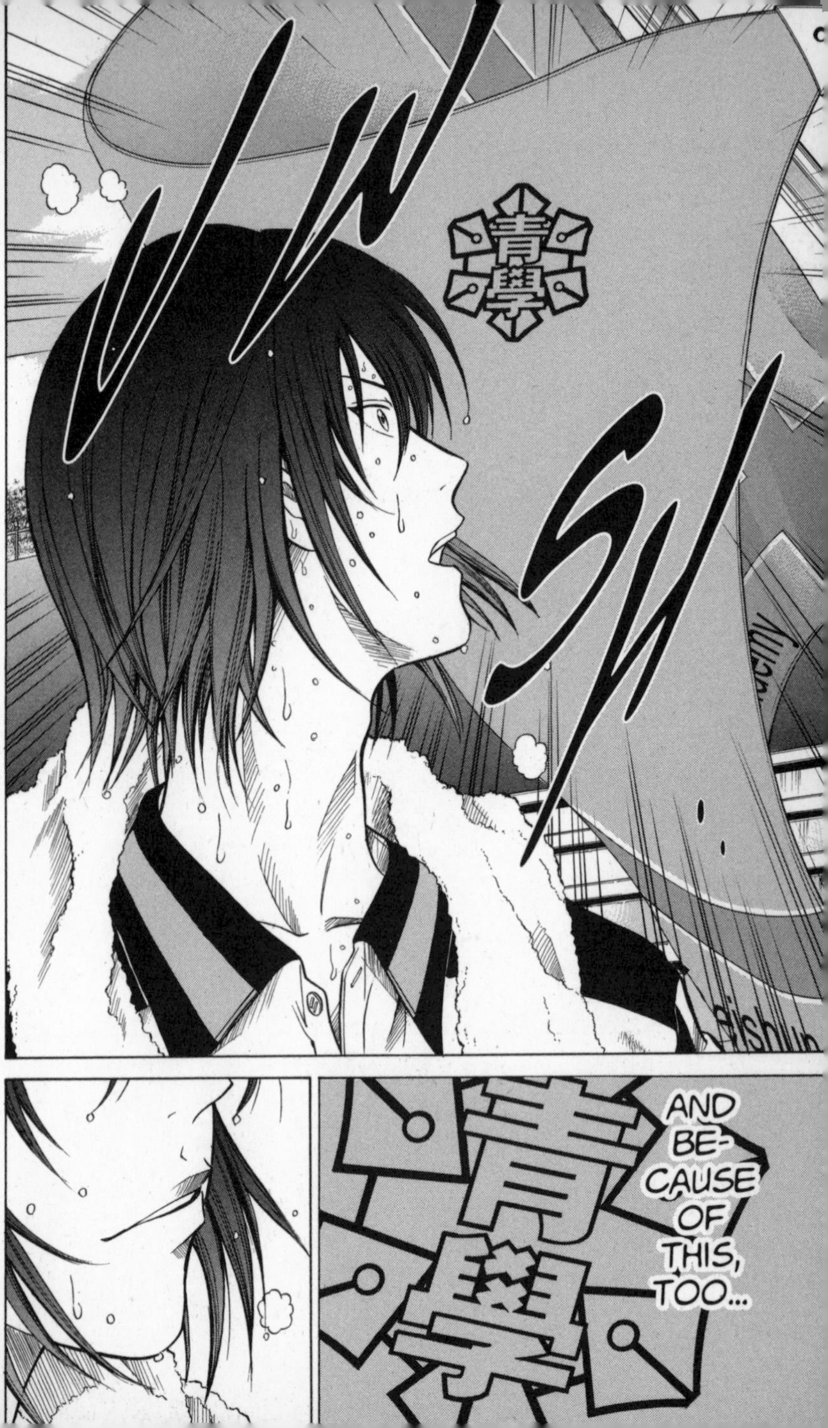
青學
AND BE-
CAUSE
OF
THIS,
TOO...

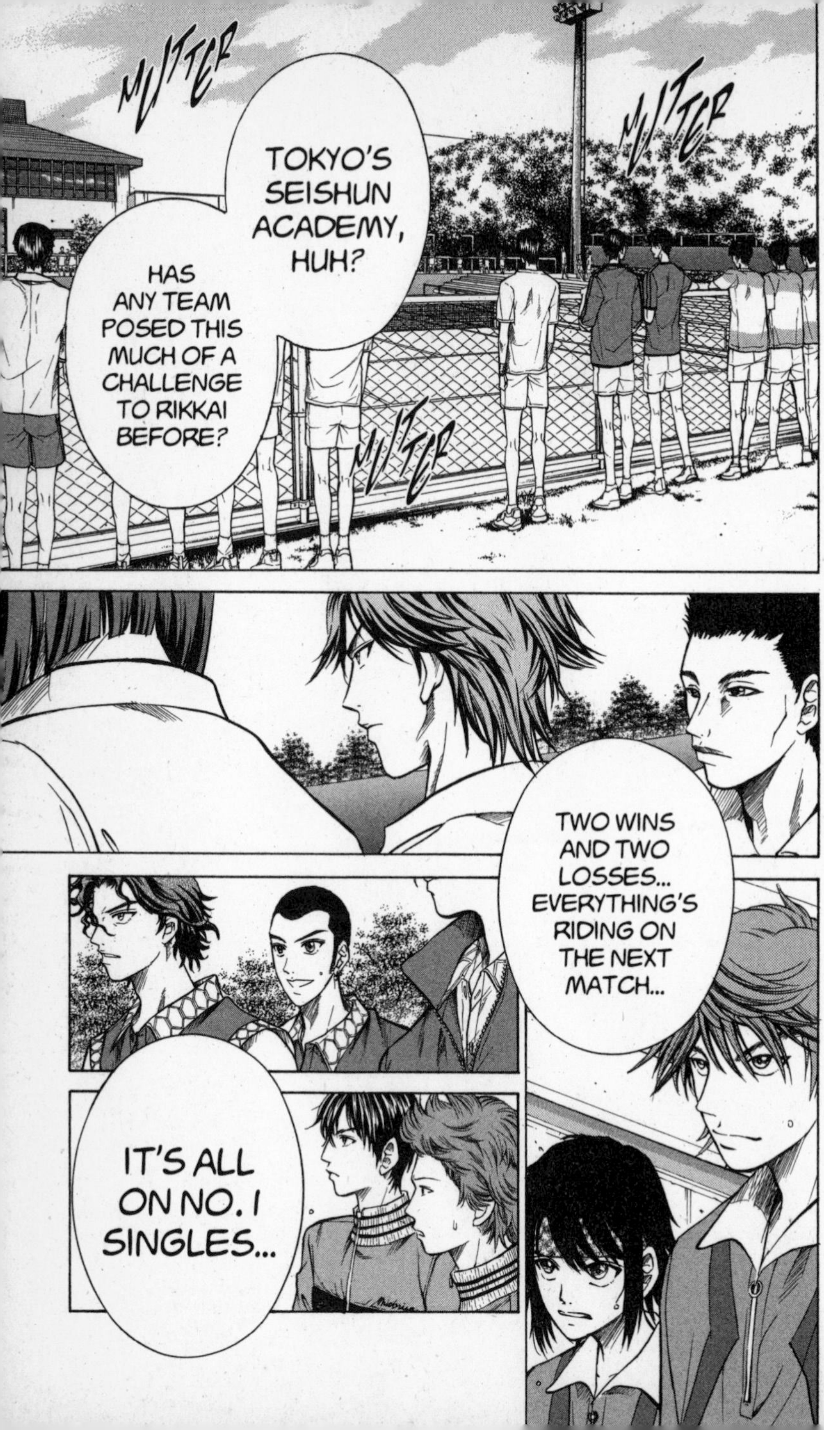
MUTTER
TOKYO'S SEISHUN ACADEMY, HUH?
MUTTER
HAS ANY TEAM POSED THIS MUCH OF A CHALLENGE TO RIKKAI BEFORE?
MUTTER
TWO WINS AND TWO LOSSES... EVERYTHING'S RIDING ON THE NEXT MATCH...
IT'S ALL ON NO. 1 SINGLES...

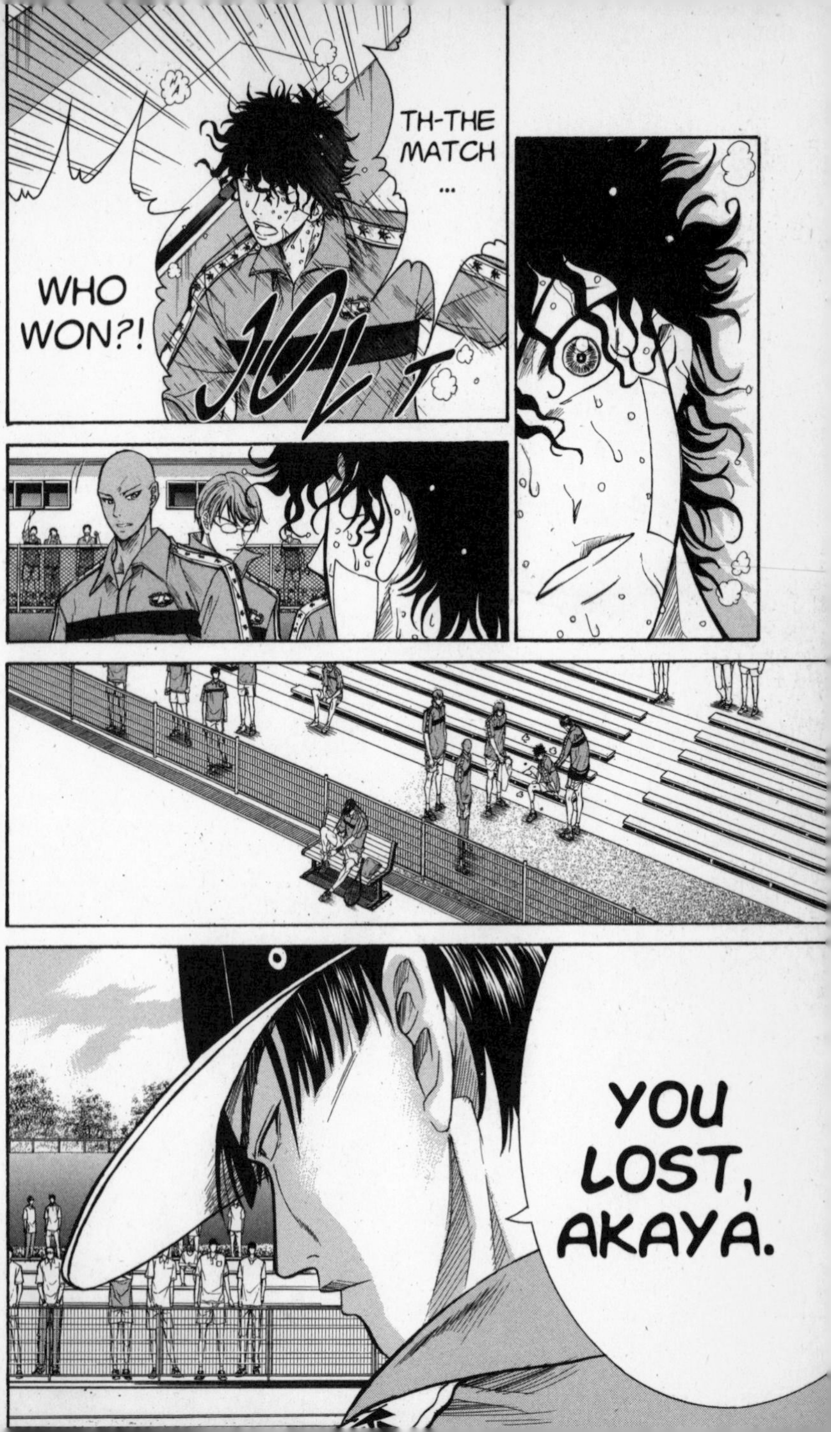
TH-THE MATCH ...
WHO WON?!
YOU LOST, AKAYA.

READ THIS WAY

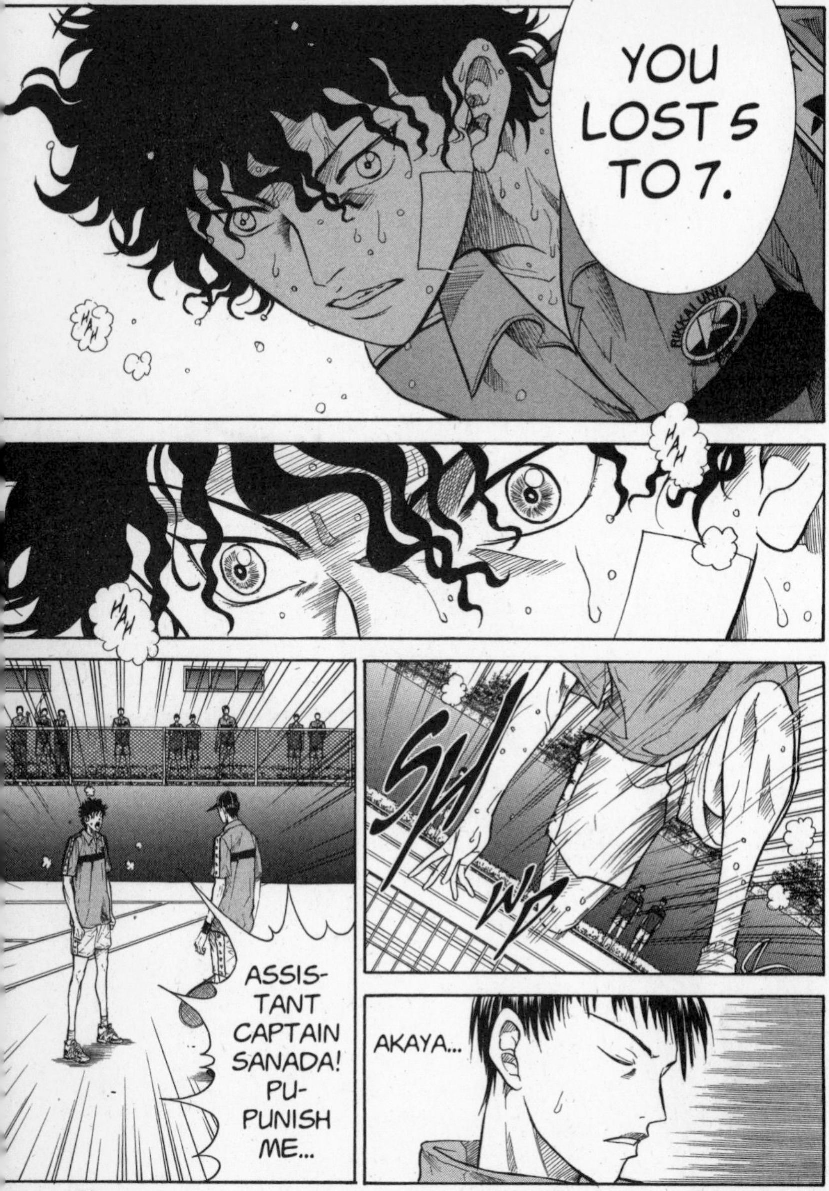
YOU LOST 5 TO 7.
HAH
HAH
HAH
AKAYA...
ASSIS-TANT CAPTAIN SANADA! PU-PUNISH ME...

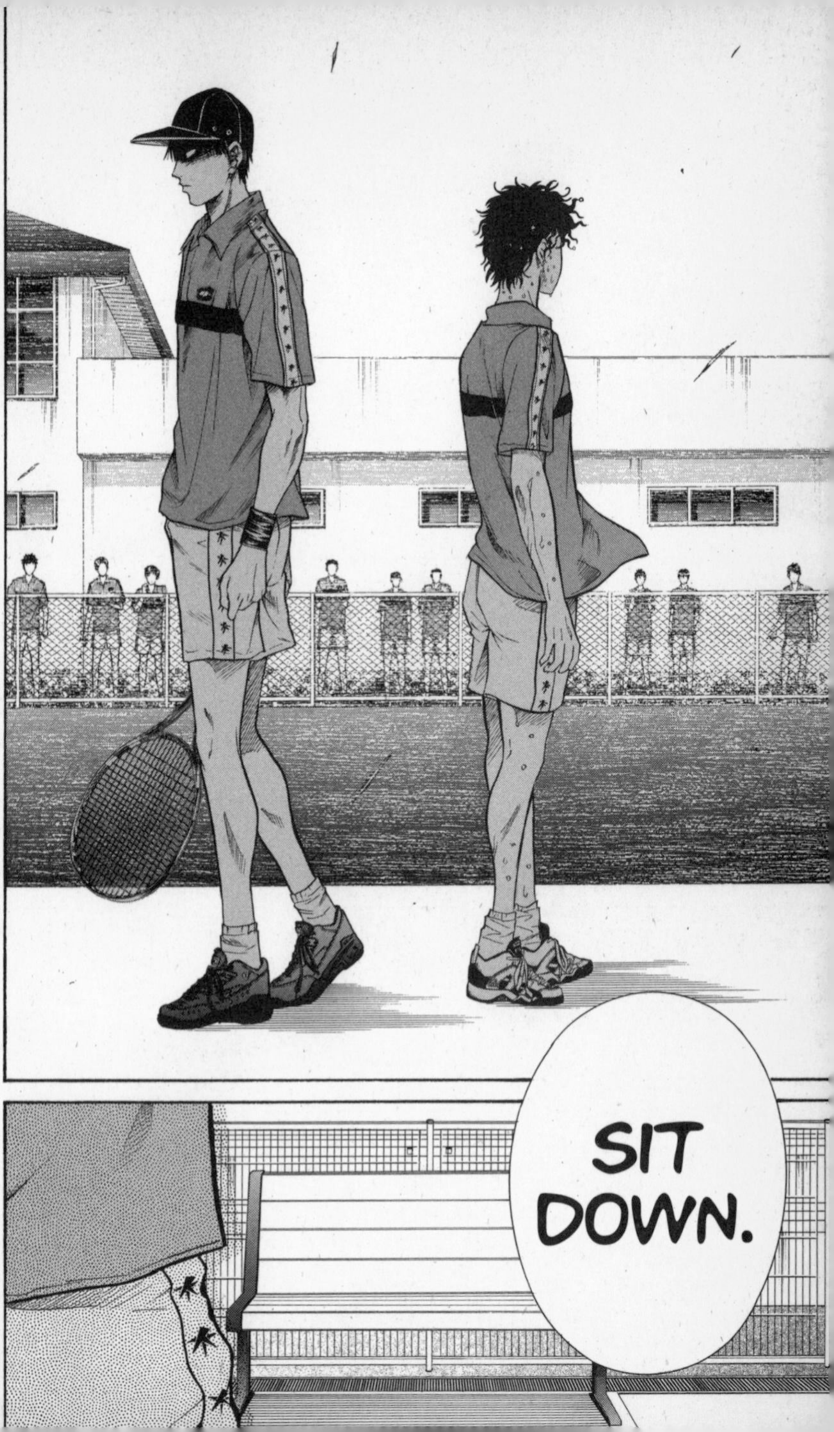
SIT DOWN.

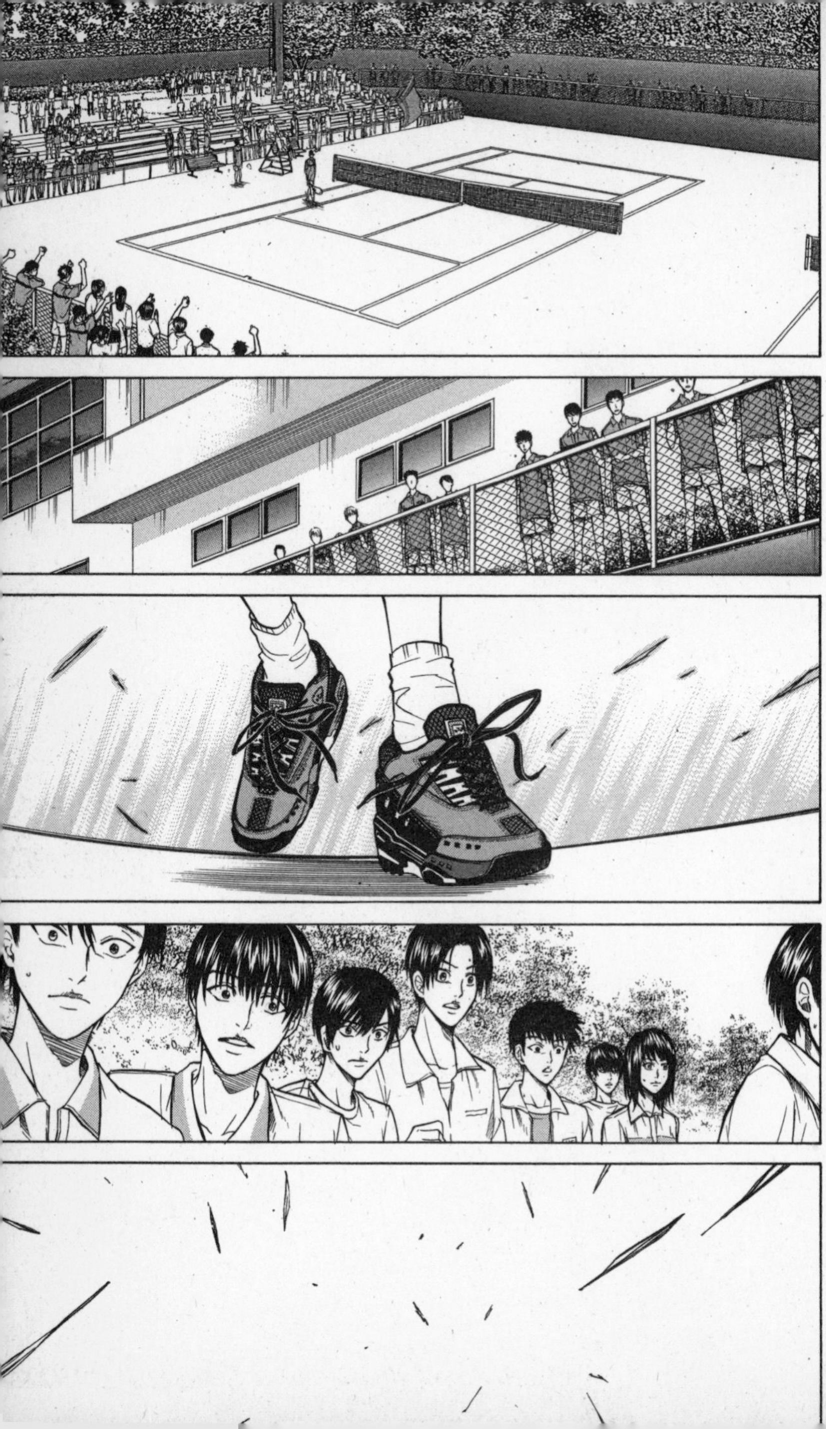

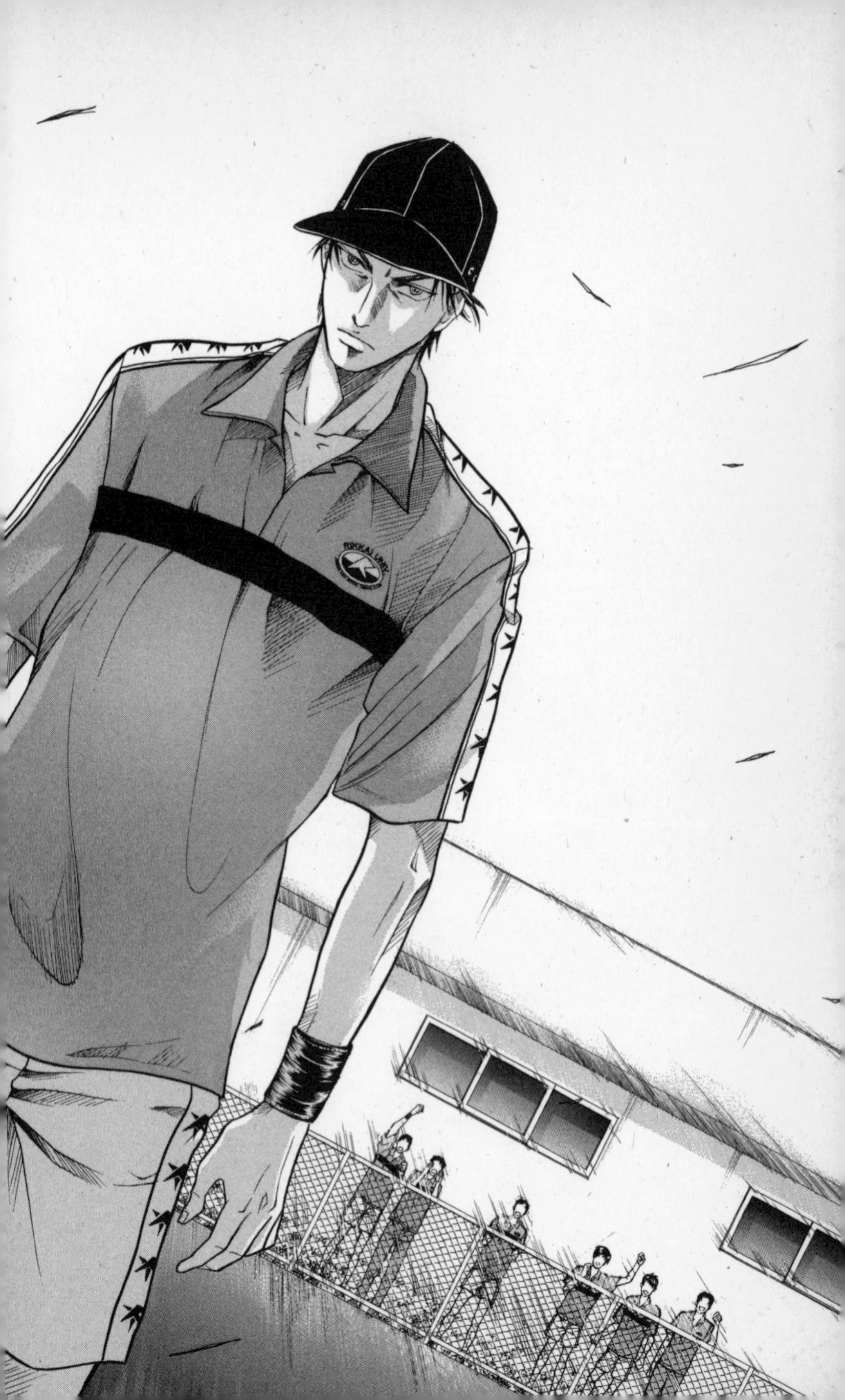
RIKKAI UNIV.

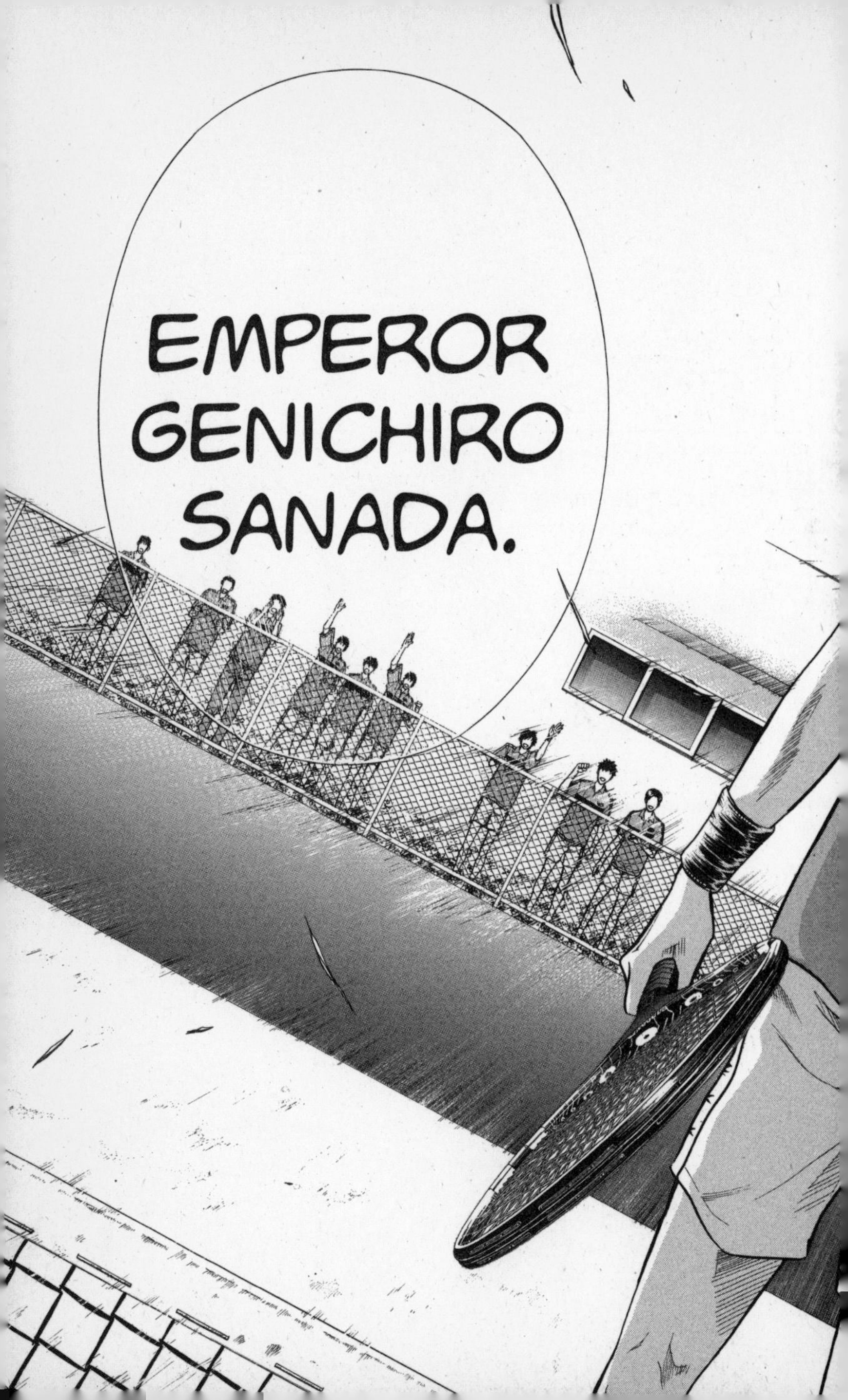
EMPEROR GENICHIRO SANADA.

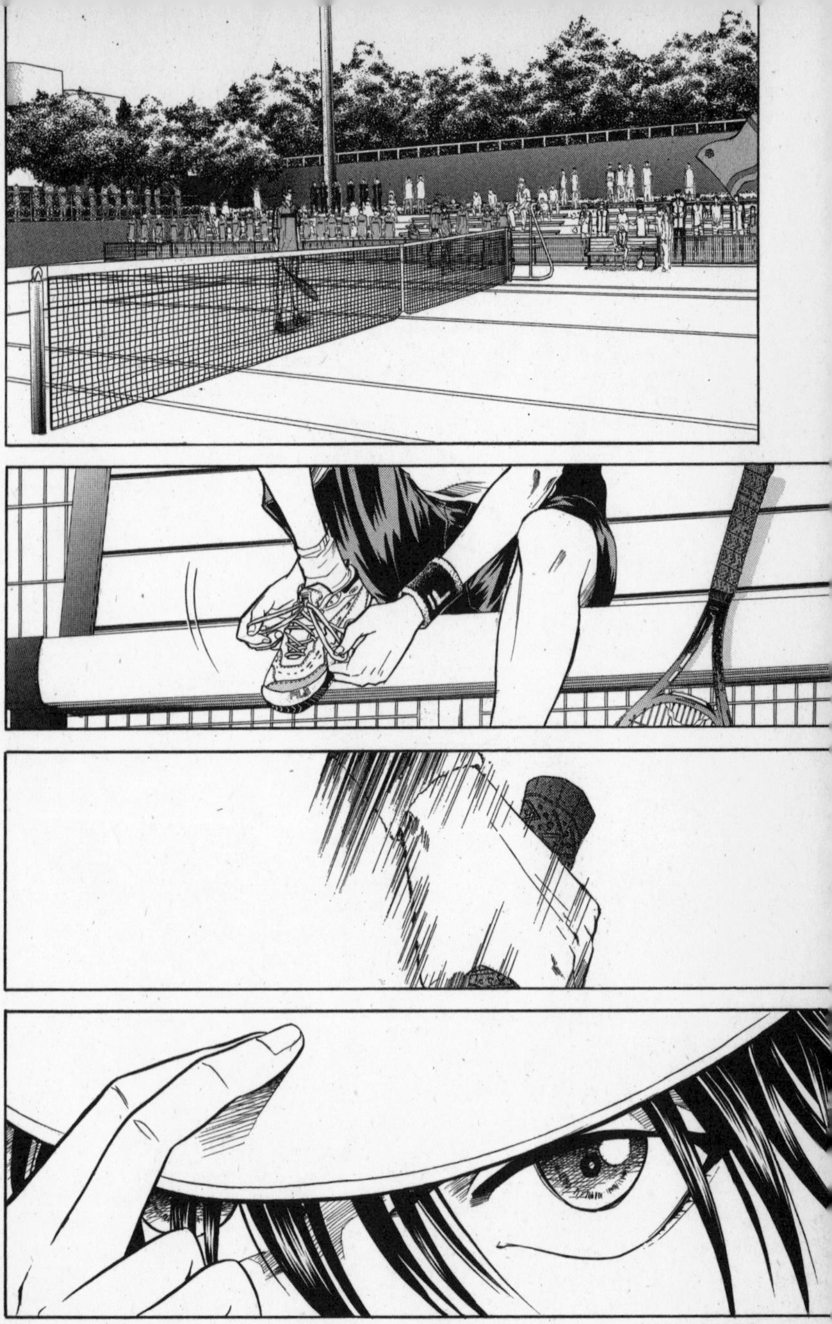

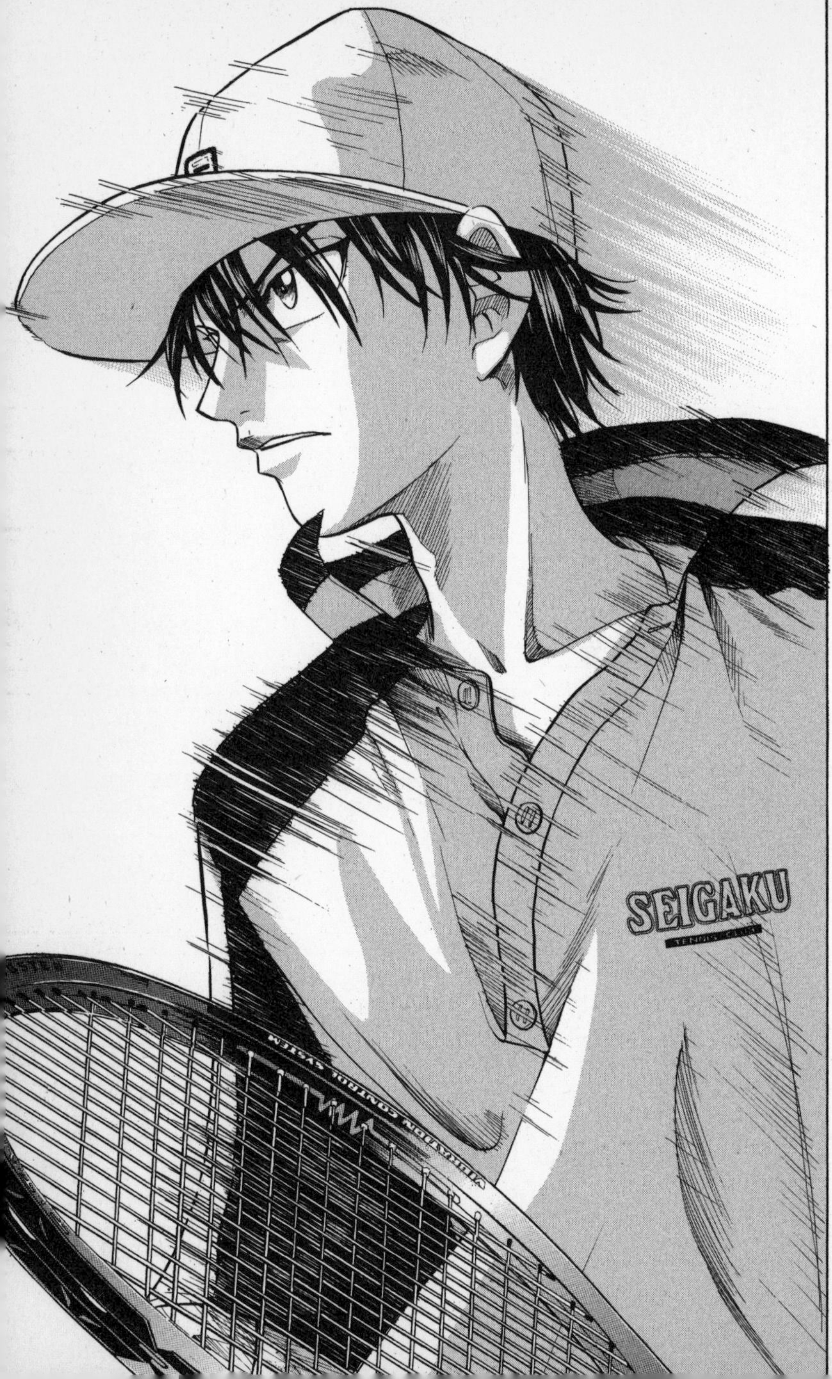
SEIGAKU

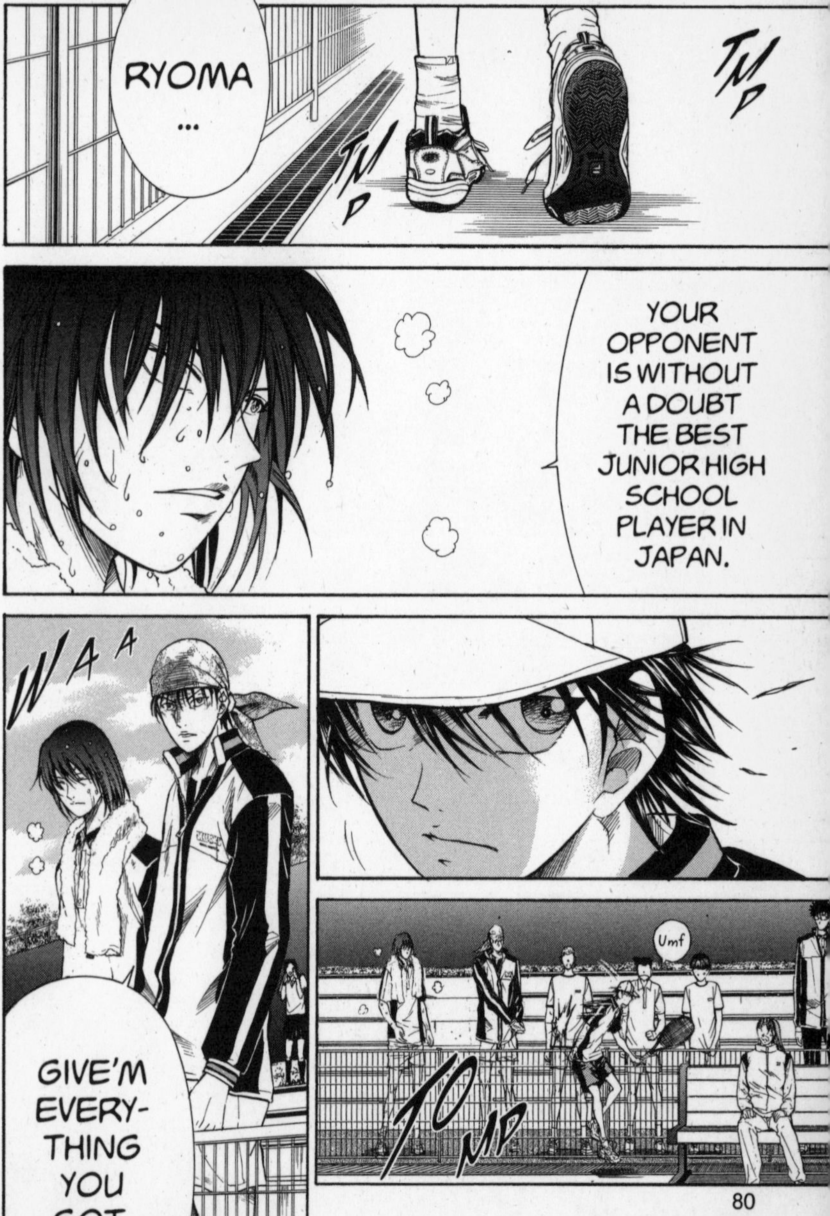
TMP
RYOMA ...
TMP
YOUR OPPONENT IS WITHOUT A DOUBT THE BEST JUNIOR HIGH SCHOOL PLAYER IN JAPAN.
Umf
TOMP
WAA
GIVE'M EVERY-THING YOU GOT.

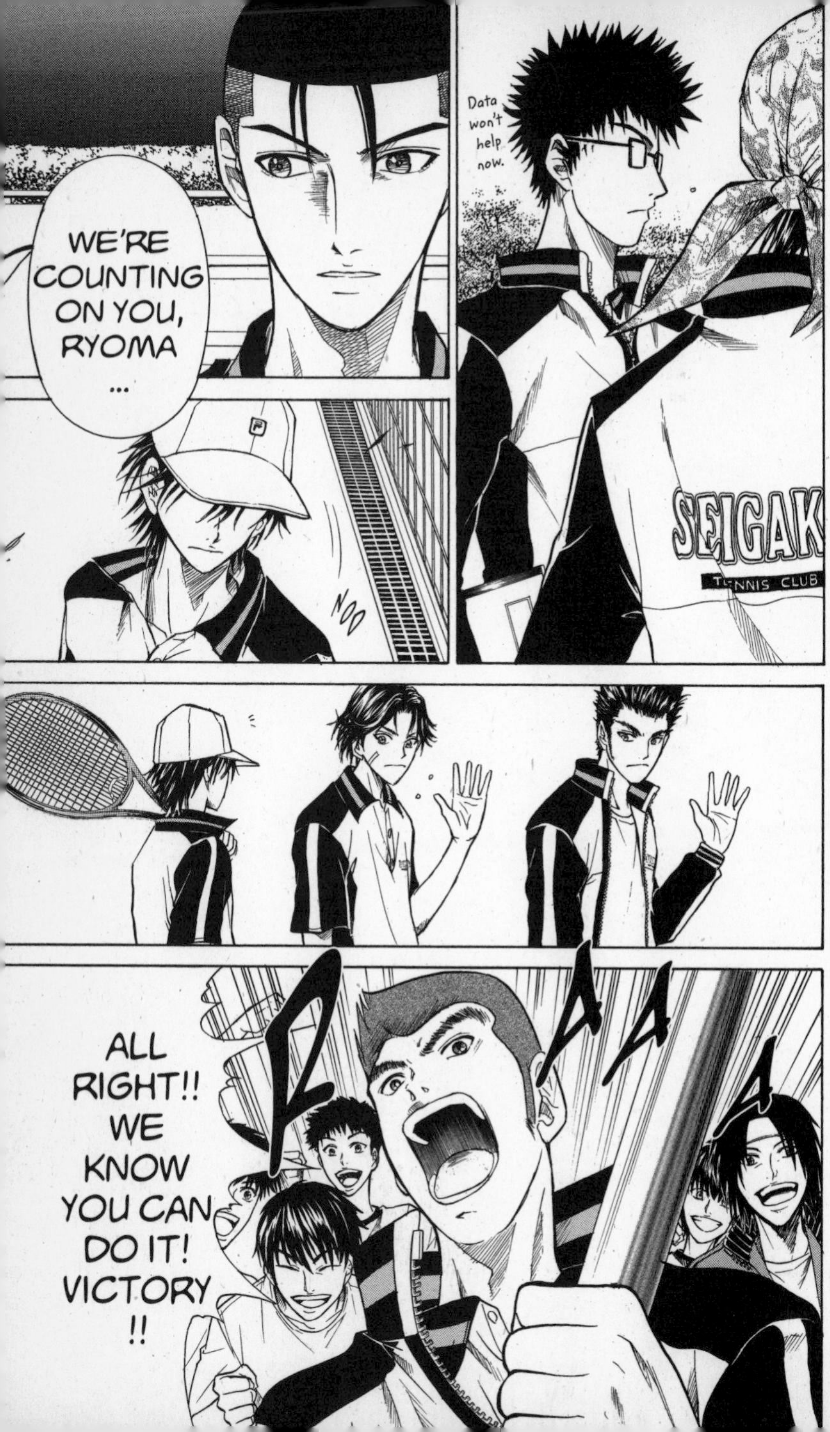
Data won't help now.
SEIGAKU
TENNIS CLUB
WE'RE COUNTING ON YOU, RYOMA ...
ALL RIGHT!! WE KNOW YOU CAN DO IT! VICTORY !!

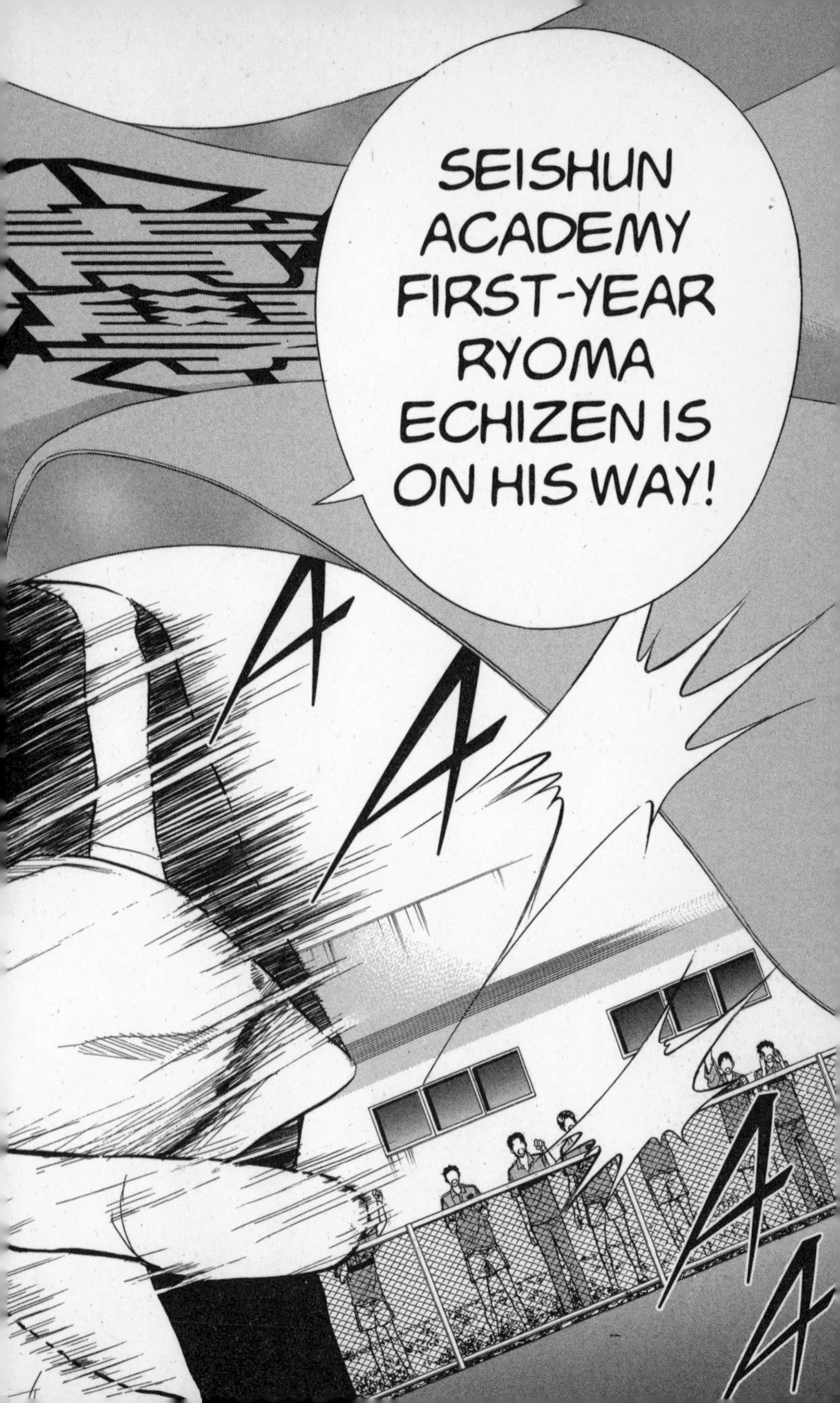
SEISHUN ACADEMY FIRST-YEAR RYOMA ECHIZEN IS ON HIS WAY!

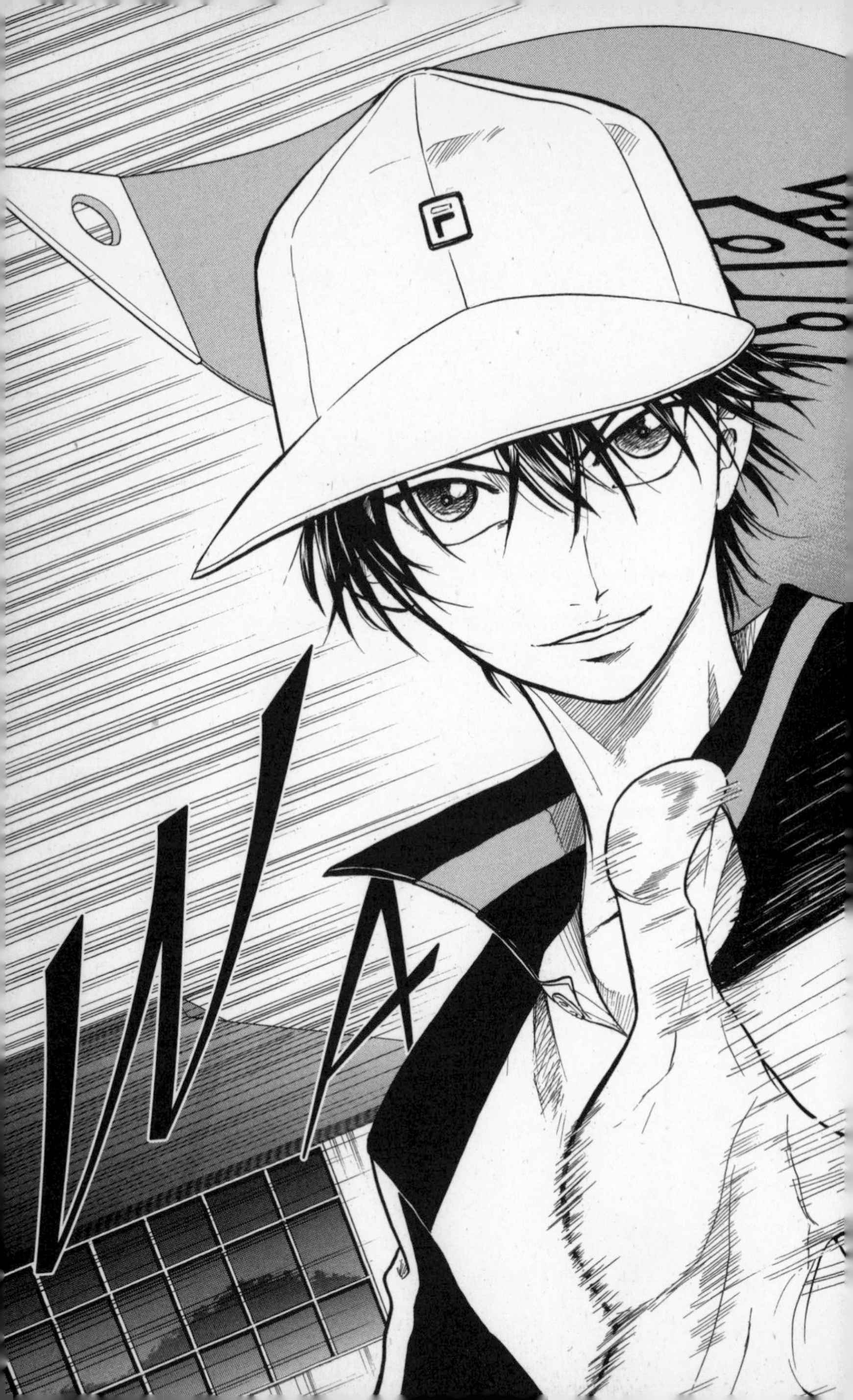
WA

RIKKAI QUESTION CORNER

Part 4

It's Back!!

We're back with another segment of the Rikkai Question Corner, the special section where members of the team answer your questions themselves!!

Q: I assume Genichiro is called "Emperor" because he's good, but if he played Kunimitsu who would win?

(R.N., Kanagawa)

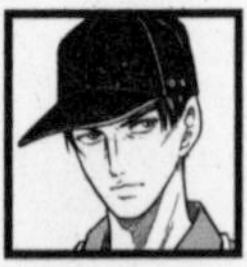

Hmph. [Brow twitches.] What a dumb question!

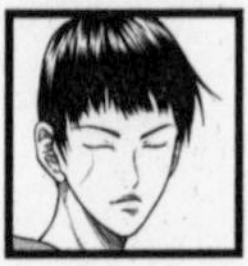

... [Silence]

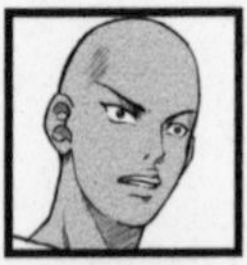

[Unable to stand the tense mood] O-Of course Gen—

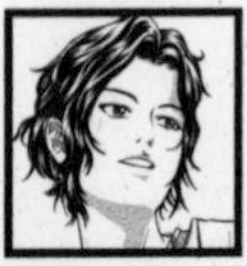

Kunimitsu? Heheh...! [Silence]

GENIUS 224: RYOMA'S UP

NATIONAL JUNIOR HIGH SCHOOL TENNIS KANTO TOURNAMENT FINALS

KANTO TOURNAMENT (BOYS' DIVISION)

1. RIKKAI JUNIOR HIGH (KANAGAWA)
2. GINKA (TOKYO)
3. NAKHIGARI ACADEMY (IBARAKI)
4. KASUMI 4TH (CHIBA)
5. FUDOMINE (TOKYO)
6. ITOGUKUMA (KANAGAWA)
7. IKARI (YAMANASHI)

ROKKANGU JUNIOR HIGH (CHIBA)
OGUCHI-MINAMI 10. (GUNMA)
KYOGIYO (TOCHIGI) 11.
AIHARA 1ST 13. (KANAGAWA)
JOSEI SHONAN 13. (KANAGAWA)
MIDORIYAMA 14. (SAITAMA)
HYOTEI ACADEMY 15. (TOKYO)
SEISHUN ACADEMY 16. (TOKYO)

RIKKAI JUNIOR HIGH (KANAGAWA) VS. SEISHUN ACADEMY (TOKYO)

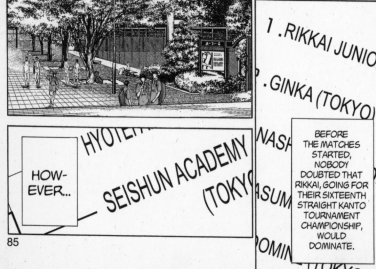

1. RIKKAI JUNIOR
2. GINKA (TOKYO)

HYOTEI
SEISHUN ACADEMY (TOKYO)

HOW-EVER...

BEFORE THE MATCHES STARTED, NOBODY DOUBTED THAT RIKKAI, GOING FOR THEIR SIXTEENTH STRAIGHT KANTO TOURNAMENT CHAMPIONSHIP, WOULD DOMINATE.

85

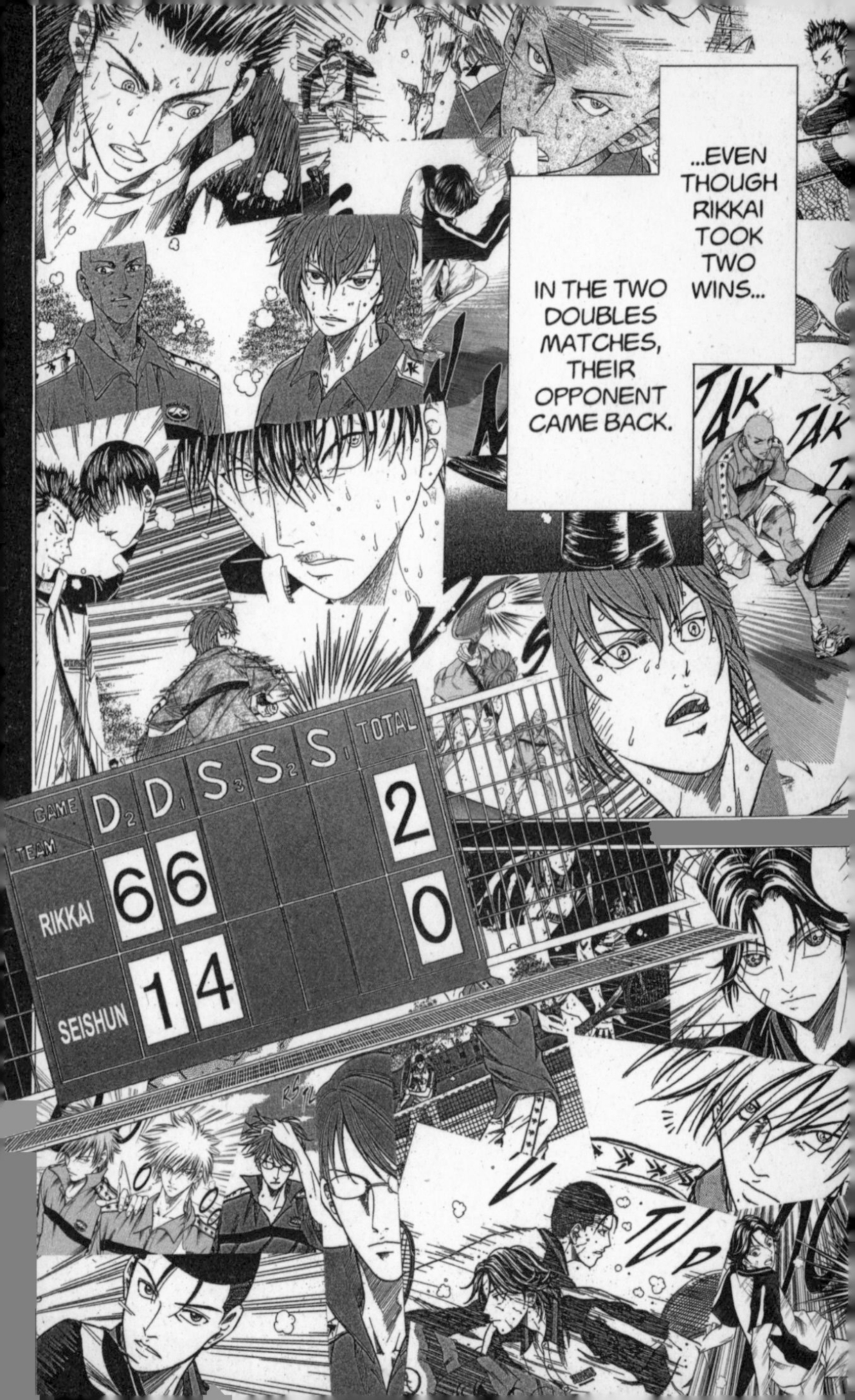
...EVEN THOUGH RIKKAI TOOK TWO WINS...
IN THE TWO DOUBLES MATCHES, THEIR OPPONENT CAME BACK.
TAK
TAK
GAME D2 D1 S3 S2 S1 TOTAL
TEAM
RIKKAI 6 6 2
SEISHUN 1 4 0

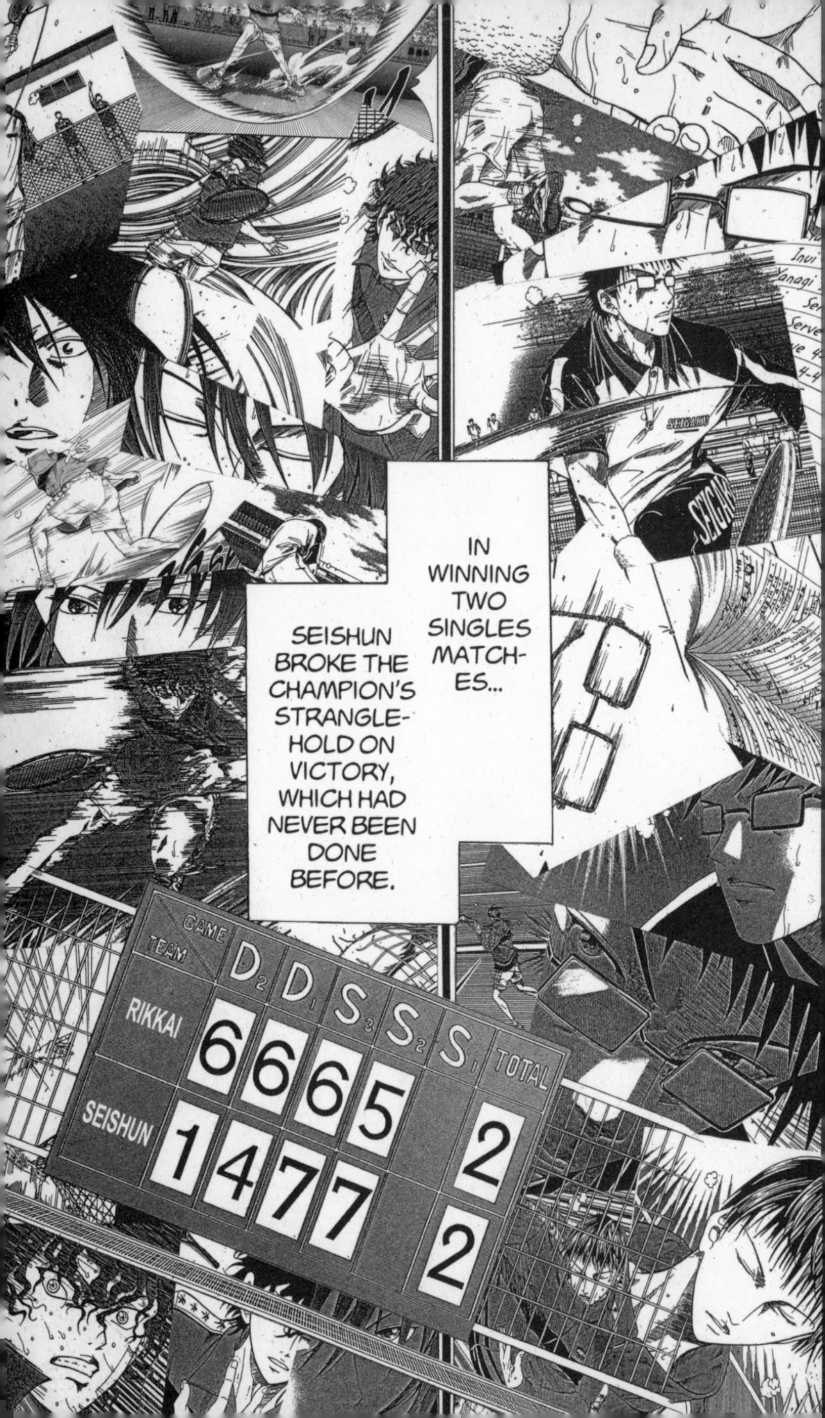
IN WINNING TWO SINGLES MATCHES...
SEISHUN BROKE THE CHAMPION'S STRANGLEHOLD ON VICTORY, WHICH HAD NEVER BEEN DONE BEFORE.
SEIGAKU
SEIGAKU
GAME TEAM D2 D1 S3 S2 S1 TOTAL
RIKKAI 6 6 6 5 2
SEISHUN 1 4 7 7 2

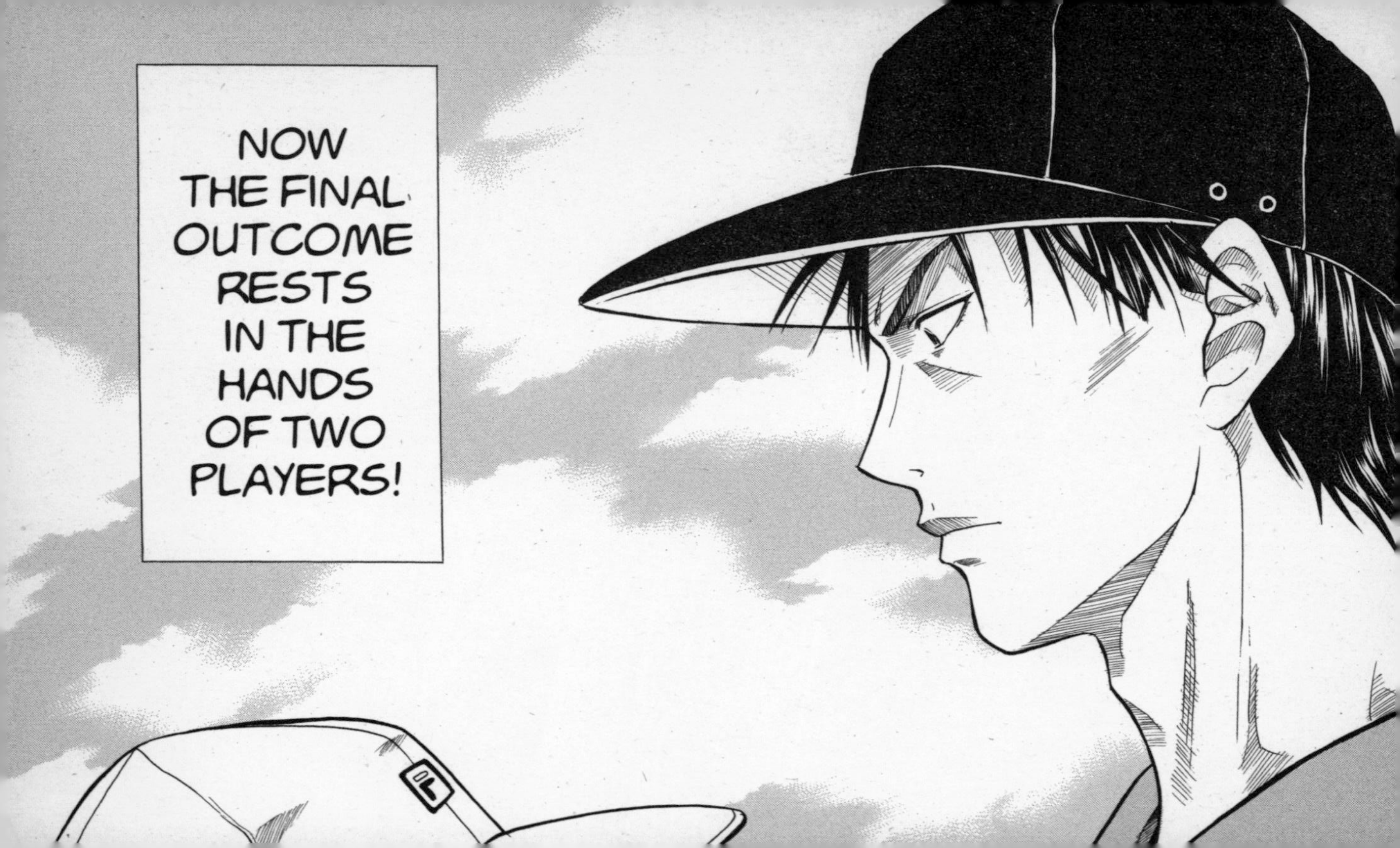
NOW THE FINAL OUTCOME RESTS IN THE HANDS OF TWO PLAYERS!

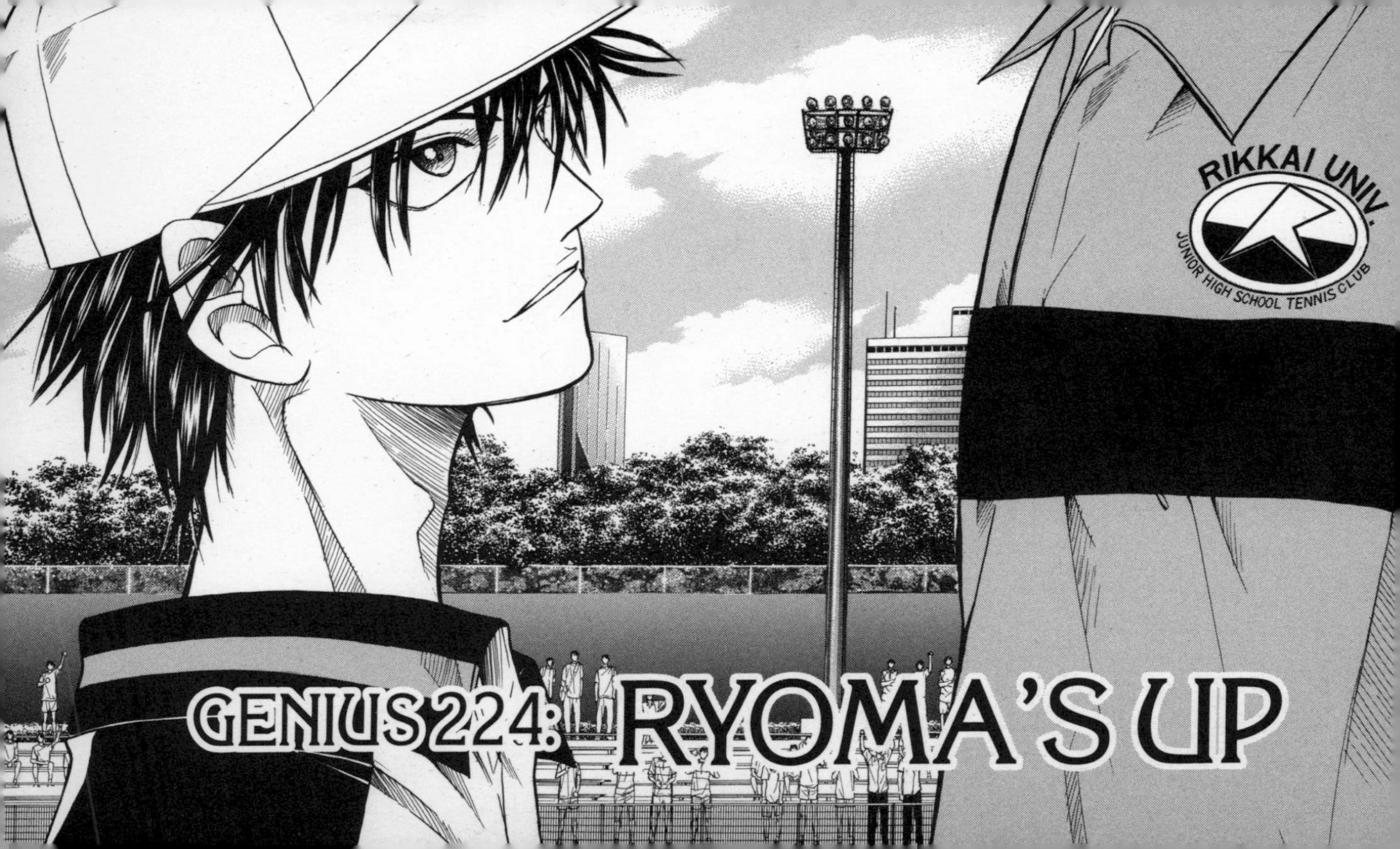
GENIUS 224: RYOMA'S UP
RIKKAI UNIV.
JUNIOR HIGH SCHOOL TENNIS CLUB

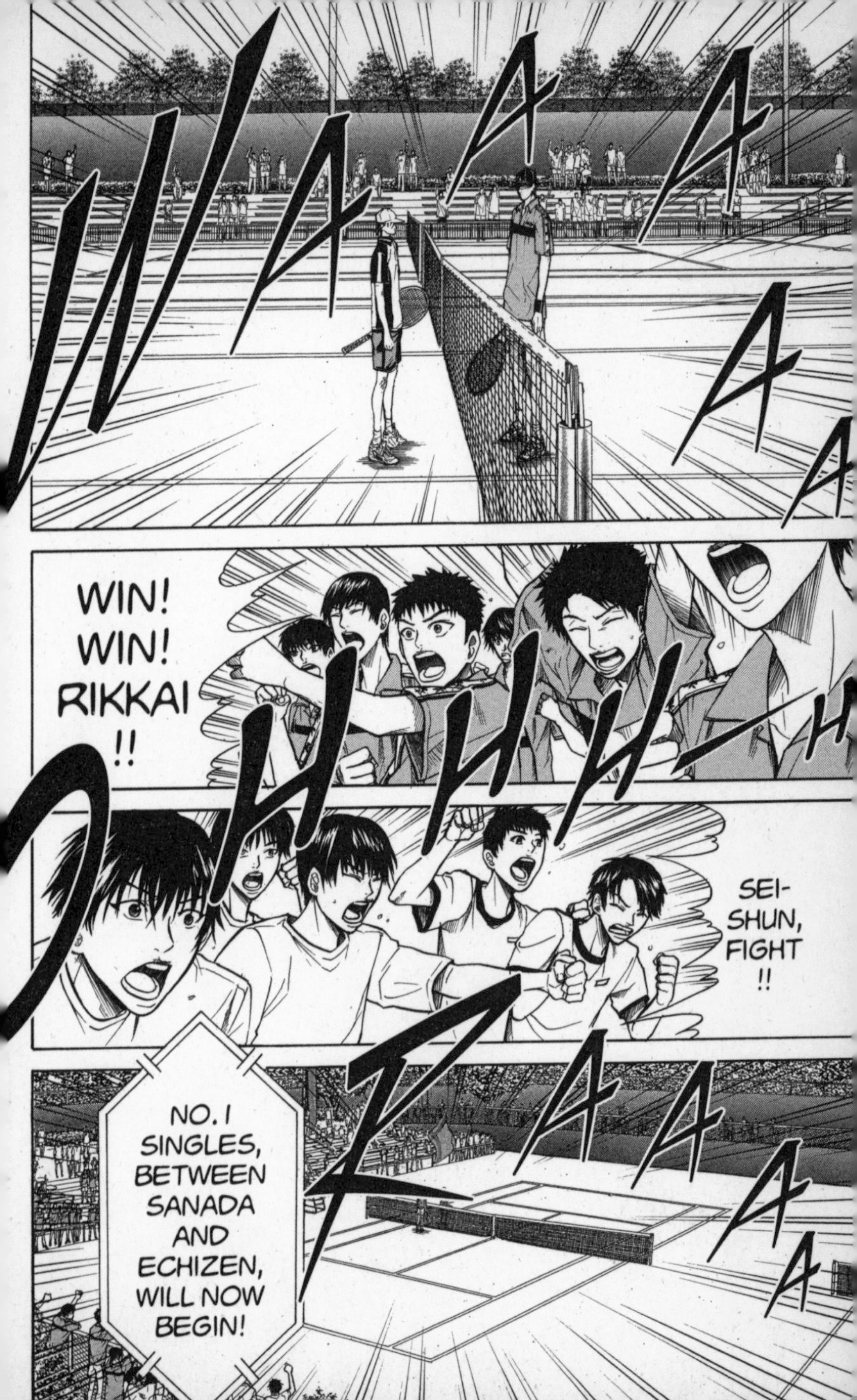
WAAAAAA
WIN! WIN! RIKKAI!!
OHHHHH
SEI-SHUN, FIGHT!!
ZAAAAAA
NO.1 SINGLES, BETWEEN SANADA AND ECHIZEN, WILL NOW BEGIN!

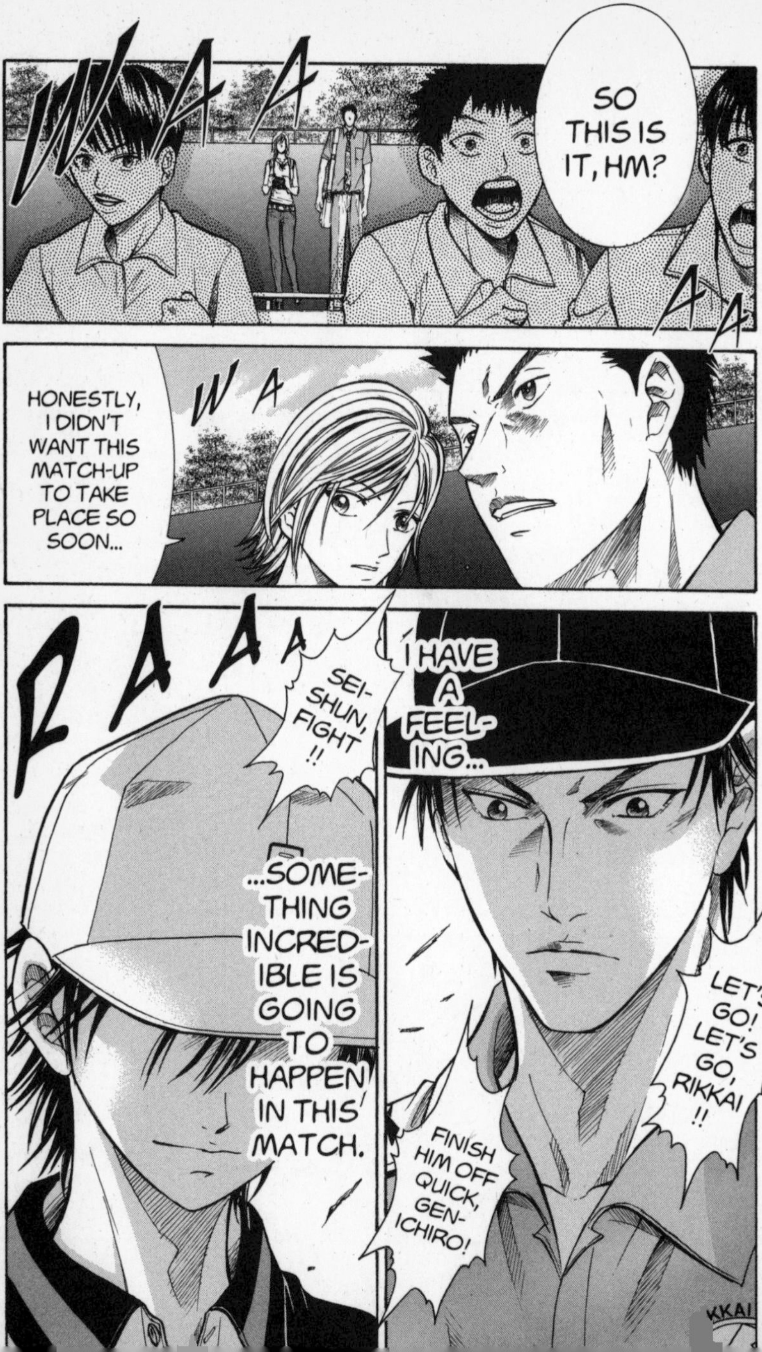
SO THIS IS IT, HM?
WAAA
AA
WA
HONESTLY, I DIDN'T WANT THIS MATCH-UP TO TAKE PLACE SO SOON...
I HAVE A FEELING...
...SOMETHING INCREDIBLE IS GOING TO HAPPEN IN THIS MATCH.
LET'S GO! LET'S GO, RIKKAI!!
FINISH HIM OFF QUICK, GEN-ICHIRO!
SEI-SHUN, FIGHT!!
RAAA

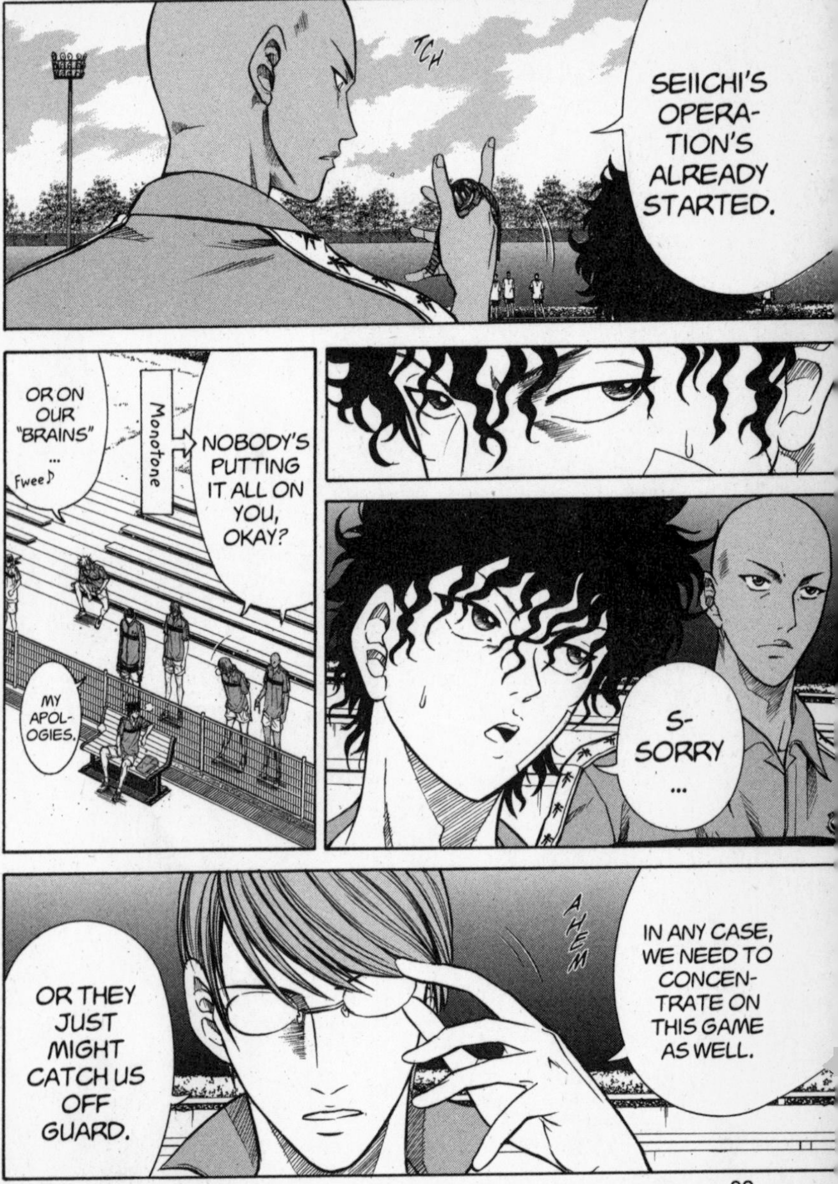
SEIICHI'S OPERATION'S ALREADY STARTED.
TCH
S-SORRY ...
NOBODY'S PUTTING IT ALL ON YOU, OKAY?
Monotone
OR ON OUR "BRAINS" ...
Fwee♪
MY APOLOGIES.
IN ANY CASE, WE NEED TO CONCENTRATE ON THIS GAME AS WELL.
AHEM
OR THEY JUST MIGHT CATCH US OFF GUARD.

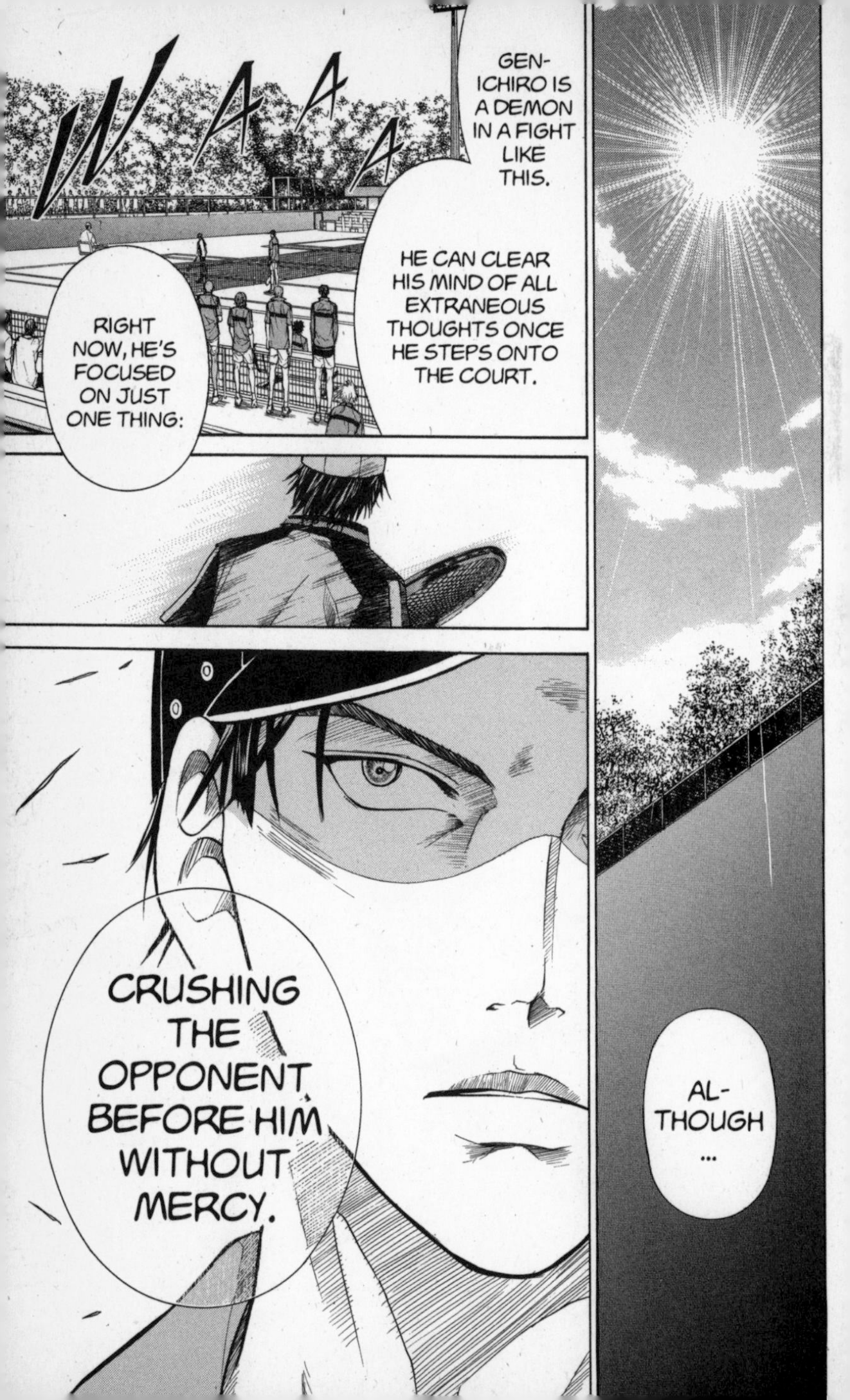

AL-THOUGH ...
WAAAA
GEN-ICHIRO IS A DEMON IN A FIGHT LIKE THIS.
HE CAN CLEAR HIS MIND OF ALL EXTRANEOUS THOUGHTS ONCE HE STEPS ONTO THE COURT.
RIGHT NOW, HE'S FOCUSED ON JUST ONE THING:
CRUSHING THE OPPONENT BEFORE HIM WITHOUT MERCY.

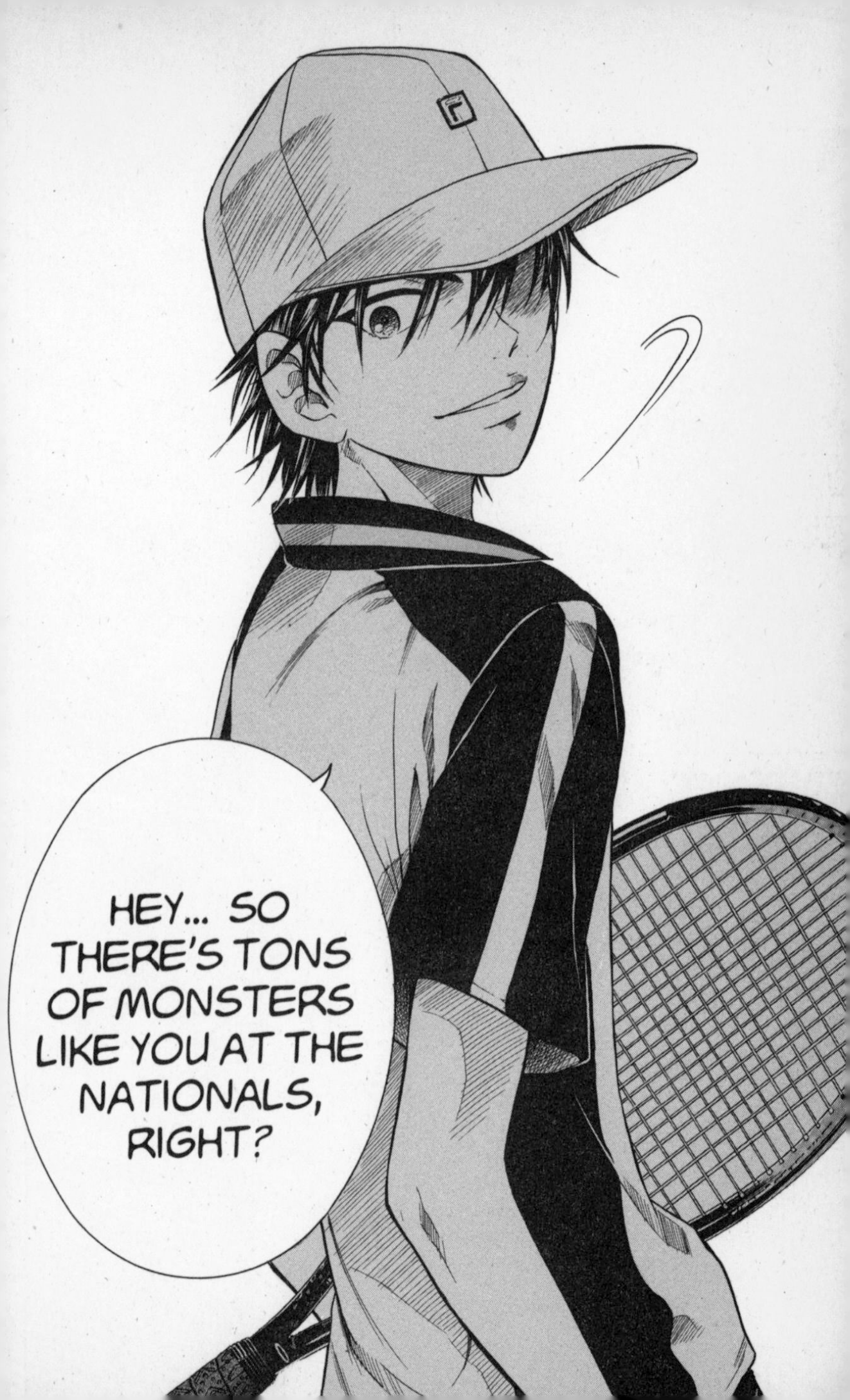
HEY... SO THERE'S TONS OF MONSTERS LIKE YOU AT THE NATIONALS, RIGHT?

READ THIS WAY

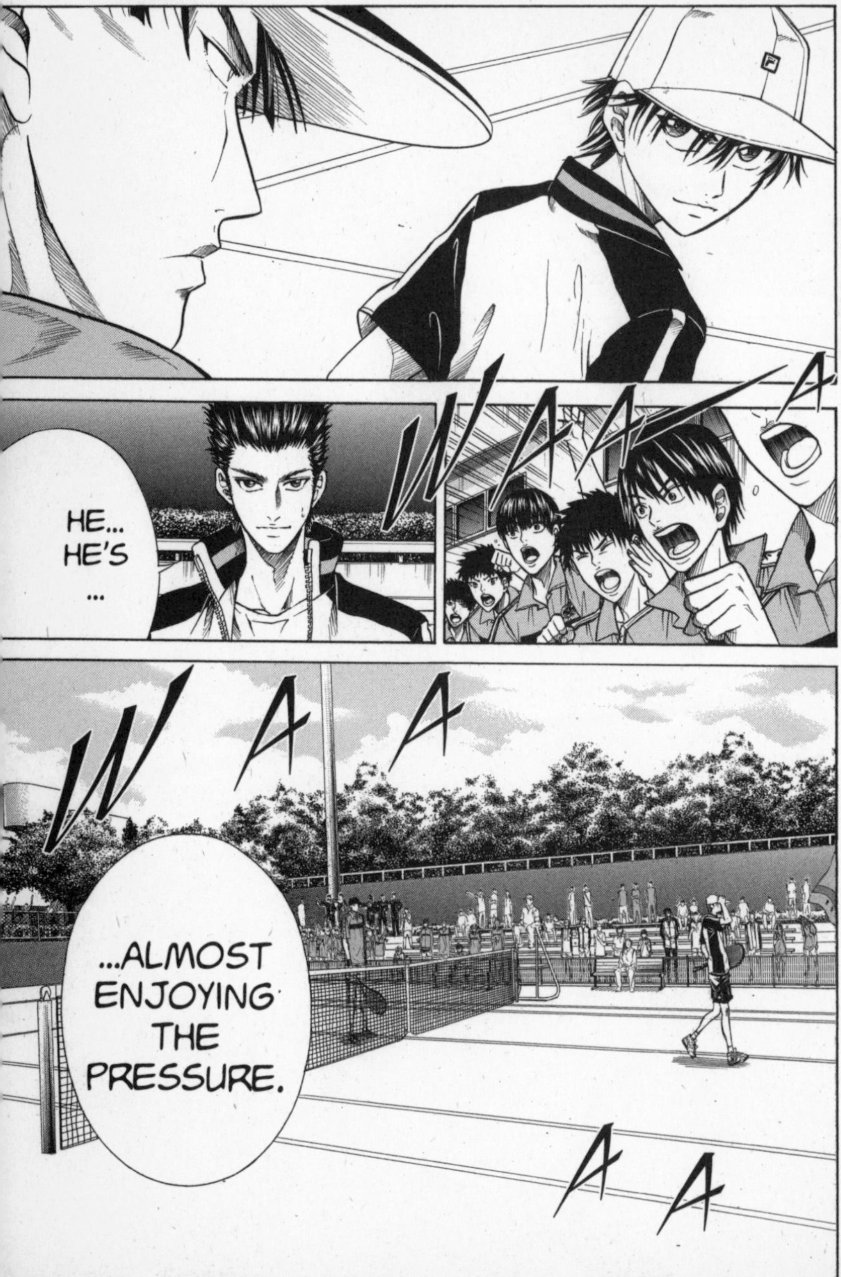
WAA–A
HE... HE'S ...
WAA
...ALMOST ENJOYING THE PRESSURE.
AA

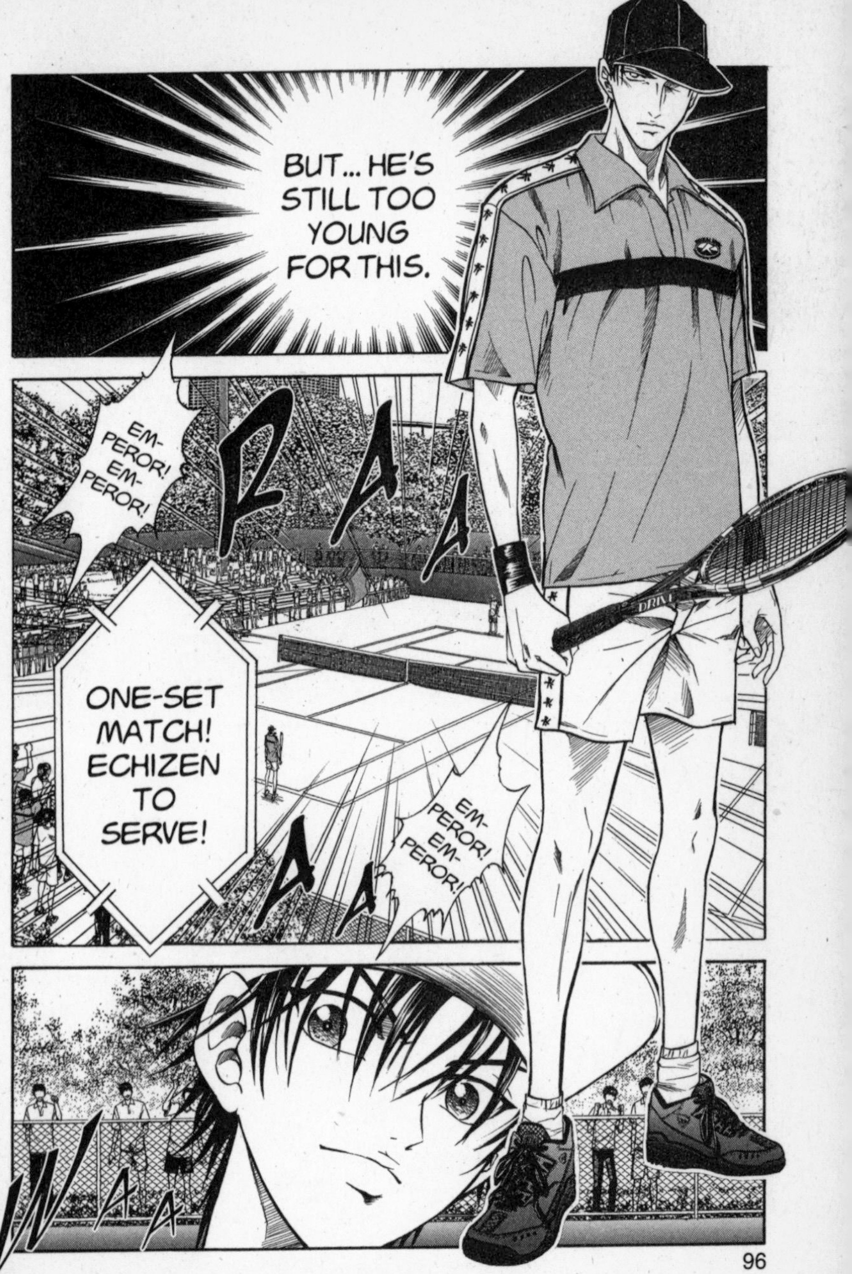
BUT... HE'S STILL TOO YOUNG FOR THIS.
EM-PEROR! EM-PEROR!
ONE-SET MATCH! ECHIZEN TO SERVE!
EM-PEROR! EM-PEROR!
RAA
RAA
WAA

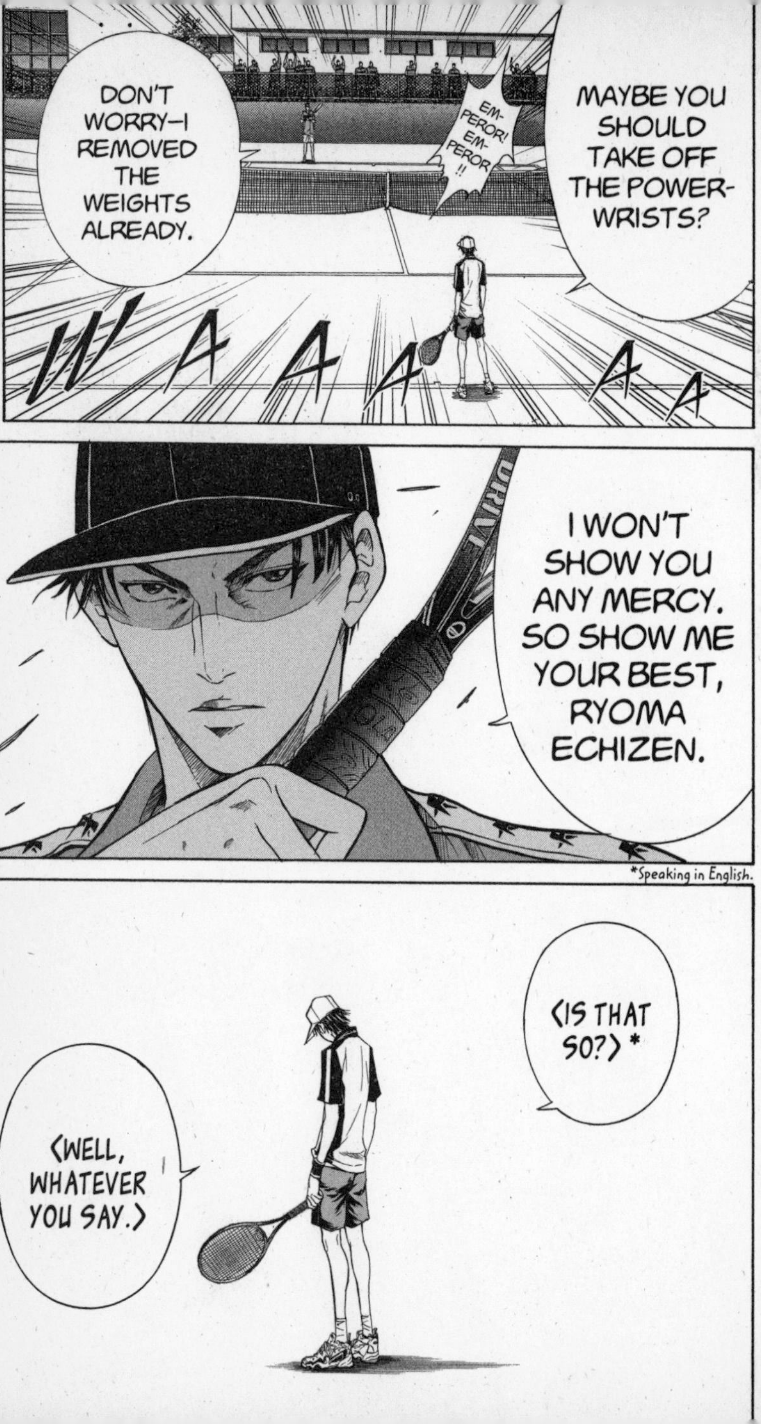
MAYBE YOU SHOULD TAKE OFF THE POWER-WRISTS?
EM-PEROR! EM-PEROR!!
DON'T WORRY—I REMOVED THE WEIGHTS ALREADY.
WAAAAAA
I WON'T SHOW YOU ANY MERCY. SO SHOW ME YOUR BEST, RYOMA ECHIZEN.
DRIVE
*Speaking in English.
<IS THAT SO?> *
<WELL, WHATEVER YOU SAY.>

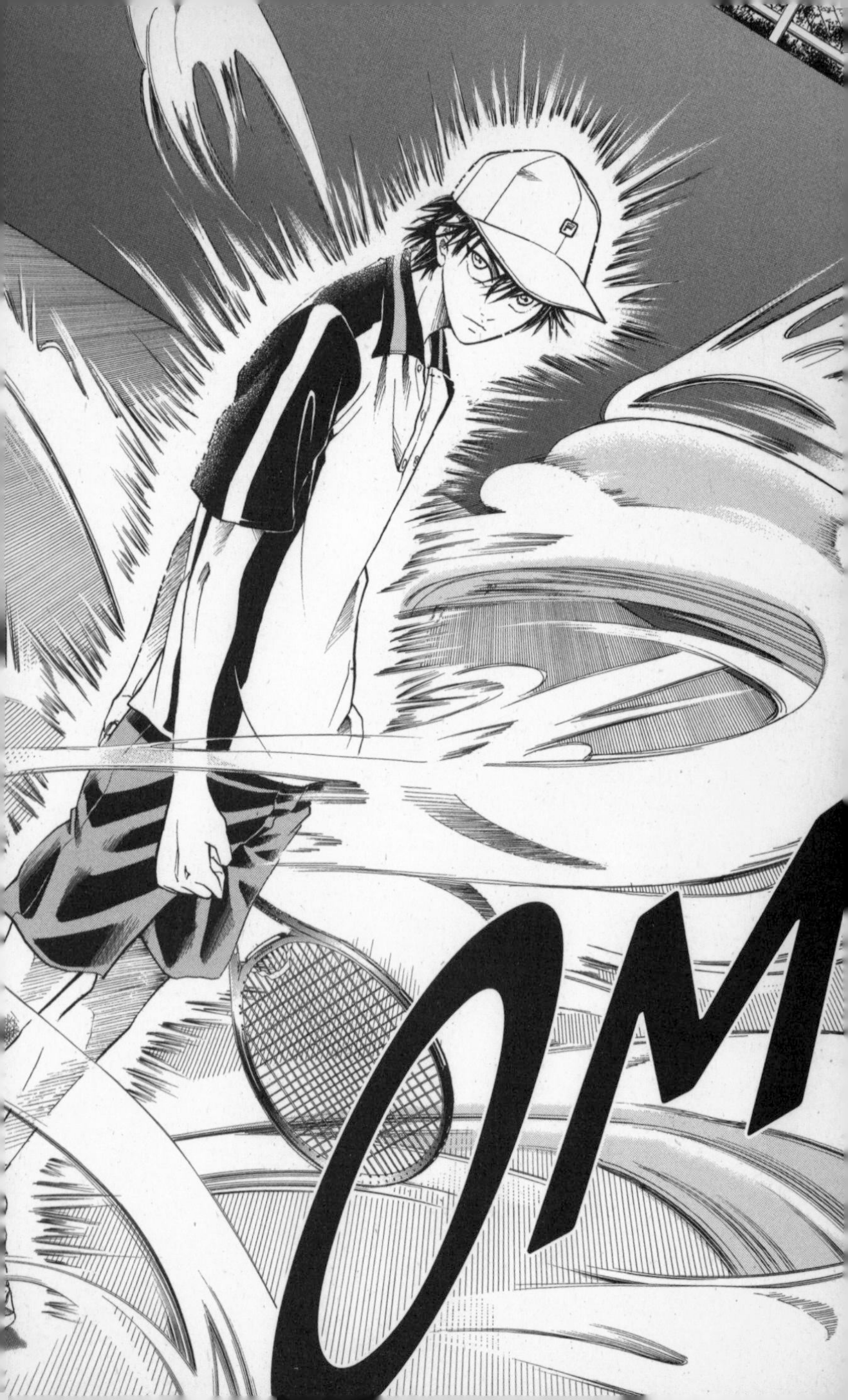
OM

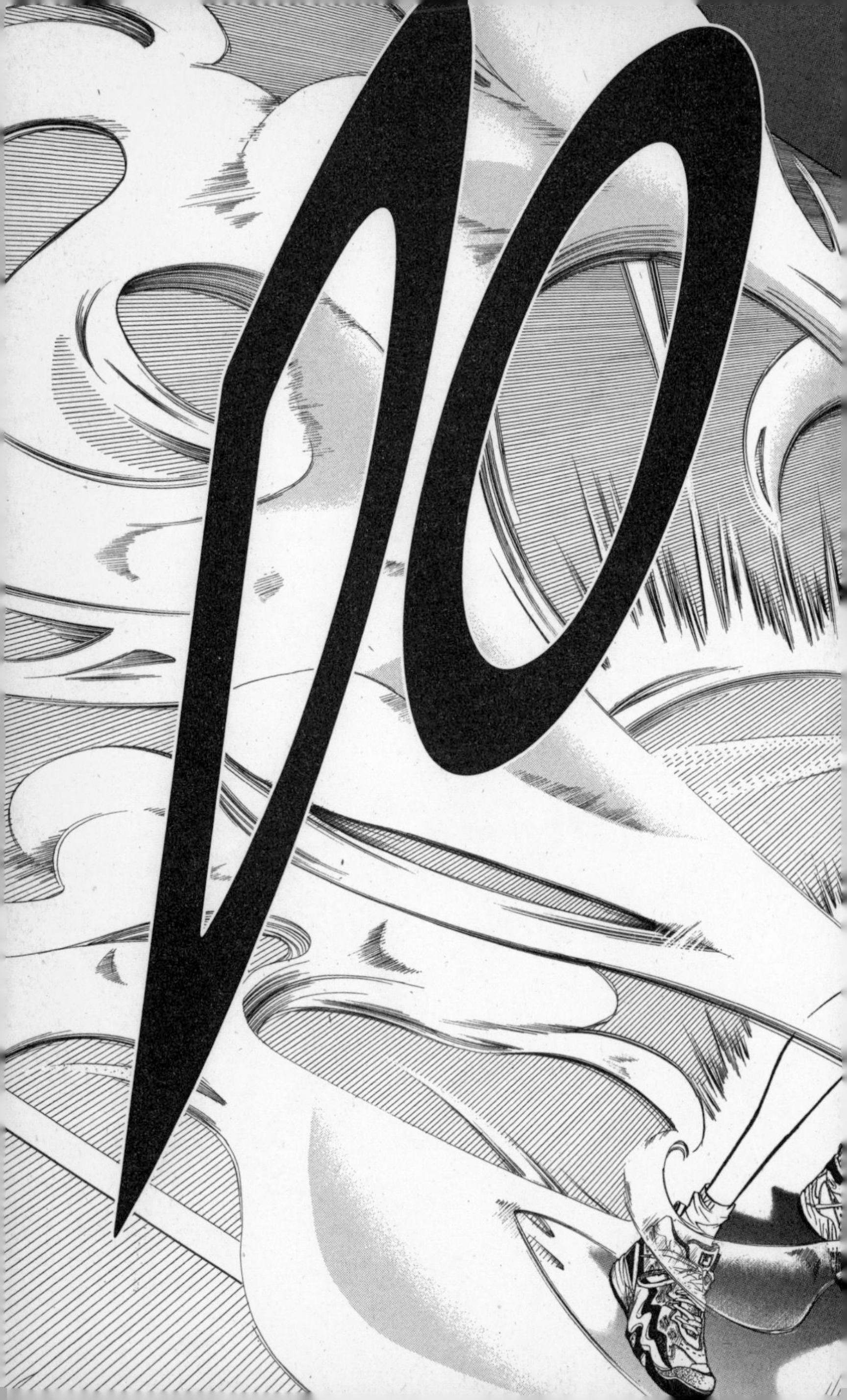

WH- WHAT THE—?!

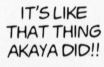
IT'S LIKE THAT THING AKAYA DID!!

LOOK AT THAT!

....!

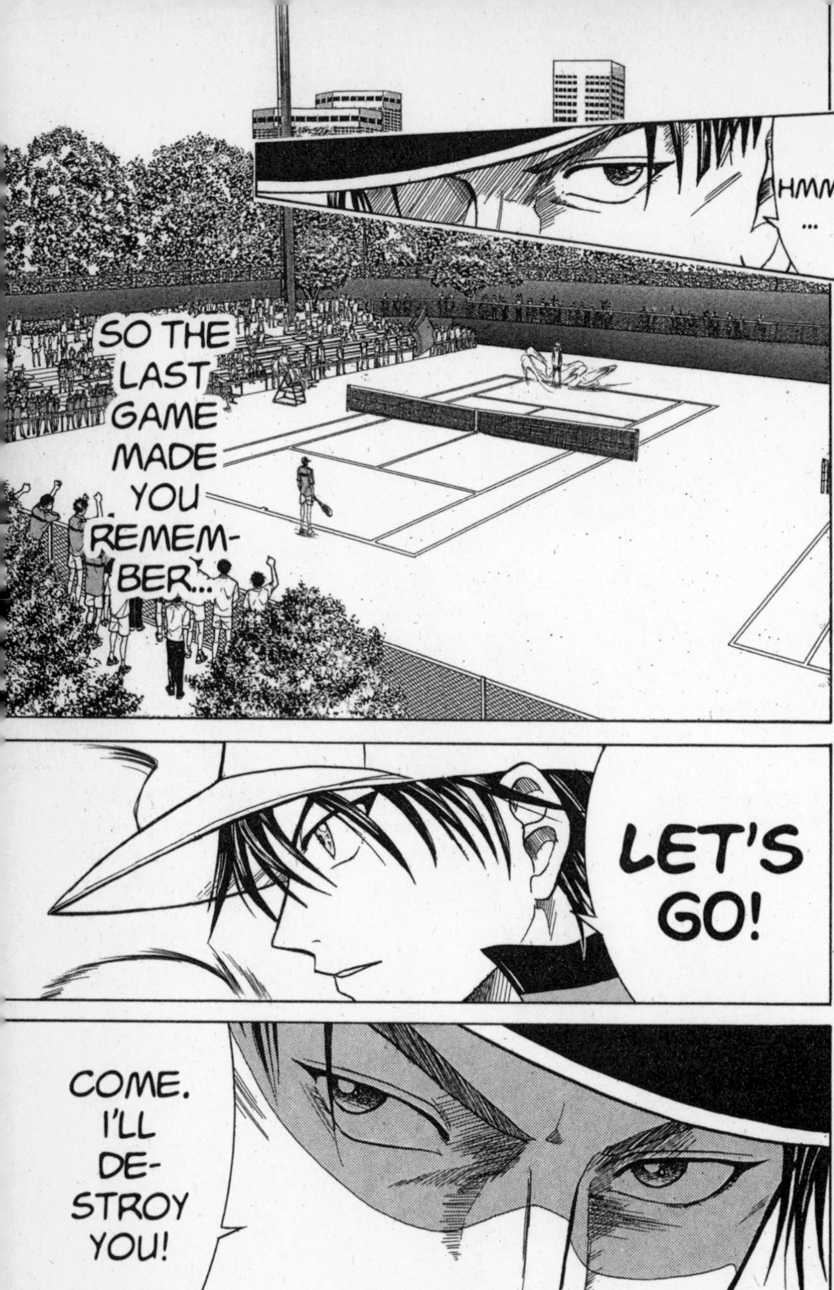
HMM ...
SO THE LAST GAME MADE YOU REMEMBER...
LET'S GO!
COME. I'LL DESTROY YOU!

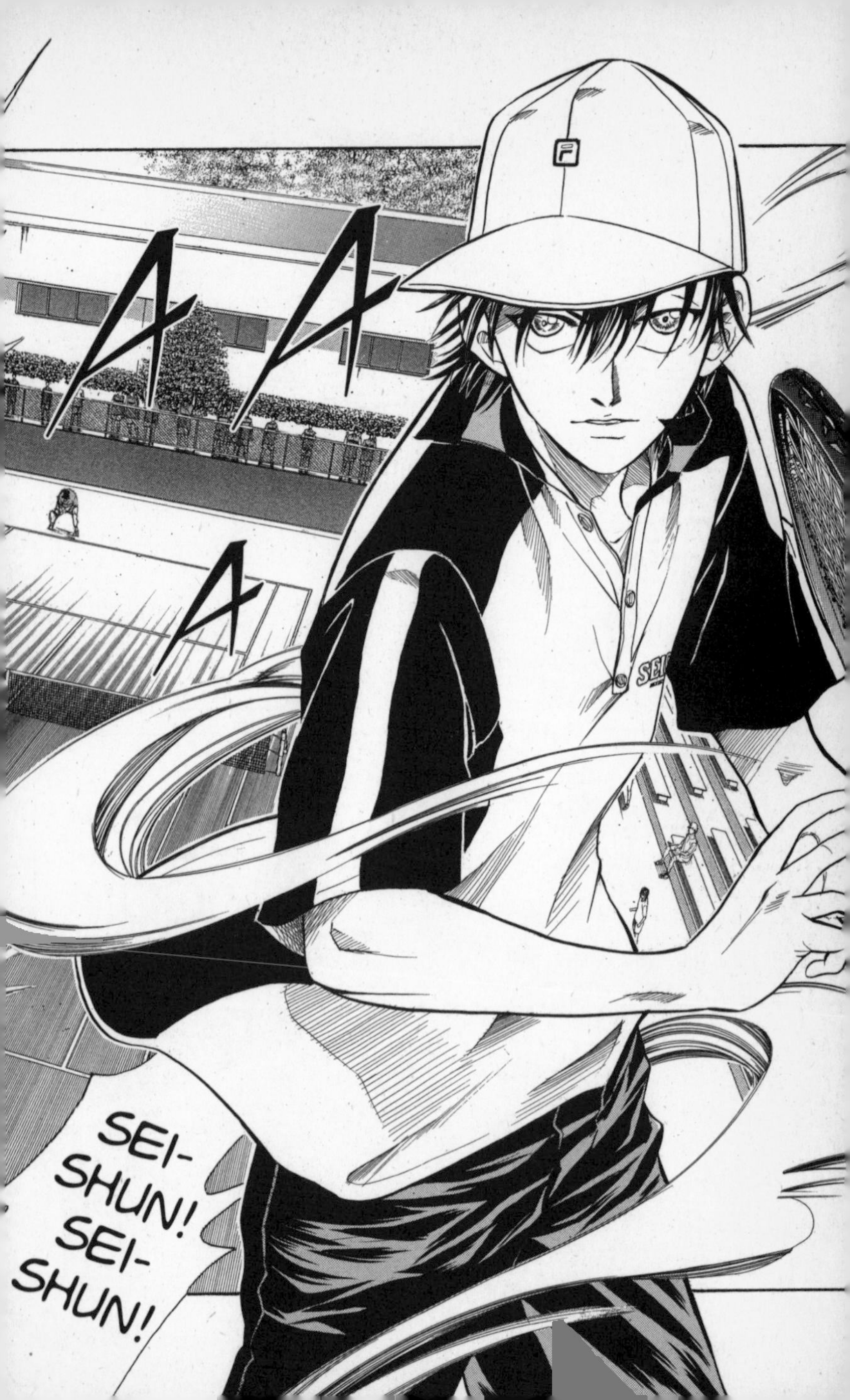
AAA
SEI-
SHUN!
SEI-
SHUN!

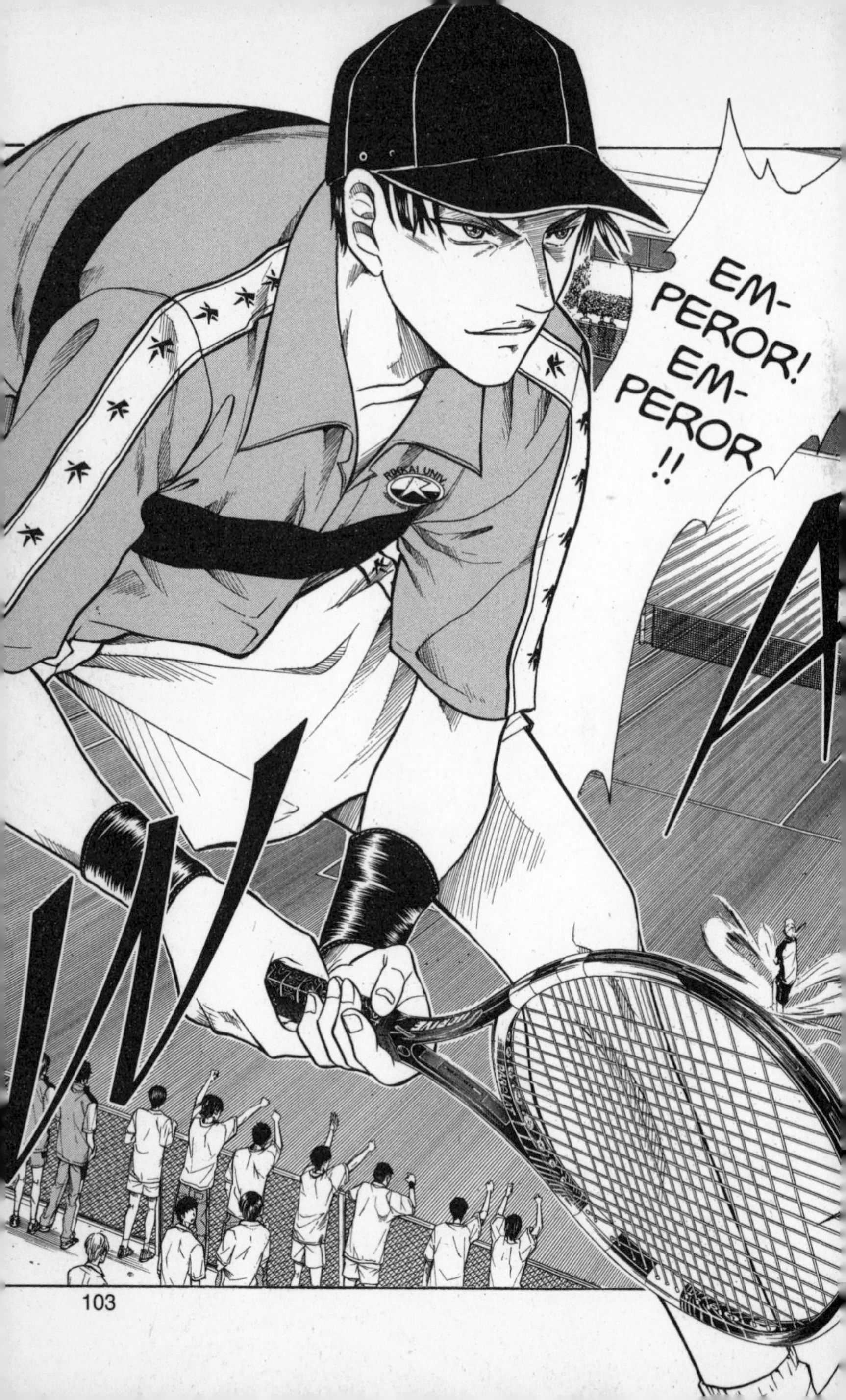
EM-
PEROR!
EM-
PEROR
!!
RIKKAI UNIV.

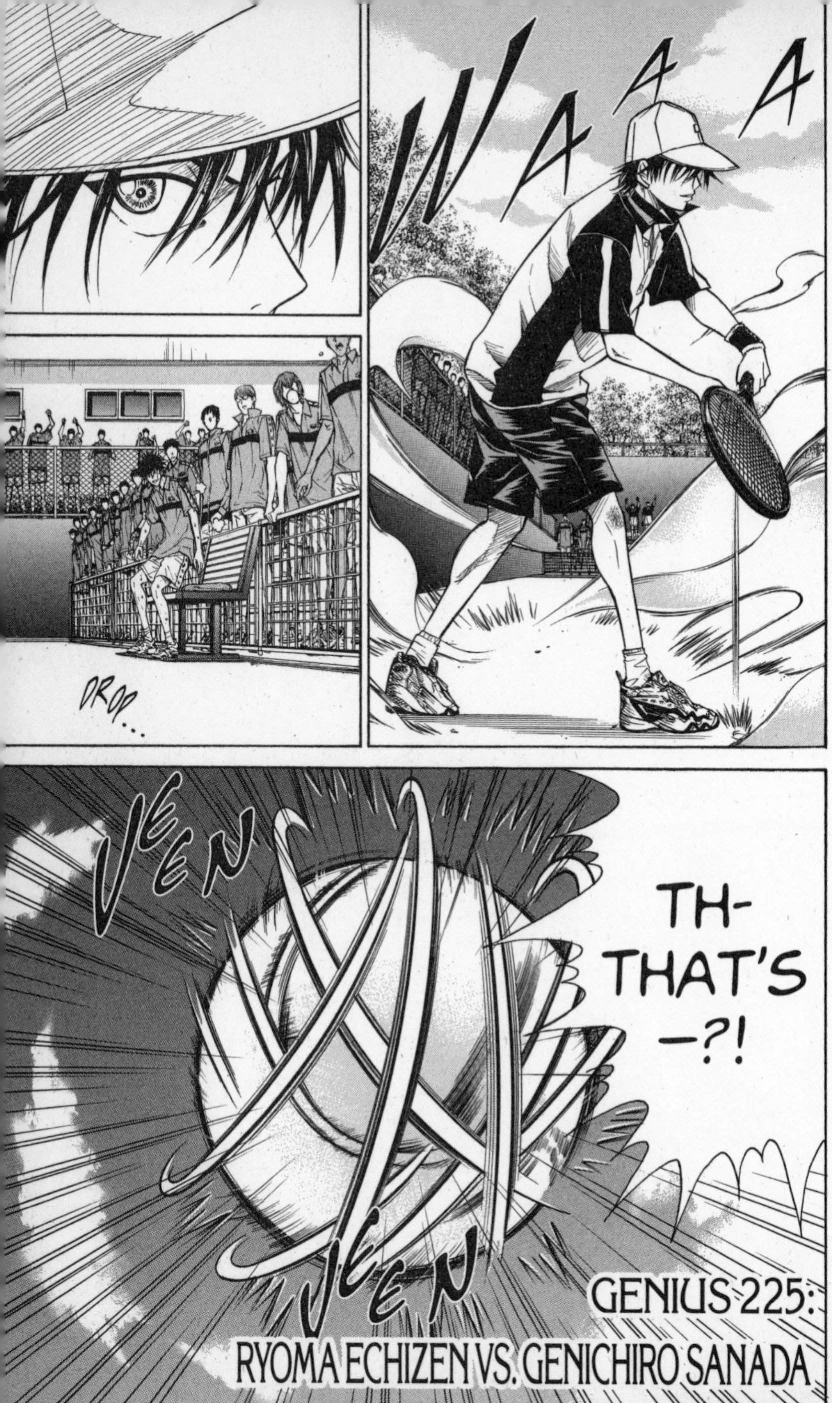
WAAAA
DROP...
VEEN
VEEN
TH-THAT'S—?!
GENIUS 225:
RYOMA ECHIZEN VS. GENICHIRO SANADA

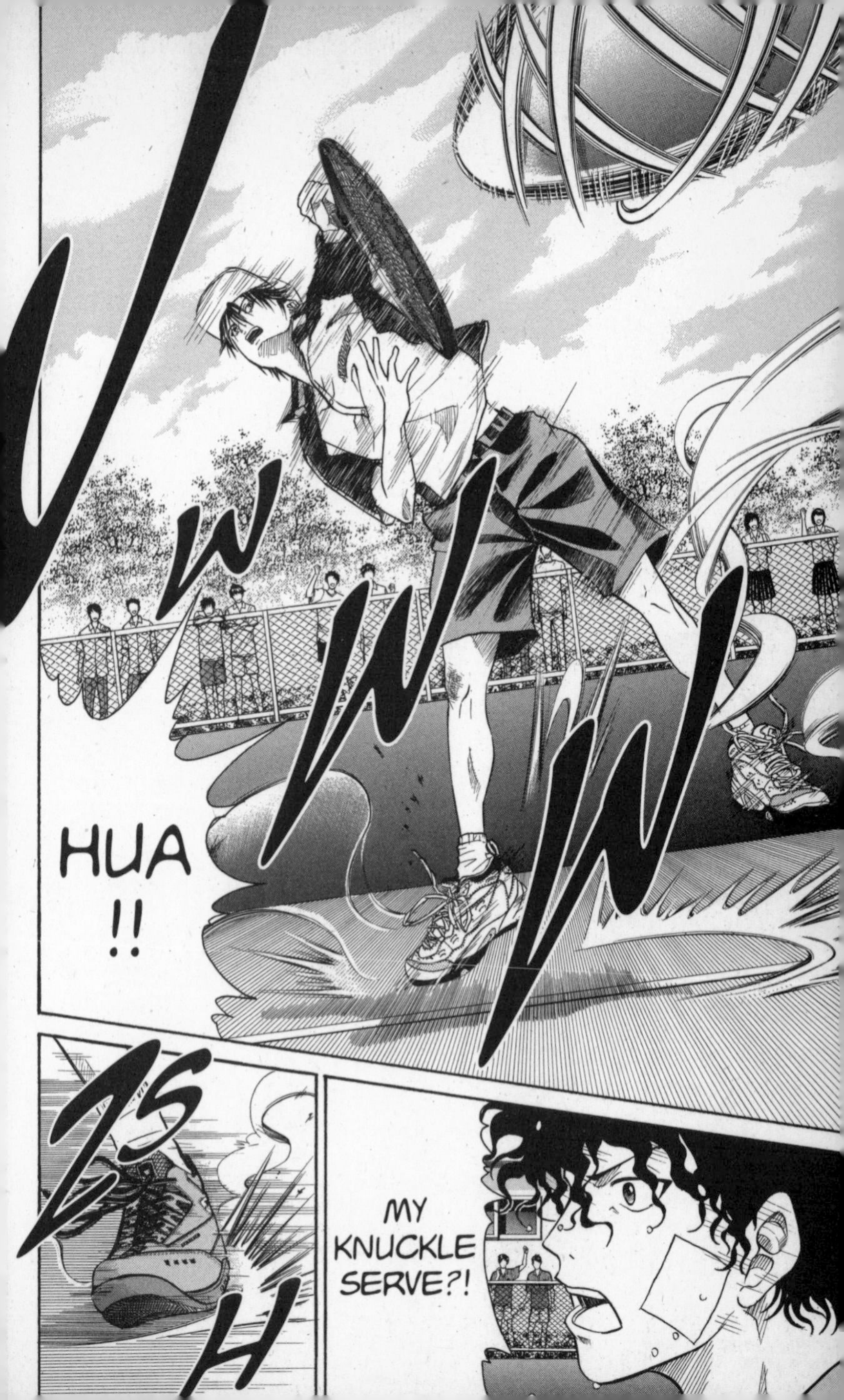
HUA !!
MY KNUCKLE SERVE?!

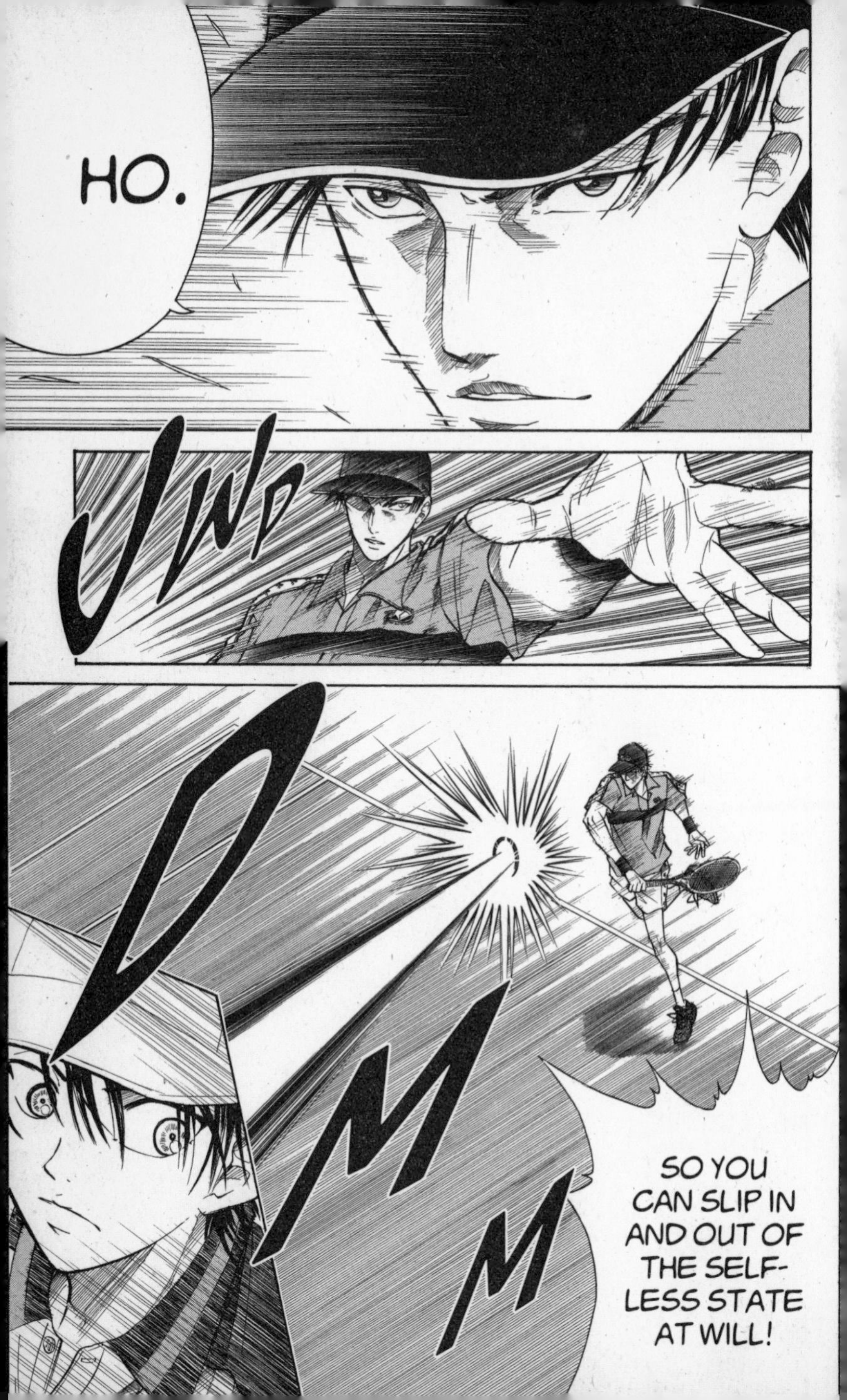
HO.
SO YOU CAN SLIP IN AND OUT OF THE SELF-LESS STATE AT WILL!

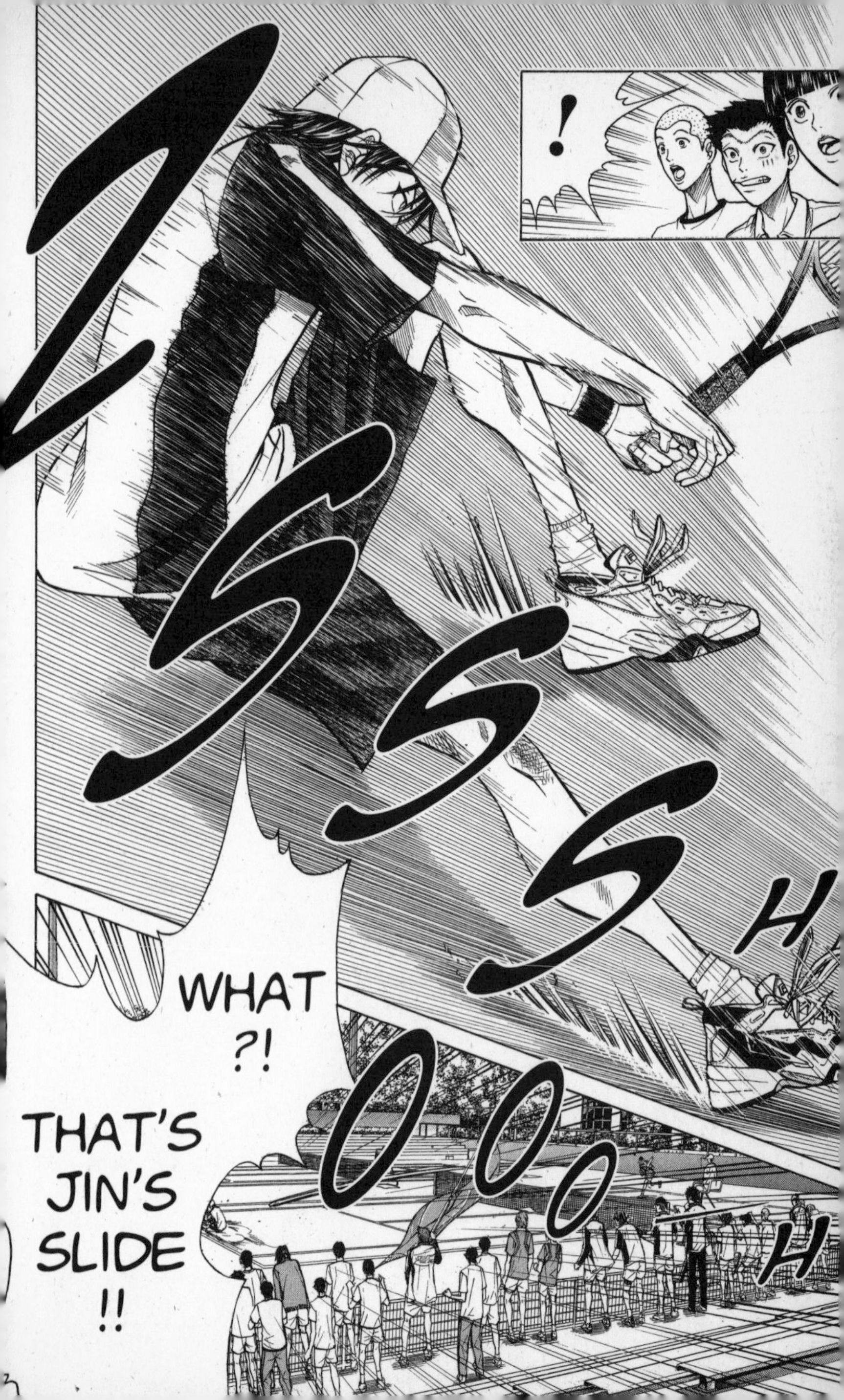
!
SSSSSHOOOOH
WHAT?!
THAT'S JIN'S SLIDE!!

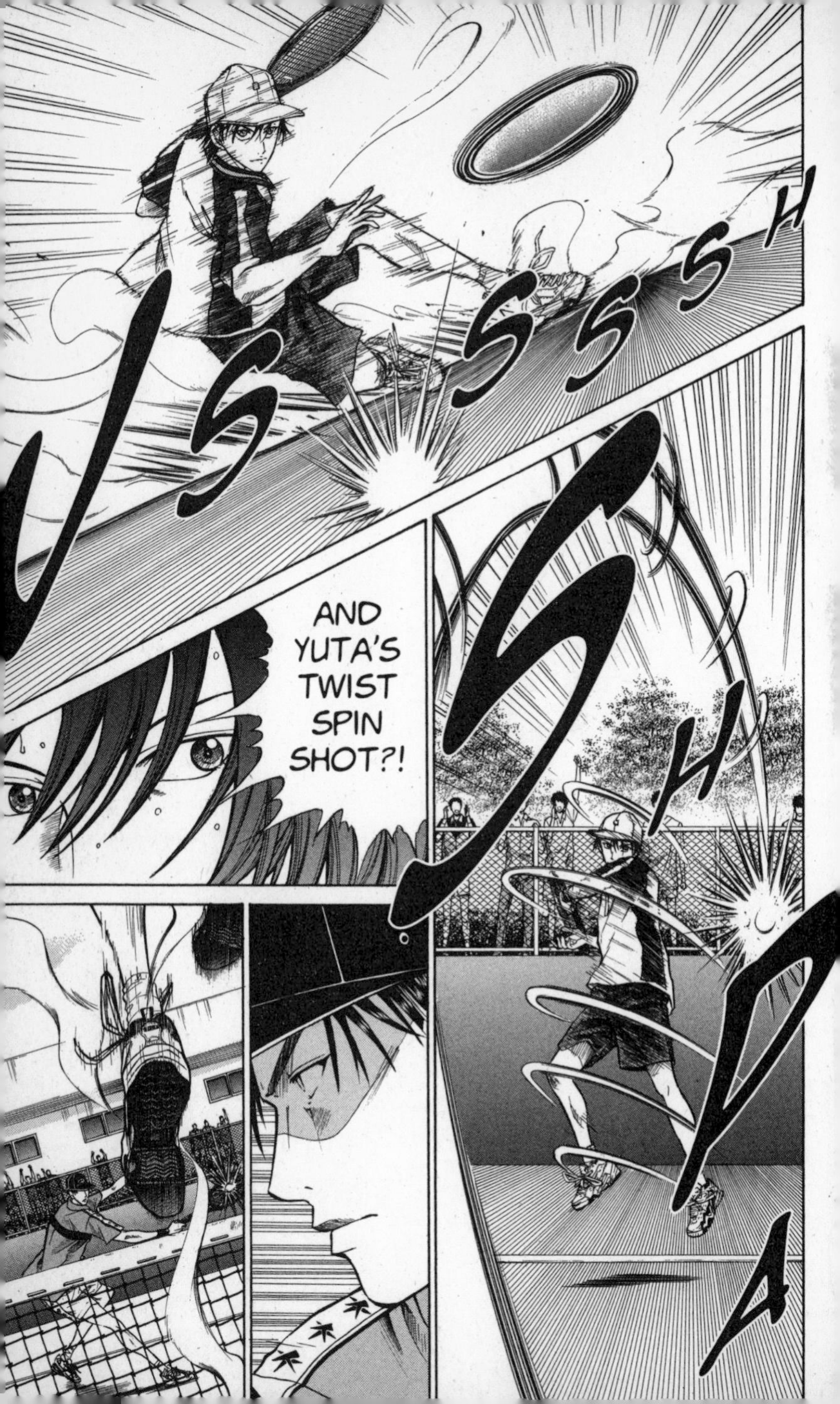

VSSSSH
AND YUTA'S TWIST SPIN SHOT?!
SSHH
VA

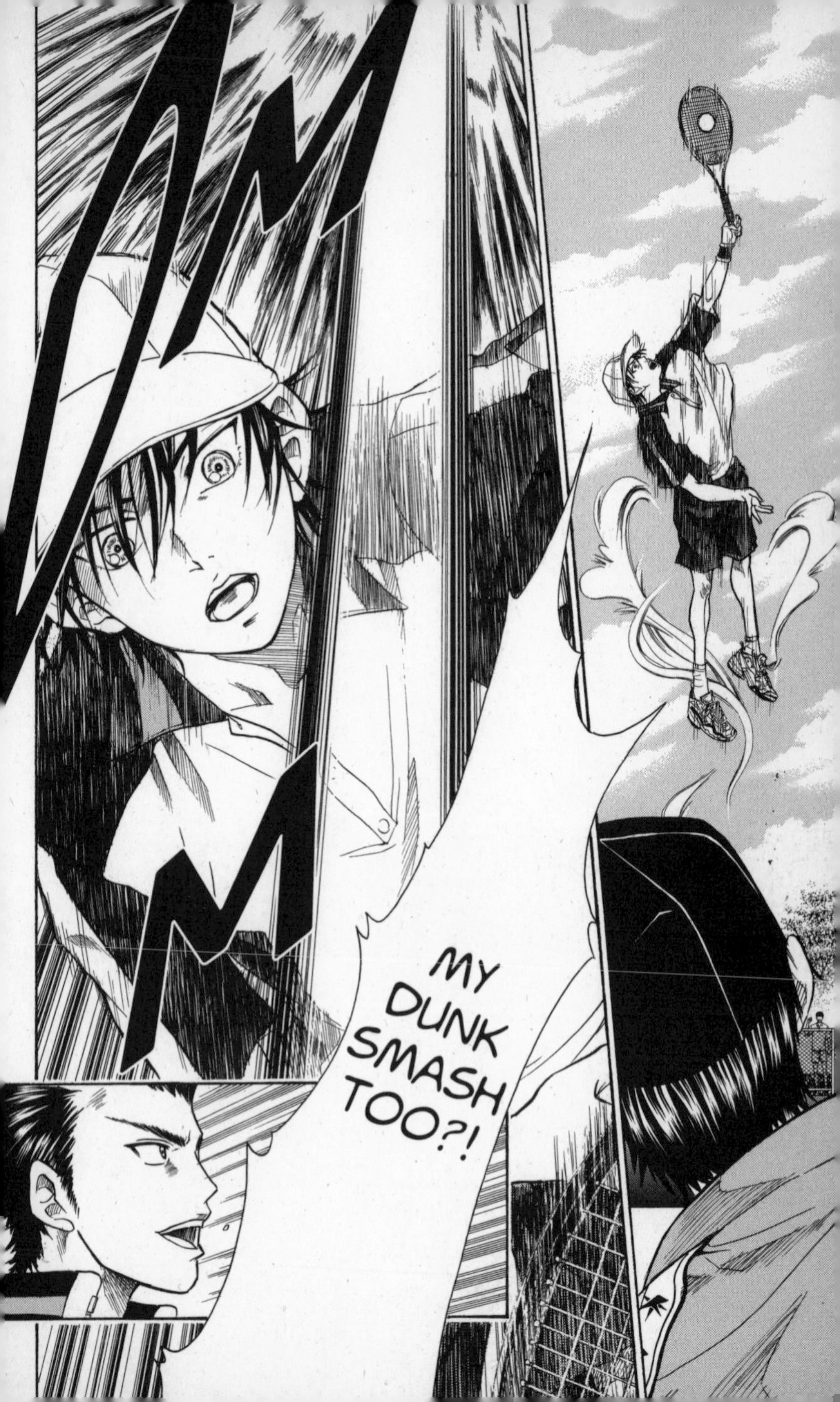
MY DUNK SMASH TOO?!

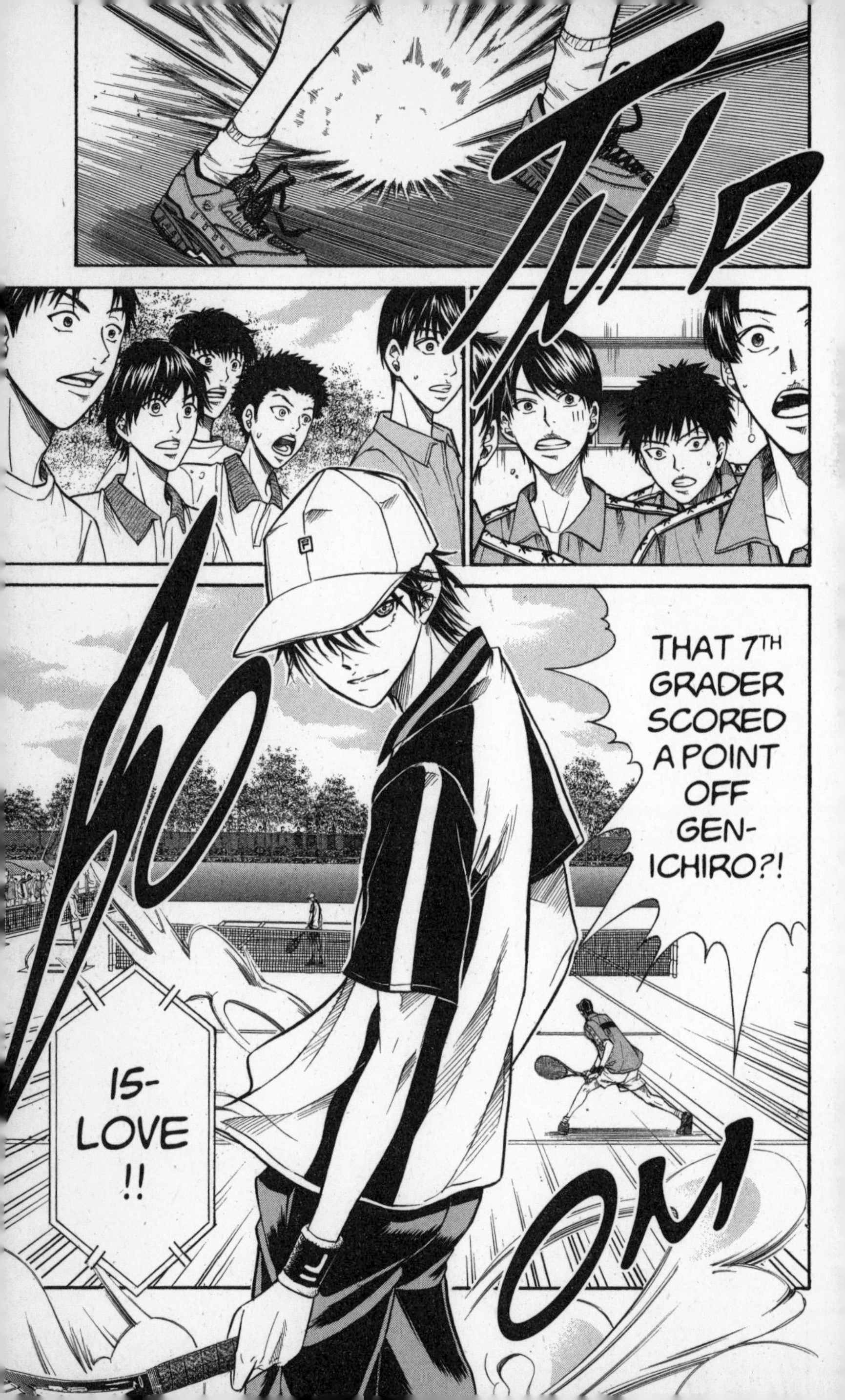
TMP
THAT 7TH GRADER SCORED A POINT OFF GEN-ICHIRO?!
15-LOVE!!

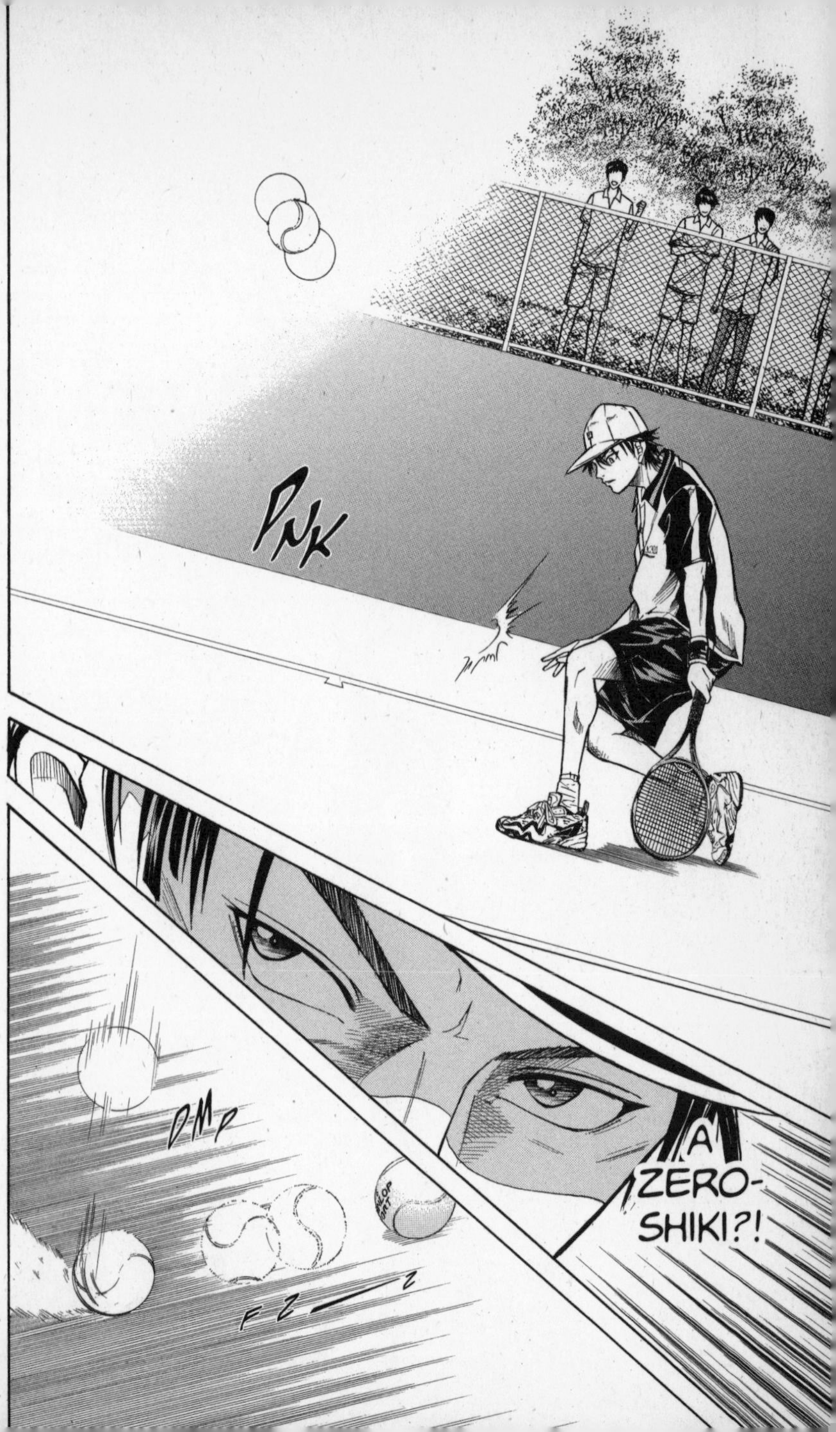
PNK
A ZERO-SHIKI?!
DMP
FZ——Z

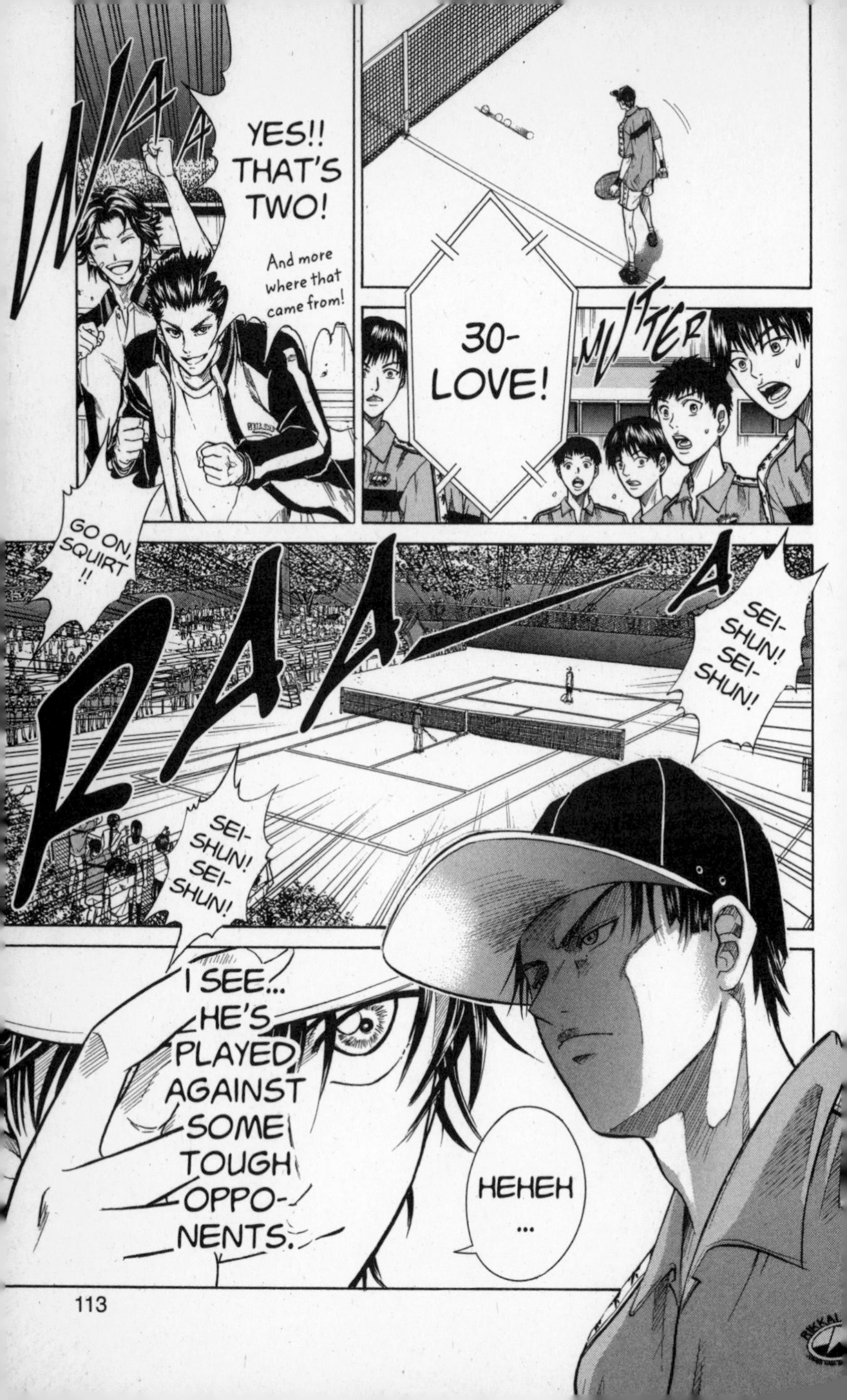
30-LOVE!
MUTTER
WAA
YES!! THAT'S TWO!
And more where that came from!
SEI-SHUN! SEI-SHUN!
GO ON, SQUIRT!!
ZAAA—A
SEI-SHUN! SEI-SHUN!
HEHEH...
I SEE... HE'S PLAYED AGAINST SOME TOUGH OPPONENTS.

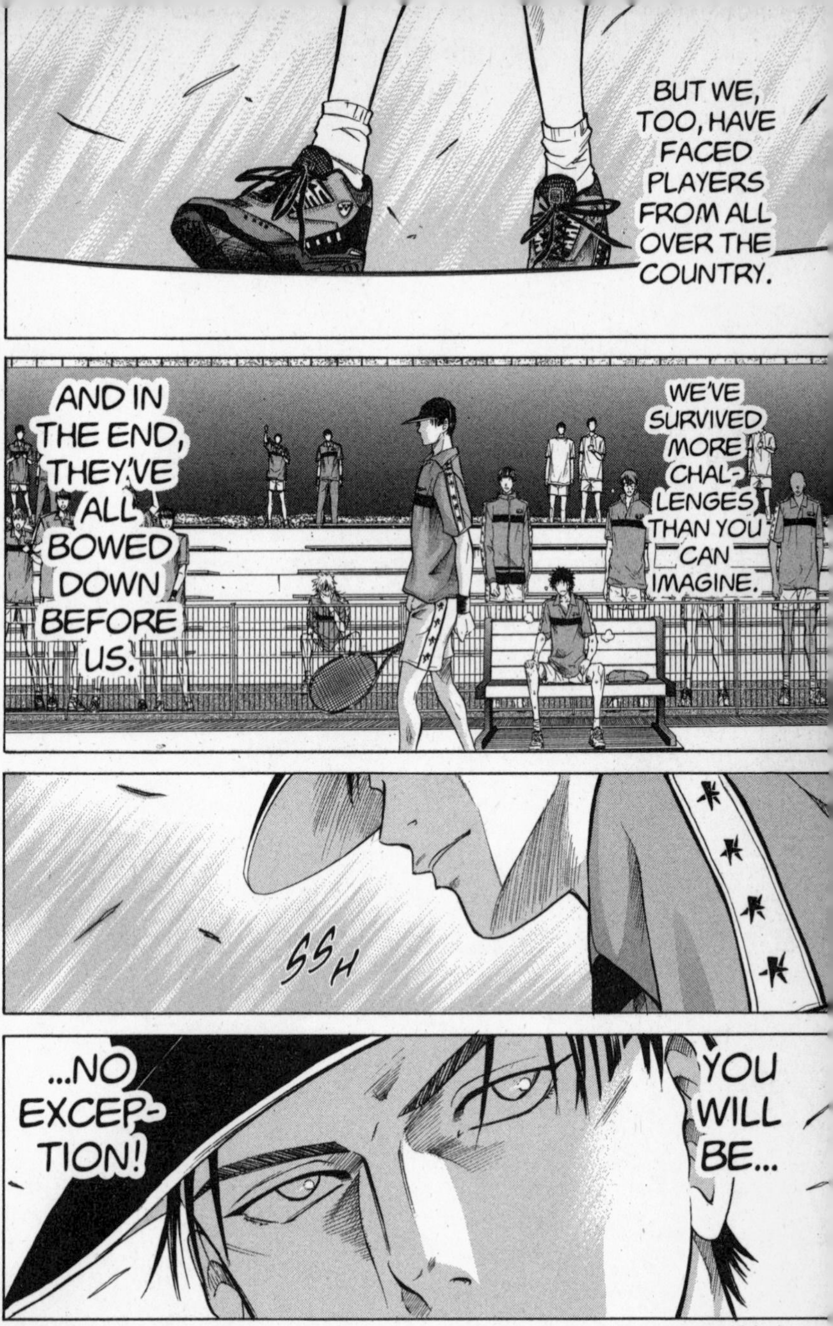
BUT WE, TOO, HAVE FACED PLAYERS FROM ALL OVER THE COUNTRY.
WE'VE SURVIVED MORE CHAL-LENGES THAN YOU CAN IMAGINE.
AND IN THE END, THEY'VE ALL BOWED DOWN BEFORE US.
SSH
YOU WILL BE...
...NO EXCEP-TION!

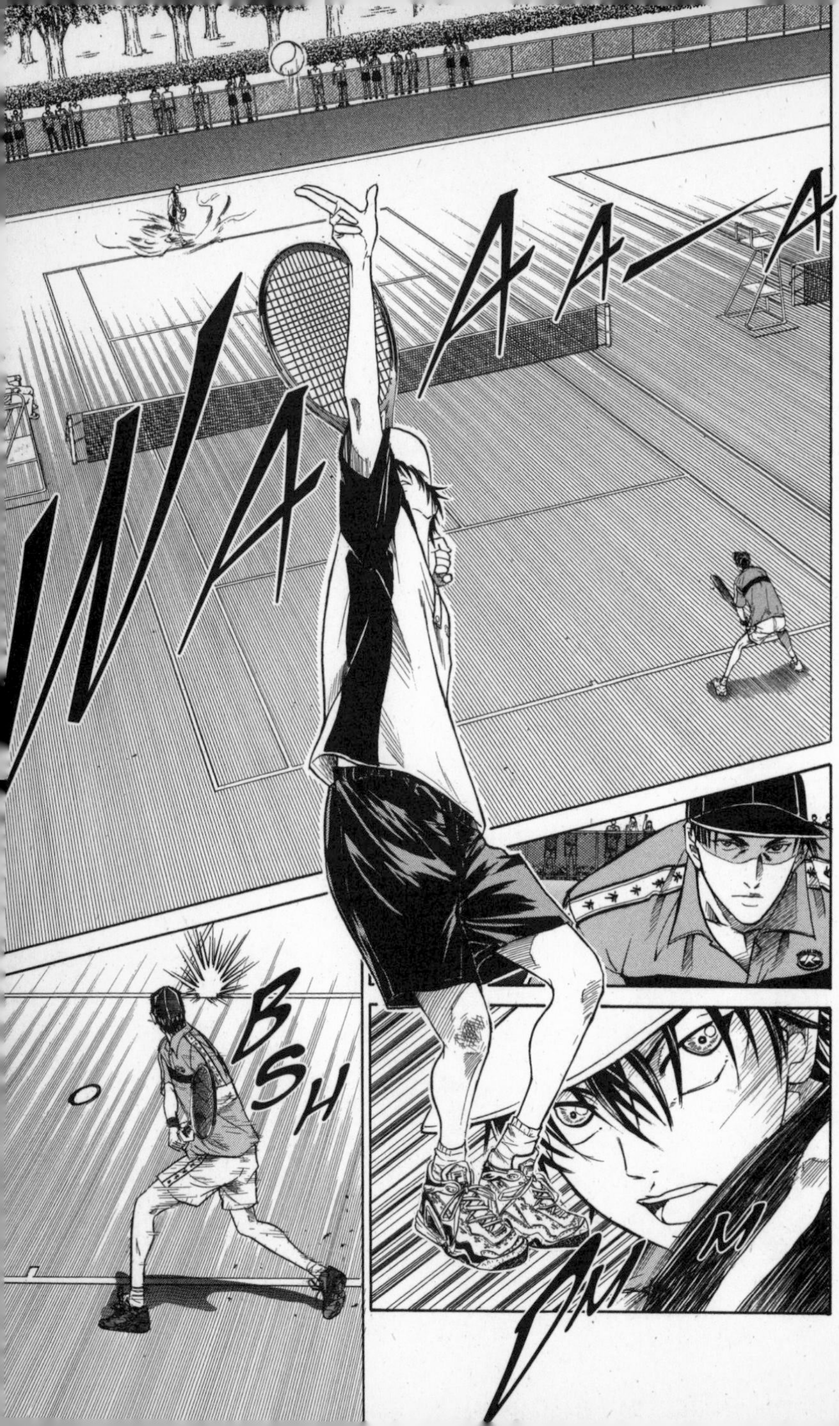
WAAA—A
BSH

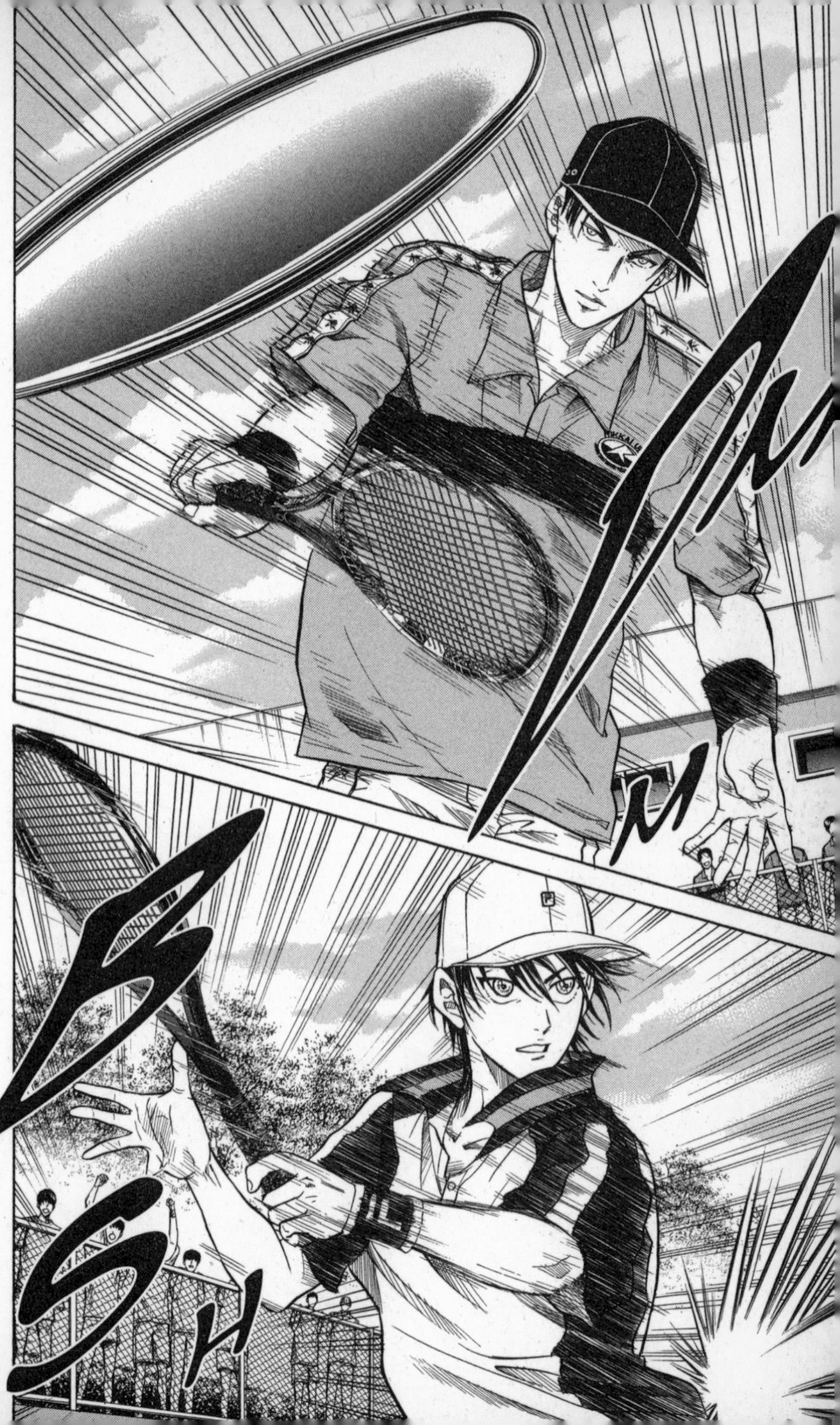

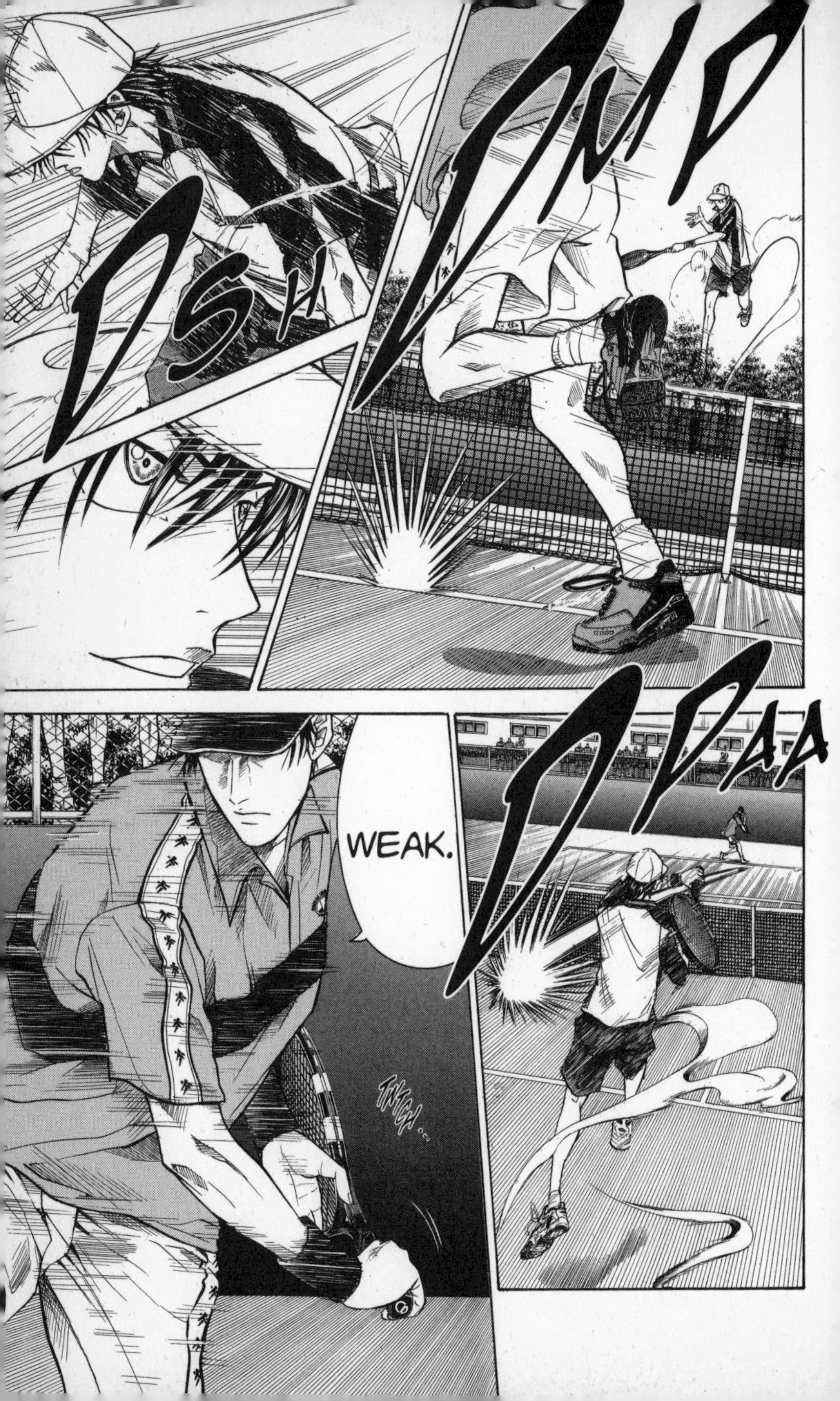
DMD
DSHU
DDAA
WEAK.

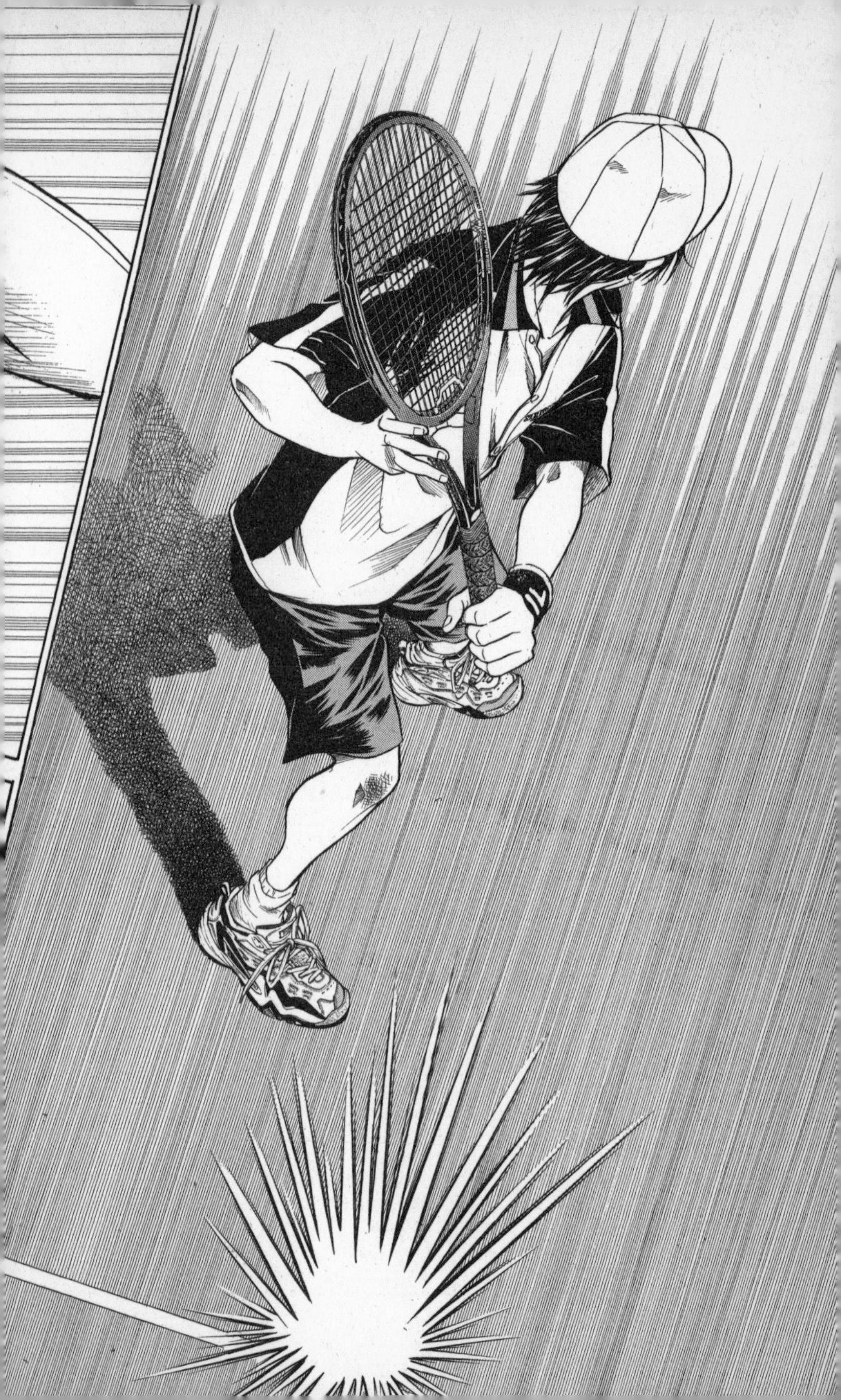

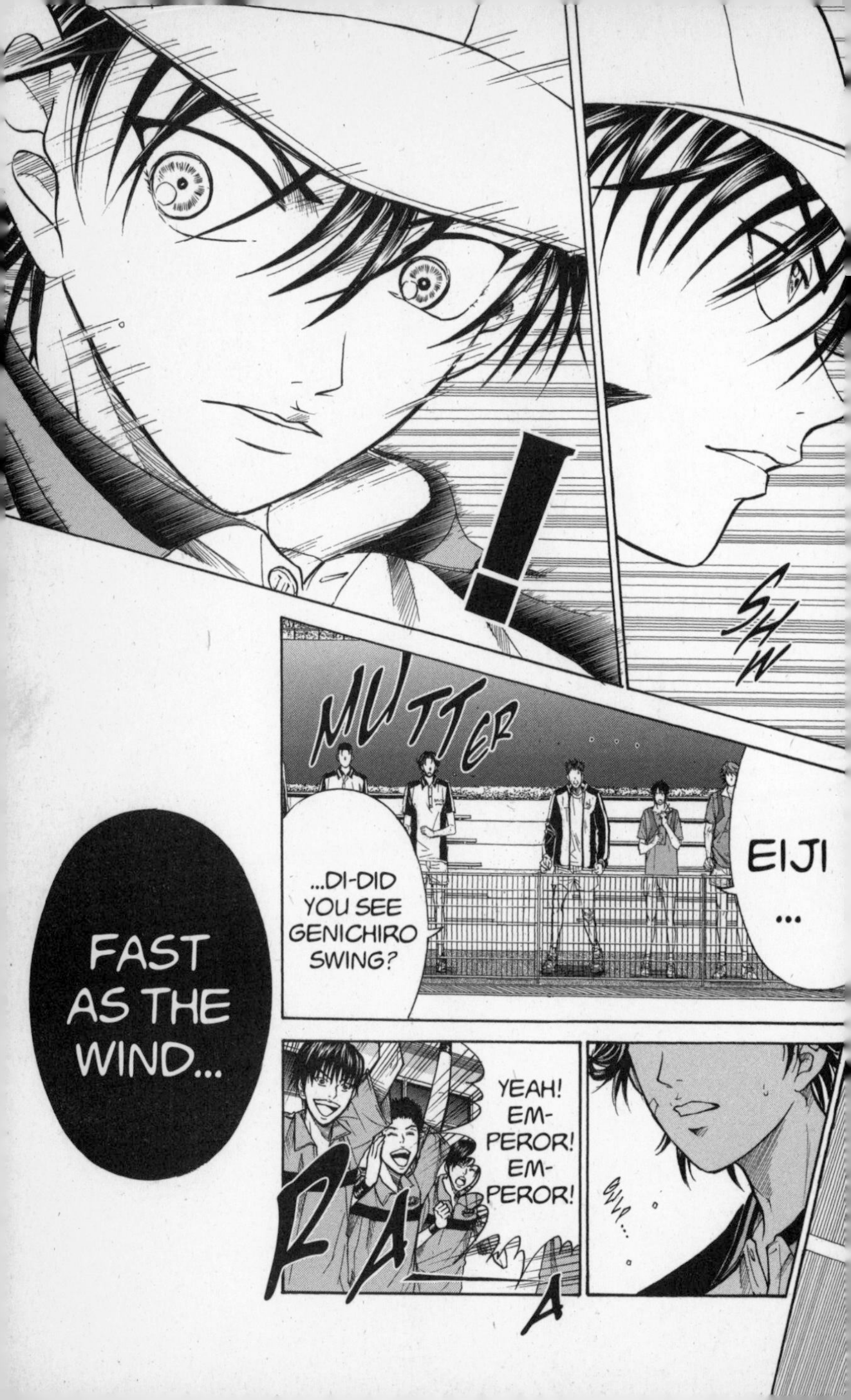
SHW
!
EIJI ...
MUTTER
...DI-DID YOU SEE GENICHIRO SWING?
GULP...
YEAH! EM-PEROR! EM-PEROR!
RAA
FAST AS THE WIND...

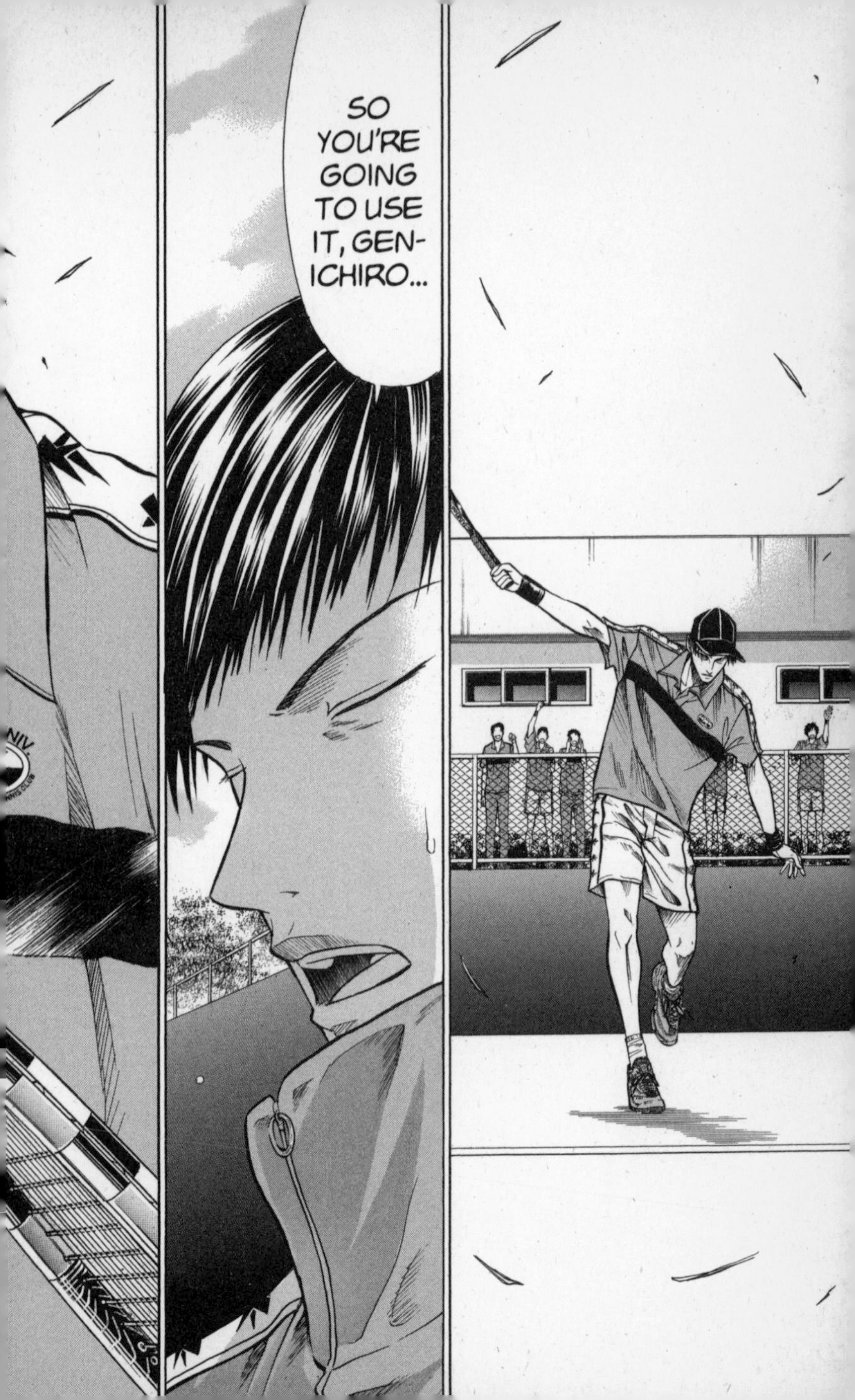
SO YOU'RE GOING TO USE IT, GEN-ICHIRO...

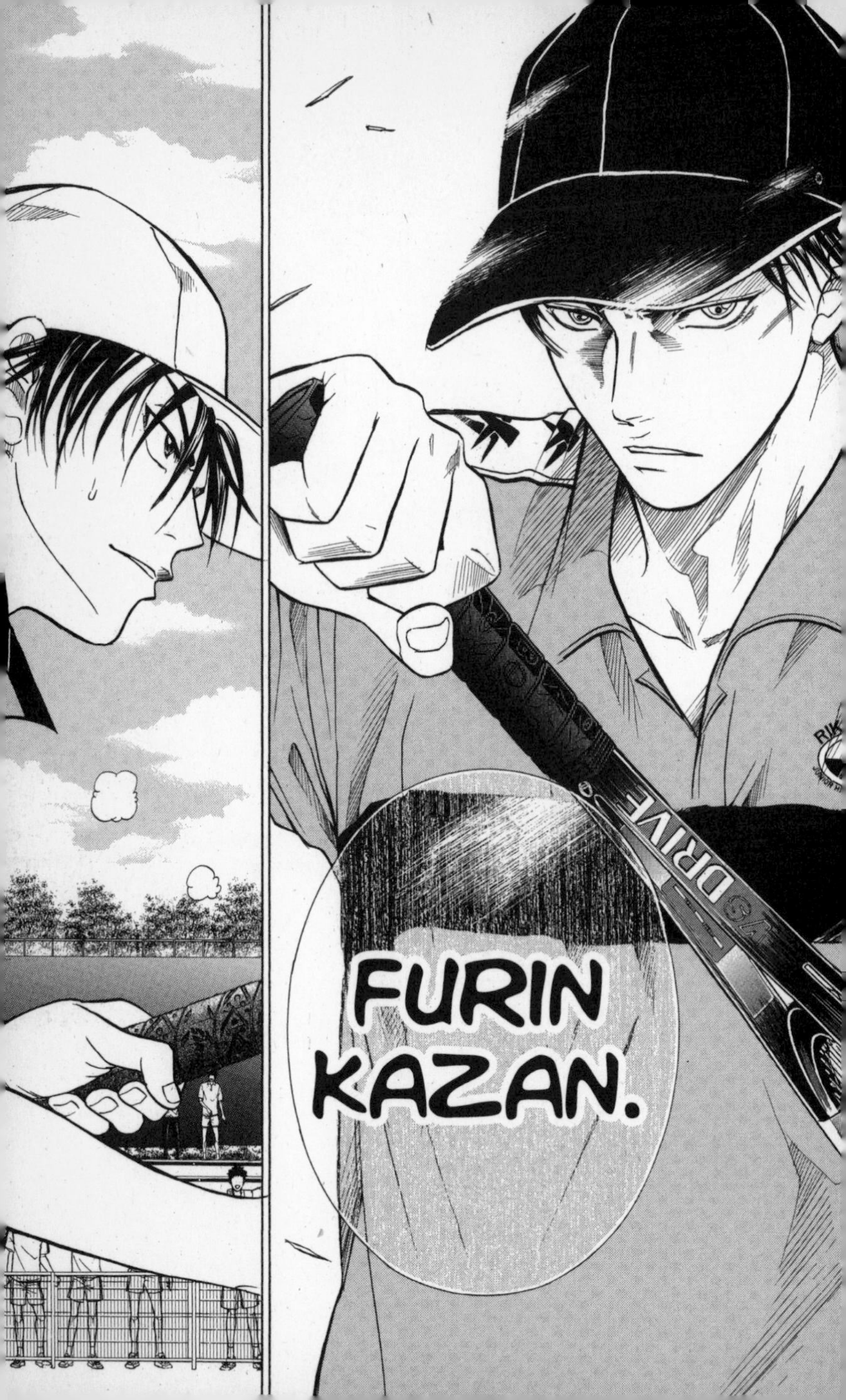
FURIN
KAZAN.

テニスの王子様

THE PRINCE OF TENNIS

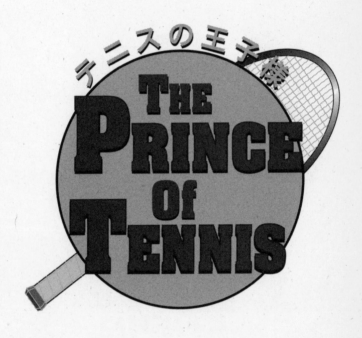

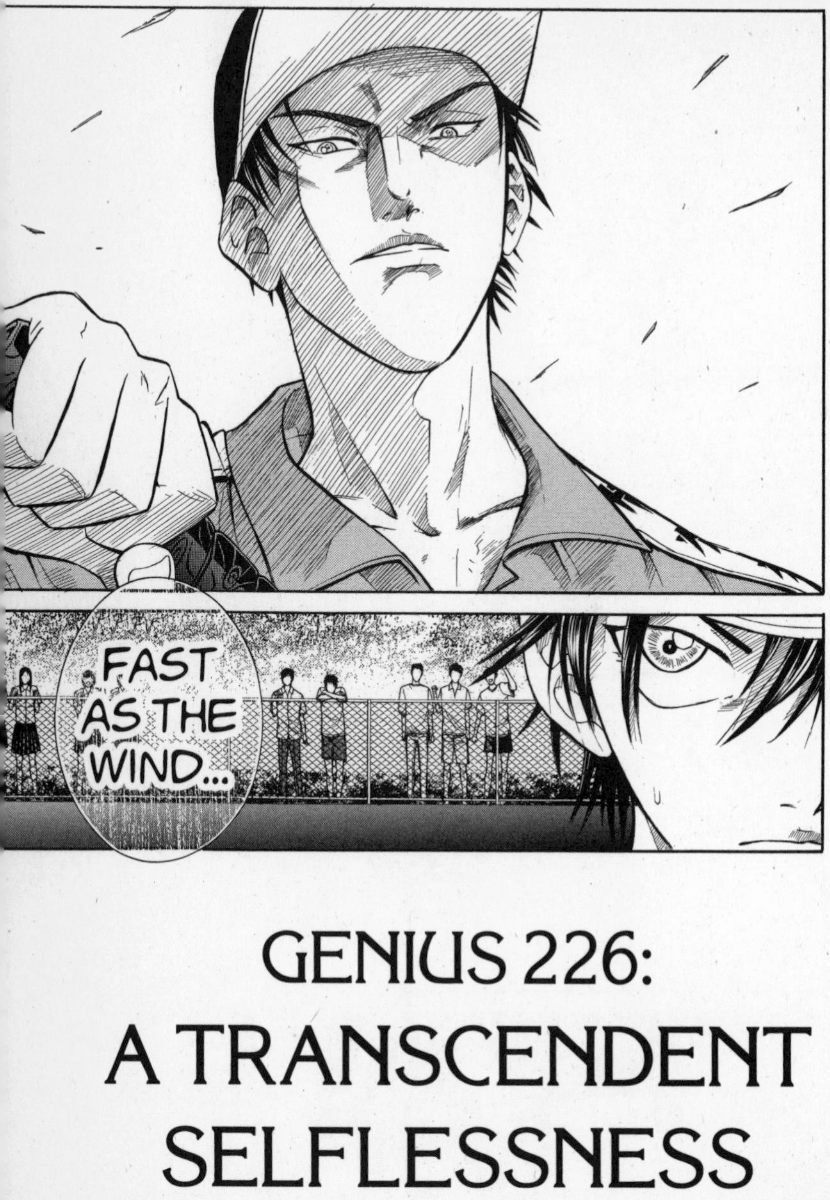
FAST AS THE WIND...

GENIUS 226: A TRANSCENDENT SELFLESSNESS

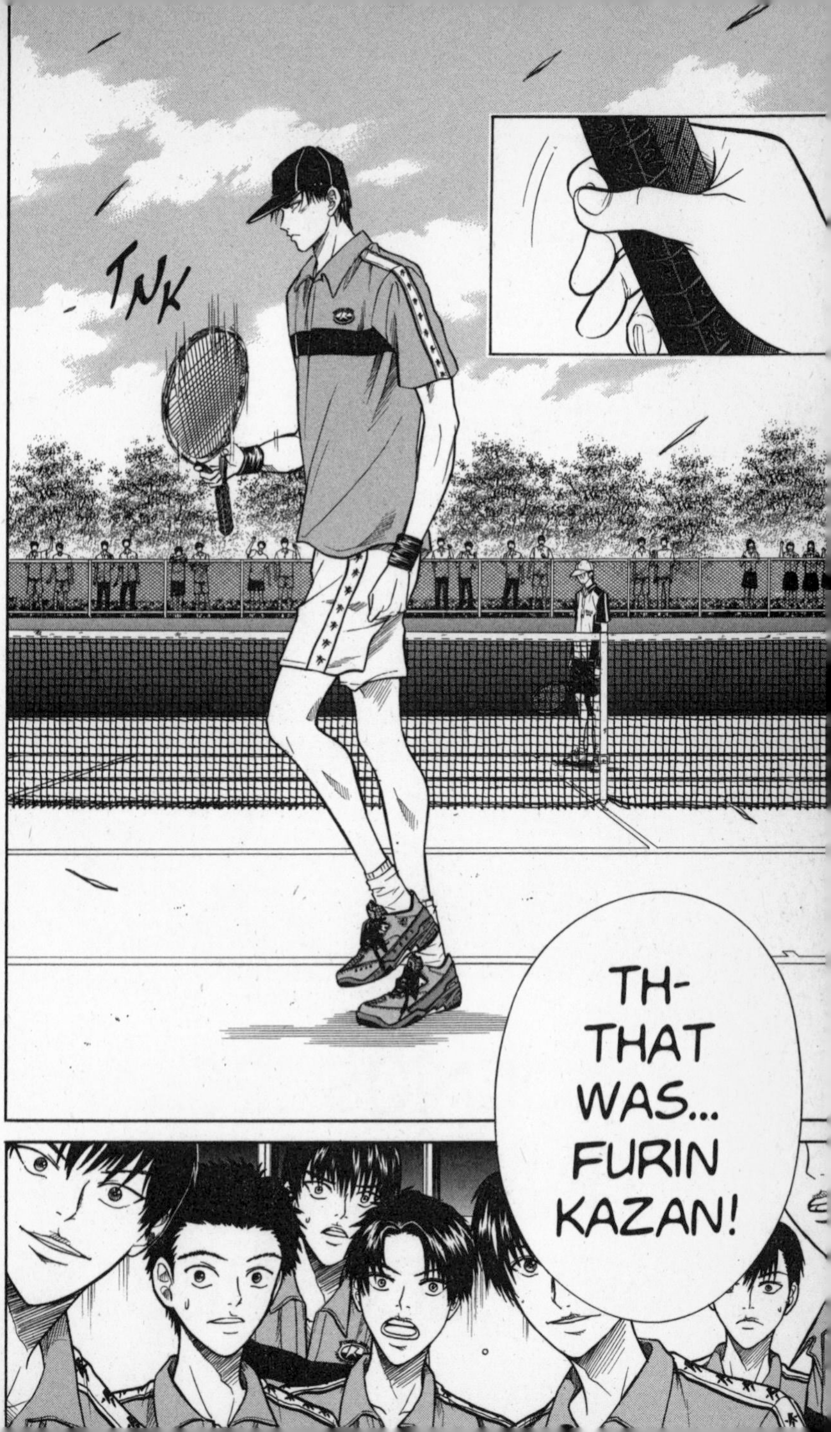
TNK
TH- THAT WAS... FURIN KAZAN!

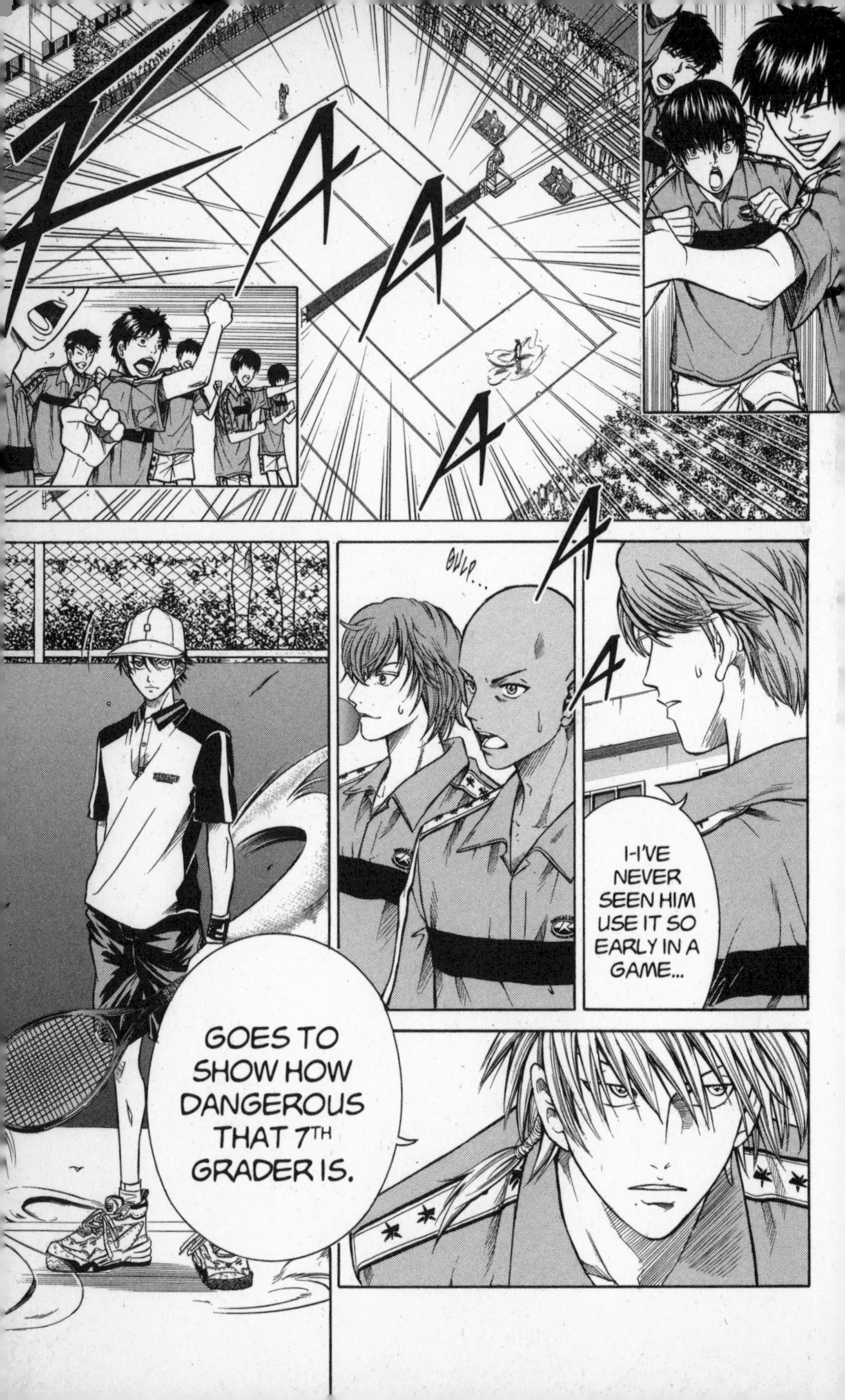
ZAAAAA
I-I'VE NEVER SEEN HIM USE IT SO EARLY IN A GAME...
GULP...
GOES TO SHOW HOW DANGEROUS THAT 7TH GRADER IS.

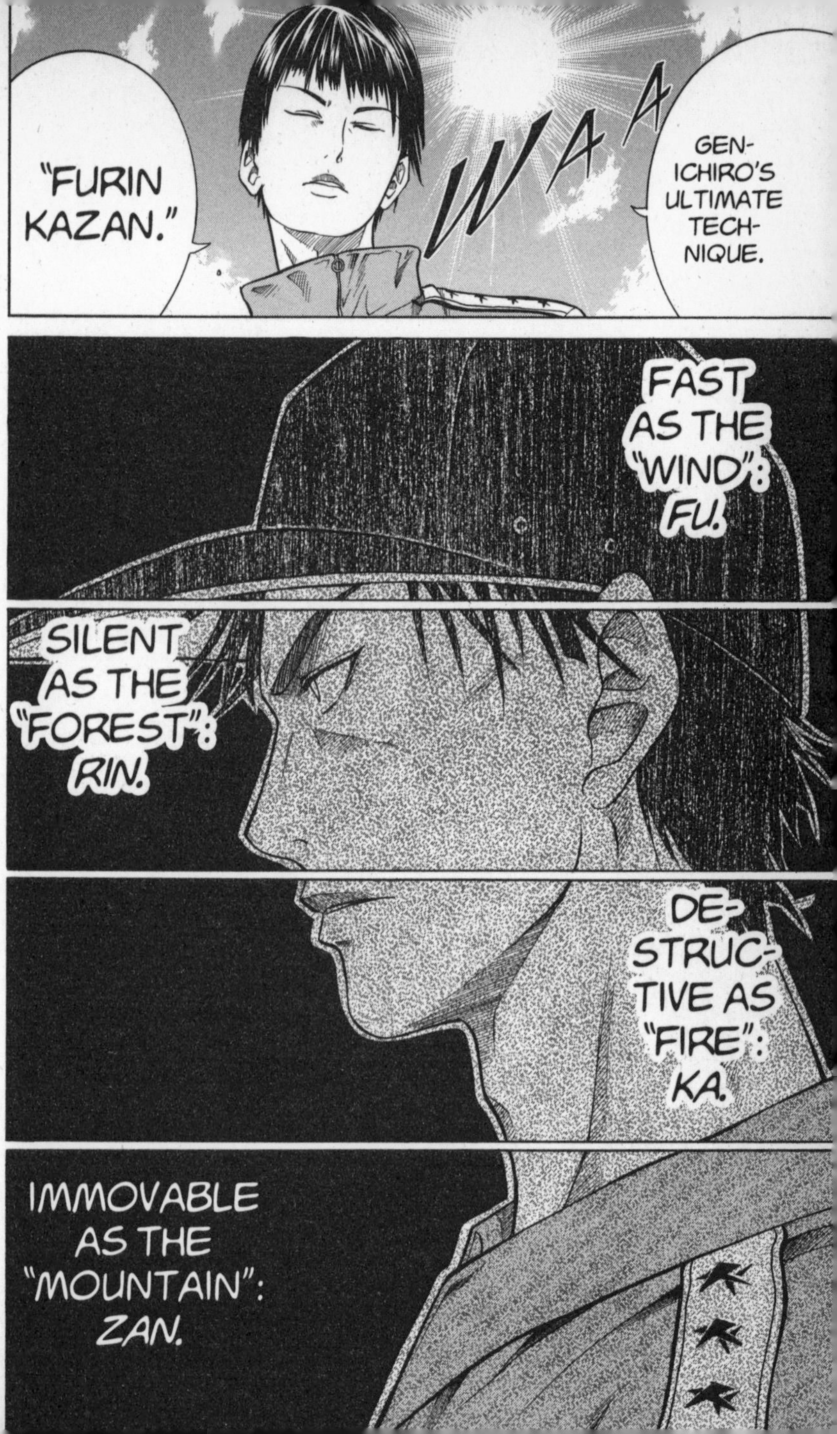
GEN-ICHIRO'S ULTIMATE TECH-NIQUE.
WAA
"FURIN KAZAN."
FAST AS THE "WIND": FU.
SILENT AS THE "FOREST": RIN.
DE-STRUC-TIVE AS "FIRE": KA.
IMMOVABLE AS THE "MOUNTAIN": ZAN.

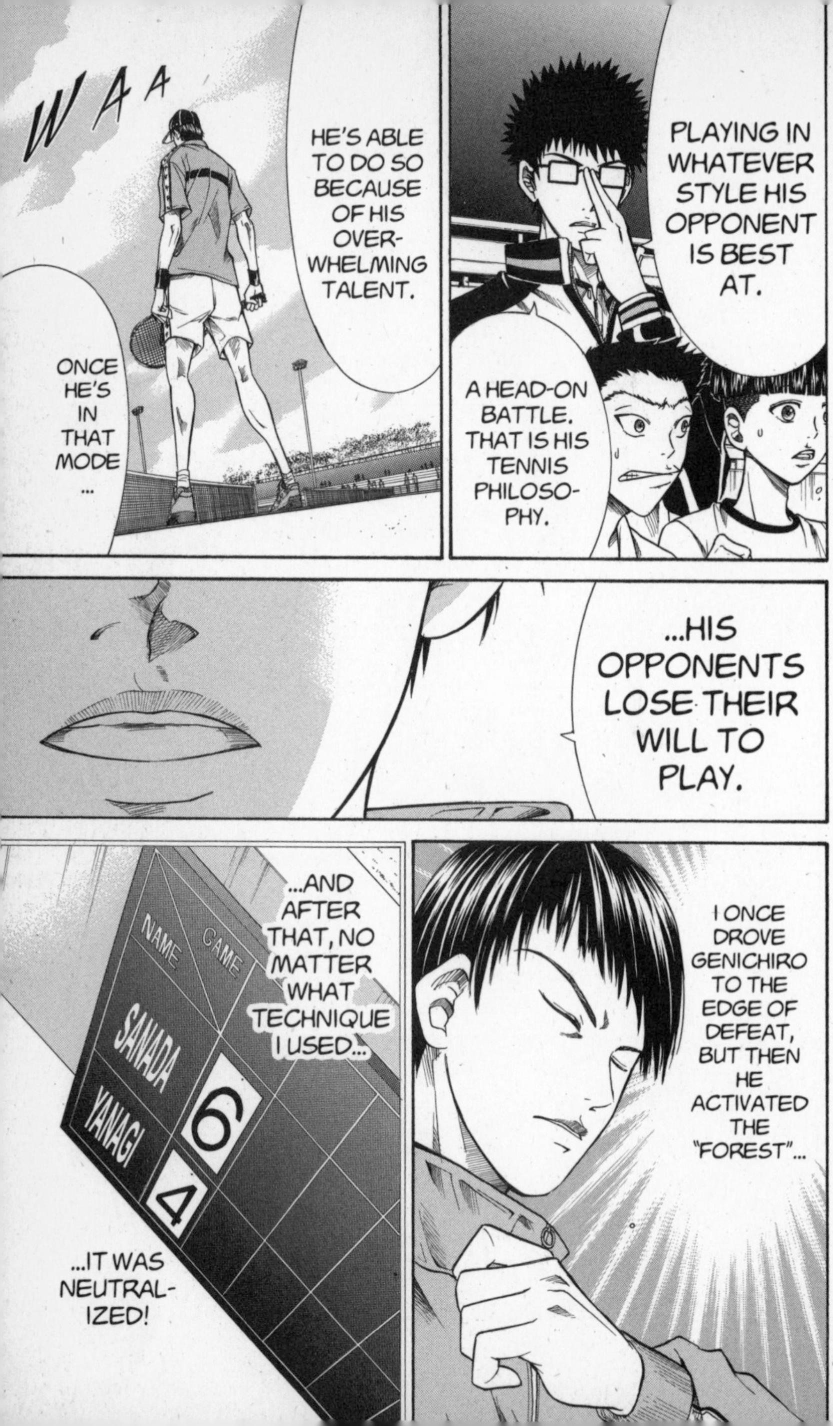
PLAYING IN WHATEVER STYLE HIS OPPONENT IS BEST AT.
A HEAD-ON BATTLE. THAT IS HIS TENNIS PHILOSOPHY.
WAA
HE'S ABLE TO DO SO BECAUSE OF HIS OVER-WHELMING TALENT.
ONCE HE'S IN THAT MODE ...
...HIS OPPONENTS LOSE THEIR WILL TO PLAY.
I ONCE DROVE GENICHIRO TO THE EDGE OF DEFEAT, BUT THEN HE ACTIVATED THE "FOREST"...
...AND AFTER THAT, NO MATTER WHAT TECHNIQUE I USED...
NAME
GAME
SANADA
YANAGI
6
4
...IT WAS NEUTRAL-IZED!

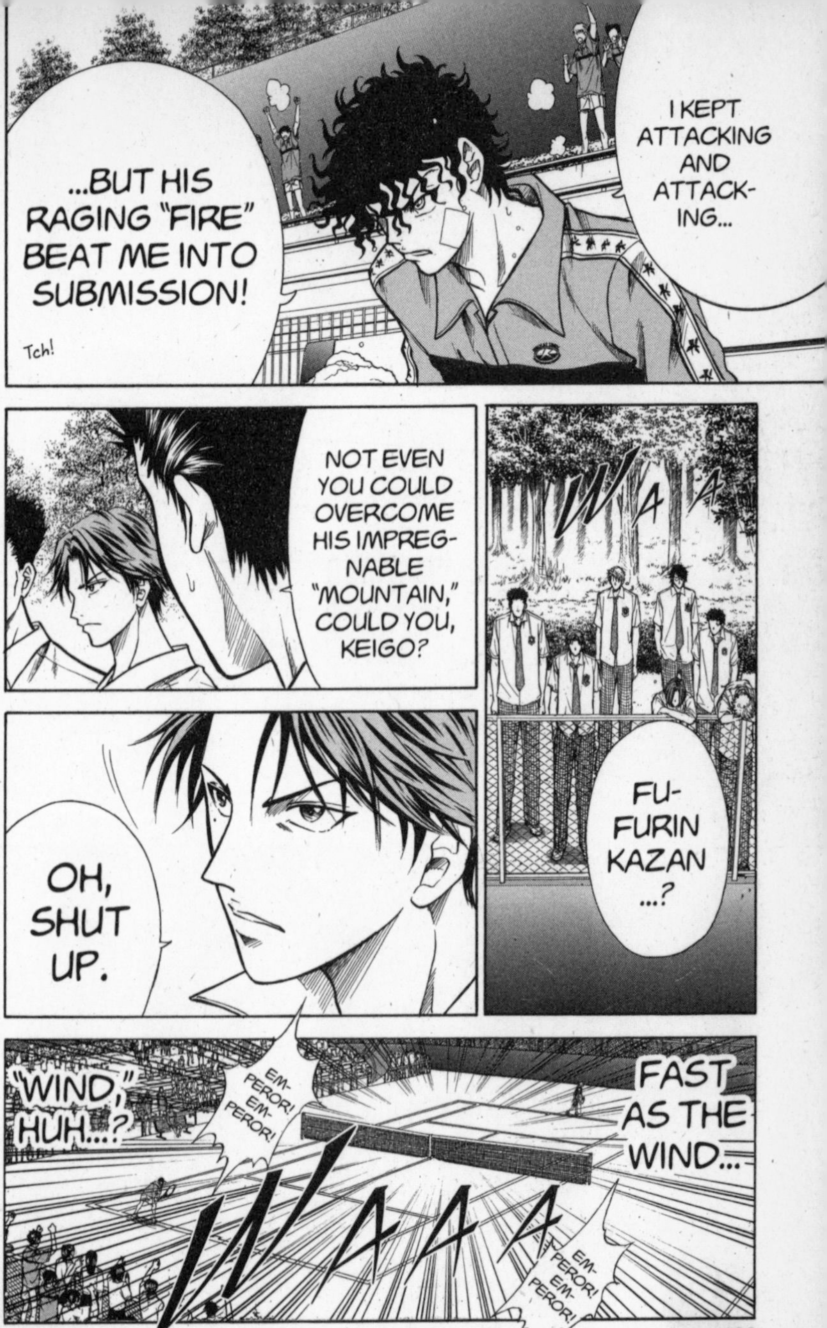

I KEPT ATTACKING AND ATTACKING...
...BUT HIS RAGING "FIRE" BEAT ME INTO SUBMISSION!
Tch!
WAA
FU-FURIN KAZAN ...?
NOT EVEN YOU COULD OVERCOME HIS IMPREGNABLE "MOUNTAIN," COULD YOU, KEIGO?
OH, SHUT UP.
FAST AS THE WIND...
EM-PEROR! EM-PEROR!
WAAA
EM-PEROR! EM-PEROR!
"WIND," HUH...?

READ THIS WAY

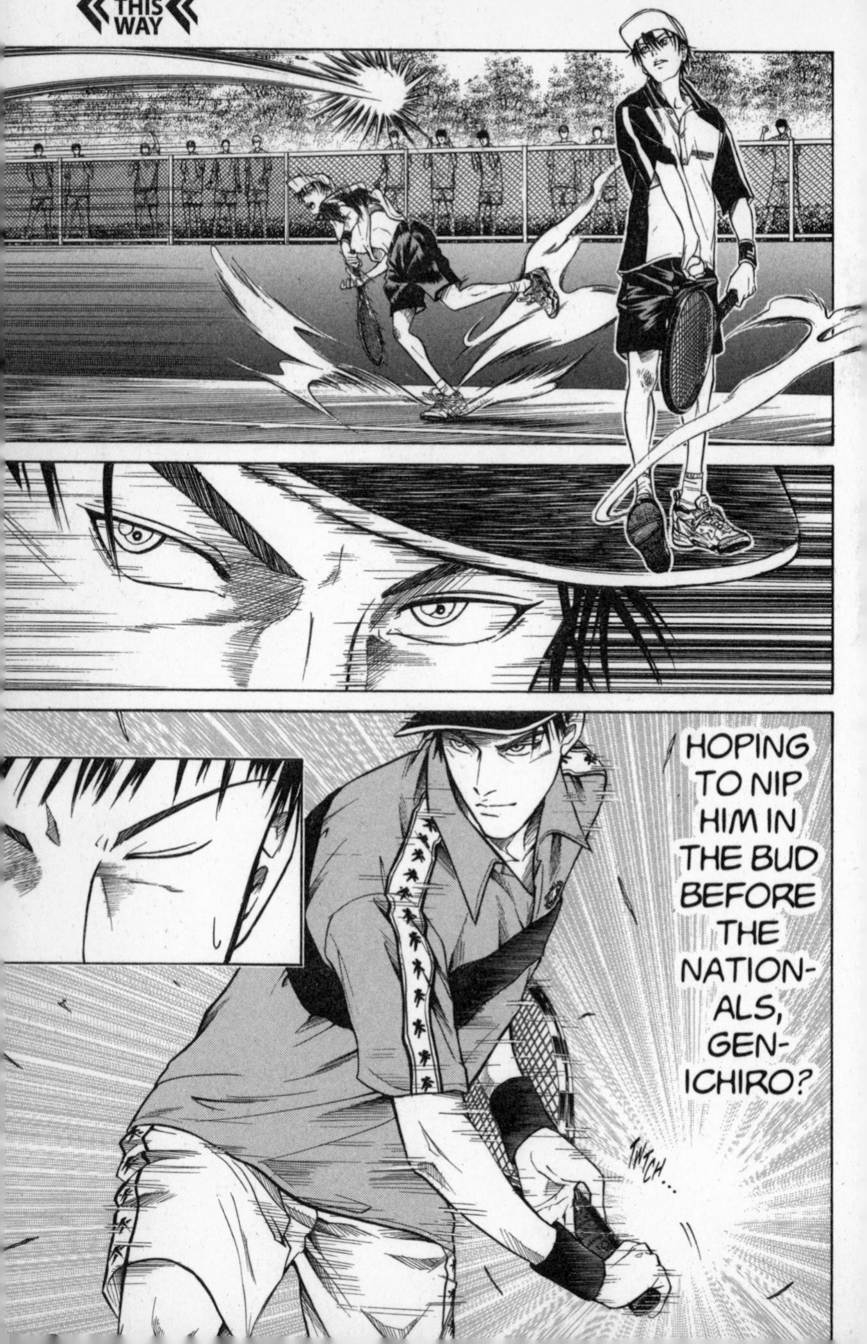
HOPING TO NIP HIM IN THE BUD BEFORE THE NATION-ALS, GEN-ICHIRO?
TWITCH...

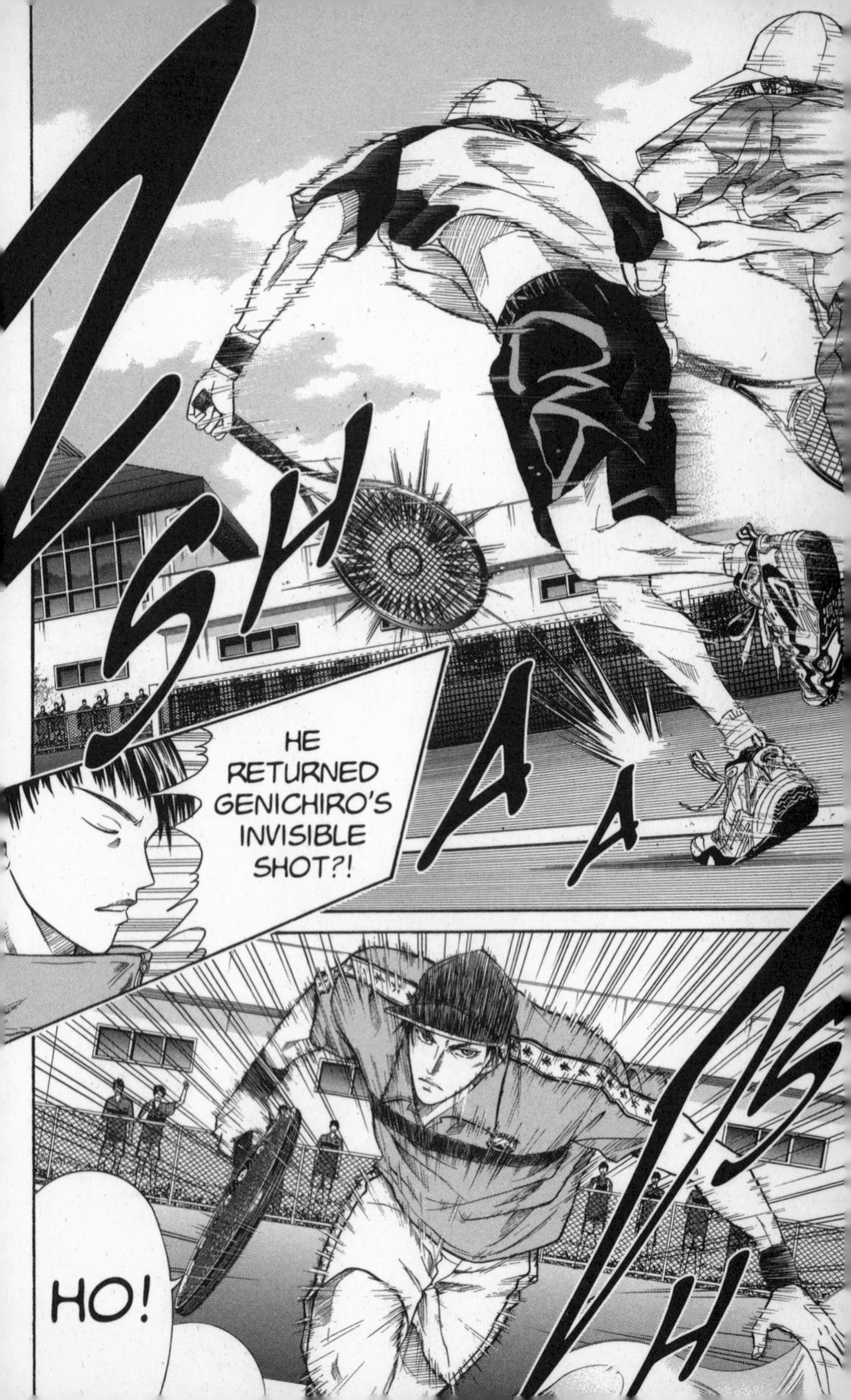
HE RETURNED GENICHIRO'S INVISIBLE SHOT?!
HO!

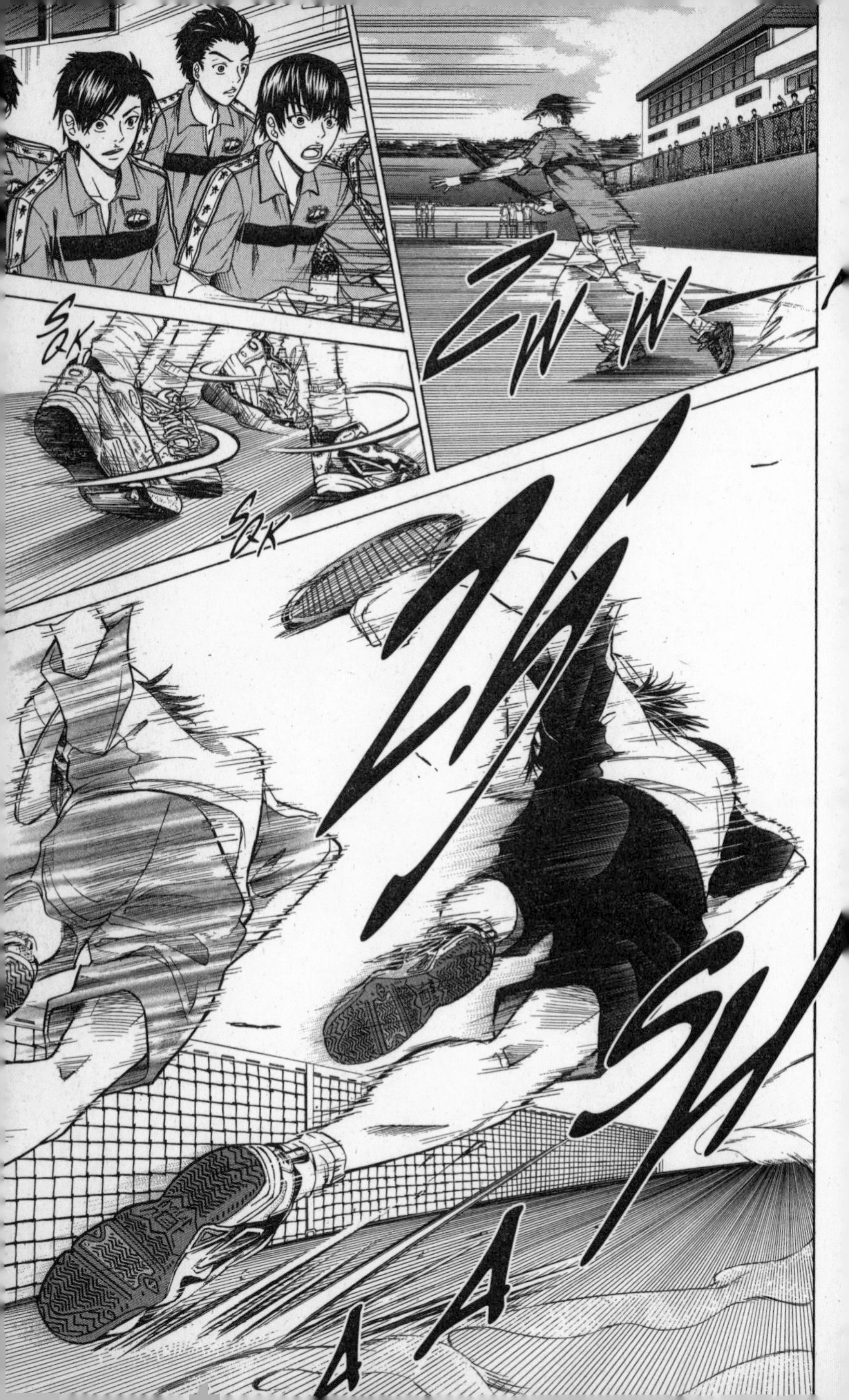
SQK
SQK

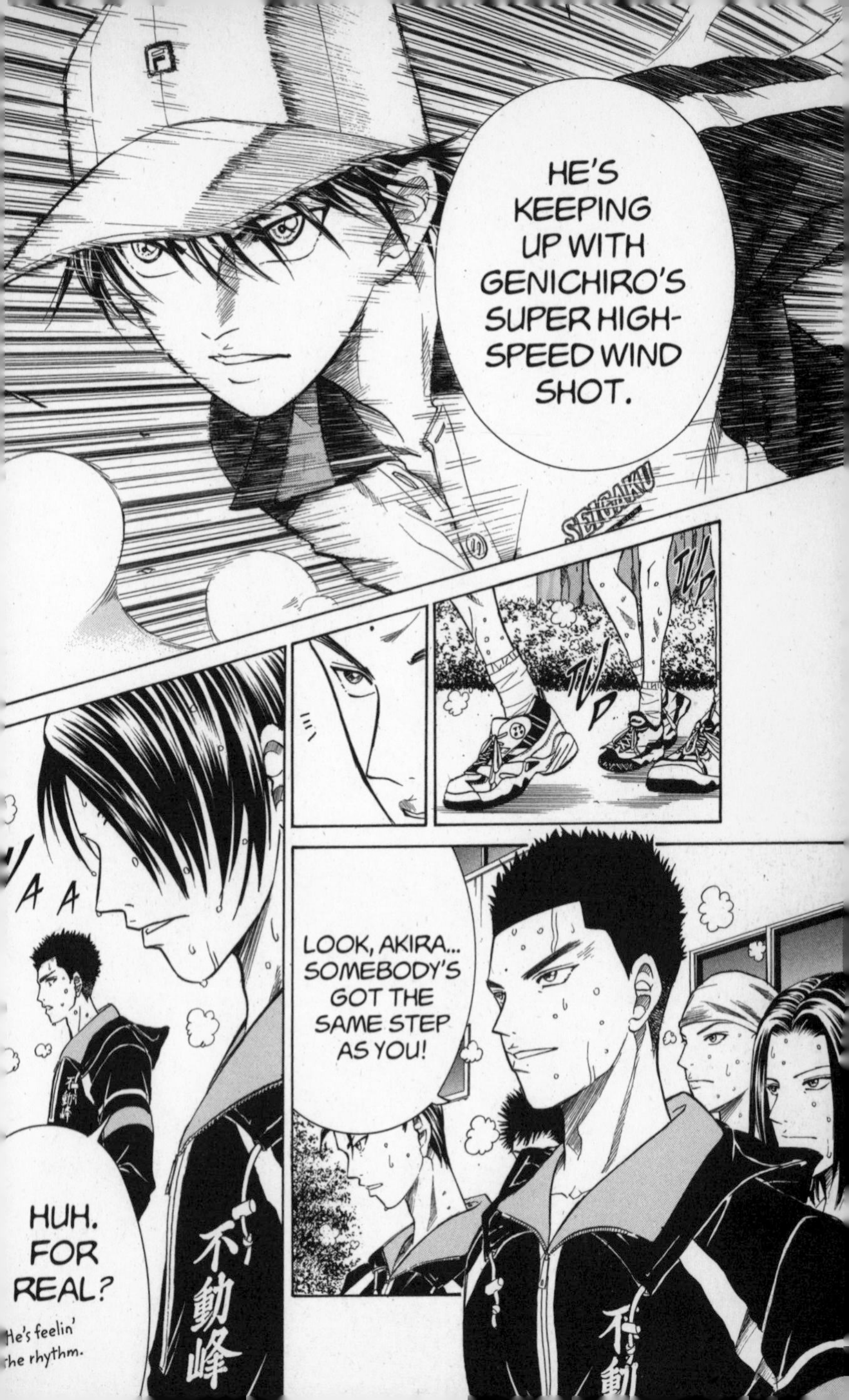
HE'S KEEPING UP WITH GENICHIRO'S SUPER HIGH-SPEED WIND SHOT.
SEIGAKU
TUP
TUP
LOOK, AKIRA... SOMEBODY'S GOT THE SAME STEP AS YOU!
HUH. FOR REAL?
He's feelin' the rhythm.
不動峰
不動峰

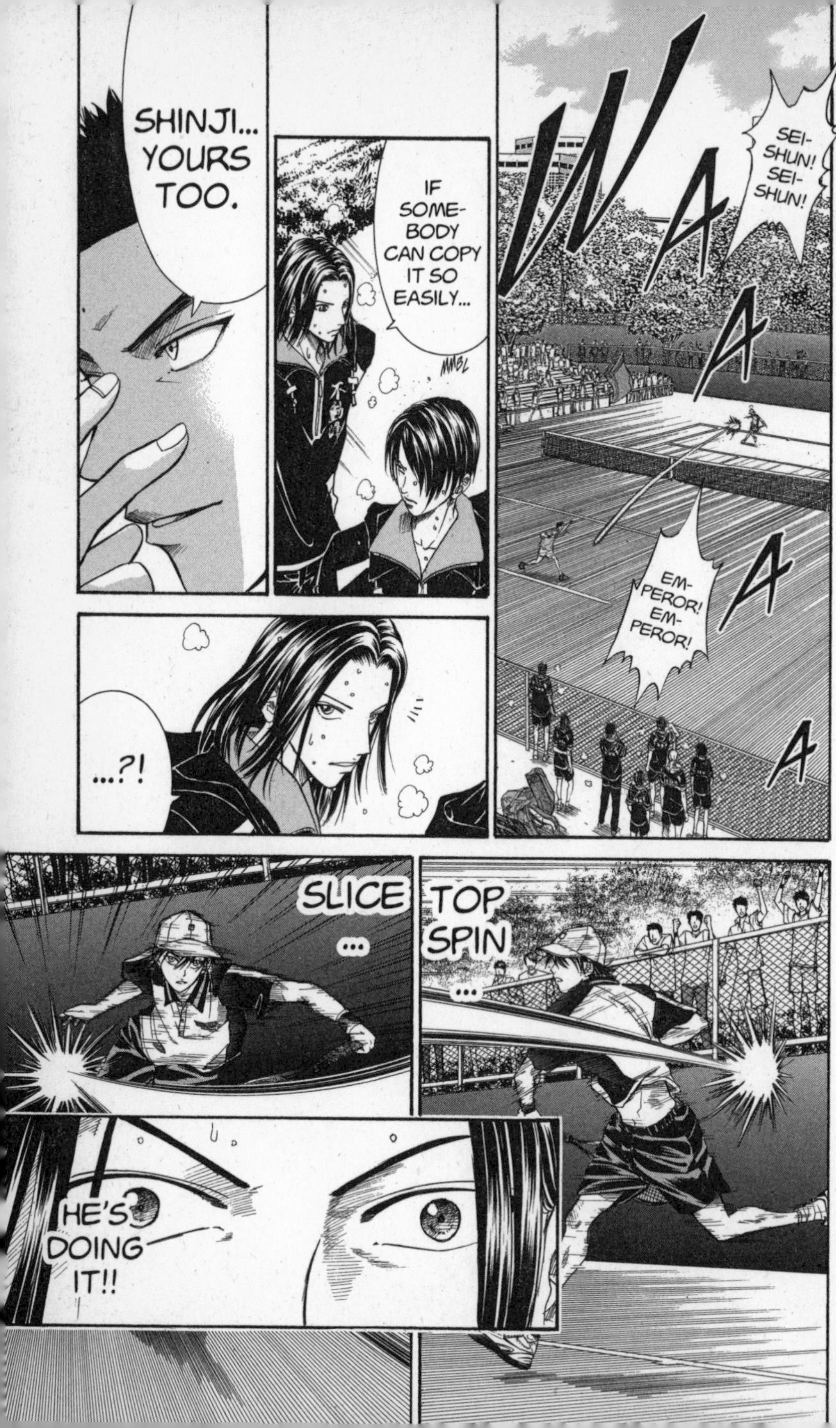
SEI-SHUN! SEI-SHUN!
WAAAA
EM-PEROR! EM-PEROR!
IF SOME-BODY CAN COPY IT SO EASILY...
MMBL
SHINJI... YOURS TOO.
...?!
TOP SPIN ...
SLICE ...
HE'S DOING IT!!

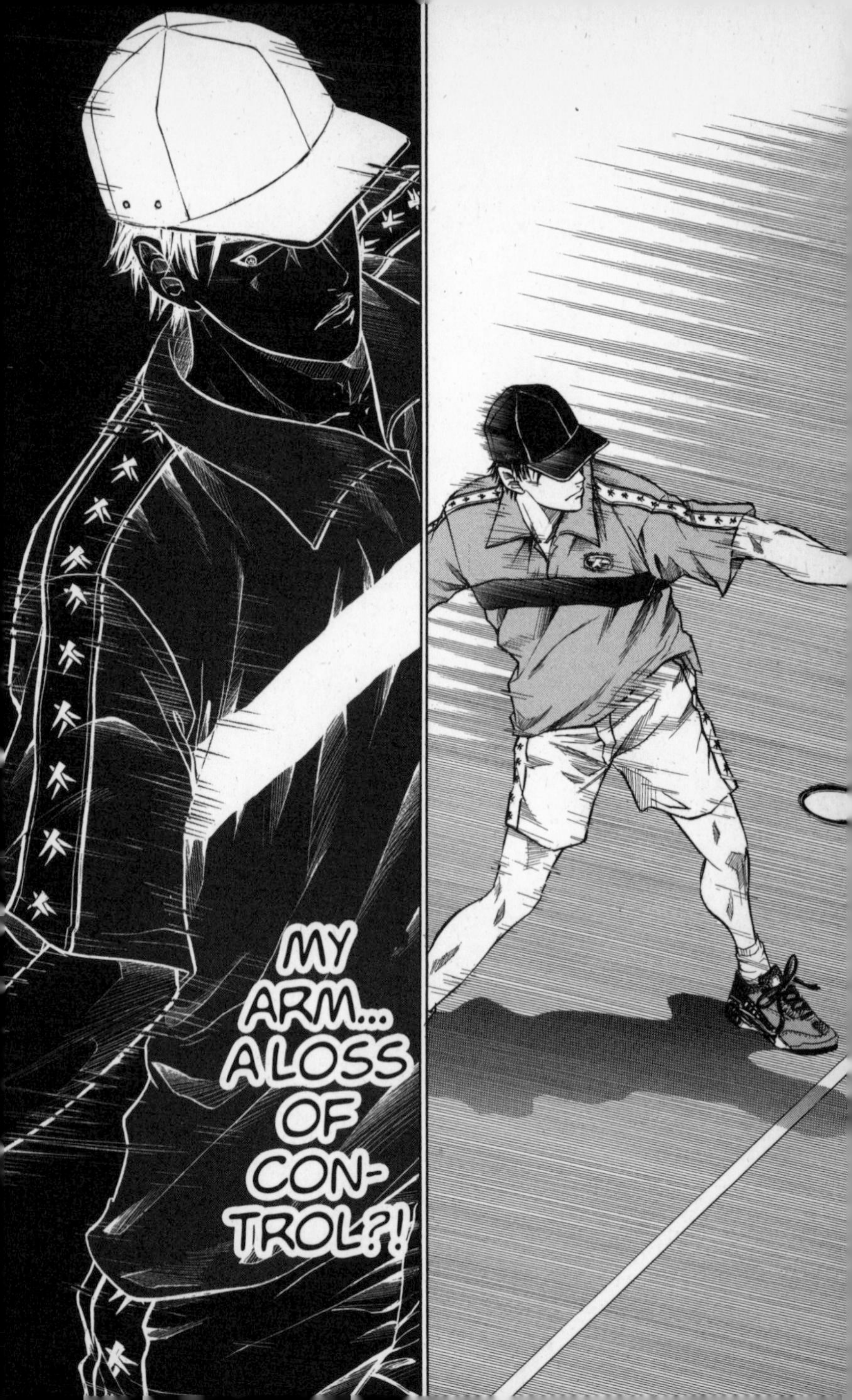
MY ARM... A LOSS OF CON-TROL?!

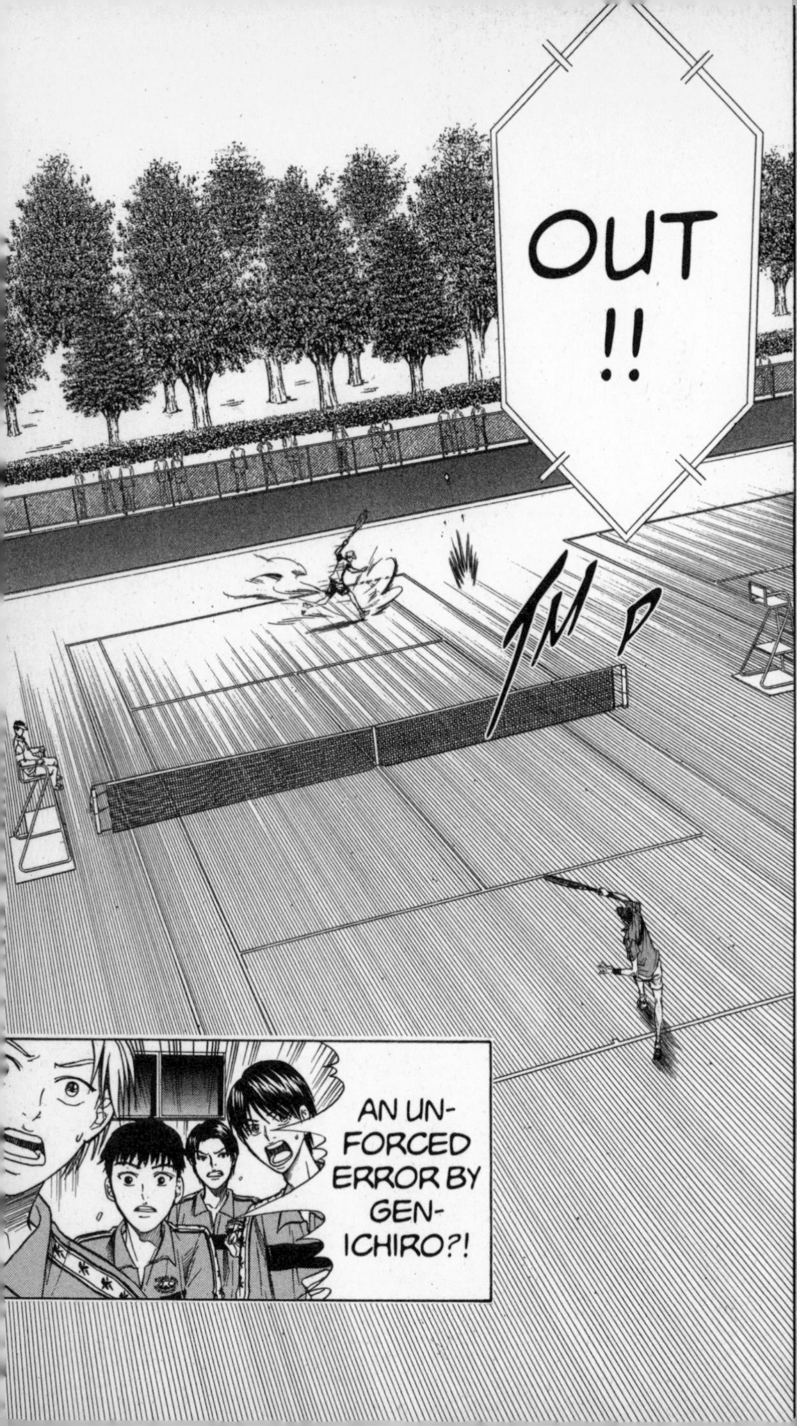
OUT!!
AN UN-FORCED ERROR BY GEN-ICHIRO?!

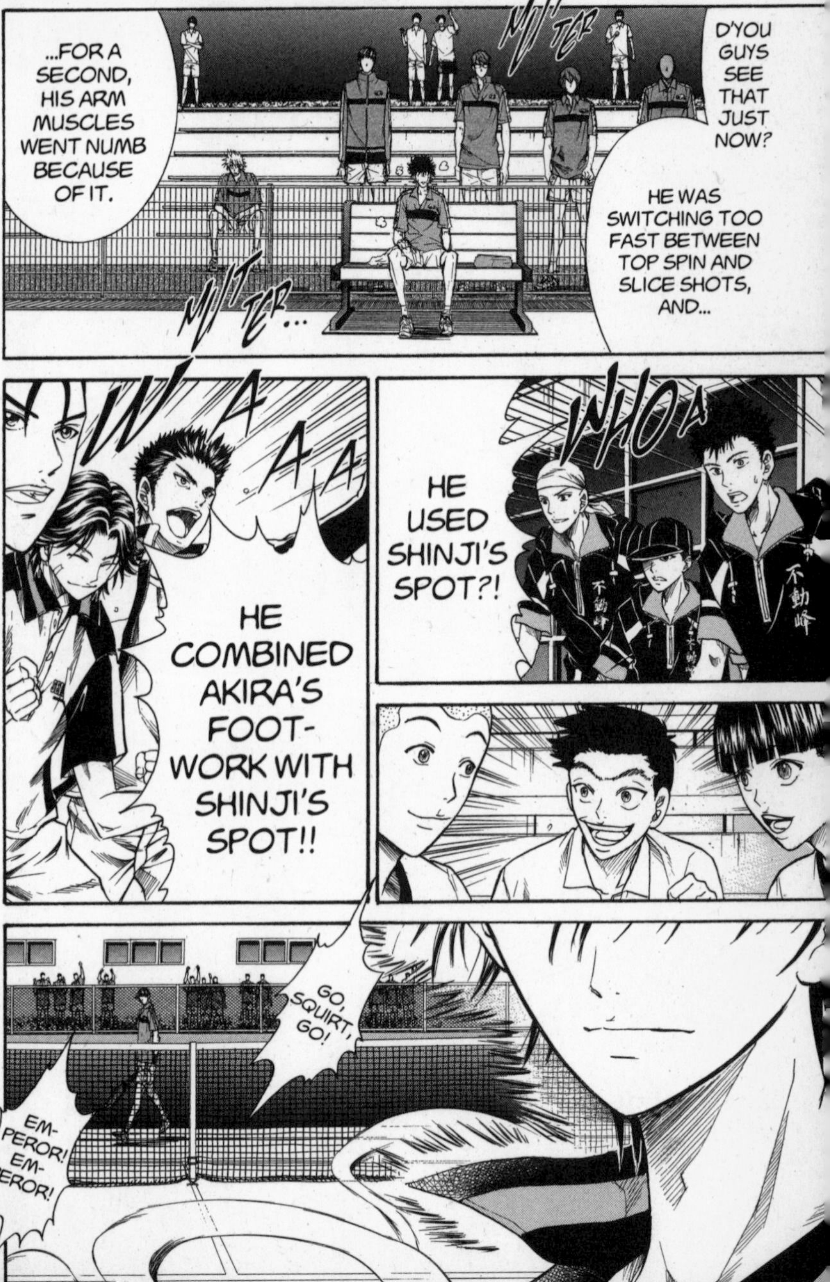

D'YOU GUYS SEE THAT JUST NOW?
HE WAS SWITCHING TOO FAST BETWEEN TOP SPIN AND SLICE SHOTS, AND...
MUTTER
...FOR A SECOND, HIS ARM MUSCLES WENT NUMB BECAUSE OF IT.
MUTTER...
WHOA
HE USED SHINJI'S SPOT?!
WAAA
HE COMBINED AKIRA'S FOOT-WORK WITH SHINJI'S SPOT!!
GO, SQUIRT, GO!
EM-PEROR! EM-PEROR!

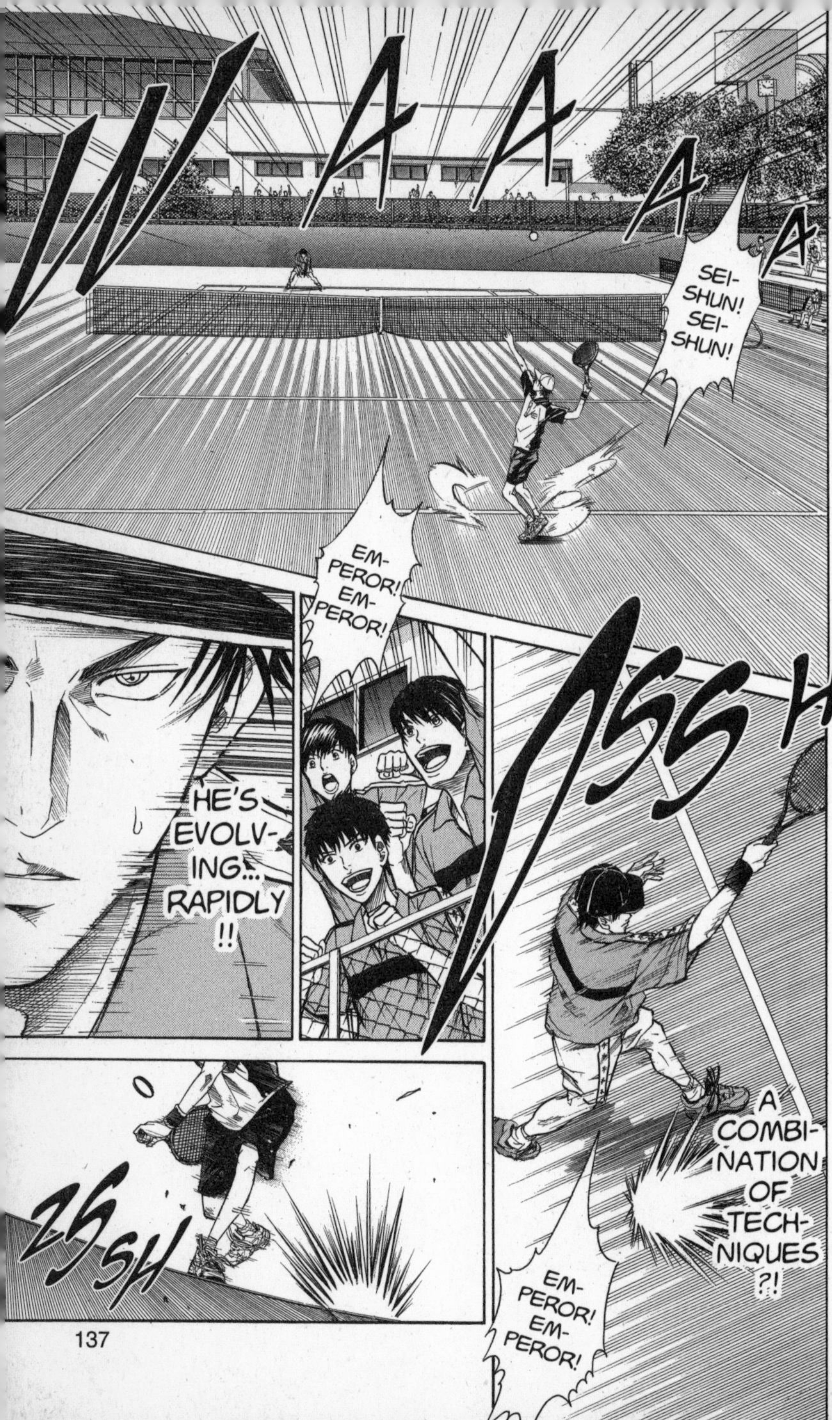
WAAAAA
SEI-SHUN! SEI-SHUN!
EM-PEROR! EM-PEROR!
A COMBI-NATION OF TECH-NIQUES?!
EM-PEROR! EM-PEROR!
HE'S EVOLV-ING... RAPIDLY!!

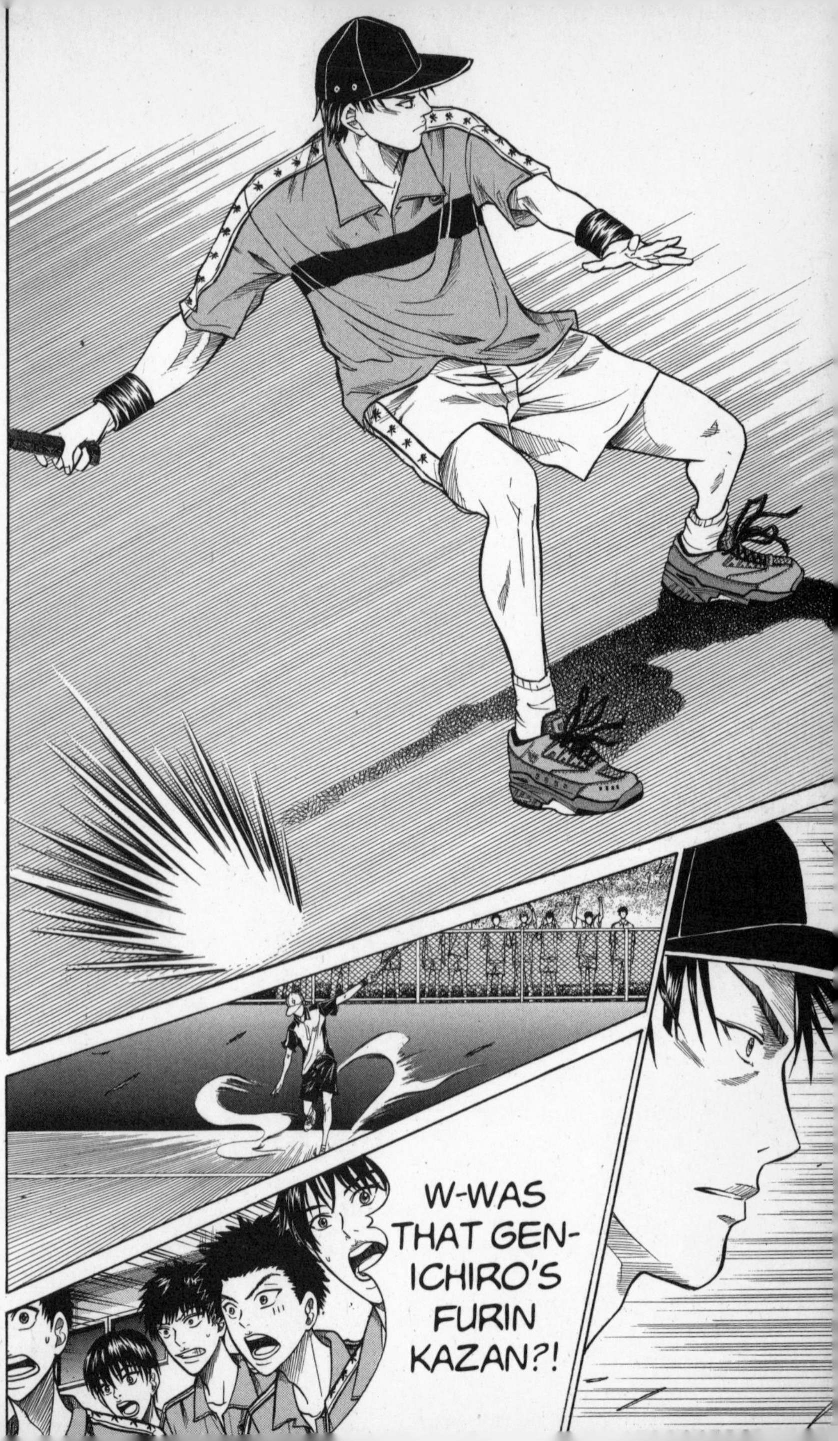
W-WAS THAT GEN-ICHIRO'S FURIN KAZAN?!

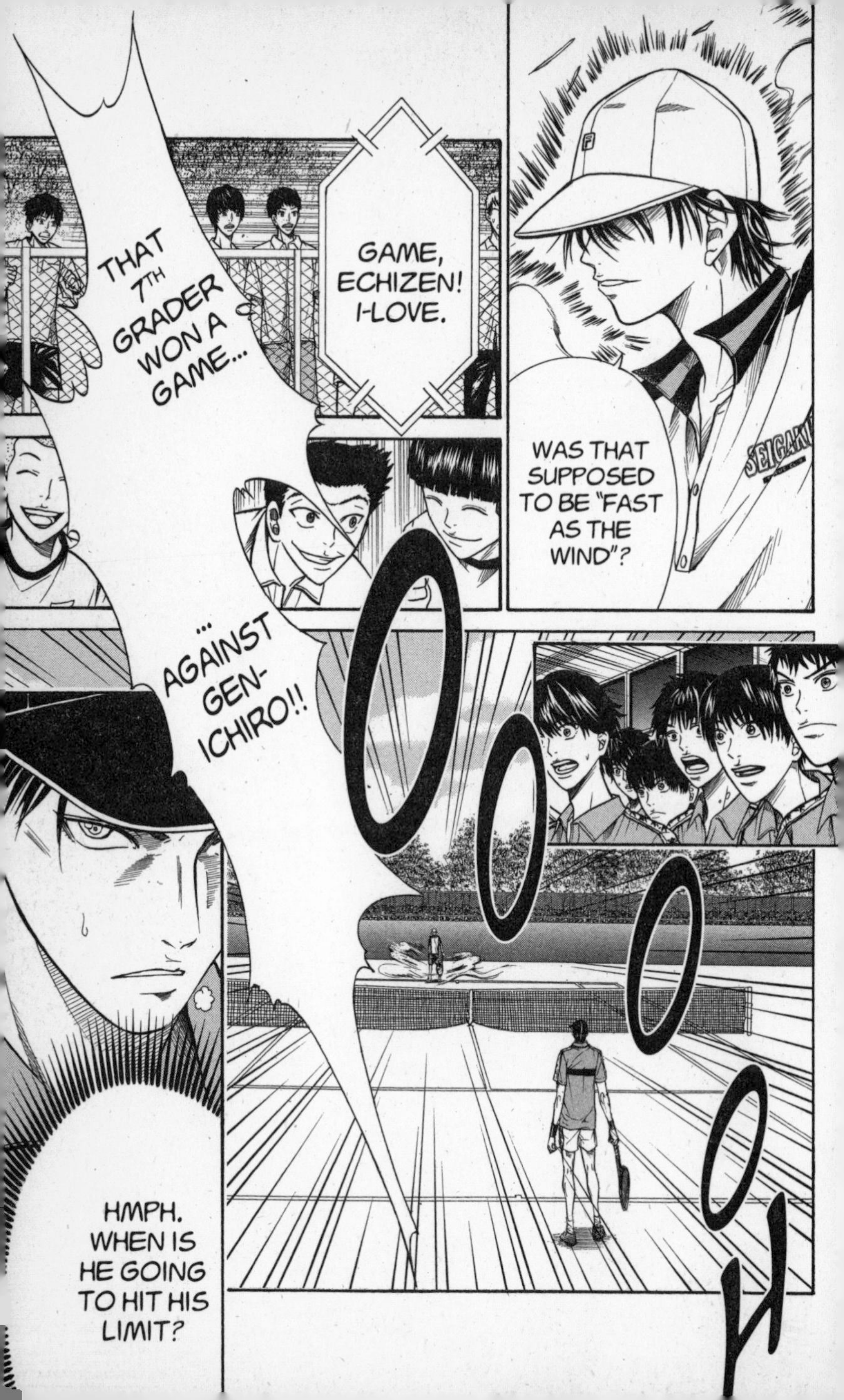

WAS THAT SUPPOSED TO BE "FAST AS THE WIND"?
GAME, ECHIZEN! I-LOVE.
THAT 7TH GRADER WON A GAME...
...AGAINST GEN-ICHIRO!!
OOOOH
HMPH. WHEN IS HE GOING TO HIT HIS LIMIT?

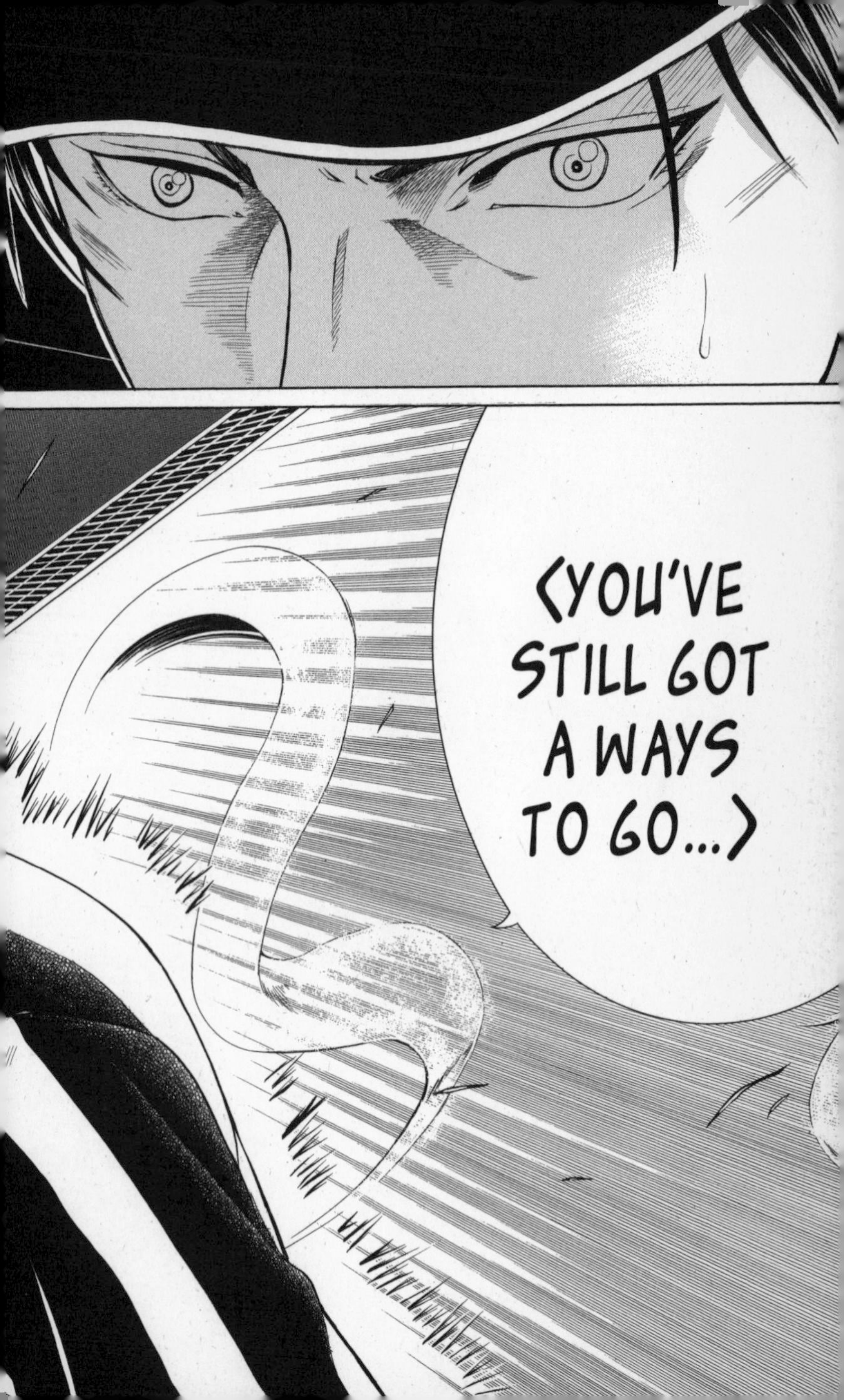
<YOU'VE STILL GOT A WAYS TO GO...>

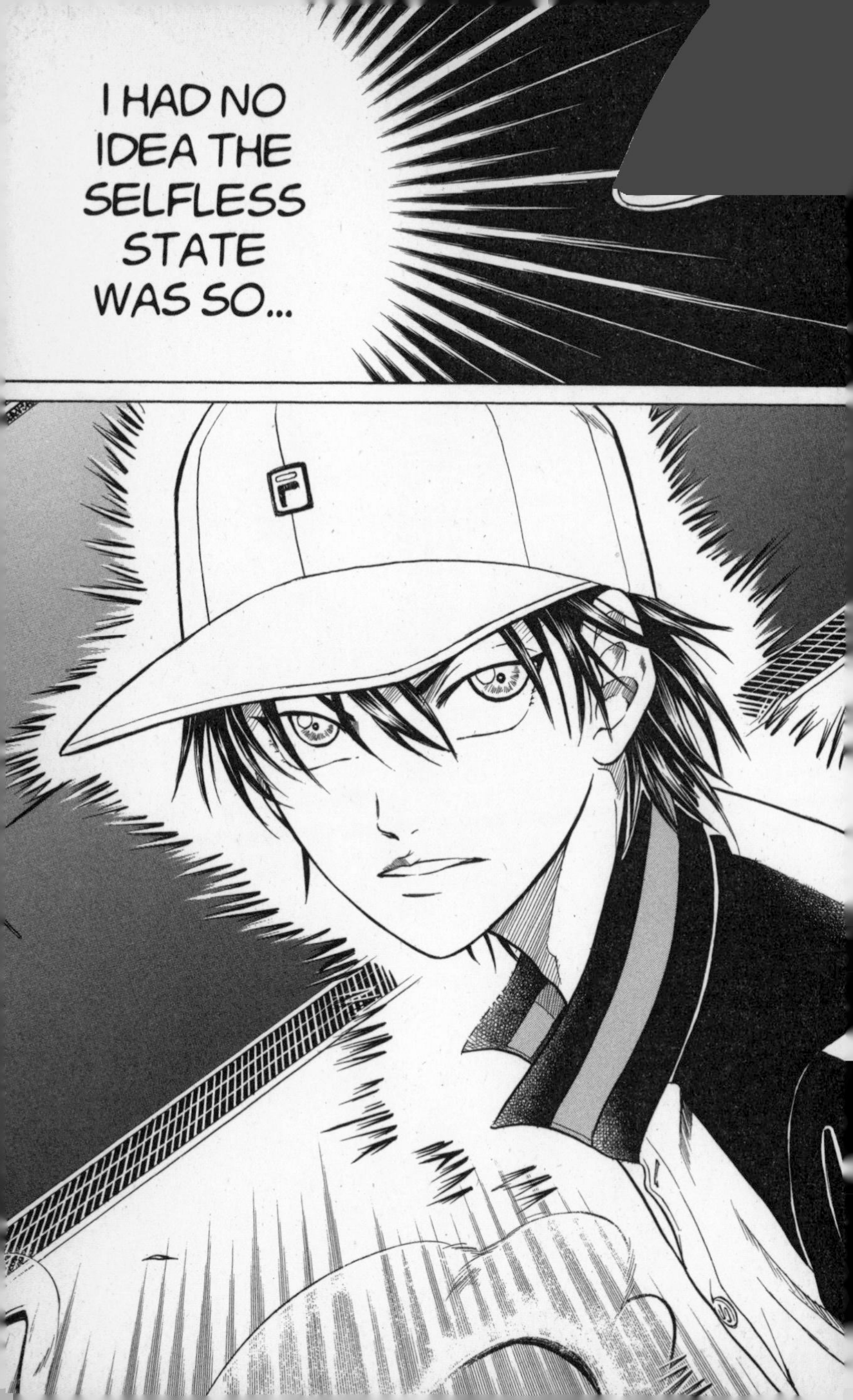
I HAD NO IDEA THE SELFLESS STATE WAS SO...

テニスの王子様

THE PRINCE OF TENNIS

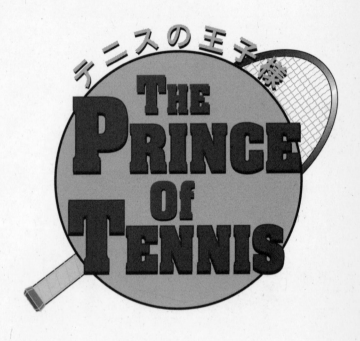

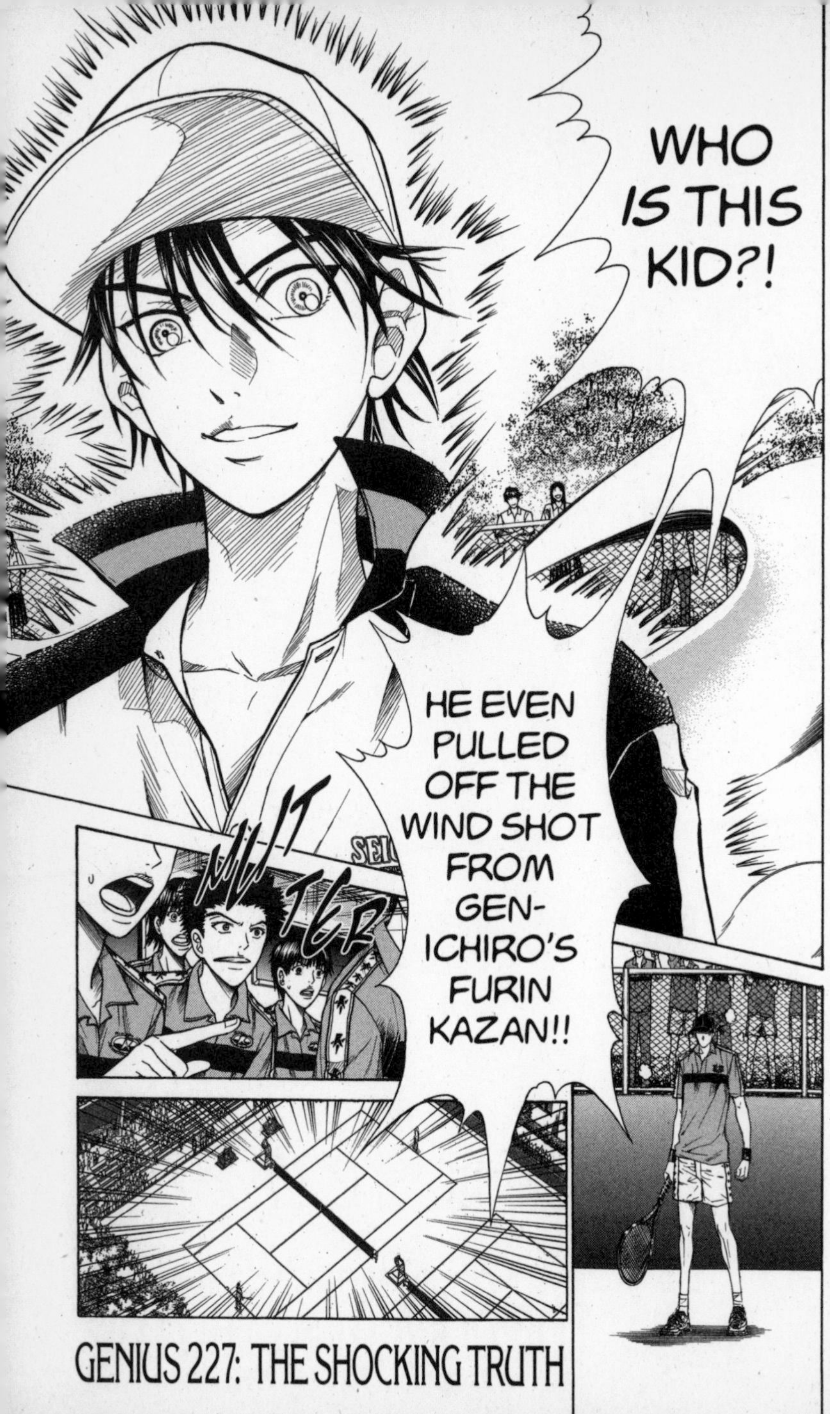
WHO IS THIS KID?!
HE EVEN PULLED OFF THE WIND SHOT FROM GEN-ICHIRO'S FURIN KAZAN!!
MUTTER

GENIUS 227: THE SHOCKING TRUTH

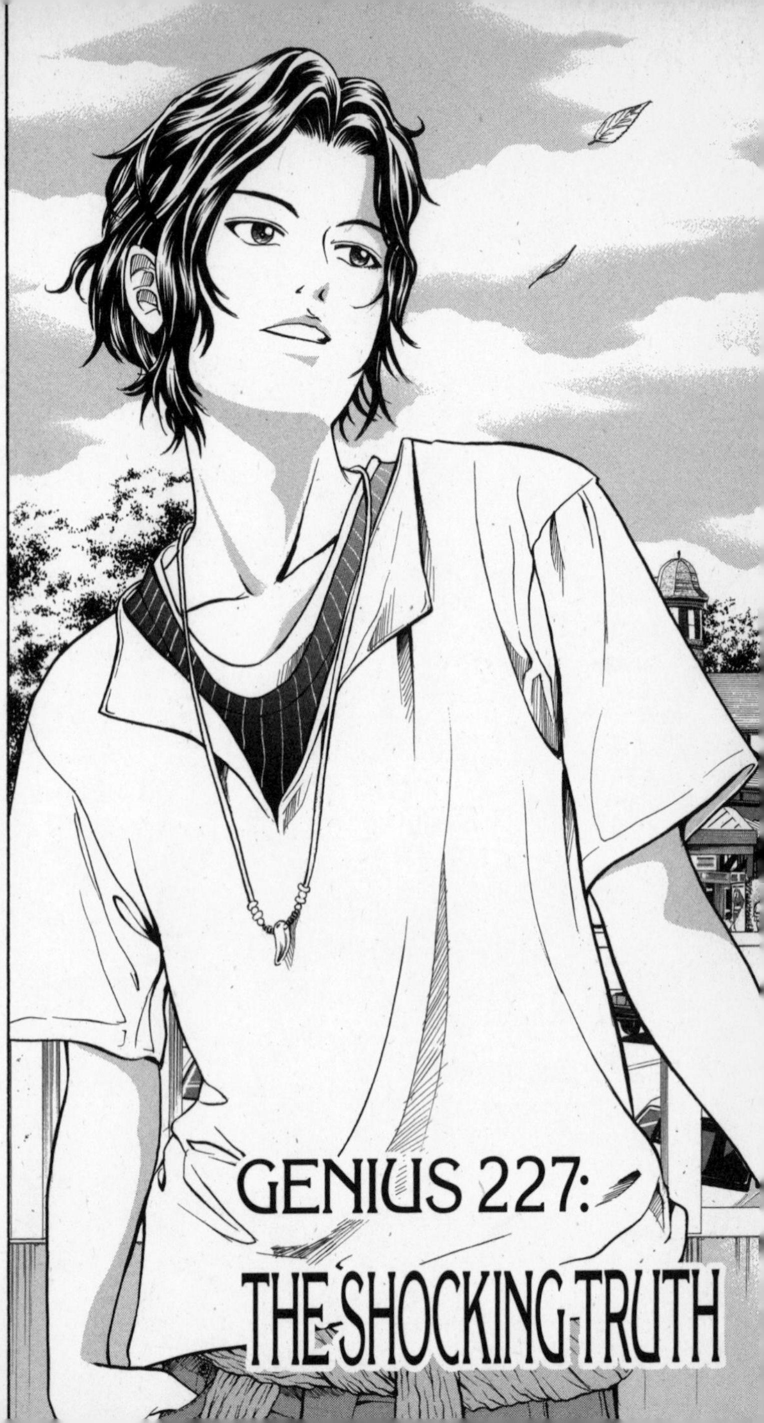
GENIUS 227:
THE SHOCKING TRUTH

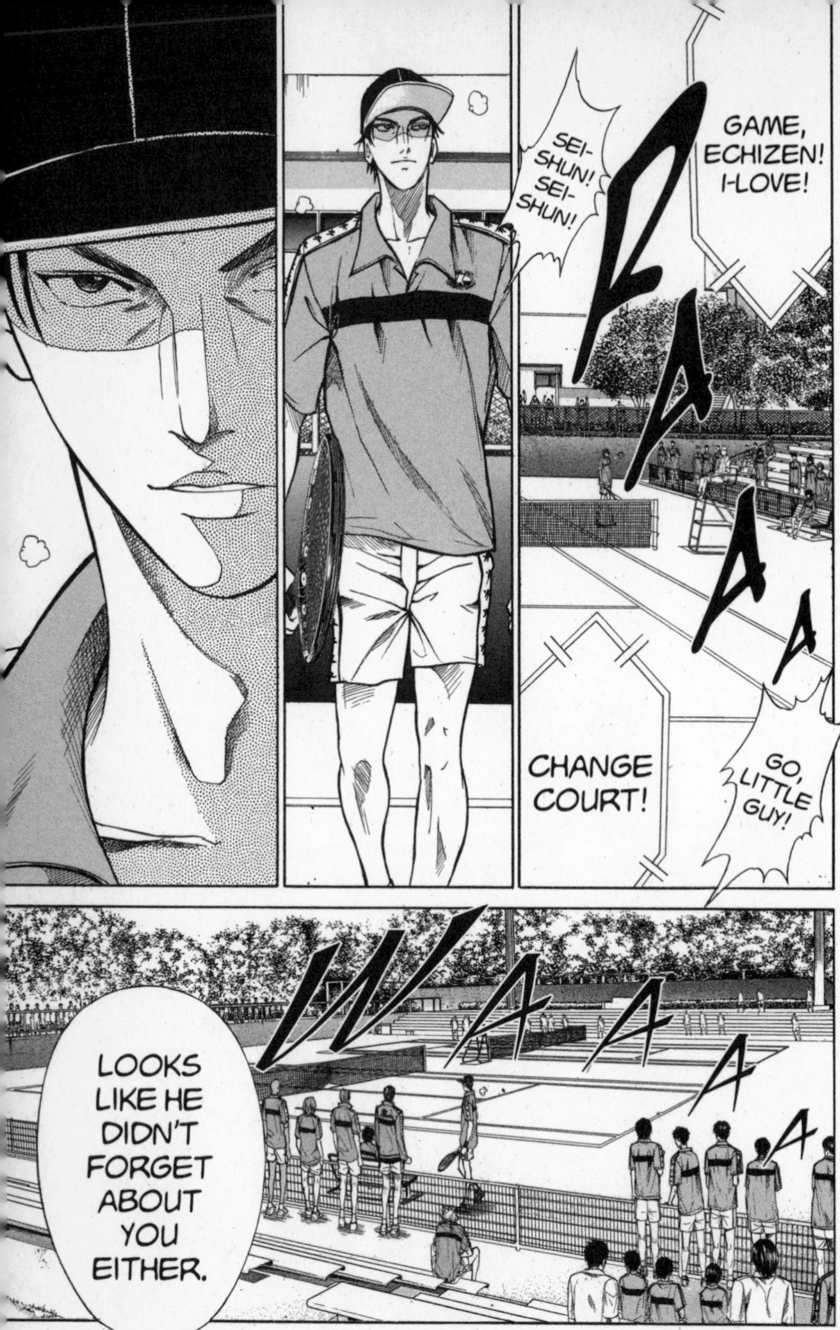
GAME, ECHIZEN! I-LOVE!
SEI-SHUN! SEI-SHUN!
CHANGE COURT!
GO, LITTLE GUY!
WAAAA
LOOKS LIKE HE DIDN'T FORGET ABOUT YOU EITHER.

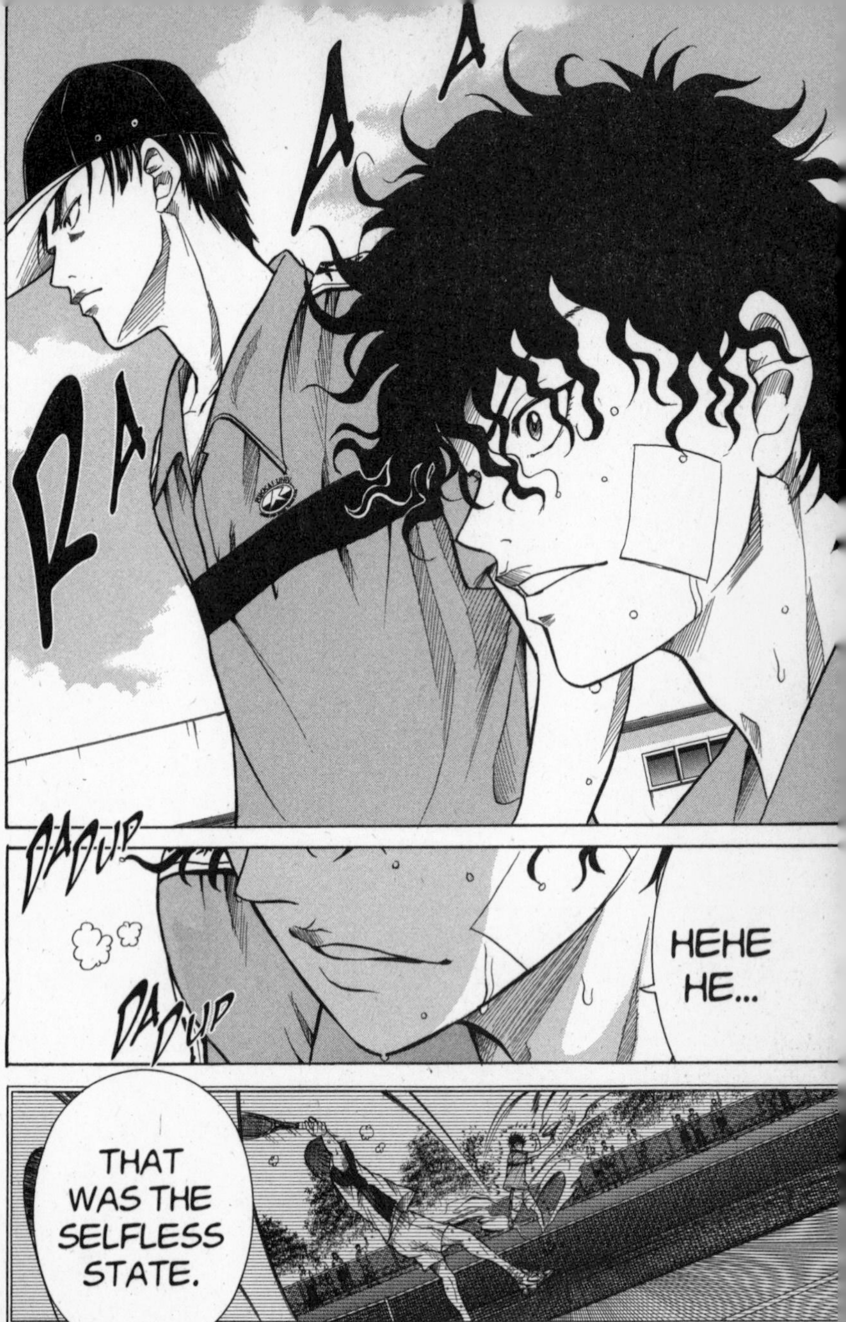
RAAAA
DADUP
DADUP
HEHE HE...
THAT WAS THE SELFLESS STATE.

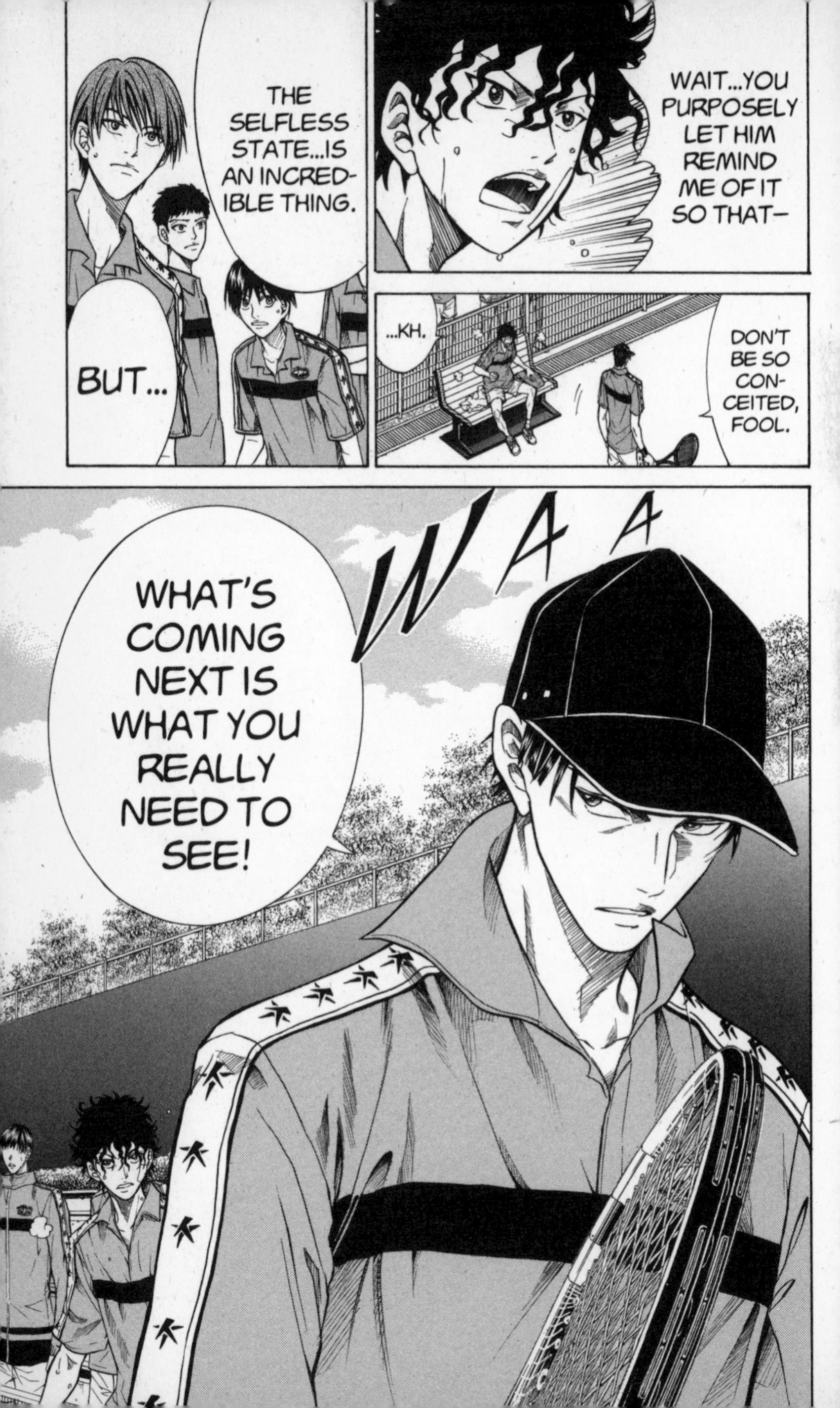

WAIT...YOU PURPOSELY LET HIM REMIND ME OF IT SO THAT—
DON'T BE SO CON-CEITED, FOOL.
...KH.
THE SELFLESS STATE...IS AN INCRED-IBLE THING.
BUT...
WAA
WHAT'S COMING NEXT IS WHAT YOU REALLY NEED TO SEE!

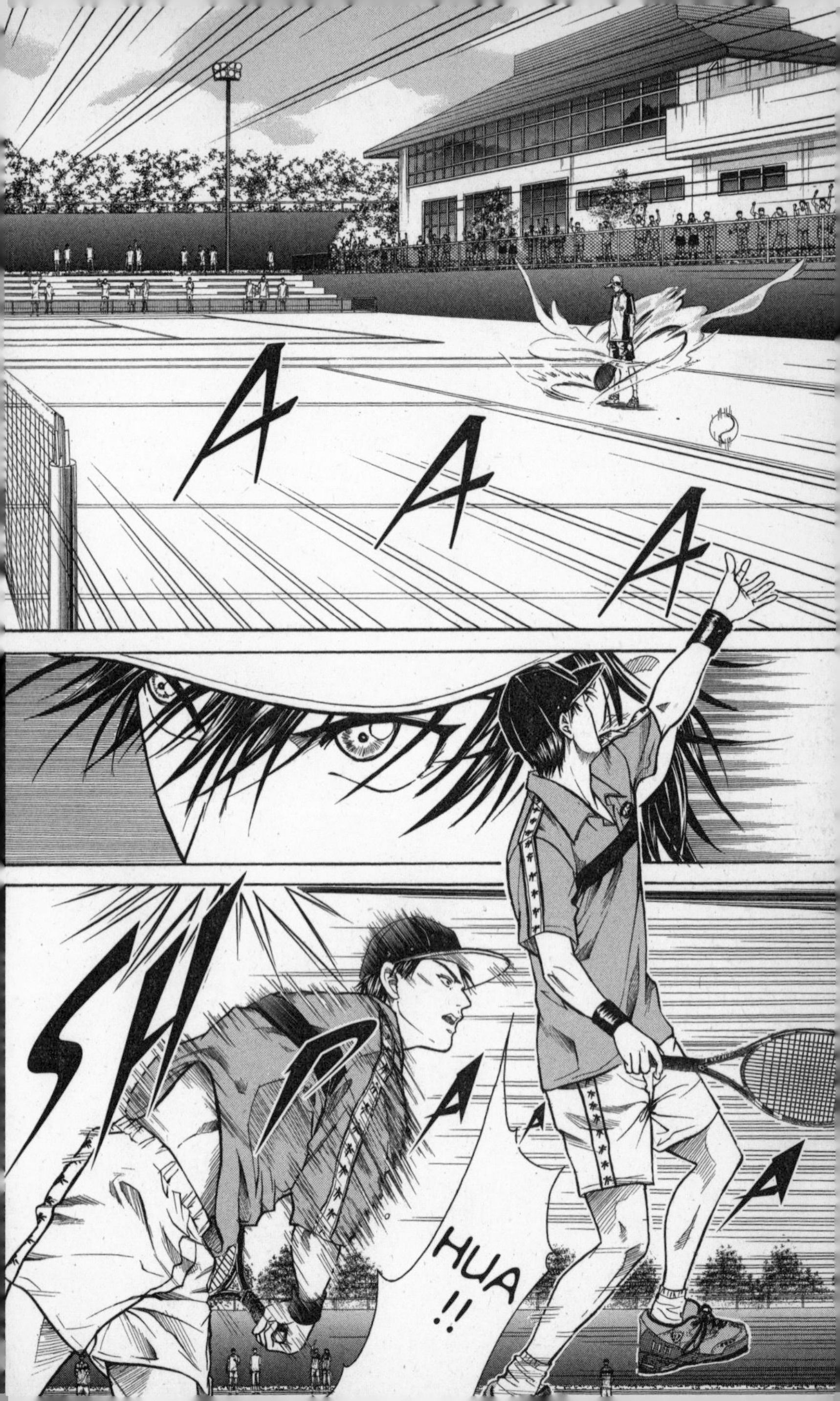
AAA
SHAAAA
HUA!!

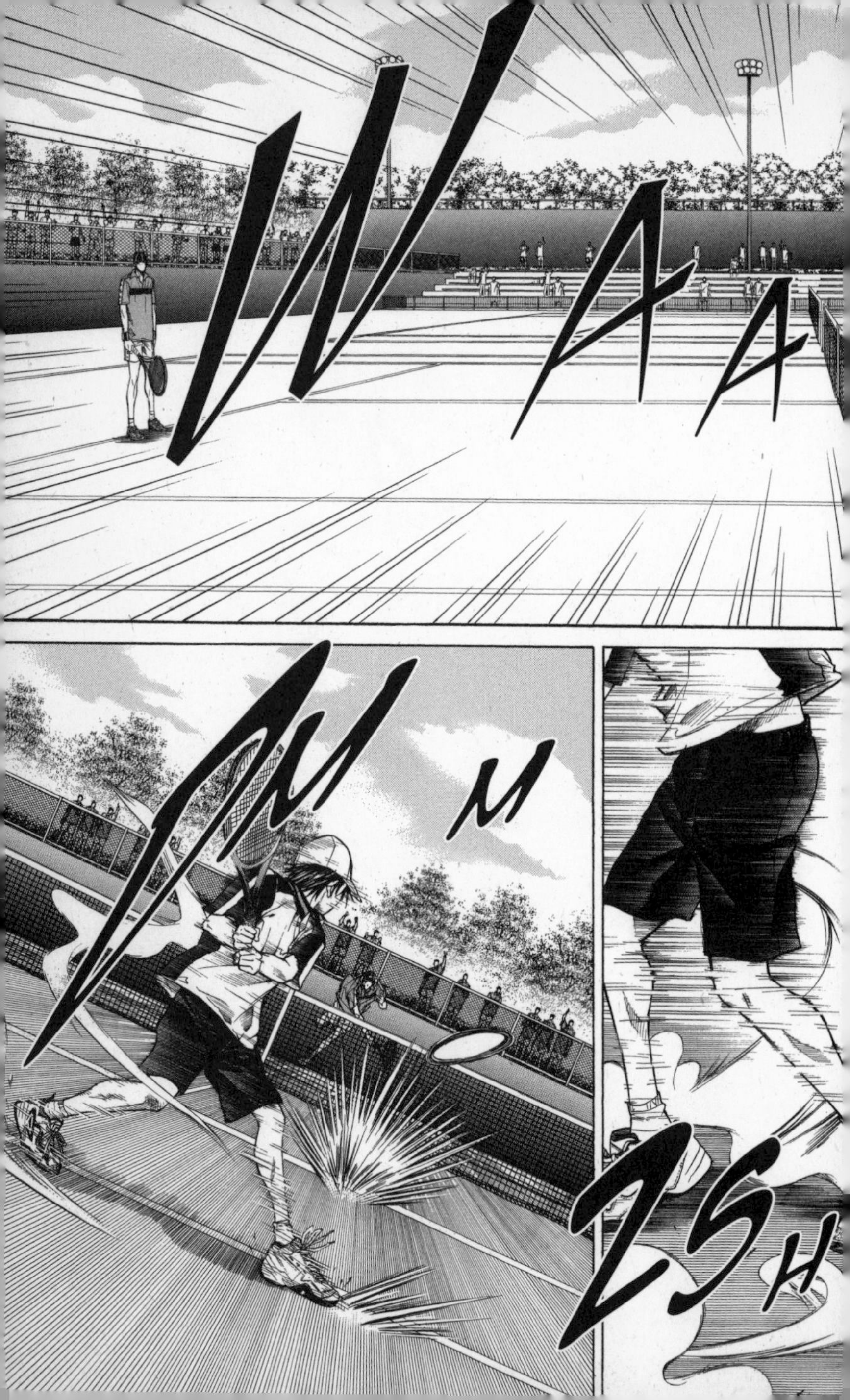
WAAA
ZSH
VMM

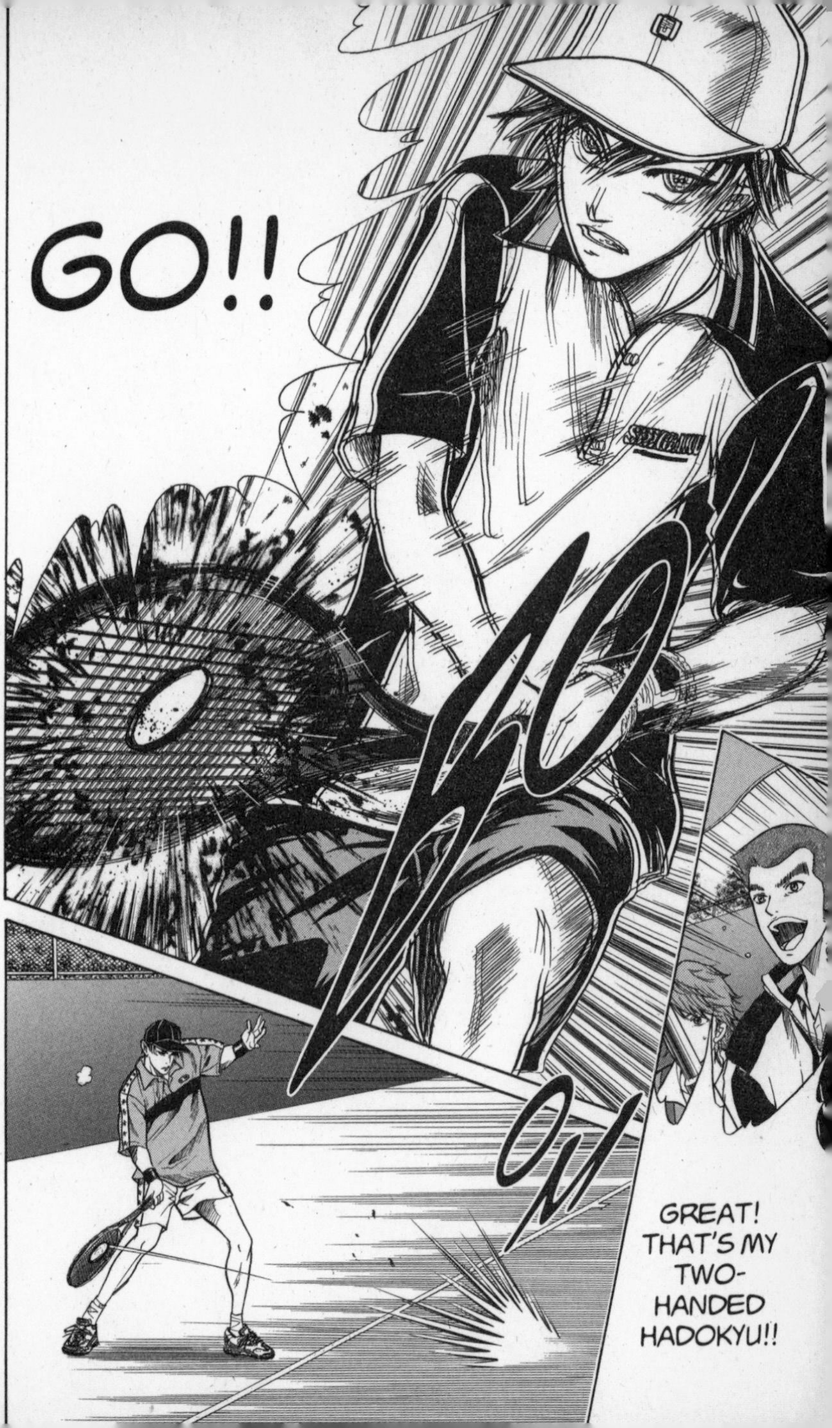
GO!!
GREAT! THAT'S MY TWO-HANDED HADOKYU!!

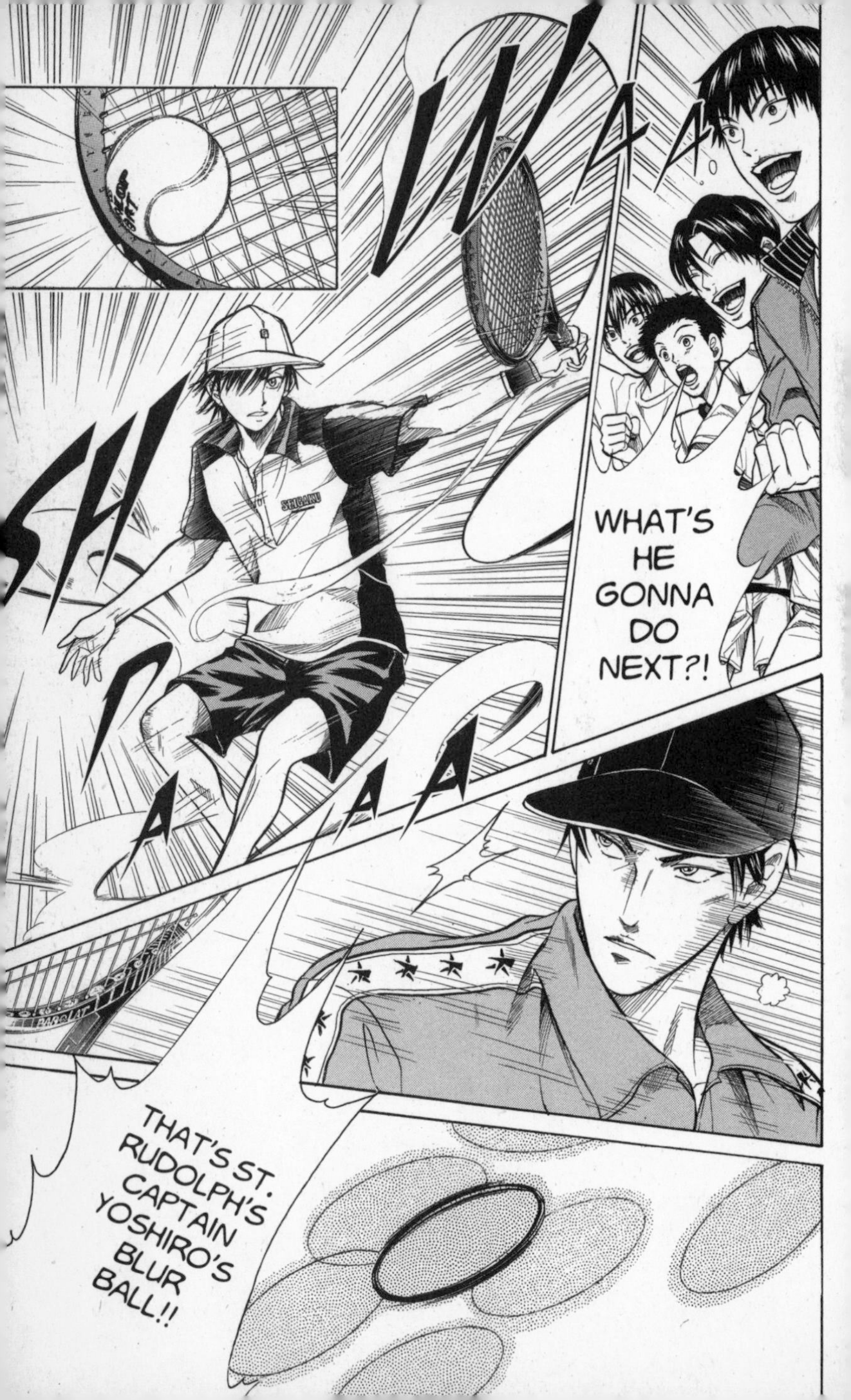
WAA
WHAT'S HE GONNA DO NEXT?!
SHAAA
THAT'S ST. RUDOLPH'S CAPTAIN YOSHIRO'S BLUR BALL!!

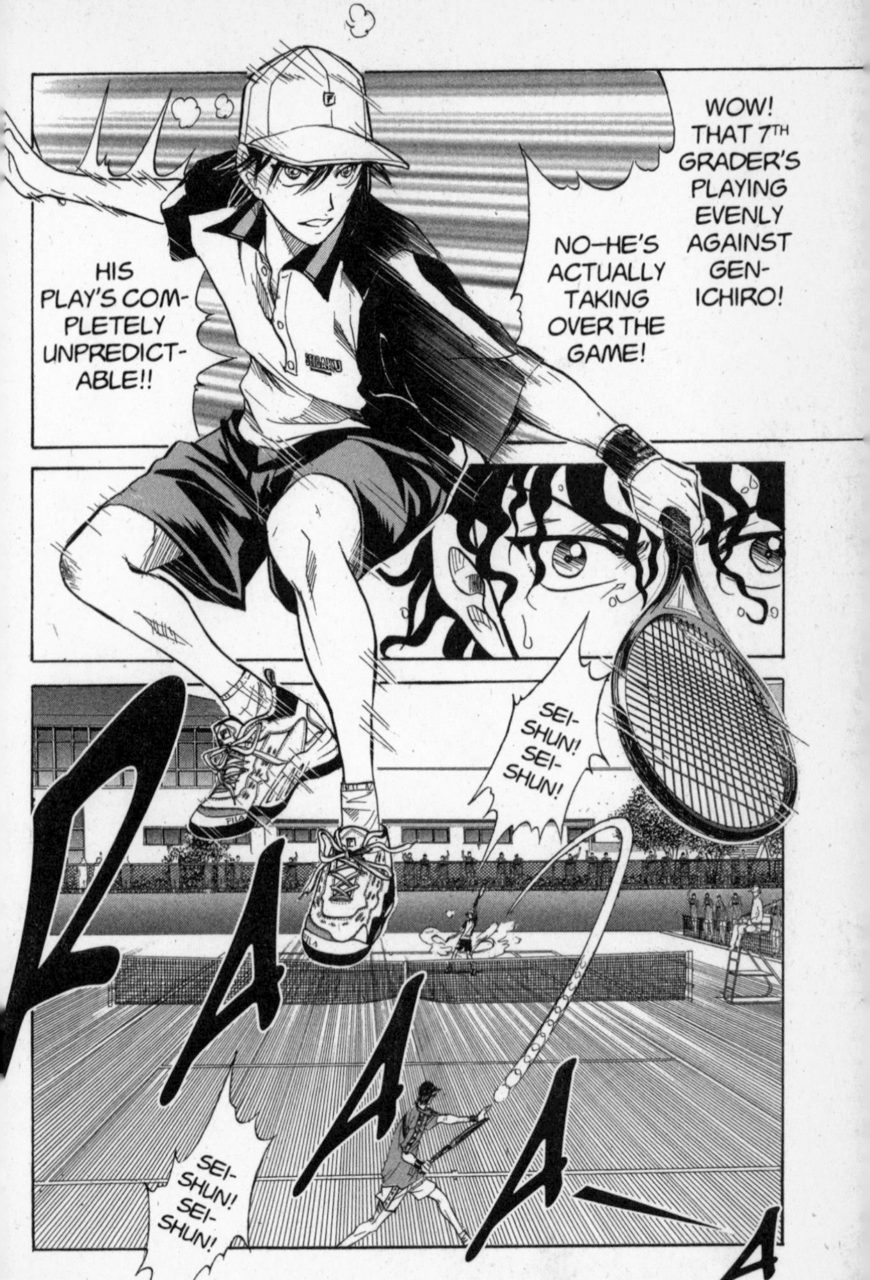
WOW! THAT 7TH GRADER'S PLAYING EVENLY AGAINST GEN-ICHIRO!
NO—HE'S ACTUALLY TAKING OVER THE GAME!
HIS PLAY'S COM-PLETELY UNPREDICT-ABLE!!
SEI-SHUN! SEI-SHUN!
SEI-SHUN! SEI-SHUN!

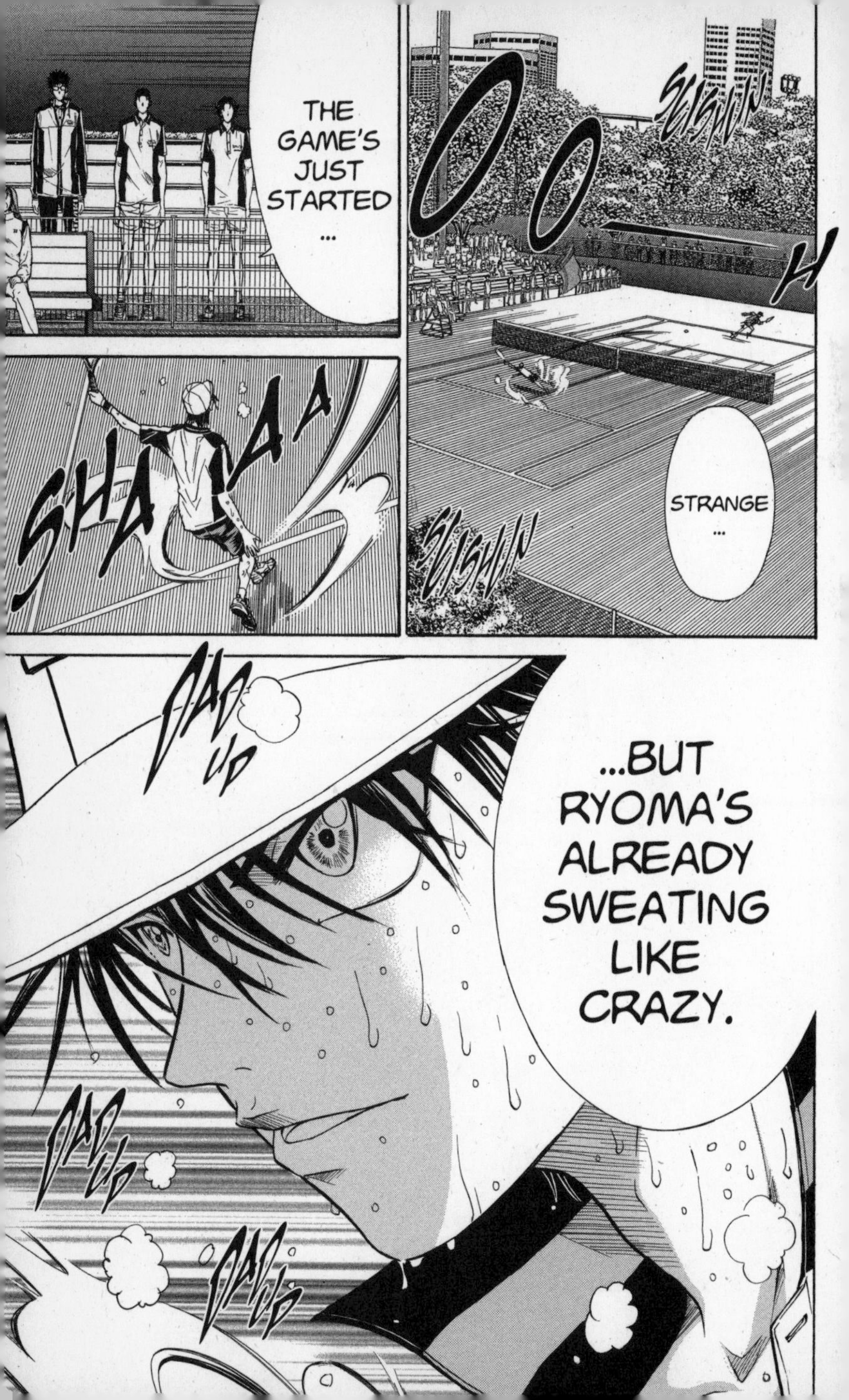

OOH
STRANGE...
THE GAME'S JUST STARTED...
SHAAA
...BUT RYOMA'S ALREADY SWEATING LIKE CRAZY.

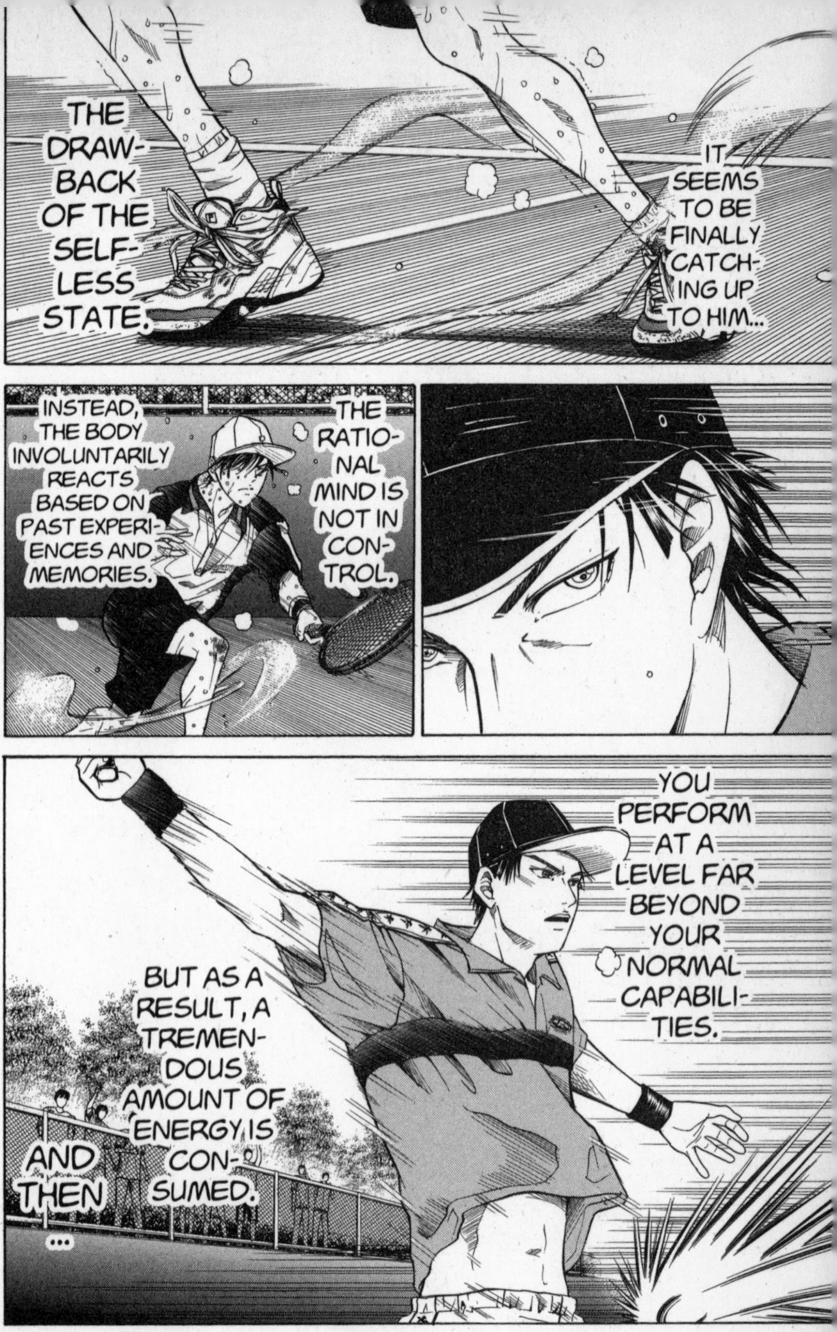
IT SEEMS TO BE FINALLY CATCHING UP TO HIM...
THE DRAWBACK OF THE SELFLESS STATE.
THE RATIONAL MIND IS NOT IN CONTROL.
INSTEAD, THE BODY INVOLUNTARILY REACTS BASED ON PAST EXPERIENCES AND MEMORIES.
YOU PERFORM AT A LEVEL FAR BEYOND YOUR NORMAL CAPABILITIES.
BUT AS A RESULT, A TREMENDOUS AMOUNT OF ENERGY IS CONSUMED.
AND THEN...

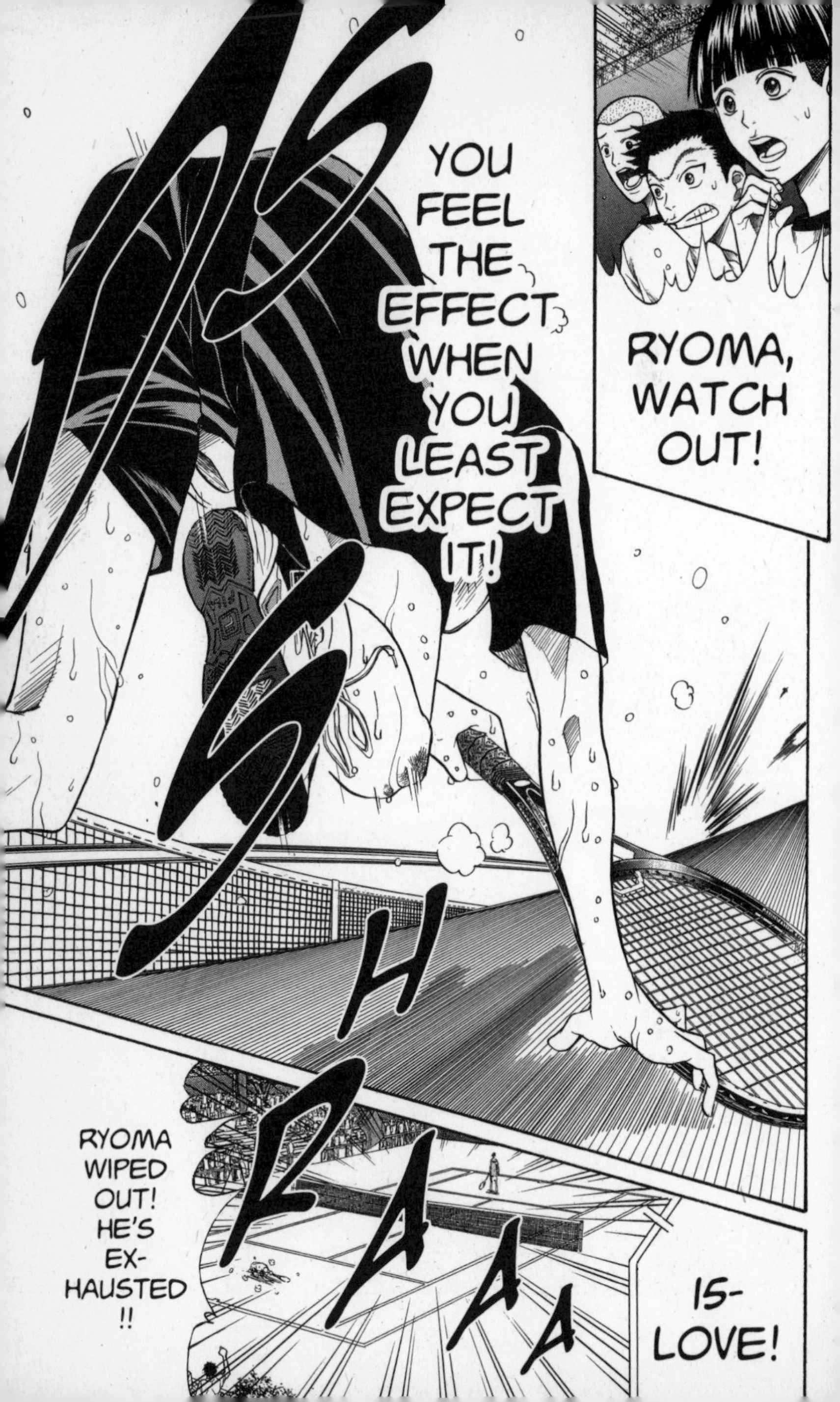
RYOMA, WATCH OUT!
YOU FEEL THE EFFECT WHEN YOU LEAST EXPECT IT!
15-LOVE!
RYOMA WIPED OUT! HE'S EX-HAUSTED!!

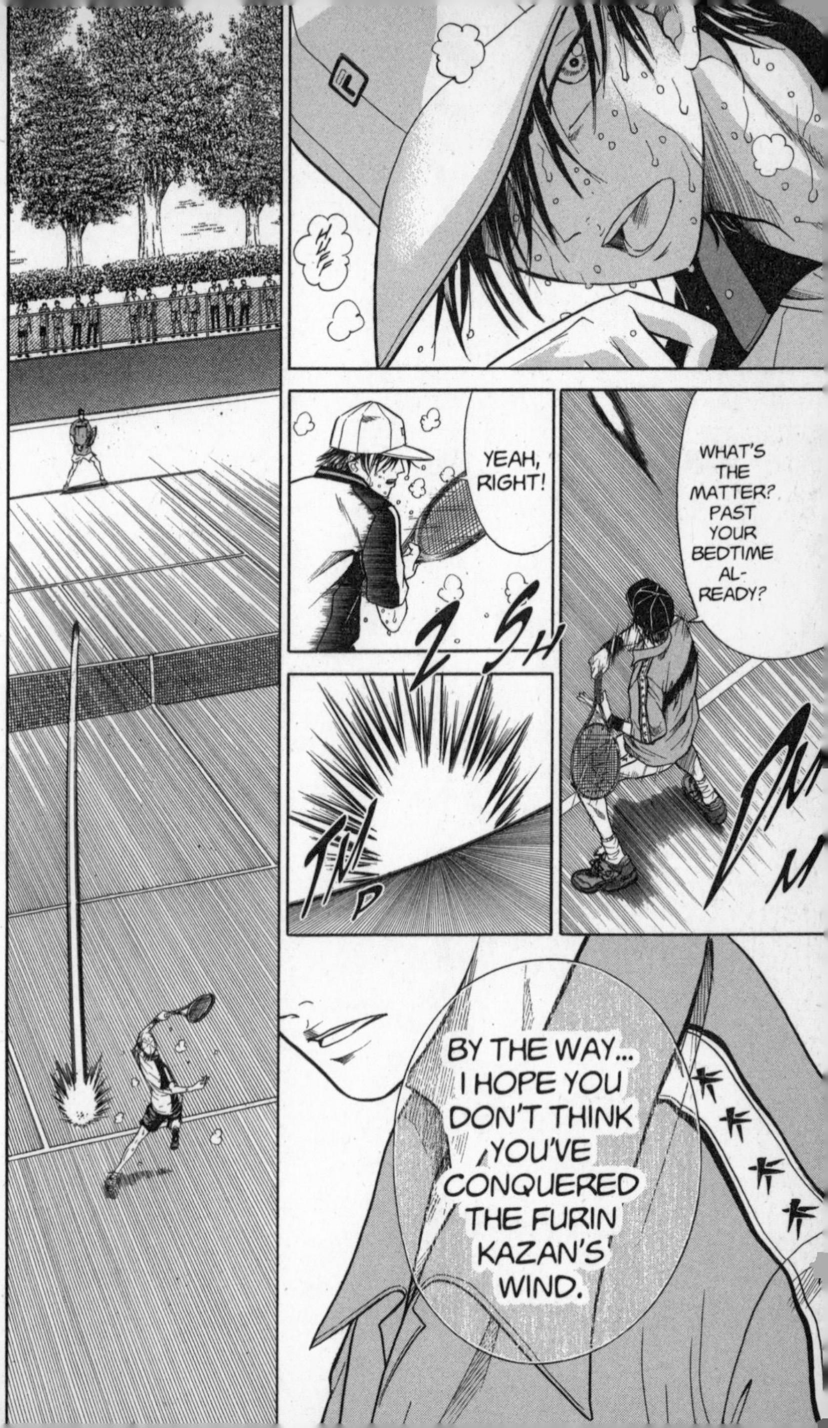
WHAT'S THE MATTER? PAST YOUR BEDTIME AL-READY?
YEAH, RIGHT!
ZSH
BY THE WAY... I HOPE YOU DON'T THINK YOU'VE CONQUERED THE FURIN KAZAN'S WIND.

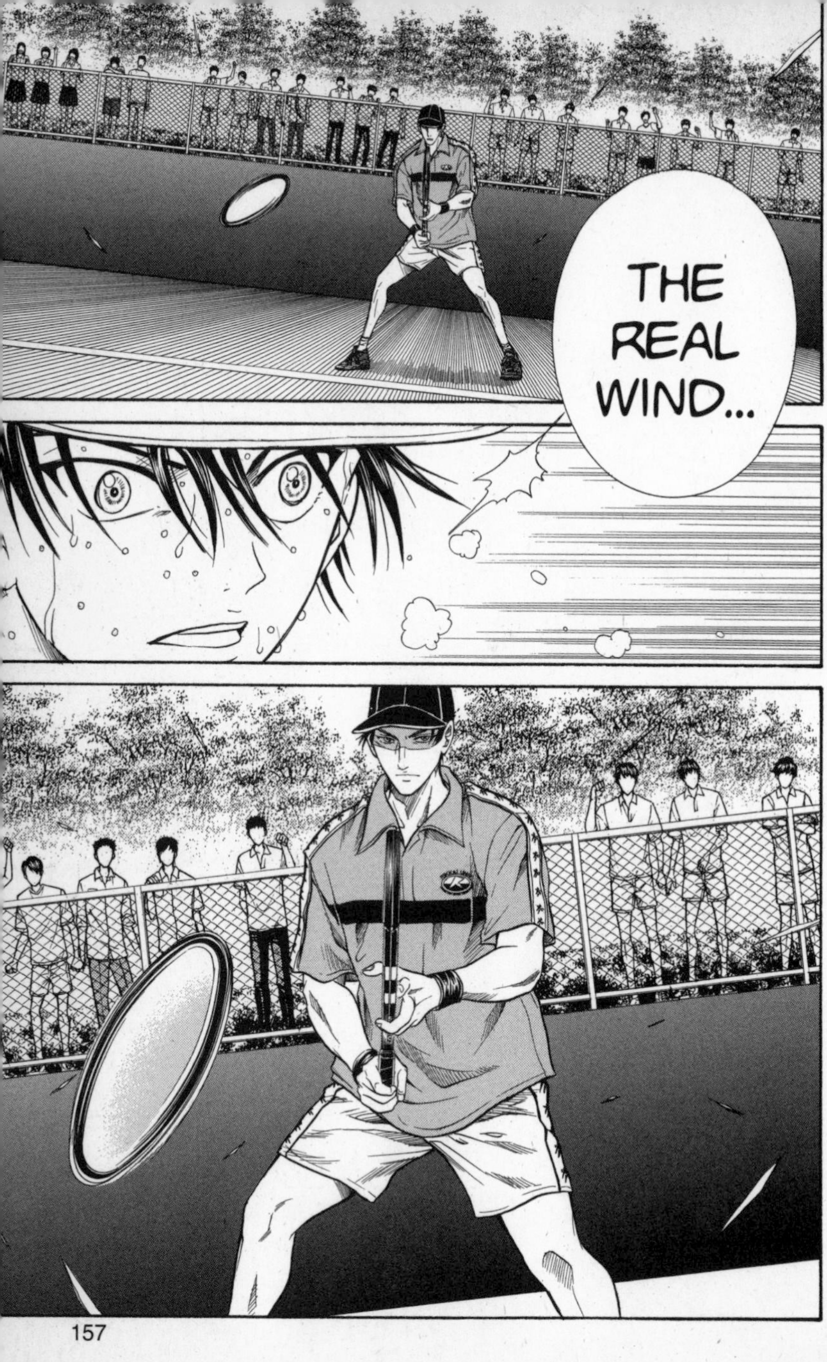
THE REAL WIND...

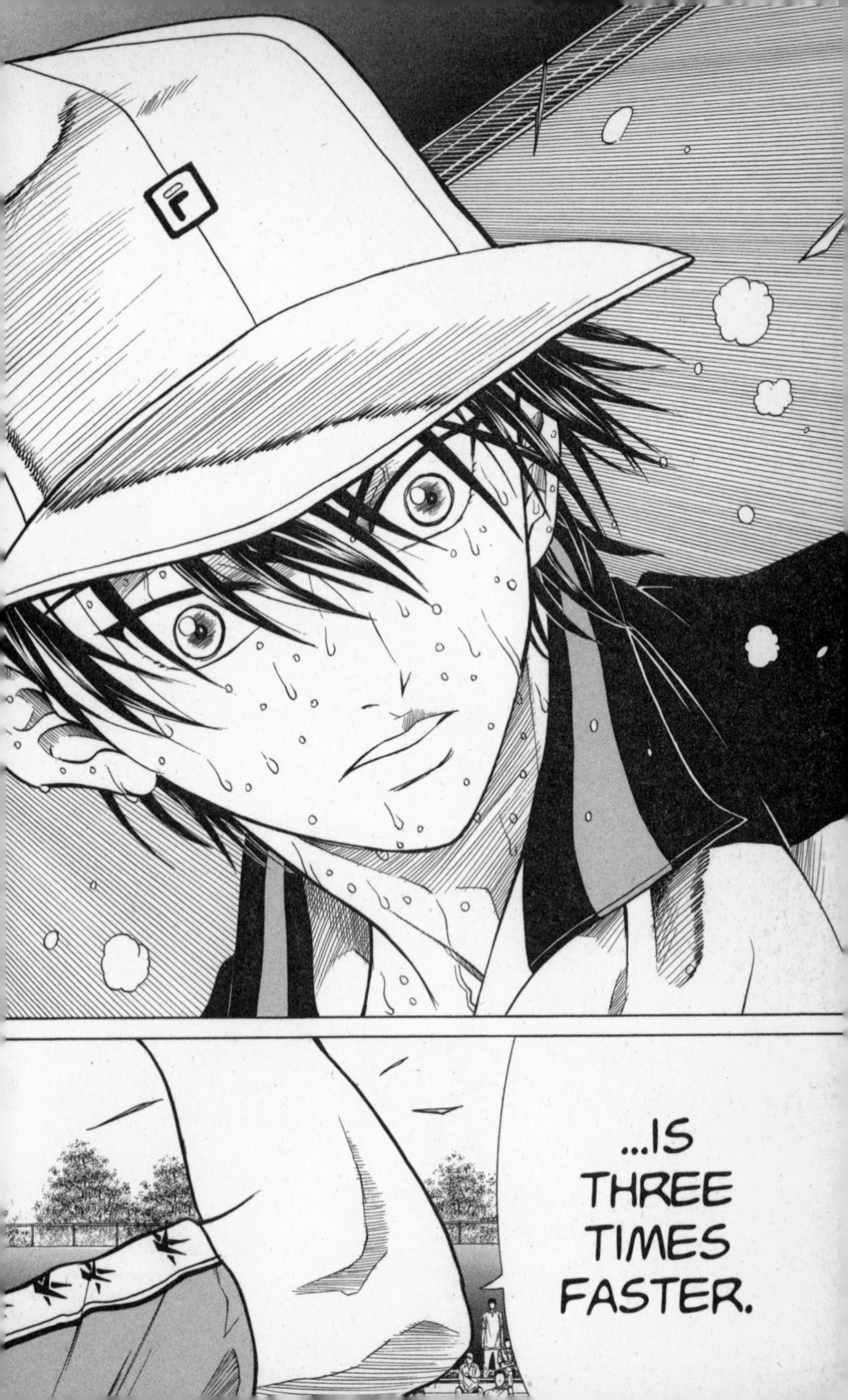
...IS
THREE
TIMES
FASTER.

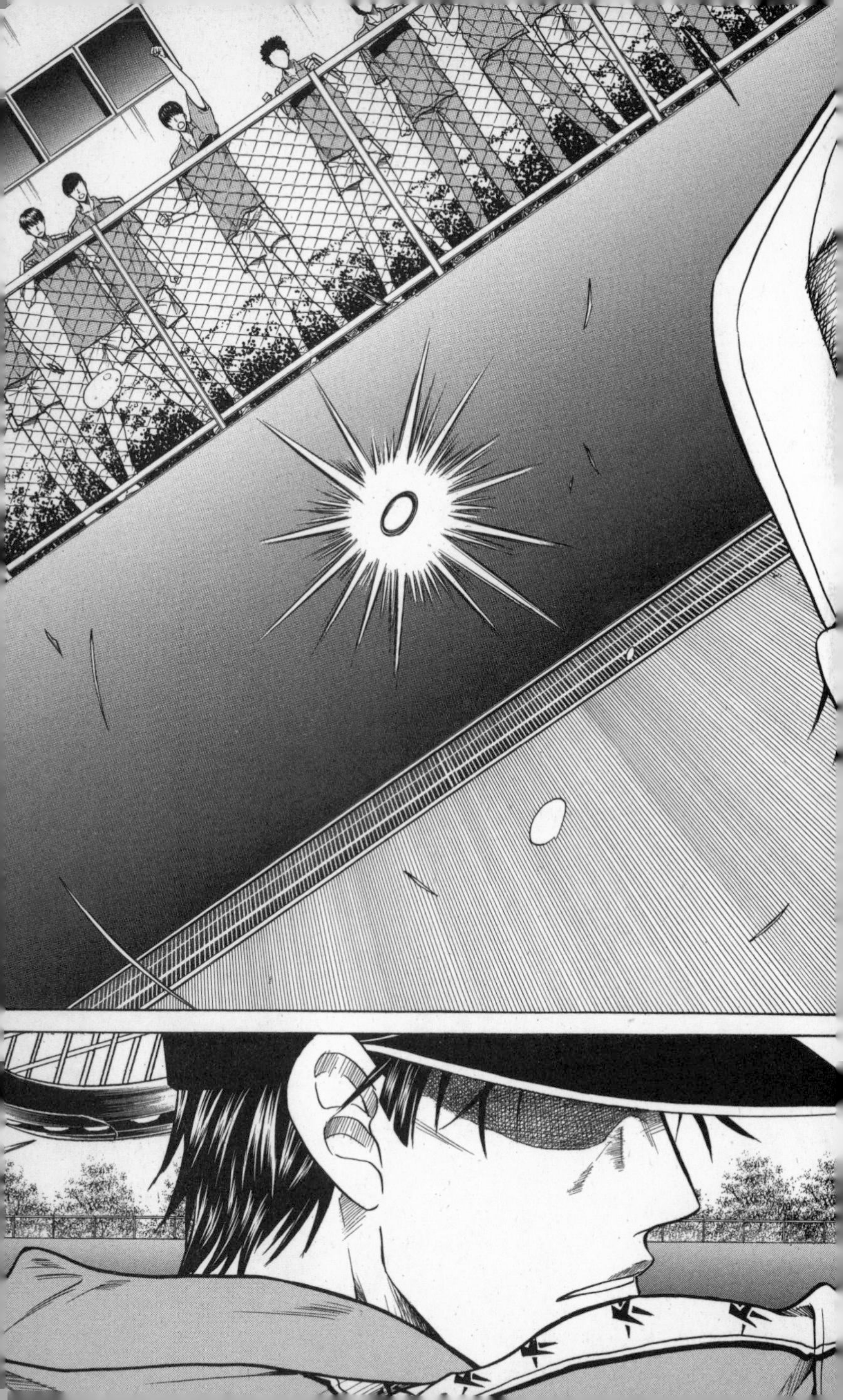

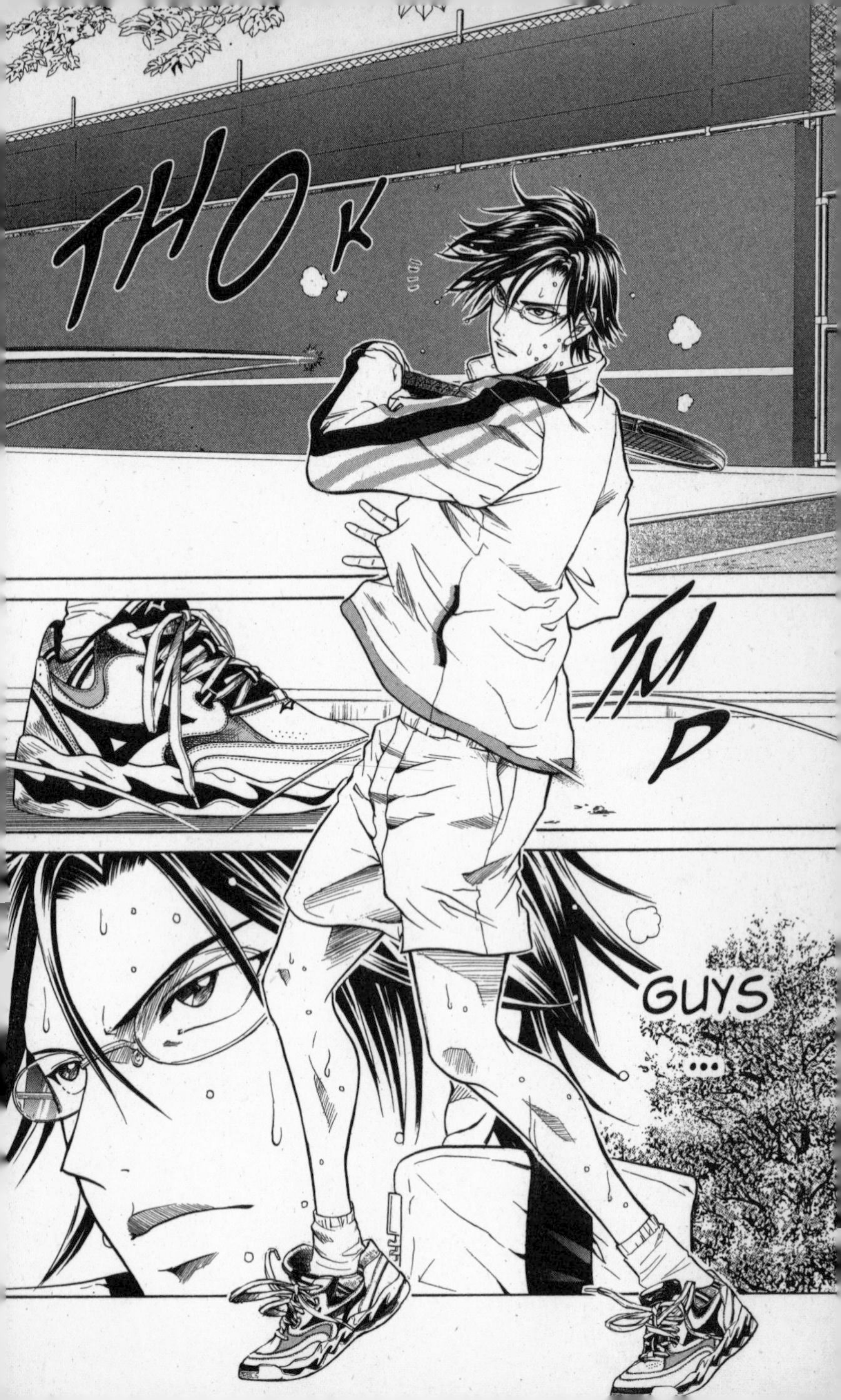
THOK
TMD
GUYS...

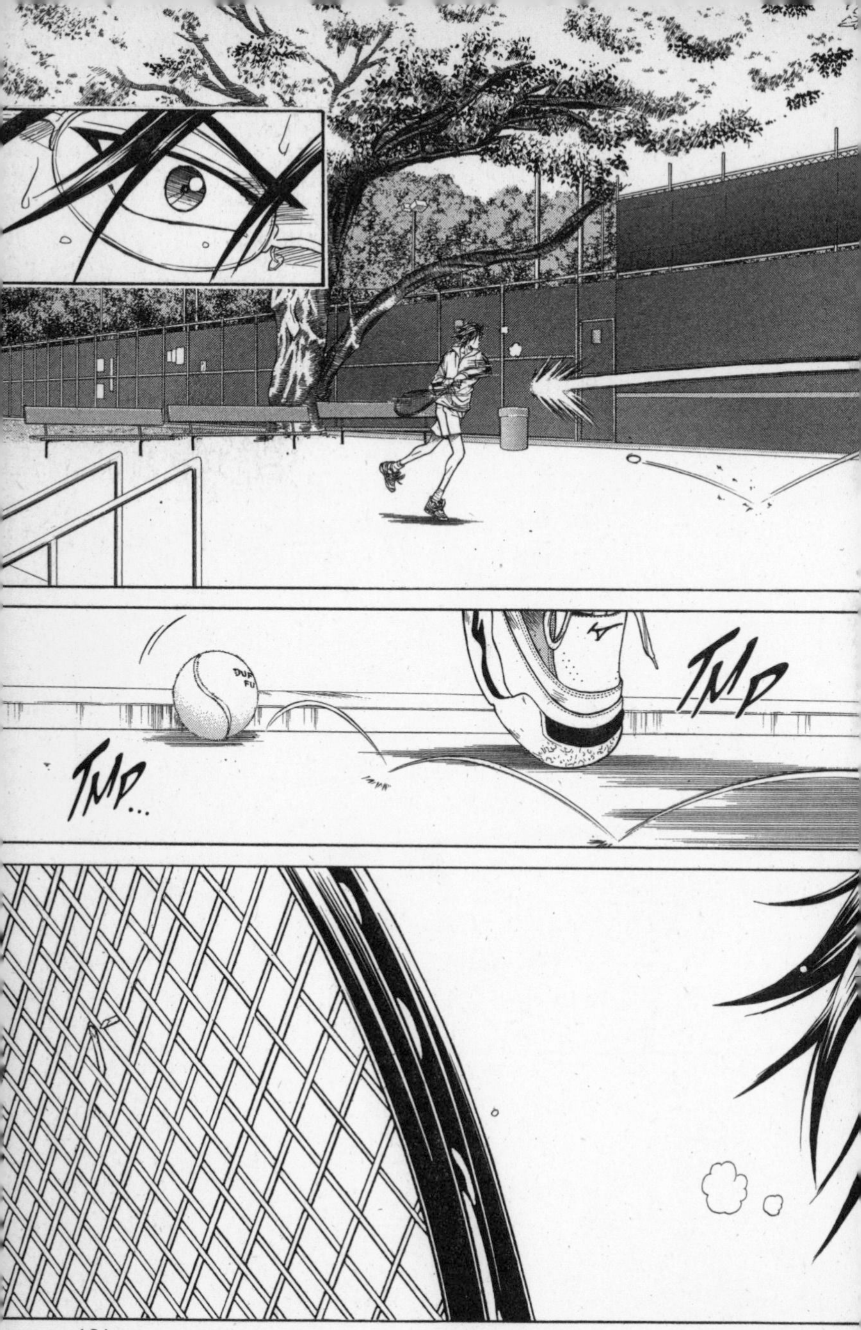
TMP
TMP...

Thank you for reading *The Prince of Tennis*, volume 26.

The last volume was finished so close to the deadline that we didn't have time to put in an Author Note. So I was touched when we received letters asking to please include a note in the next volume.

The movie is only a month and a half away from release! The fantastic crew that's been developing the anime version for a little over three years worked really hard on it. (I did too.) I'm sure all of you will enjoy it. And more great news! Volume 27 will be released earlier than normal! It'll be out next month!! (Waa! What am I gonna do?!)

Thanks for all your warm support this year, and keep your eyes open for more exciting tennis coming next year!!

T. Konomi
2004. 11. 2

Send fan letters to: Takeshi Konomi, *The Prince of Tennis*, c/o VIZ Media LLC, P.O. Box 77010, San Francisco, CA 94107

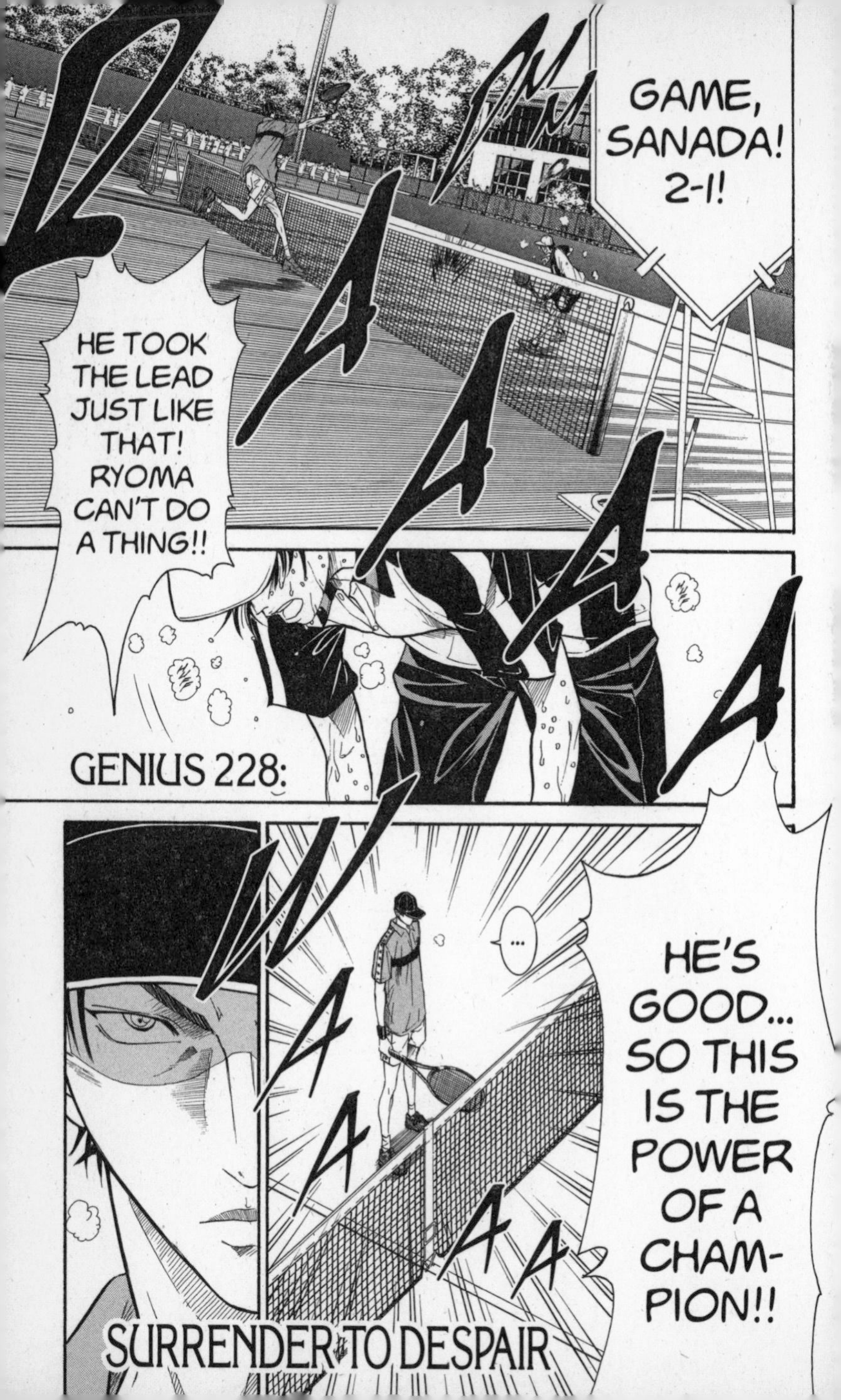
GAME, SANADA! 2-1!
HE TOOK THE LEAD JUST LIKE THAT! RYOMA CAN'T DO A THING!!
GENIUS 228:
...
HE'S GOOD... SO THIS IS THE POWER OF A CHAMPION!!
SURRENDER TO DESPAIR

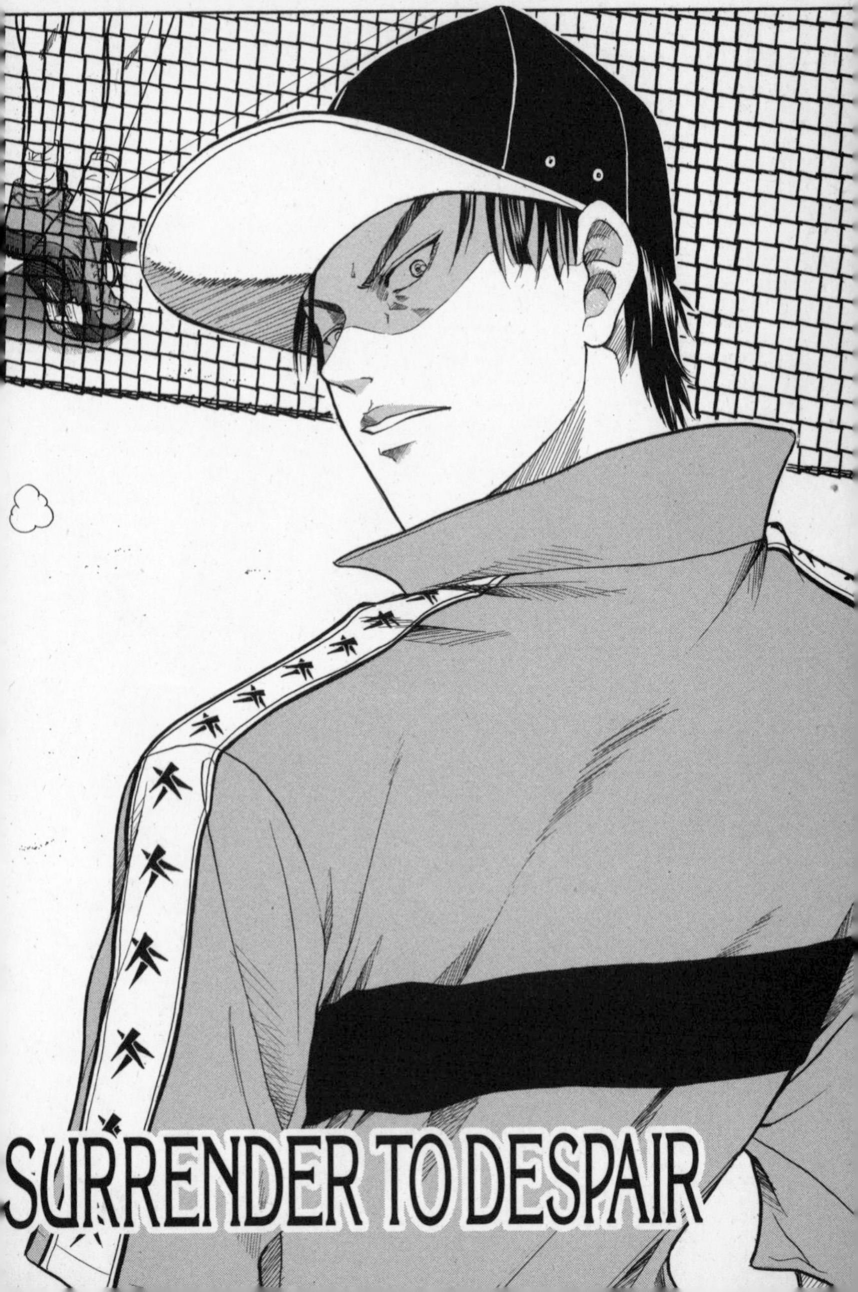
SURRENDER TO DESPAIR

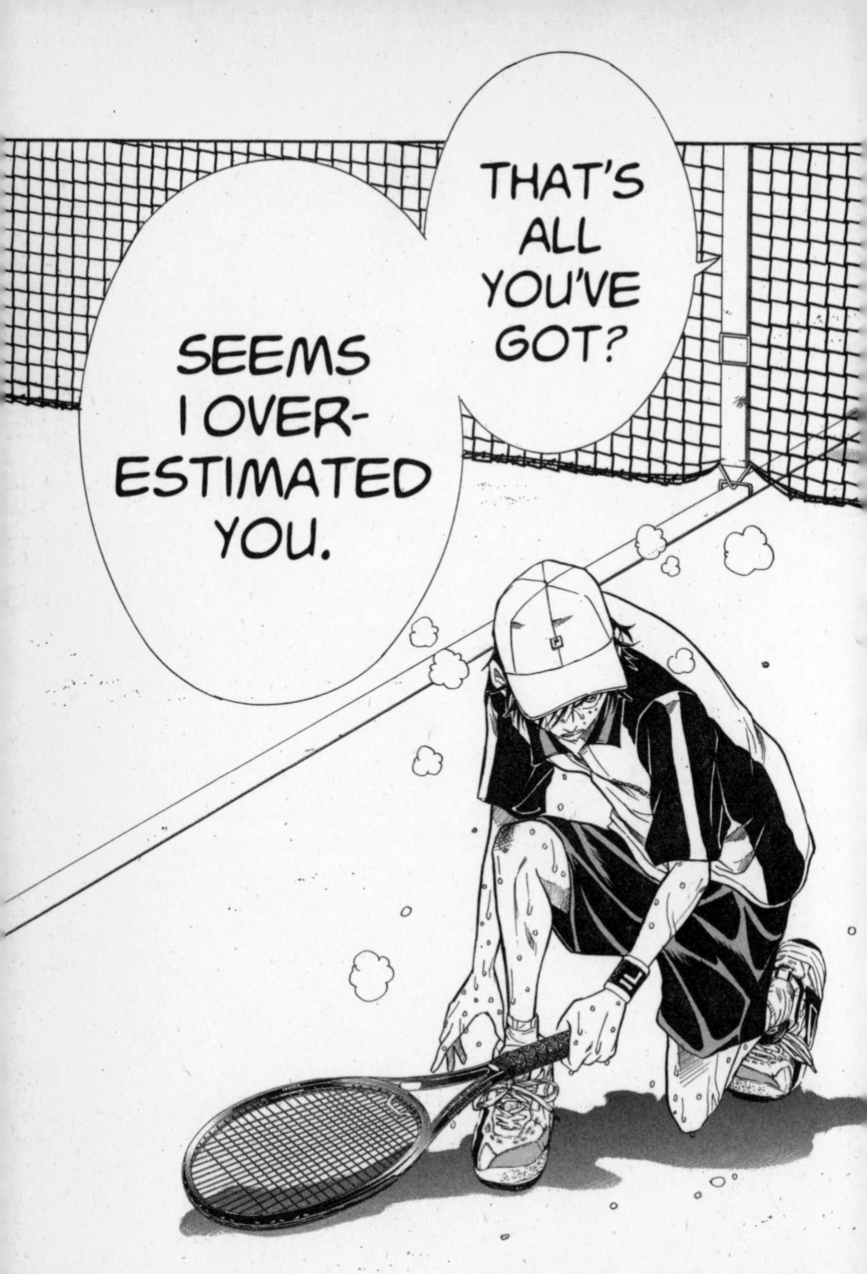
THAT'S ALL YOU'VE GOT?
SEEMS I OVER-ESTIMATED YOU.

GENIUS-228:

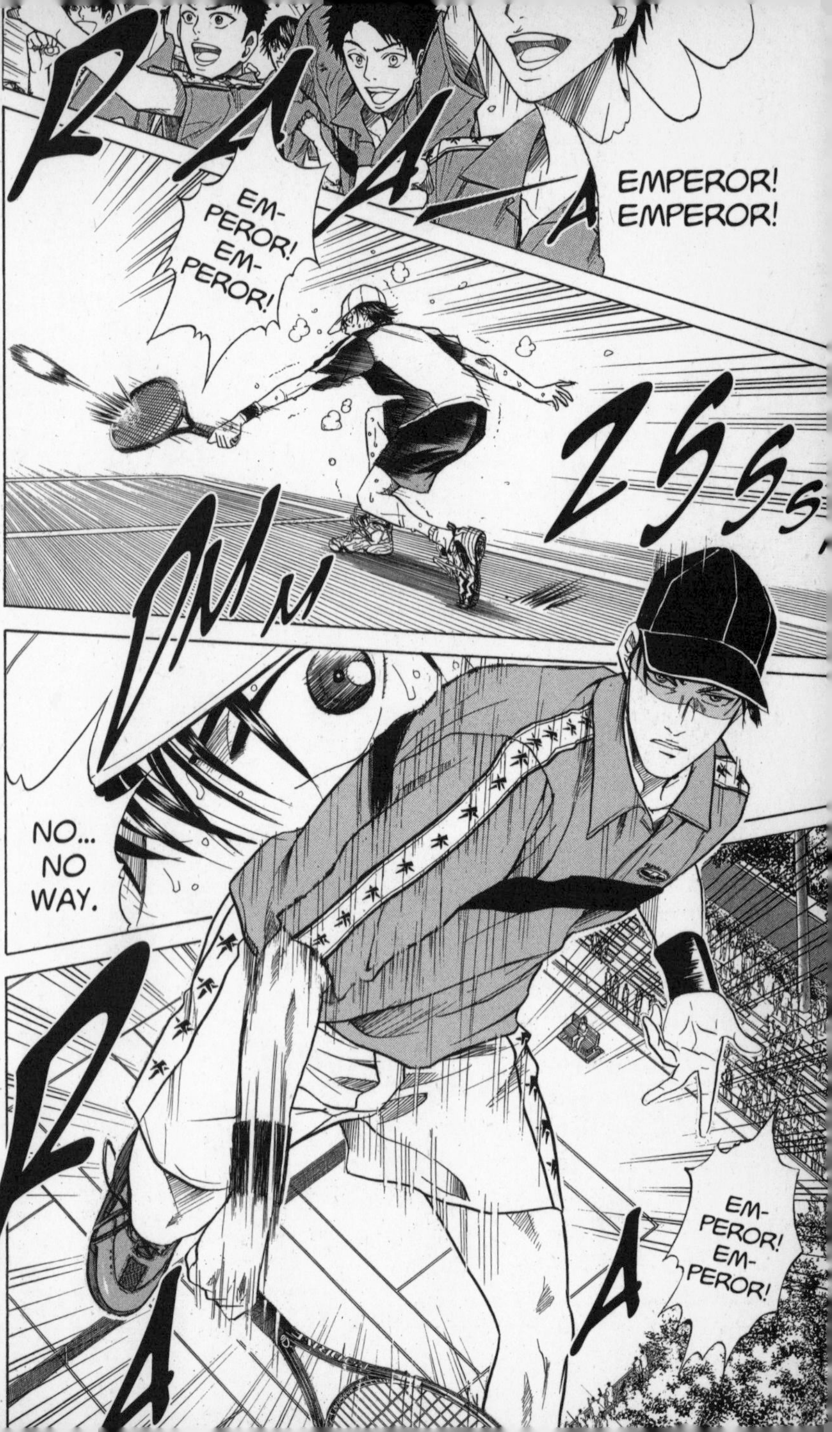
EMPEROR! EMPEROR!
EM-PEROR! EM-PEROR!
NO... NO WAY.
EM-PEROR! EM-PEROR!

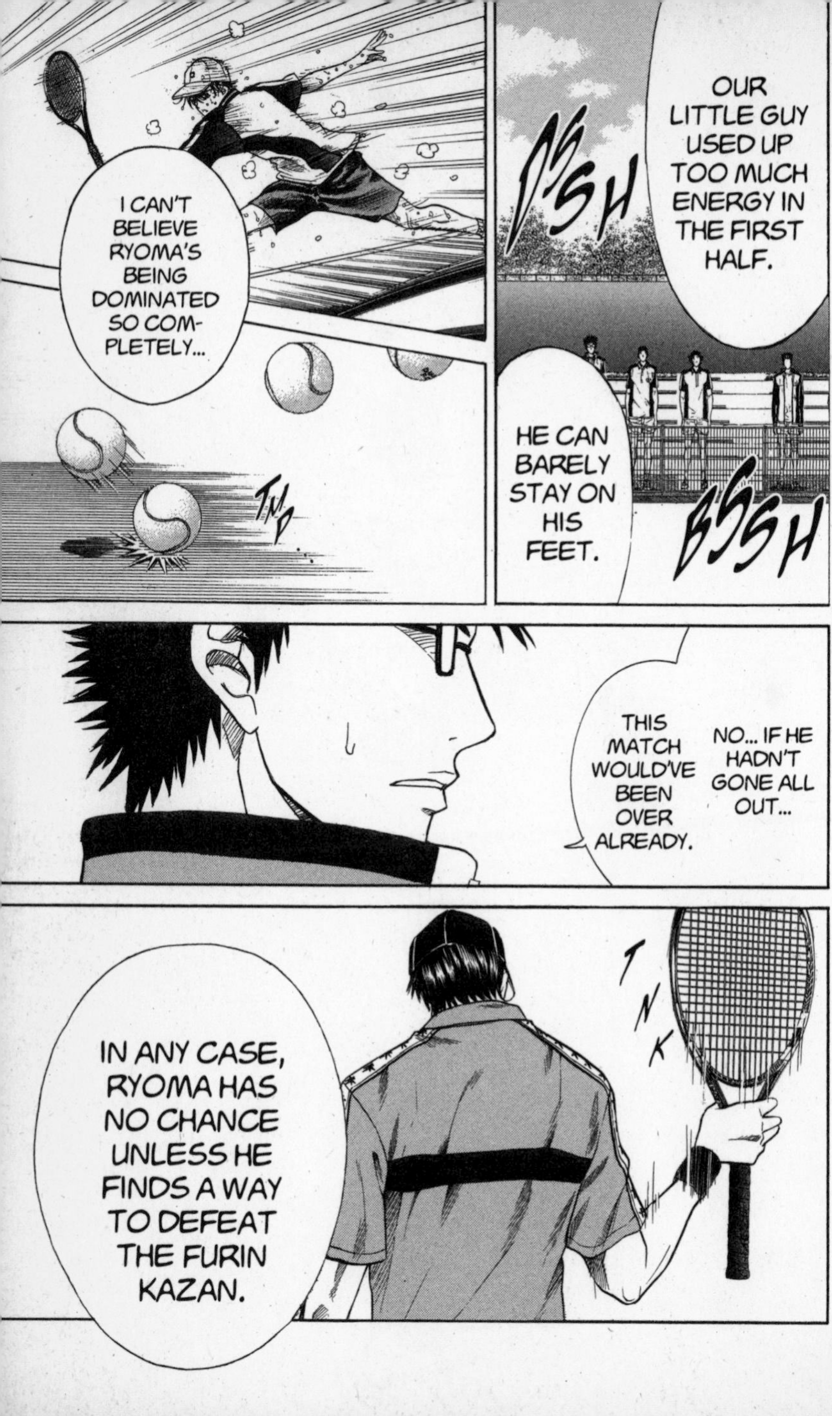
OUR LITTLE GUY USED UP TOO MUCH ENERGY IN THE FIRST HALF.
HE CAN BARELY STAY ON HIS FEET.
BSSH
I CAN'T BELIEVE RYOMA'S BEING DOMINATED SO COM-PLETELY...
TMP
NO... IF HE HADN'T GONE ALL OUT...
THIS MATCH WOULD'VE BEEN OVER ALREADY.
TNK
IN ANY CASE, RYOMA HAS NO CHANCE UNLESS HE FINDS A WAY TO DEFEAT THE FURIN KAZAN.

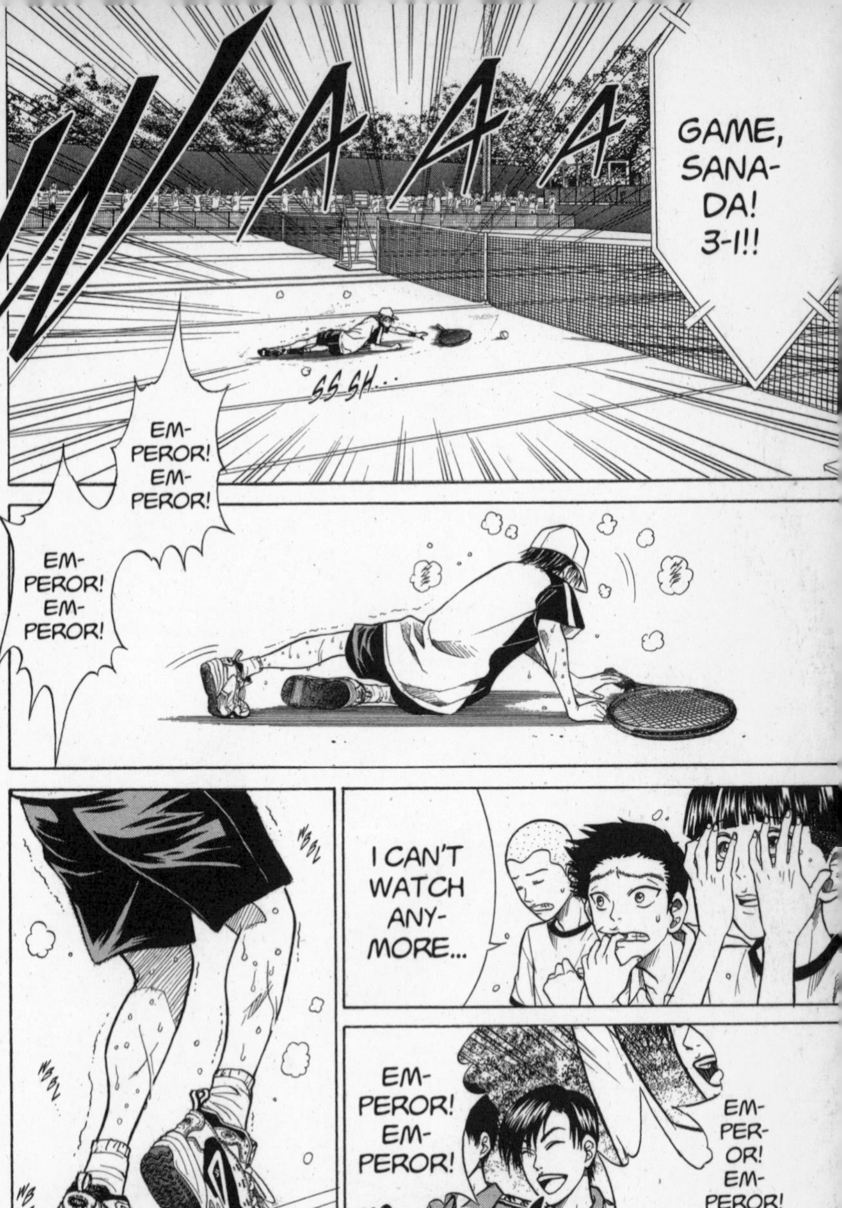
WAAAA
GAME, SANA-DA! 3-1!!
SS SH...
EM-PEROR! EM-PEROR!
EM-PEROR! EM-PEROR!
I CAN'T WATCH ANY-MORE...
EM-PER-OR! EM-PEROR!
EM-PEROR! EM-PEROR!
EM-PEROR! EM-PEROR!
RAA

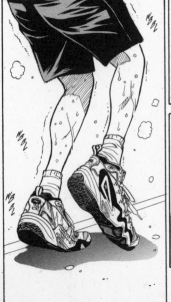

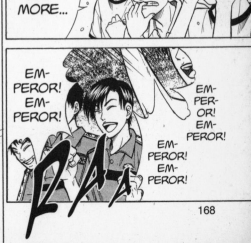

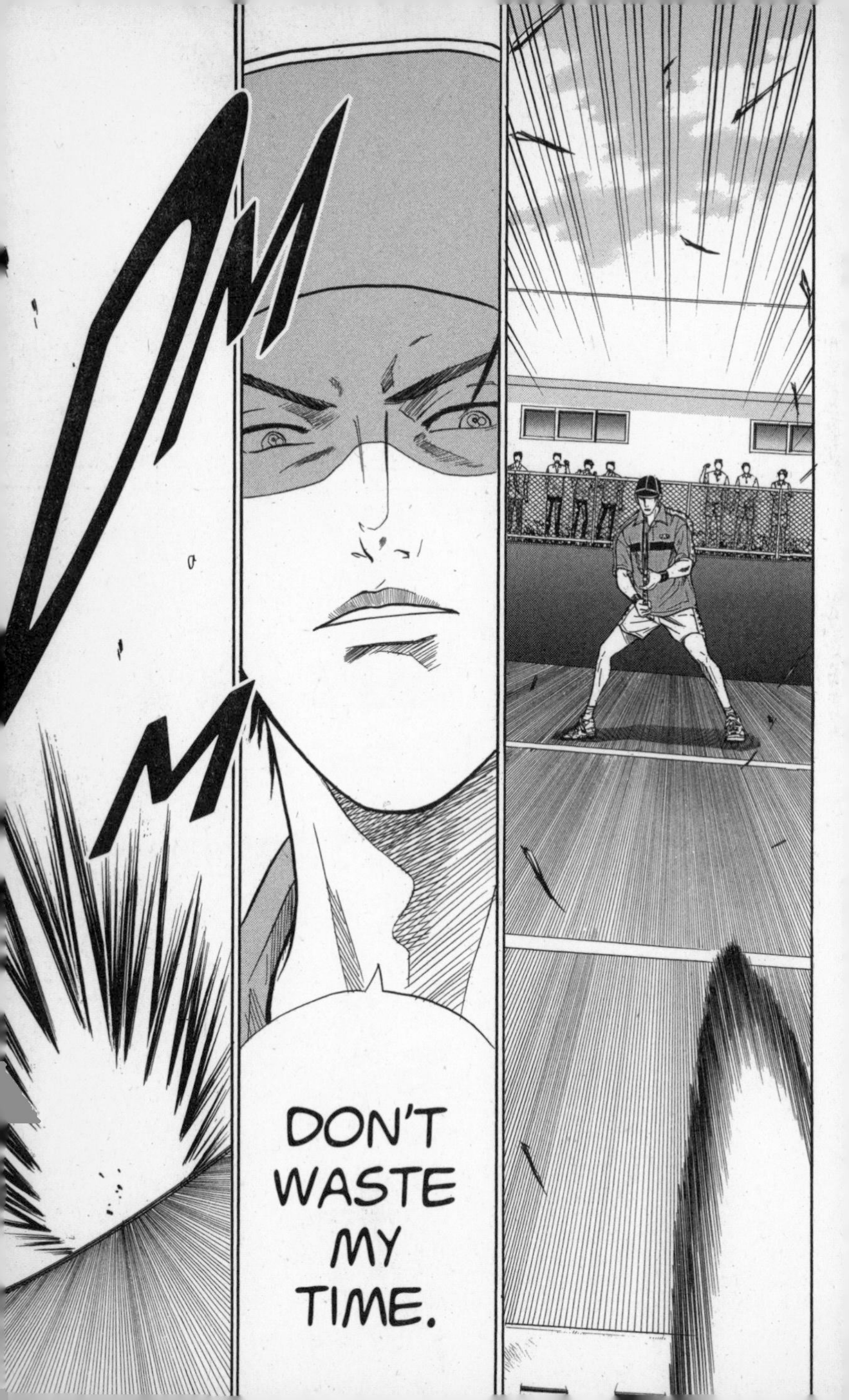
DON'T WASTE MY TIME.

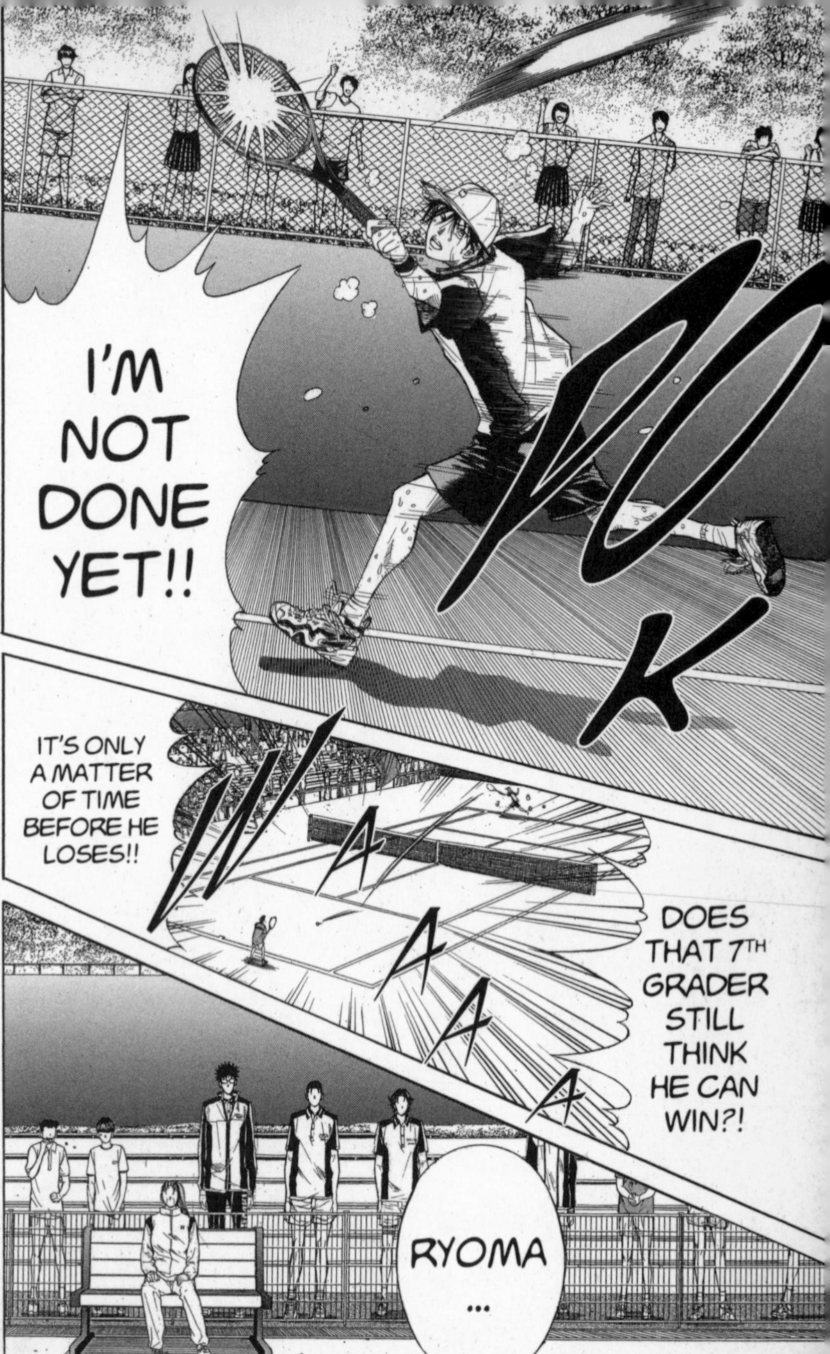
I'M NOT DONE YET!!
DOES THAT 7TH GRADER STILL THINK HE CAN WIN?!
IT'S ONLY A MATTER OF TIME BEFORE HE LOSES!!
WAAAA
RYOMA ...

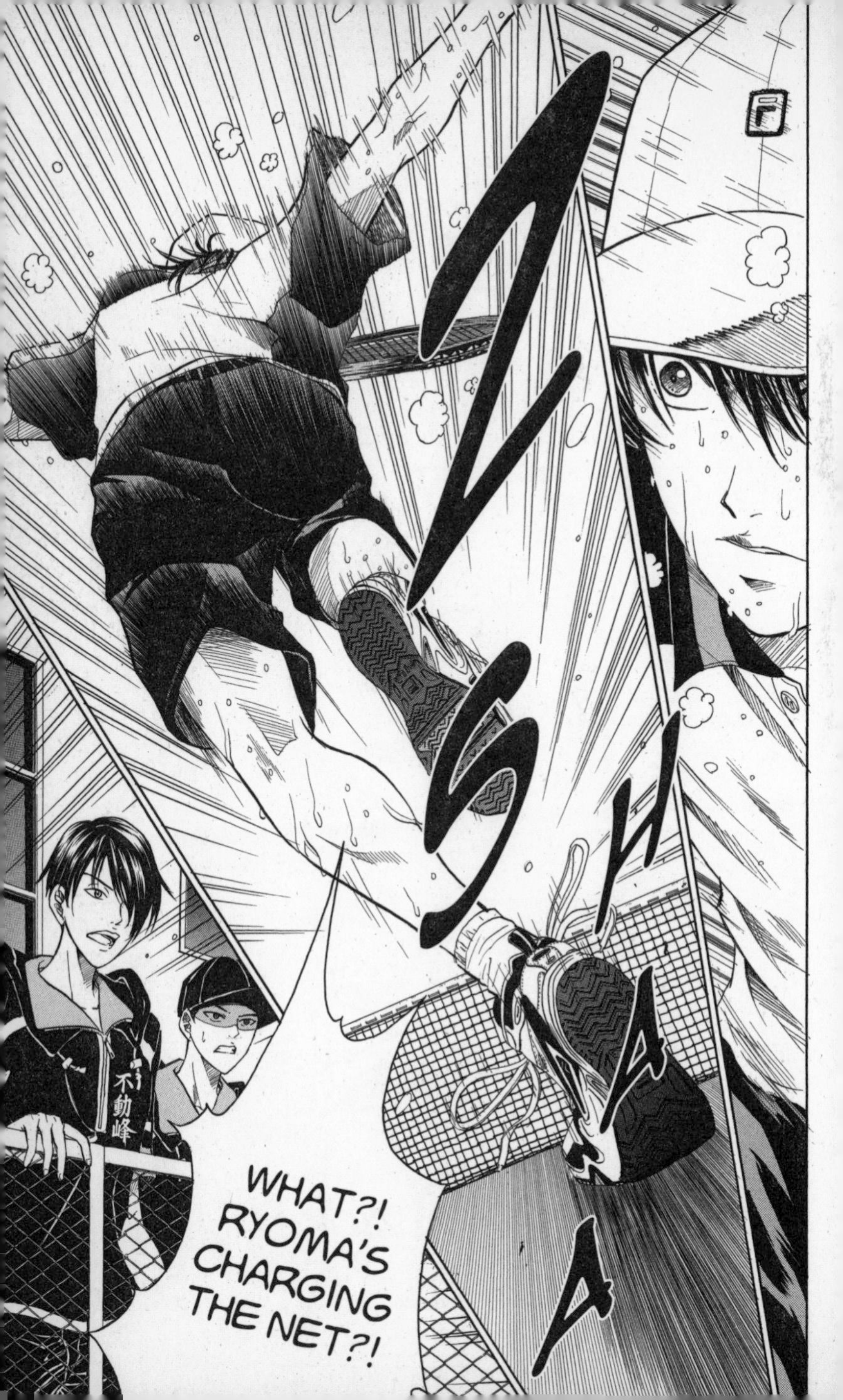
WHAT?! RYOMA'S CHARGING THE NET?!
不動峰

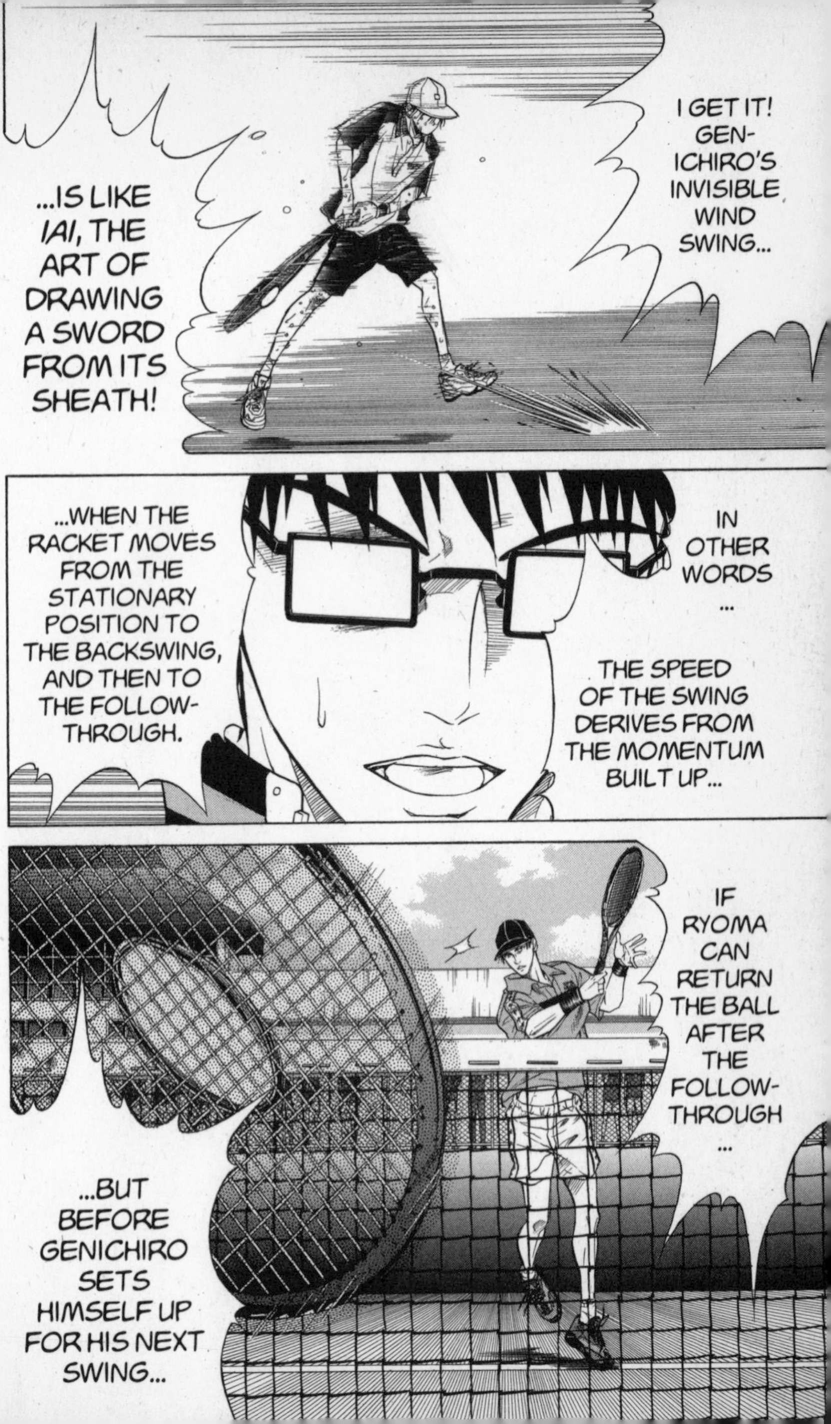
I GET IT! GEN-ICHIRO'S INVISIBLE WIND SWING...
...IS LIKE *IAI*, THE ART OF DRAWING A SWORD FROM ITS SHEATH!
IN OTHER WORDS...
THE SPEED OF THE SWING DERIVES FROM THE MOMENTUM BUILT UP...
...WHEN THE RACKET MOVES FROM THE STATIONARY POSITION TO THE BACKSWING, AND THEN TO THE FOLLOW-THROUGH.
IF RYOMA CAN RETURN THE BALL AFTER THE FOLLOW-THROUGH...
...BUT BEFORE GENICHIRO SETS HIMSELF UP FOR HIS NEXT SWING...

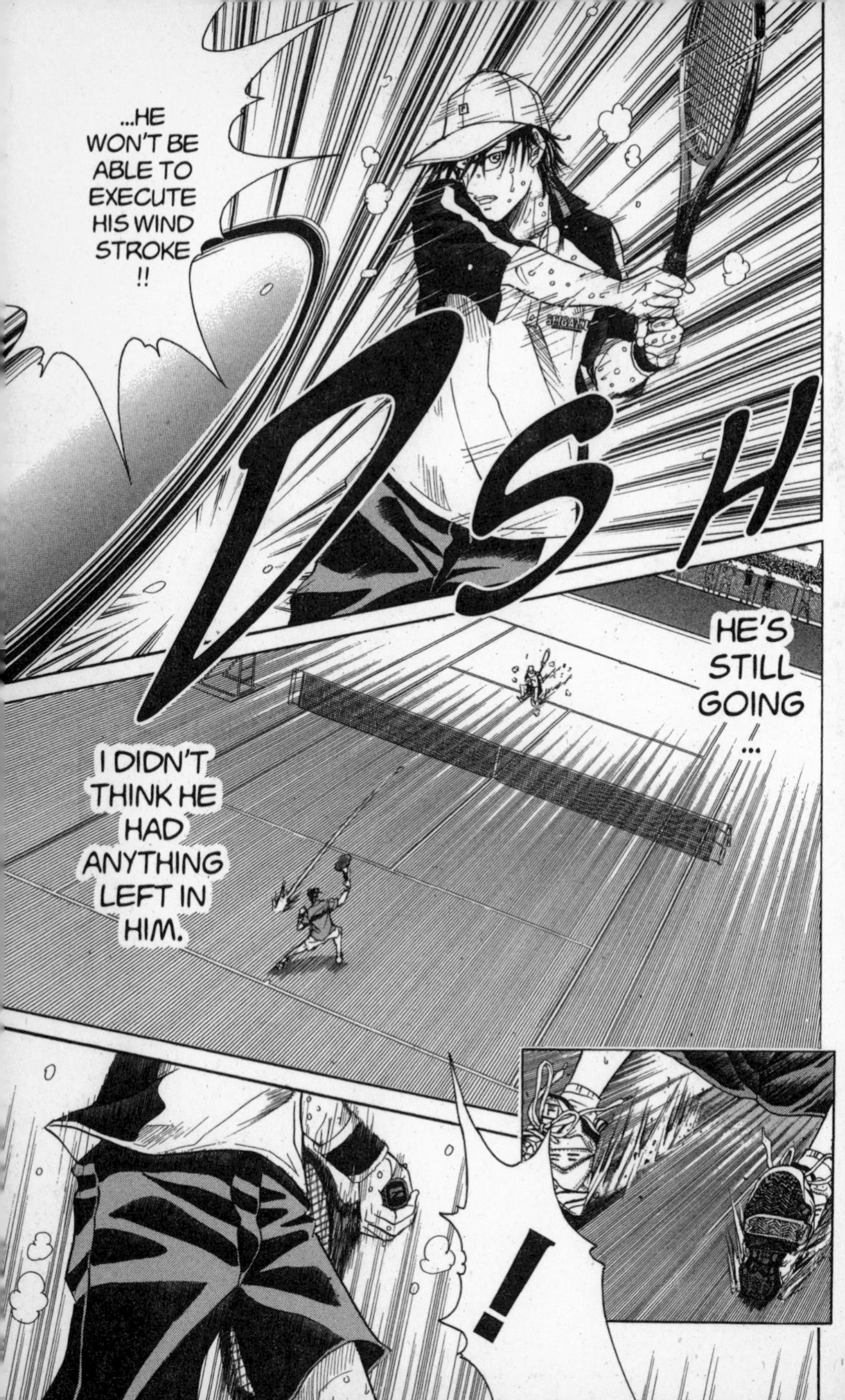
...HE WON'T BE ABLE TO EXECUTE HIS WIND STROKE !!
DSH
HE'S STILL GOING ...
I DIDN'T THINK HE HAD ANYTHING LEFT IN HIM.
!

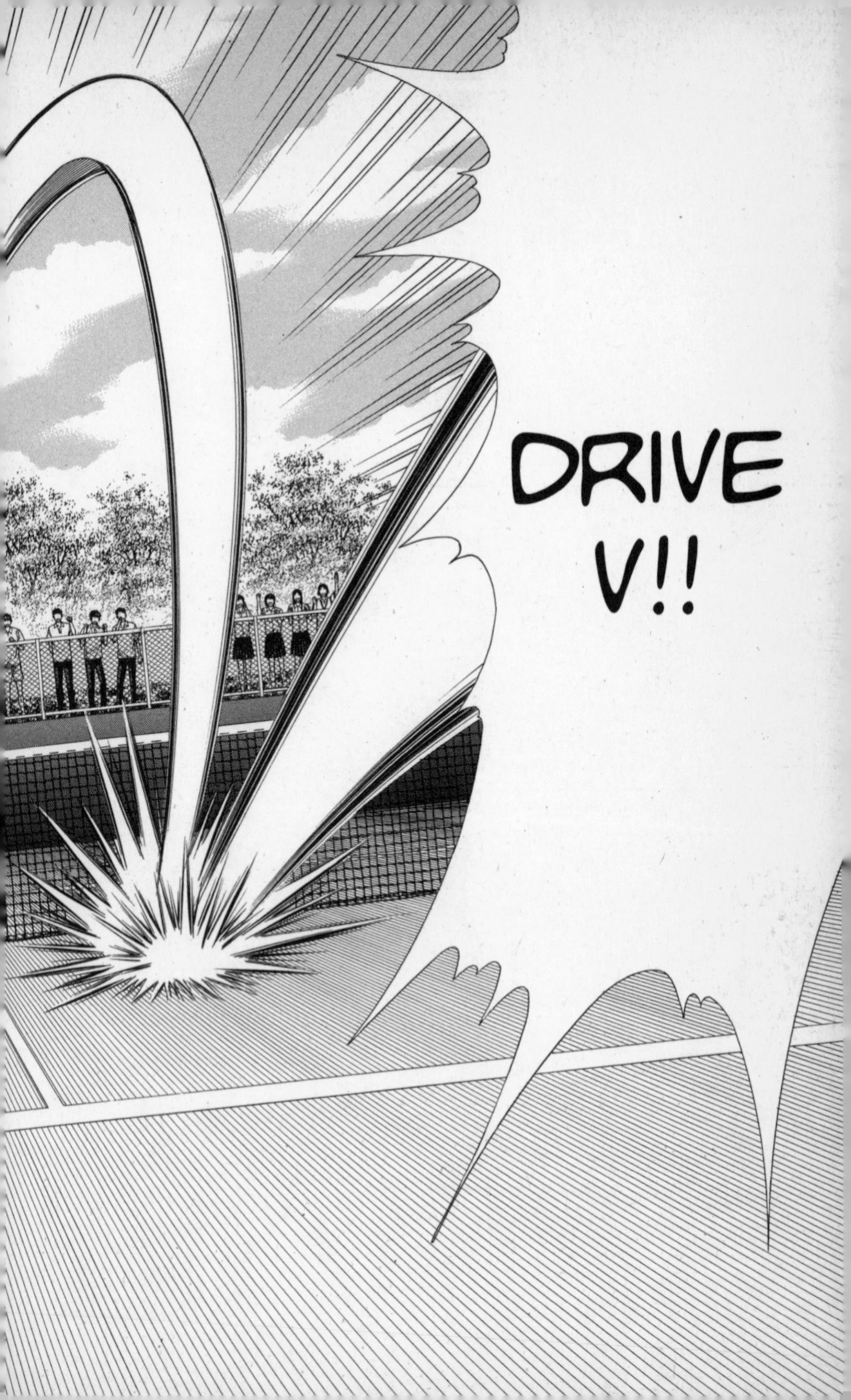
DRIVE V!!

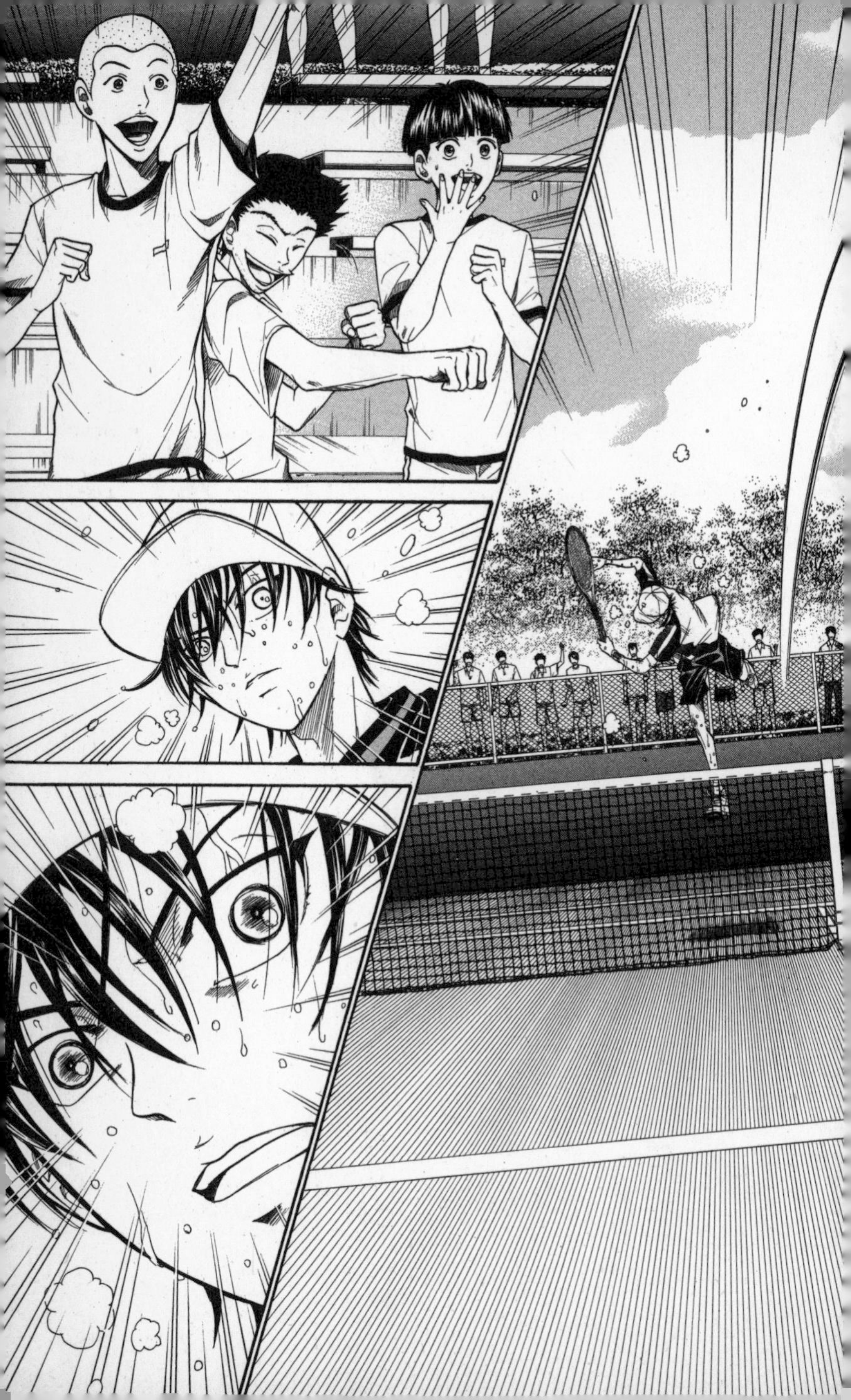

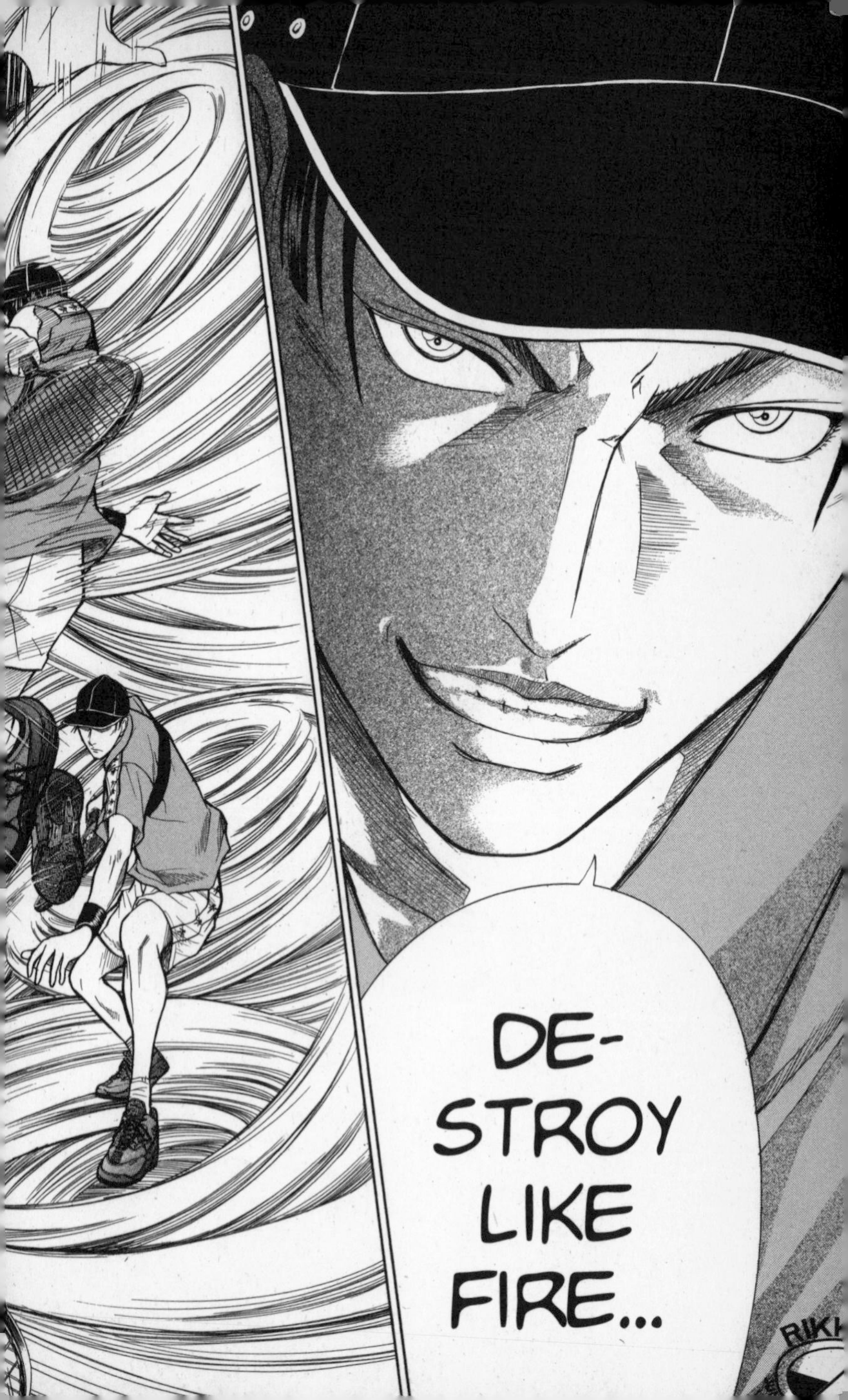
DE-STROY LIKE FIRE...

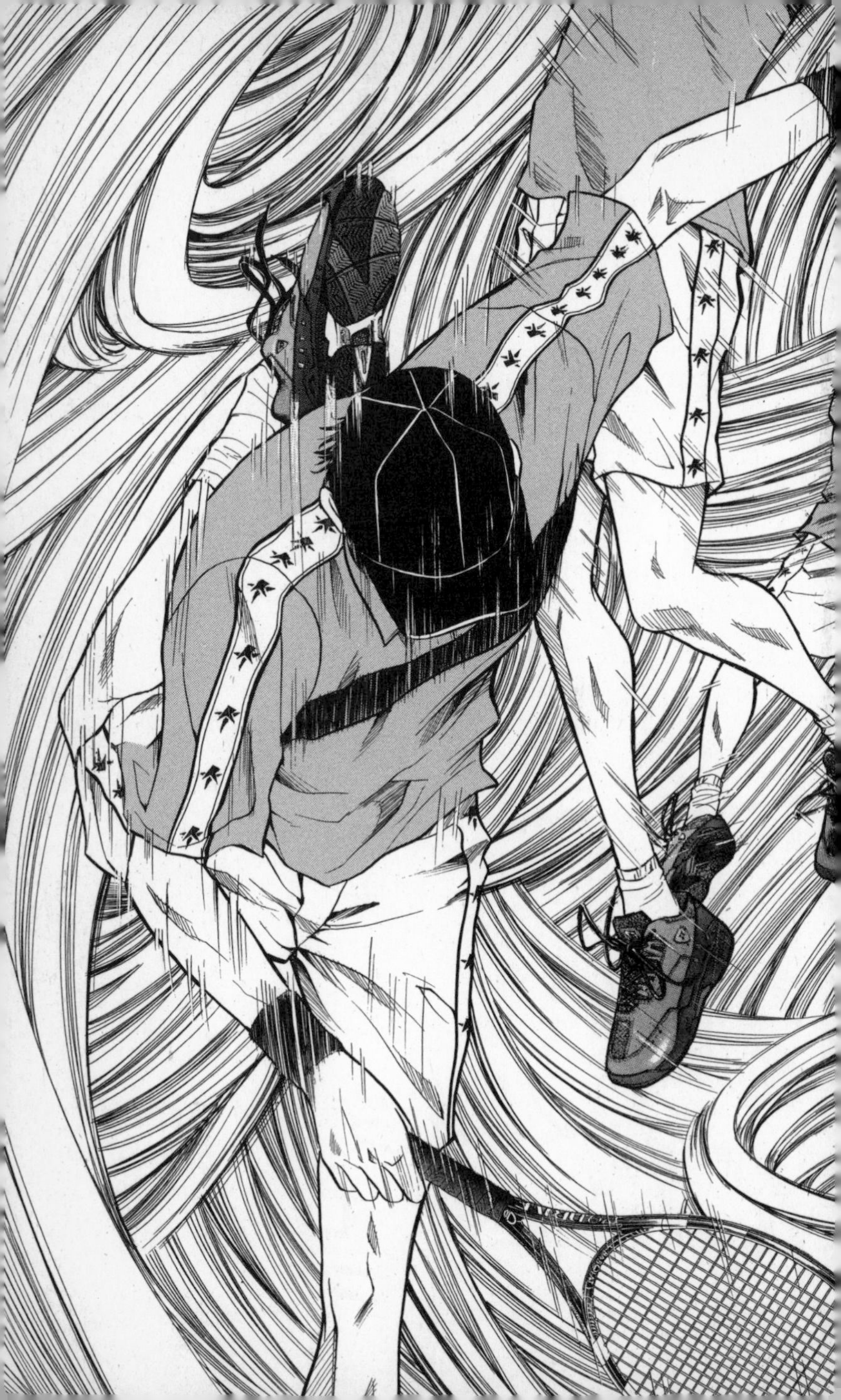

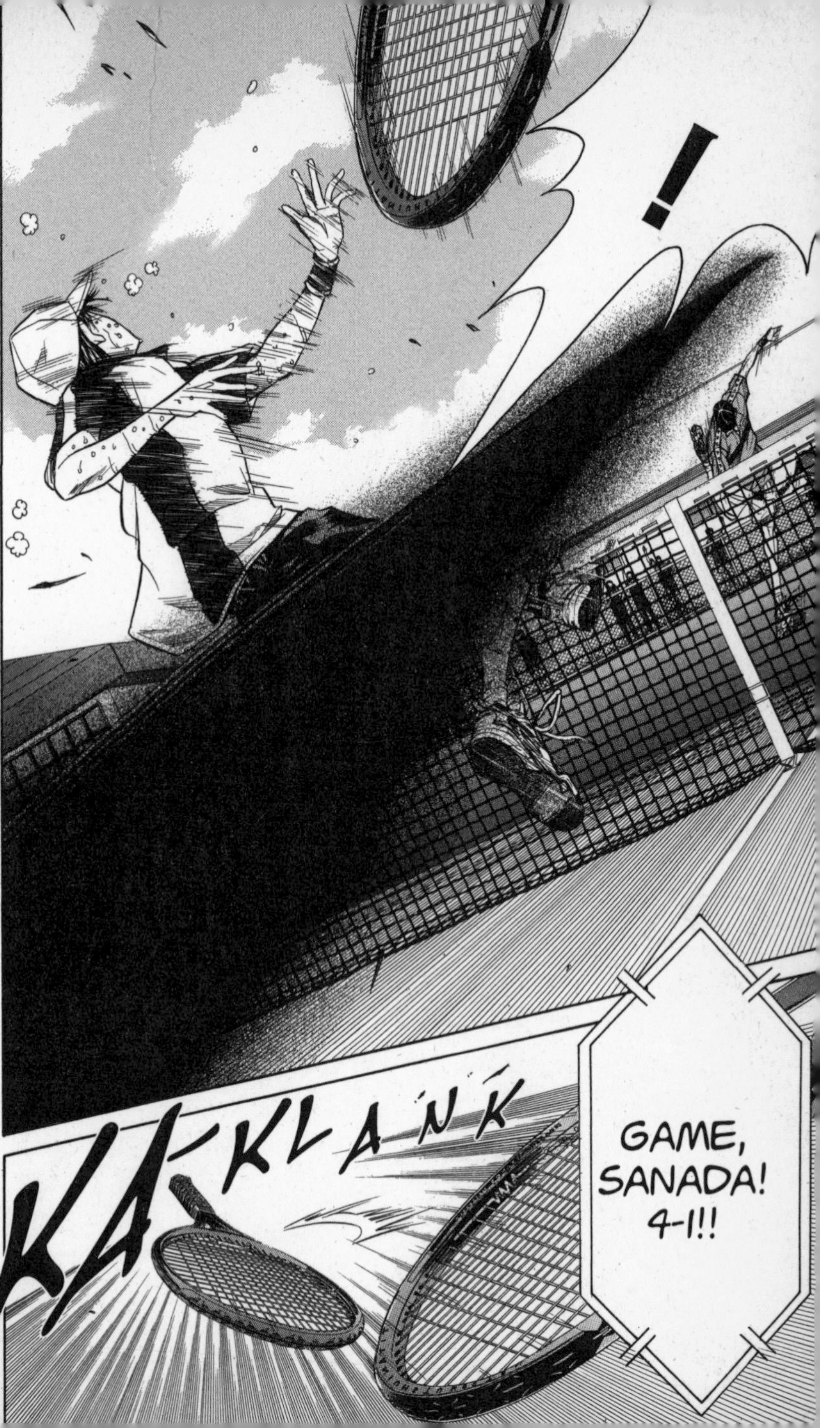
!
KA-KLANK
GAME, SANADA! 4-1!!

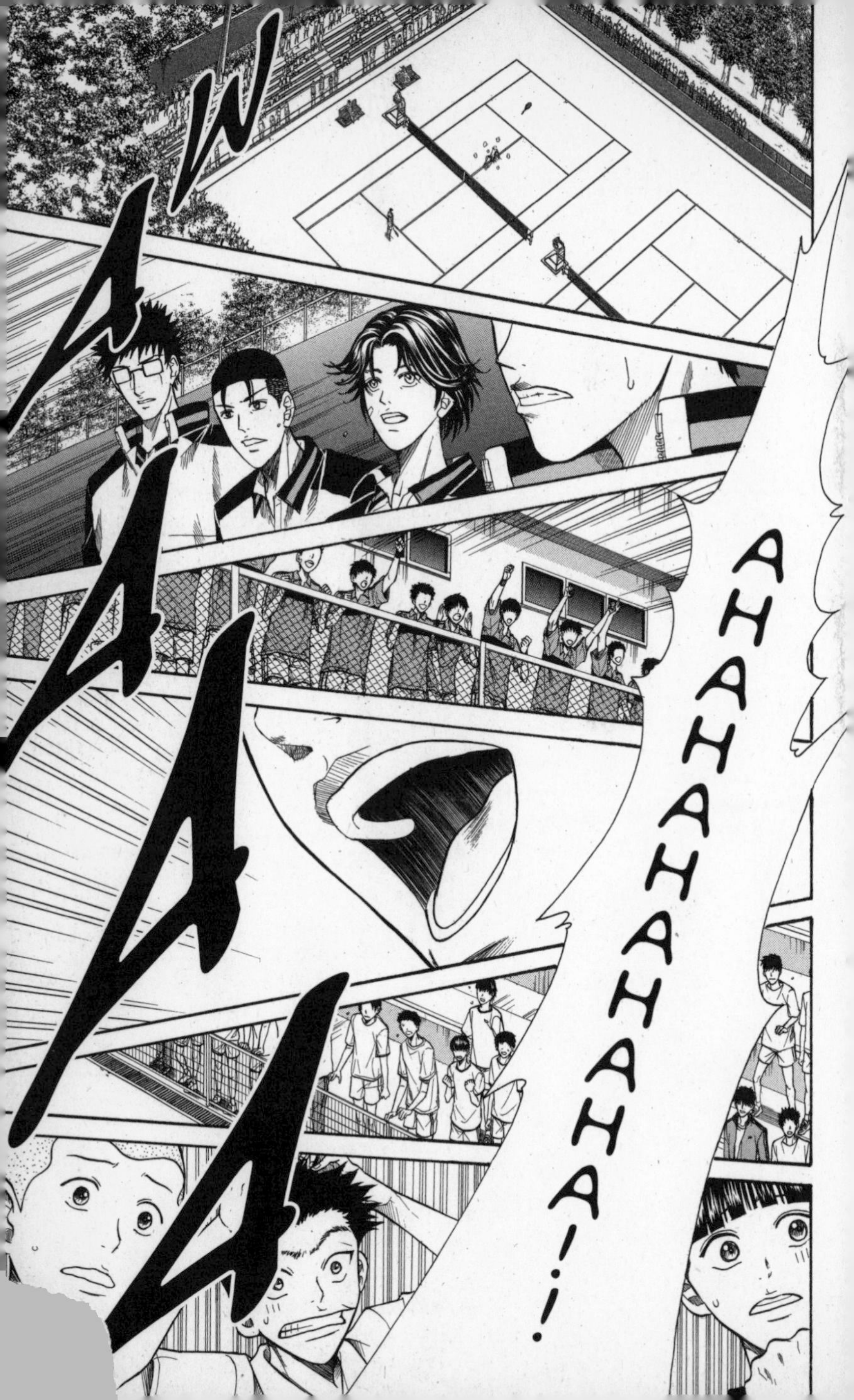
AHAHAHAHAHA!!

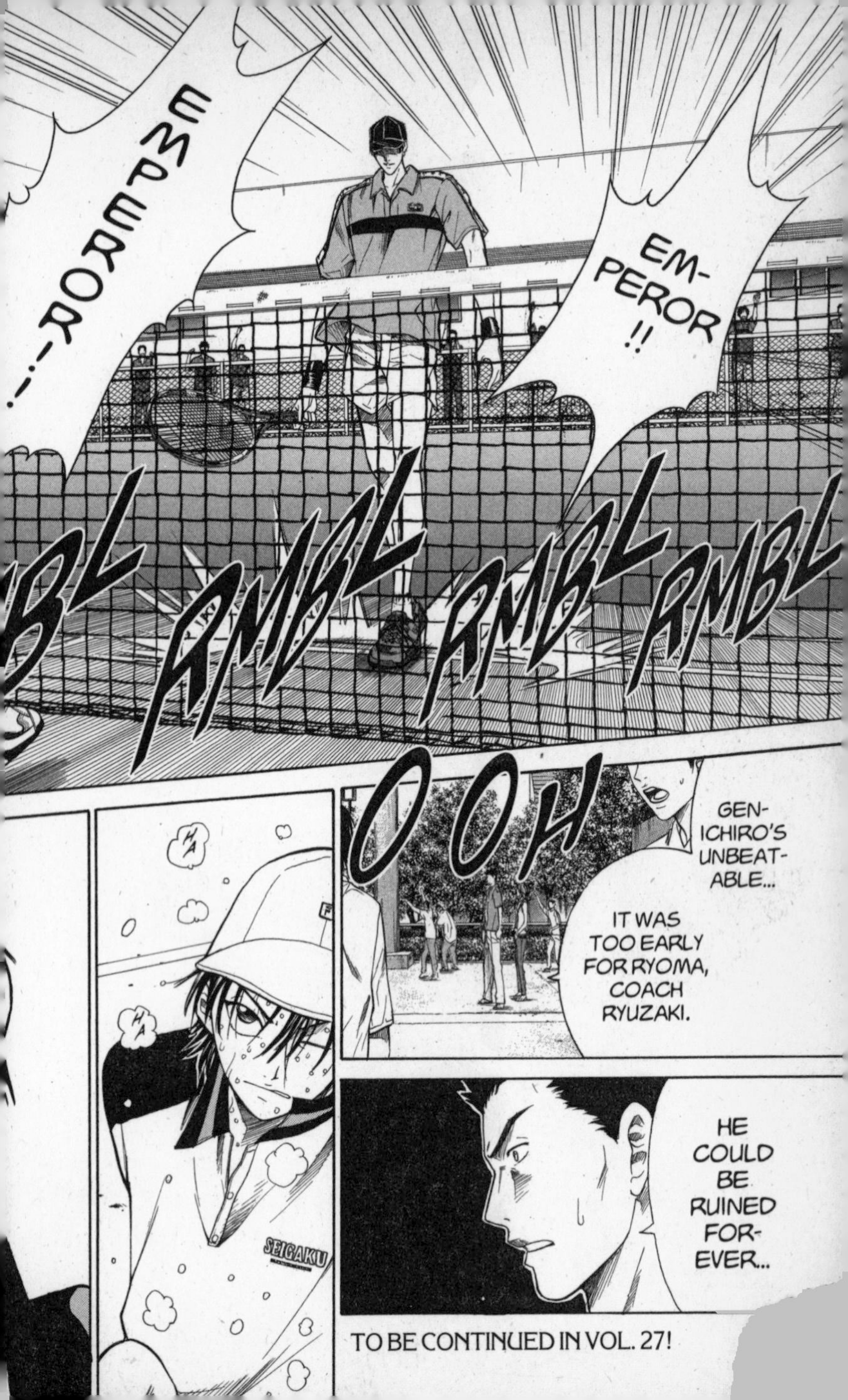
EM-PEROR!!
EMPEROR...!!
RMBL RMBL RMBL RMBL
OOH
GEN-ICHIRO'S UNBEAT-ABLE...
IT WAS TOO EARLY FOR RYOMA, COACH RYUZAKI.
HE COULD BE RUINED FOR-EVER...
HA
HA
SEIGAKU

TO BE CONTINUED IN VOL. 27!

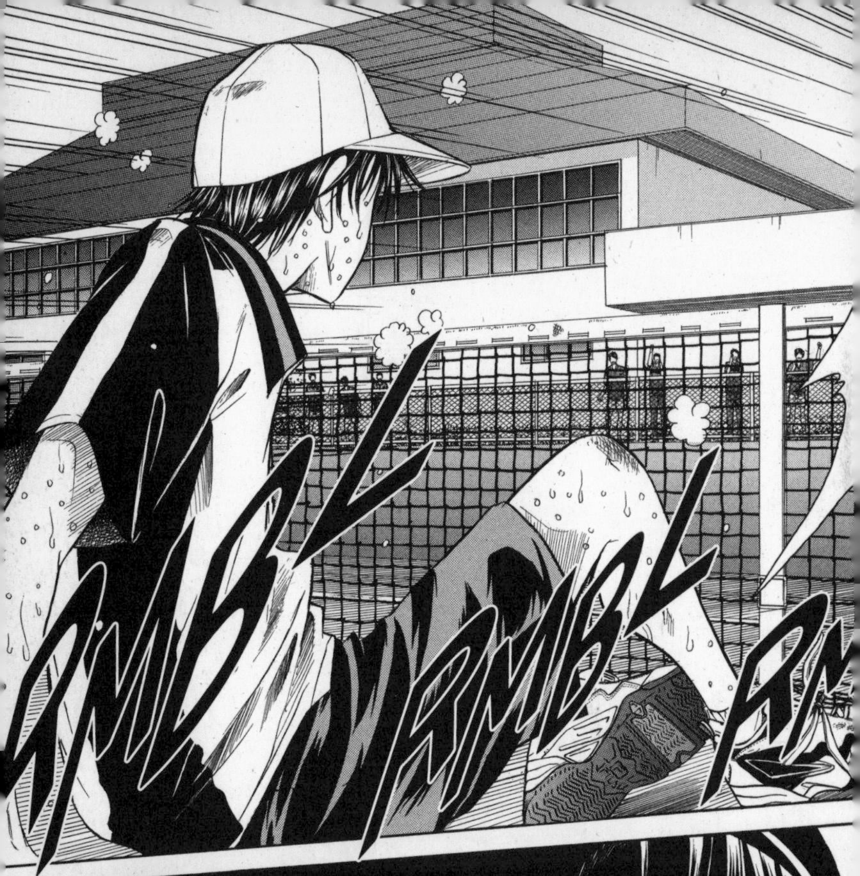
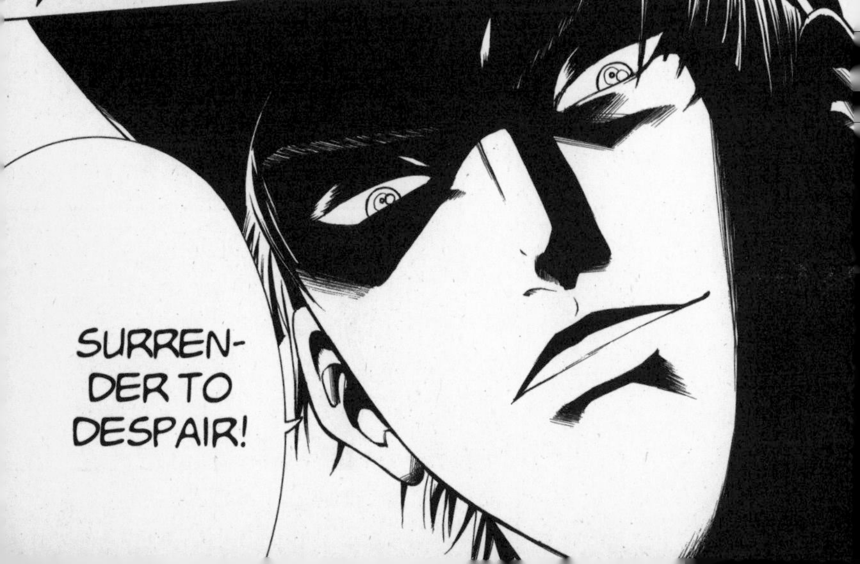
SURREN-
DER TO
DESPAIR!

In the Next Volume...

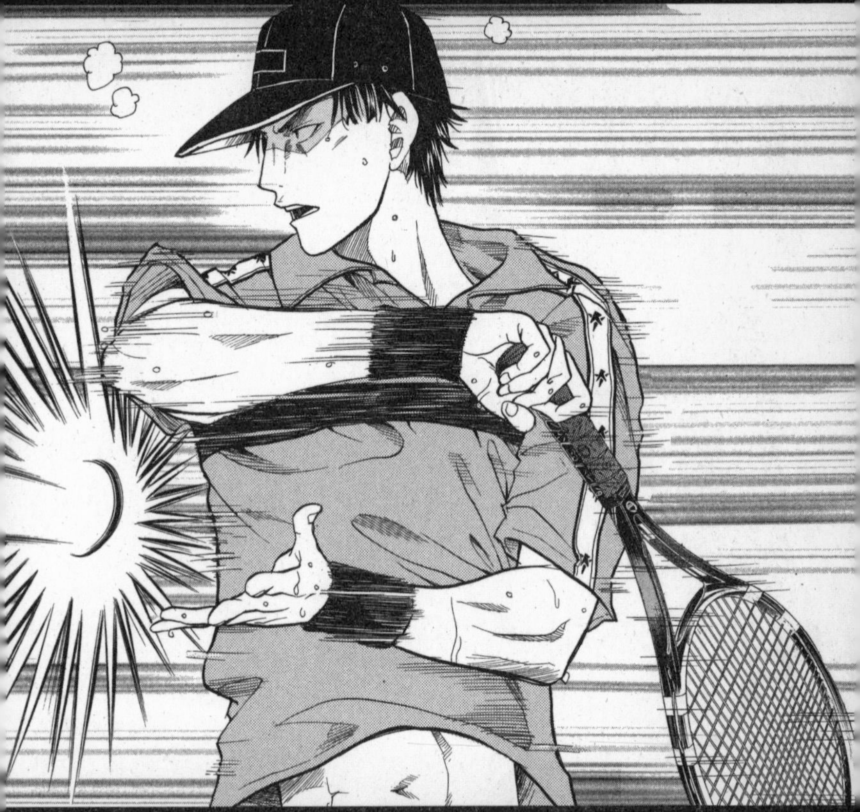

Until the Very Last Shot

Determined to regain Rikkai's dominance, Genichiro continues to pound away at Ryoma with his "Furin Kazan" shots, which seem to be too powerful for any player to overcome. Everybody believes the match is over—everyone but the Seishun players, who know Ryoma won't give up until the very last shot.

Available September 2008!

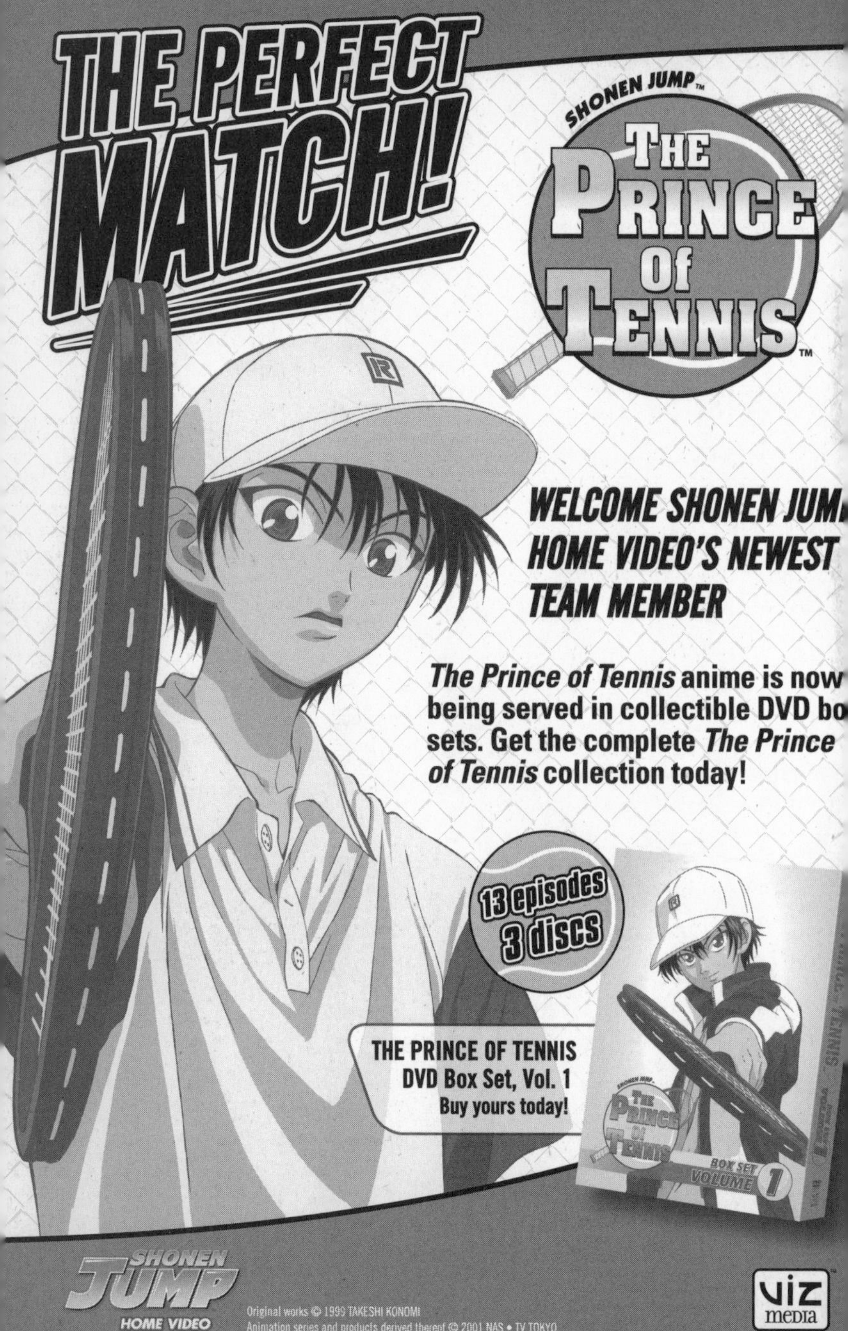

THE PERFECT MATCH!
SHONEN JUMP™
THE PRINCE OF TENNIS™
WELCOME SHONEN JUM
HOME VIDEO'S NEWEST
TEAM MEMBER
The Prince of Tennis anime is now being served in collectible DVD bo sets. Get the complete *The Prince of Tennis* collection today!
13 episodes 3 discs
THE PRINCE OF TENNIS
DVD Box Set, Vol. 1
Buy yours today!
SHONEN JUMP
HOME VIDEO
www.shonenjump.com
Original works © 1999 TAKESHI KONOMI
Animation series and products derived thereof © 2001 NAS • TV TOKYO
All Rights Reserved.
VIZ media
www.viz.com

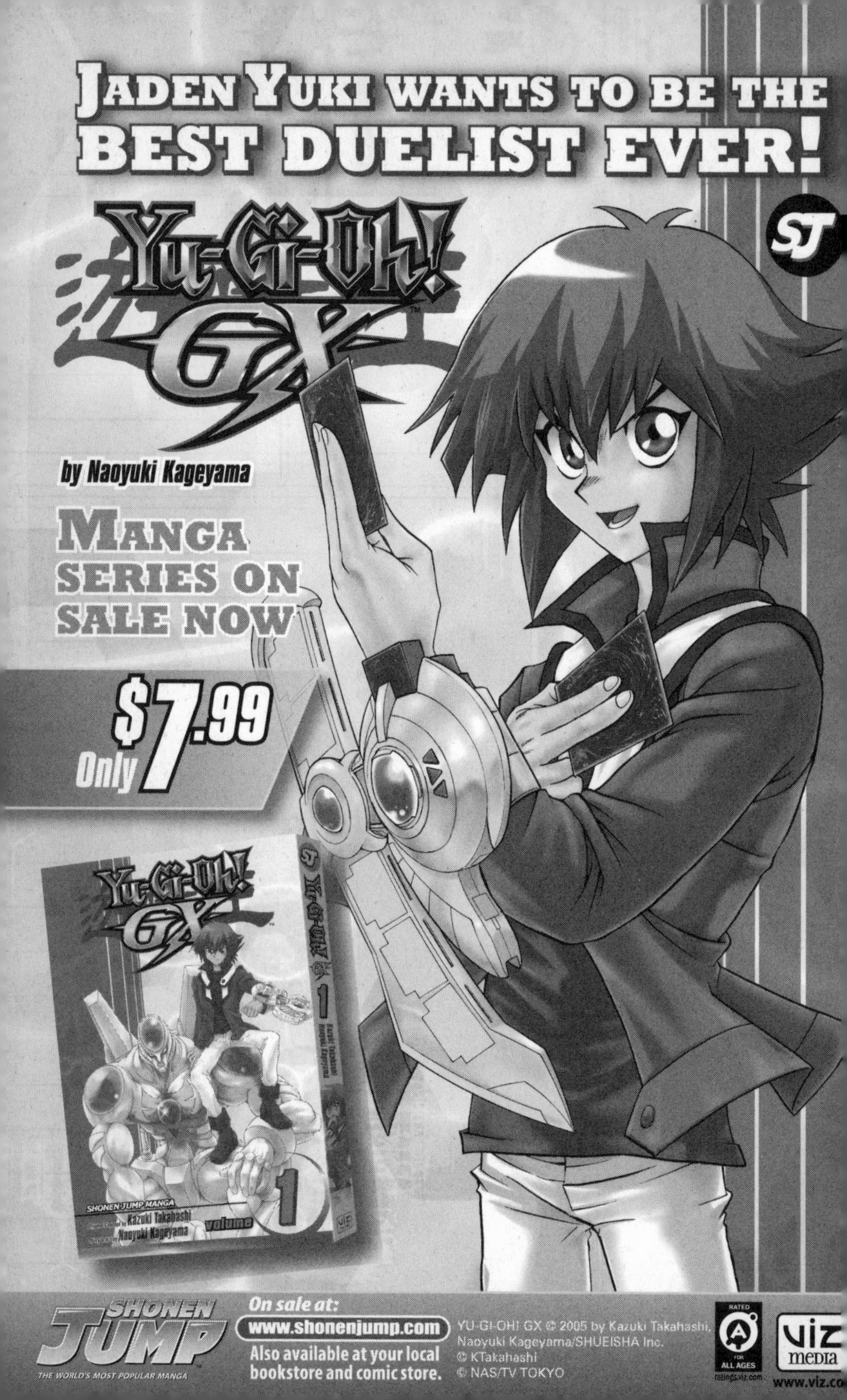
JADEN YUKI WANTS TO BE THE
BEST DUELIST EVER!
SJ
YU-GI-OH! GX™
by Naoyuki Kageyama
MANGA
SERIES ON
SALE NOW
Only $7.99
YU-GI-OH! GX
1
SHONEN JUMP MANGA
Kazuki Takahashi
Naoyuki Kageyama
volume 1
SHONEN JUMP
THE WORLD'S MOST POPULAR MANGA
On sale at:
www.shonenjump.com
Also available at your local bookstore and comic store.
YU-GI-OH! GX © 2005 by Kazuki Takahashi, Naoyuki Kageyama/SHUEISHA Inc.
© KTakahashi
© NAS/TV TOKYO
RATED A FOR ALL AGES
ratings.viz.com
viz media
www.viz.co

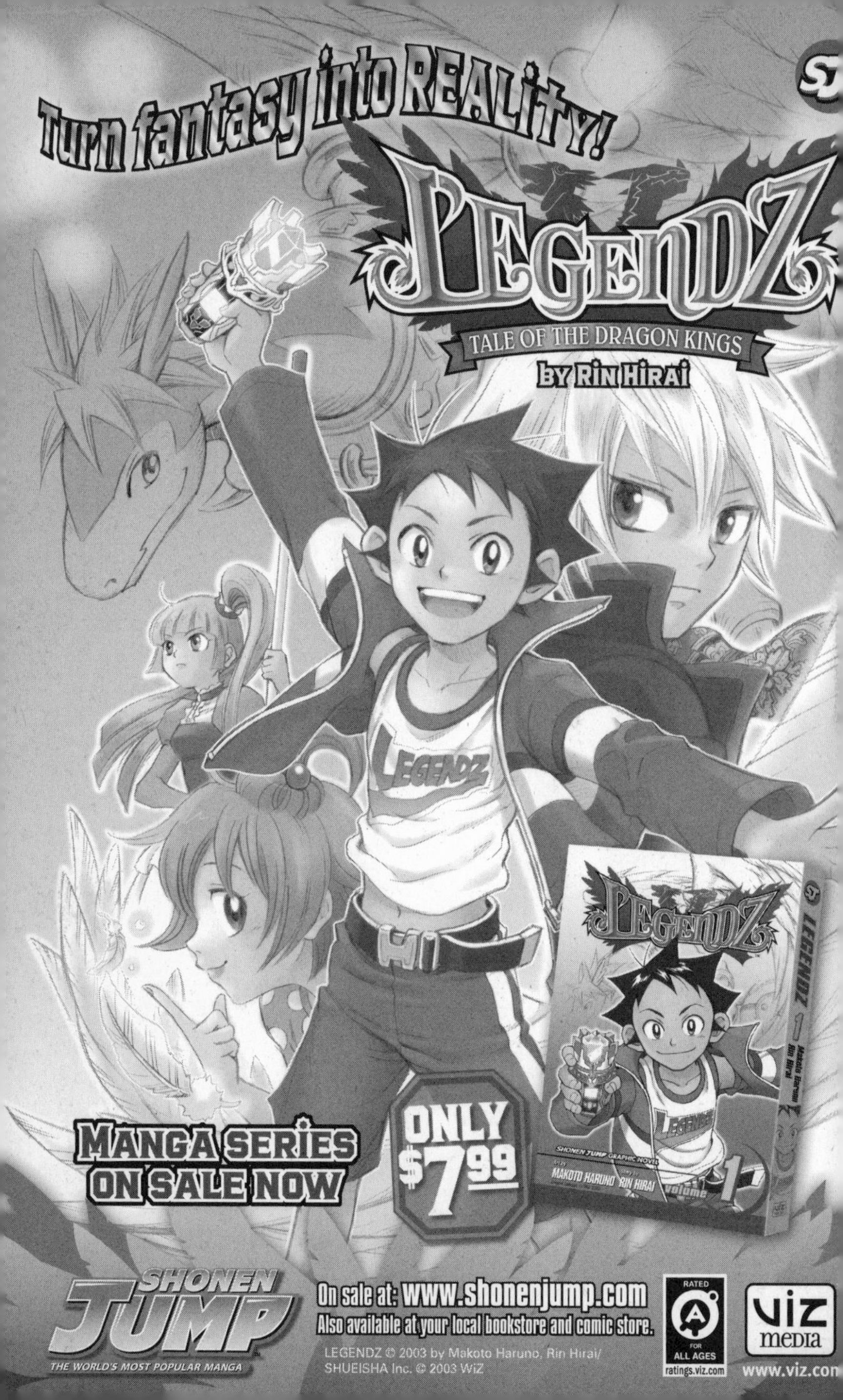
SJ
Turn fantasy into REALity!
LEGENDZ
TALE OF THE DRAGON KINGS
BY RIN HIRAI
LEGENDZ
MANGA SERIES ON SALE NOW
ONLY $7.99
LEGENDZ
LEGENDZ 1 Makoto Haruno Rin Hirai
SHONEN JUMP GRAPHIC NOVEL
MAKOTO HARUNO RIN HIRAI volume 1
SHONEN JUMP
THE WORLD'S MOST POPULAR MANGA
On sale at: www.shonenjump.com
Also available at your local bookstore and comic store.
LEGENDZ © 2003 by Makoto Haruno, Rin Hirai/
SHUEISHA Inc. © 2003 WiZ
RATED A FOR ALL AGES
ratings.viz.com
viz media
www.viz.com

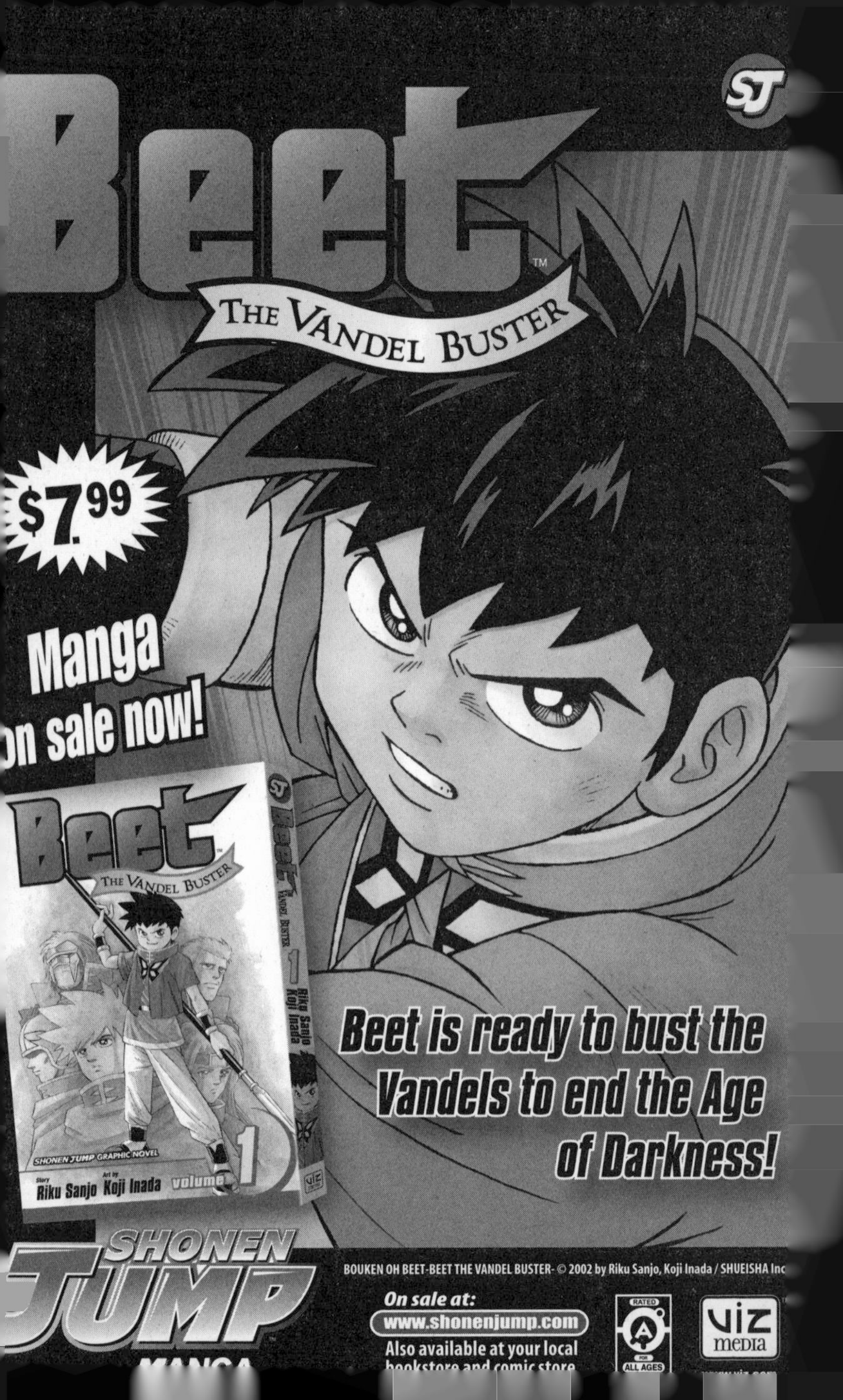
Beet™
THE VANDEL BUSTER
$7.99
Manga
on sale now!
Beet
THE VANDEL BUSTER
Riku Sanjo
Koji Inada
SHONEN JUMP GRAPHIC NOVEL
Story
Riku Sanjo
Art by
Koji Inada
volume 1
Beet is ready to bust the Vandels to end the Age of Darkness!
SHONEN JUMP
BOUKEN OH BEET-BEET THE VANDEL BUSTER- © 2002 by Riku Sanjo, Koji Inada / SHUEISHA Inc
On sale at:
www.shonenjump.com
Also available at your local
RATED
FOR
ALL AGES
VIZ media

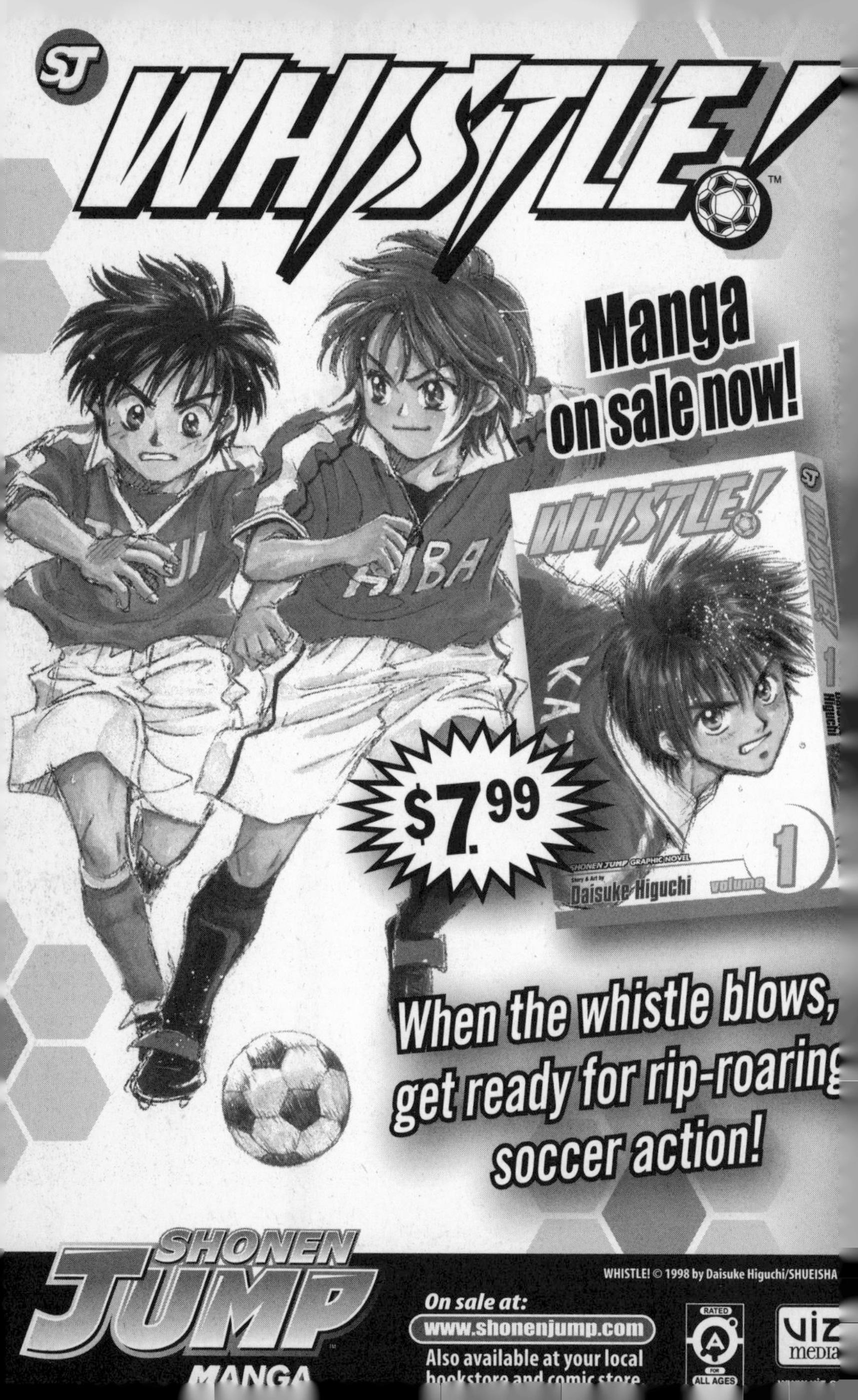

SJ
WHISTLE!™
Manga on sale now!
WHISTLE!
$7.99
SHONEN JUMP GRAPHIC NOVEL
Story & Art by
Daisuke Higuchi
volume 1
When the whistle blows, get ready for rip-roarin soccer action!
SHONEN JUMP MANGA
WHISTLE! © 1998 by Daisuke Higuchi/SHUEISHA
On sale at:
www.shonenjump.com
Also available at your local bookstore and comic store.
RATED A FOR ALL AGES
viz media